James Blair *of* Virginia

James Blair was at the height of his powers when he went to England in 1703 to seek the removal of Lieutenant Governor Francis Nicholson. There in 1705 he engaged J. Hargreaves to paint portraits of his wife and himself.

James Blair
of
Virginia

by

Parke Rouse, Jr.

The University
of
North Carolina Press

Chapel Hill

Printed by Heritage Printers, Inc., Charlotte, N.C.
Manufactured in the United States of America
ISBN 0–8078–1175–0
Library of Congress Catalog Card Number 70–159559

For my daughters
ELIZABETH MARSHALL *and* SARAH DASHIELL ROUSE

Contents

Illustrations

Acknowledgments

◄ᙆ The author acknowledges his gratitude to many persons for the materials from which this book was written.

He is indebted beyond measure to Mrs. Jacqueline Chapman, his associate at the Jamestown Foundation, for her skill and care in preparing the manuscript and for her assistance with the many details of research and documentation. He acknowledges also his debt to the American Philosophical Society for a grant that made possible examination of sources in Scotland and England. Among those who gave help in Scotland, he is especially grateful to Marcus Milne, librarian emeritus of Aberdeen, and the Reverend John L. Blair, present minister of Alvah Parish at Banff. In London he was assisted by E. K. Timings of the Public Records Office.

Thanks are extended also to several friends who read all or part of the manuscript, though the author accepts full responsibility for what appears here. These include Mrs. Mary Mordecai Goodwin of Colonial Williamsburg; Herbert Ganter, archivist of the College of William and Mary; George H. Reese, director of the Center for Textual and Editorial Studies in Humanistic Sources at the University of Virginia; the Reverend George J. Cleaveland, registrar of the Episcopal Diocese of Virginia; the Reverend Carter Henry Harrison, retired, of the Diocese of Southern Virginia; his wife, Margaret Scott Harrison, herself the author of a master of arts thesis in 1958 on Blair; the Honorable Lewis Archer McMurran, Jr., longtime student of colonial history; the Reverend Arthur Pierce Middleton, rector of St. James's Church, Great Barrington, Massachusetts; and the Reverend Walter Kennedy, pastor of the First Presbyterian Church of Newport News.

He acknowledges a special debt to Samuel R. Mohler, professor of history at Central Washington State College, for his study of Blair in his doctoral thesis, "Commissary James Blair, Churchman, Educator and Politician of Colonial Virginia," submitted to the University of Chicago in 1940. The author found Dr. Mohler's work the most comprehensive study of Blair, far surpassing Daniel Esten Motley's *Life of Commissary James Blair*, published in 1901.

Thomas E. Thorne, chairman of the Department of Fine Arts of the College of William and Mary, provided information on the portraits of James and Sarah Blair. William C. Pollard, librarian of the college, kindly obtained copies of all Blair correspondence in the files of the Society for Promoting Christian Knowledge in London. Miss Margaret Cook of the library's Rare Book Room uncovered a Blair letter and a deed previously unknown to the author. Two physicians, Dr. Kurt Schmidt of Williamsburg and the late Dr. George D. Vaughan, Jr., of Richmond, were helpful in explaining the pathology of Blair's last illness.

Courteous help was provided by the staff of the William and Mary College library, including Henry C. Hoar, Henry Grunder, Miss Marie Ellis, Miss Suzanne Foley, and Miss Lynn Thaxton. Similar assistance in the Research Department of Colonial Williamsburg came from Edward M. Riley, director, and Mrs. Rose Belk, Miss Dorothy Shipman, Miss Jane Carson, and Miss Susanne Neale. James H. Hutson of the Institute of Early American History and Culture made helpful suggestions.

Gratitude is acknowledged to John Jennings, director of the Virginia Historical Society, for permitting reproduction of a likeness of Francis Nicholson; and to Howson Cole, curator of manuscripts at the society, for providing copies of deeds between Blair and the Ludwells from the society's manuscript collection. Similar help was provided at the Virginia State Library by William J. Van Schreeven, who was then state archivist, and by John Dudley and Thomas J. Headlee, Jr. In locating and deciphering early Henrico court records relating to Blair, the author was greatly assisted by Young Tyree of Richmond. Latin phraseology in early documents was translated by J. Ward Jones, professor of ancient languages at the College of William and Mary. Mrs. Evelyn Danner kindly checked footnotes.

Charles E. Hatch, Jr., of Colonial National Historical Park, provided information on early Jamestown—Middle Plantation settlement, and Miss Mary Stephenson of Williamsburg supplied data on the Harrison family in Surry County. Hugh DeSamper and Ross Weeks, Jr., directors respectively of the press bureaus of Colonial Williamsburg and of the College of William and Mary, kindly provided many of the prints and photographs that appear as illustrations. The source of each is indicated individually.

Manuscripts and books referred to are listed in the bibliography, but the author would like to express particular appreciation for several works that proved of special usefulness. In addition to Dr. Mohler's aforementioned dissertation, they include Samuel Yonge's *The Site of Old "James Towne"*; William Stevens Perry's *Historical Collections Relating to the American Colonial Church*; George MacLaren Brydon's *Virginia's Mother Church*; Lyon Gardiner Tyler's *The Cradle of the Republic* and his collections of college data; Mary Mordecai Goodwin's Colonial Williamsburg research reports on the Wren Building and on Archibald Blair's store, as well as her compilation of data on the early college; W. A. R. Goodwin's *Historical Sketch of Bruton Church* and *The Record of Bruton Parish Church*; Earl G. Swem's *Virginia Historical Index*, and Richard L. Morton's *Colonial Virginia*.

Finally, the author extends thanks to Louis B. Wright, former director of the Folger Shakespeare Library, who offered encouragement when he set out to follow James Blair; and to Betsy Rouse, who shared his enthusiasm along the way.

James Blair *of* Virginia

There is no man that hath left house, or brethren, or sisters, or father, or mother, or wife, or children, or lands, for my sake, and the gospel's,

But he shall receive a hundredfold now in this time, houses, and brethren, and sisters, and mothers, and children, and lands, with persecutions; and in the world to come eternal life.

MARK 10:29–30

CHAPTER I

A Youth in Scotland
1655-1685

⌐᷄ England in 1603 stood on the threshold of worldwide colonization. A succession of strong Tudor monarchs had curbed the power of feudal lords, infused national spirit, and launched a navy that had defeated the Spanish Armada in 1588. Now, as Queen Elizabeth lay dying and Tudor rule neared its end, the island kingdom was impatient to extend its control to the rich lands in the New World, as Portugal and Spain had done.

Shrewdly, Elizabeth chose her successor. He was her cold-eyed cousin, King James VI of Scotland. Although he sadly lacked the magnetism of Elizabeth and her earthy father, Henry VIII (his great, great uncle), James as a Protestant would assure England's continued defiance of Rome and of its adherents on the thrones of France and Spain.

Moreover, Elizabeth saw that England needed Scotland to realize her imperial ambitions. Against Spain's 8 million people, or France's 15 million, Elizabeth's England held only 5 million.

Scotland would add a million more to the oncoming contest for world dominion. With one monarch—even the lacklustre James Stuart—at their head, the neighbor kingdoms might end their ceaseless warring and unite against larger foes. The "new English nation" that Sir Walter Raleigh envisioned in the New World could make good use of Scottish brains and resourcefulness.

Thus it was that James VI of Scotland was enthroned in London in 1603 as James I of England to reign for twenty-two years. And though a new English nation did indeed begin to take shape overseas, discontent continued to divide Scotland and England at home. Poets George Chapman and John Marston expressed English discontent in their drama of New World exploration, *Eastward Ho*, produced in 1605. "Only a few industrious Scots . . . are dispersed over the face of the whole earth," one English character therein remarked. "And for my own part, I would a hundred thousand of them were there [in Virginia]; for we are all one countrymen now, ye know, and we should find ten times more comfort of them there than we do here."[1]

For this aspersion against their Scottish king, James had the authors clapped into prison and ordered pages containing the passage removed and reprinted. Nevertheless, Stuart misrule continued to embitter both England and Scotland. In the Puritan Revolution of 1649, James's son and successor, Charles I, was beheaded, and for eleven years the Commonwealth forces of Oliver Cromwell held power. Even after Charles I's son was enthroned in the restoration of the monarchy of 1660, it was evident that he had inherited the peculiar Stuart insensitivity to popular will, which for nearly a century kept both nations in a torment.

Religious conflict repeatedly swept both countries in these formative years. In Scotland it was the Stuarts' efforts to reform the church along English lines which chiefly inflamed the people. Since Henry VIII, England's monarch had headed the Church of England and carried the title "Defender of the Faith," conferred on Henry by Pope Leo X in reward for his opposition to Martin Luther. As a sort of viceroy of Christ in England, the king governed the spiritual life of his people through his nomination of bishops, or "lords spiritual," whose authority the church claimed to have derived from Christ's commission to Peter, "upon this rock I build my church," and thence through the succession of apostles and bishops.

The Church of Scotland, on the other hand, had developed a more democratic character during the Reformation, under the influence of John Calvin and of John Knox. It was governed not by bishops but by democratically chosen presbyters of equal rank. The Anglican doctrine of prelacy, or church government by bishops and archbishops, was objectionable to Presbyterians as popish.

In an effort to extend royal control over the Church of Scotland and to unify his kingdoms, James I after his accession to England's throne had imposed bishops over the presbyteries. His action so inflamed many of his countrymen that Charles I in 1641 was forced to approve Scotland's return to Presbyterian church government. Nevertheless, many Scottish Presbyterians joined forces with the Roundhead armies of Oliver Cromwell in 1642 to defeat the Cavaliers and to install Oliver Cromwell in 1649 as Lord Protector of England.

It was in this disturbed period of Scottish life that James Blair was born. The event occurred during the Cromwellian protectorate, between May 1655 and May 1656.[2] His father was Robert Blair, minister of the parish of Alvah in Banffshire on the bleak northeastern coast and facing the North Sea.

Scotland's history contains many well-known Blairs, but the minister of Alvah was not one. After attending Marischal College in Aberdeen from 1616 to 1618,[3] the elder Blair had been ordained to the ministry of the Church of Scotland, served in several parishes, and been installed in his native parish of Forglen in Banffshire in 1634. In that year he had appeared with others to testify to the Lords of the Privy Council about "the disorders in the North, which afford . . . pregnant evidence of the prostration of law and authority."[4] Two years later he became minister of nearby Alvah, serving for forty-three years, until 1679 or later.[5]

Alvah was a rural parish, four miles south of the county seat of Banff on the North Sea. Then as now most parishioners were small farmers, raising grain and livestock on hills that drained into the river Deveron and the sea. Alvah's church had been built in medieval times. Tradition had it that Saint Columba, coming from the island of Iona off western Scotland in the seventh century, had stopped there; Saint Combe's well near Alvah commemorated his supposed visitation.

To Alvah's minister, Robert Blair, and his wife, one daughter and four sons were born. Nothing is known of the daughter, Marjory, except that she was accused in 1661 of "immorality" but found not guilty by the Presbytery of Fordyce,[6] which governed the parish of Alvah. In the puritanical Scotland of 1661, however, "immorality" might have been nothing more heinous than chronic absence from church.

The eldest of Robert Blair's sons, William, was born about 1644, received his master of arts from Marischal College in 1663, was ordained about 1667, and became minister of Fordyce Parish in 1675. He removed to Aberdeen in 1680, became minister of St. Nicholas Church, and was rector of Marischal College from 1688 to 1690.[7] He died in Aberdeen about 1716.

John Blair, probably the third-born son, went south to Edinburgh and was established as an apothecary before November 10, 1682.[8] On August 15 of the following year, John was recorded as a "Burgess and Guild Brother," meaning enfranchised citizen and tradesman, and as a "prentice to John Kennedy, apothecar."[9] On April 30, 1686, warrant for his marriage to Mary M'Lurge was given by the bishop of Edinburgh to the Reverend Alexander Malcome who performed the ceremony. Fourteen years later, John Blair remarried, this time to Elizabeth Pearson, daughter of the late Archibald Pearson of West Hall.[10]

John Blair rose to minor eminence, being appointed postmaster of Edinburgh by the town council on April 4, 1690. For this he received £6 per year and was made responsible for supplying the city fathers with "news letters and gazets." Nine years later, on October 20, 1699, he was granted an annual pension of 200 marks Scots for himself and for the education of his children. On June 6, 1707, he was one of four respected apothecaries who petitioned the council to appoint a "visitor" from their ranks to examine the qualifications of new entrants to the craft in Edinburgh.[11]

The youngest of James Blair's brothers, Archibald, born about 1665, graduated from the University of Edinburgh in 1685 and became a physician before emigrating to Virginia about 1690.[12] He alone of Blair's Scottish family was to remain close to James throughout his life, as will appear in the following pages.

The Banffshire of James Blair's youth was a land of fishing villages, nestled in inlets along a bold coast. The Moray Firth, the shallow bay that indents the Banffshire shore, is warmed by the current of the Gulf Stream that moderates the climate and brings year-round rainfall. Out of sight to the north, the Orkney Islands trail off toward the North Pole. Forty miles to the east around Kinnaird's Head is Aberdeen, then a thriving port and commercial city. Sailing ships from Denmark, Norway, and Sweden plied Scottish waters, exchanging their cargo for the beef, mutton, wool, whiskey, and leather that Scotland produced.

James Blair as a boy knew the chores of a rural minister's household: keeping hearthfires of peat and logs, tending livestock, and shearing sheep each spring. These prepared him for hardships later in Virginia. His father probably taught him to read and write in a parish school of the type instituted by John Knox a century earlier. At the age of nine or ten, he probably entered Latin grammar school at Banff.[13]

The Alvah church has been partly rebuilt since Blair's day, but the small structure typifies the austerity of rural Scotland. Fashioned of native whenstone, it is surrounded by moss-covered tombstones of generations of farmers, weavers, shoemakers, and distillers. No evidence remains of the Abercrombies, who were the lairds of the area. Scattered across the rolling hills are small stone farmhouses, enclosed by neat fields of grain and pasturage.

James Blair grew up speaking the Buchan Scottish of Banff and Aberdeen, its accents betraying the influence of Norwegian immigration. Forty or fifty miles inland, the Highlands nourished a more rural and warlike society, where Roman Catholicism and medieval folkways survived from pre-Reformation times. Southward, in the lowlands and in Ayrshire where most of Scotland's Blairs had originated, the "broad Scots" dialect prevailed. To a greater extent than most of Scotland then, coastal Banffshire and Aberdeenshire produced a mixture of accents and cultures, civilized by the effects of trade. Like many Britons of his era, James Blair looked beyond the horizon.

From its rocky coast, Banffshire undulates upwards to the Highlands. It was in such coastal regions that the Protestant Reformation had begun to nurture a middle class. The medieval holdings of lairds were giving way to small farms called crofts. Though the growing season was brief in this northern clime, the land produced abundant grain for cattle and malt for ale. Narrow rivers like the Deveron, plunging down from the Highlands to the sea, cut the coastal lowlands into a fringe of glens and provided water for distilling. Each glen was a world unto itself.

The dead hand of John Knox lay heavily upon Scotland, and it is not surprising that James Blair's life was directed toward the church. As John Malcolm Bulloch wrote in *A History of the University of Aberdeen, 1495–1895,* "Scottish thought in the 17th century was exclusively monopolized by the pulpit." In addition, Blair's father and his elder brother were clergymen in a land where the ministry was regarded as the noblest and most rewarding of all vocations. By the time he was eleven or twelve, James had absorbed enough Latin and Greek to become a preparatory student at college, which was the prerequisite to theological study.

In 1667 young James applied for and won a Crombie bursarship, or scholarship, to Marischal College at Aberdeen, a Protestant institution of some hundred students. As he was only twelve at the time, it is probable that he entered its preparatory grammar school. In late summer he left Alvah and journeyed southward for fifty miles to the grey coastal city, then the chief port of Scotland. Presumably he went on foot or on horseback, for stage coaches did not yet exist there.

Crossing the river Don into the town over the Brig o' Balgownie (Bridge of Dawn), the youth found himself in a town of about ten thousand people, some on one side of the river in the Old City and others in the New. At the entrances were gates manned in time of war: Gallow Gate, Upper Kirk Gate, Nether Kirk Gate, Shiprow, Justice Street, and the Futty Port.

The city had a dull grey cast, from its dirt streets to its slate roofs that were seldom brightened by sunshine. Houses and shops were built of stone, roughly quarried and joined. A few wooden structures with thatched roofs stood along the outskirts, but these were outlawed after a fire had wasted the city. Of the seven or eight principal thoroughfares, one came to be known, after Blair's day, as Virginia Street for the tobacco shipments that entered Aberdeen from that colony.

Though it was later supplanted by Edinburgh and Glasgow, Aberdeen then was the center of Scottish commerce with the world. From its docks and those of nearby Futty (named for Saint Fotin, patron saint of fishermen), Scotland exported woolen and linen cloth, stockings, hats, and beef. In return she received tobacco and furs from the American colonies, sugar from the West Indies, and a few Negro slaves. From Norway she imported timber, from Sweden iron, and from Danzig and Königsberg flax and hemp. France and the Netherlands sent luxury goods and silks.

Scottish trade with English colonies in the New World, once so promising, had lagged since the English Parliament in 1660 had imposed the Navigation Act restricting trade with the American colonies to English ships and ports. Aberdonian merchants were incensed, as Blair was later to find the Virginians also were, and they readily evaded the law. As Professor Gordon Donaldson has pointed out: ". . . in spite of the English exclusive policy, a certain trade between Scotland and the plantations did develop, sometimes legitimately by special licence or by way of an English port, more usually by illicit means. Clearance papers could be forged, colonial ships could call at Scottish ports on their way between England and the colonies, load Scottish goods, and land them in America on the strength of their English clearance papers."[14]

In the fall of 1667 young Blair became a "bajan,"[15] or new student, at Marischal, a strongly Calvinist institution founded in 1593 by George Keith, fifth Earl Marischal. It occupied a former Grey Friers monastery that had been seized during the Reformation and bestowed by the town council of Aberdeen in 1593 on the Keiths, one of the three noble families that ruled Aberdeenshire. It was, as Scottish historian John Malcolm Bulloch wrote, "aggressively Protestant."[16]

Blair found Marischal demanding, from the time he rose in the darkness of dawn until he fell into bed at night. Students were required to "lie in the college," and Crombie bursars did the housekeeping. They were required to "wear white gowns, girt with a white leather belt four fingers broad," college regulations directed, "and it shall be their duty at about five o'clock to go round the apartments of all sleeping within the Academia, to awaken the students for their work, and to bring light in winter and also not to decline other lighter duties in the dining hall or at supper time, particularly in placing the dishes on the table and in supplying water."[17]

As a twelve-year-old grammar school student, James became acquainted with the master of arts course that lay ahead of him. The curriculum, which was Aristotelian in outlook, prescribed philosophy, Hebrew, Greek, Latin, and arithmetic the first year; logic, disputations, geometry, public declamations, and sacred lessons the second; general physiology, natural philosophy, morality, and ethics the third; and metaphysics, special physiology, and astronomy the last.[18] These subjects constituted the humanities, which prepared the student for the chief objective of university life in a church-centered age—the study of divinity.

James and his fellow bajans were to be "diligent in their studies and pure in their morals."[19] After six days of study, they spent Sunday reading the New Testament in Greek. St. Luke's gospel was prescribed for the entering class, the Acts of the Apostles for the second, the Epistle to the Romans for the third, and the Epistle to the Hebrews for the fourth. Finally, students were required to: "undergo a trial and examination of their proficiency in all the four years' courses open to the Principal and Masters, and thereafter do emit public theses, which they defend in a solemn manner in presence of all the Doctors, Professors, and learned men of the University. And thereafter, after they have solemnly bound themselves by oath to the Protestant

Religion, and to be grateful to their Alma Mater, they do conform to their several qualifications [and] receive the degree of Master of Arts."[20]

Along with other students and masters, twelve-year-old James was required to remain celibate. It had been stipulated in 1626 that a master at Marischal "remain a single person and noways marry nor take any wife so long as he remains in the said office."[21] Other rules were directed against the "Cunning of Satan," who endeavors to "lead youth away from the Gospel back to the darkness of Popery."[22] Every student had to swear to uphold the Covenant of 1638 to oppose episcopacy in Scotland: first before the principal on entrance, then before the rector on matriculation, and finally before the dean of the faculty on graduation. The oath was required at least once each year.[23]

Despite these severities, Marischal students had their small pleasures. One Aberdonian complained to the town council in 1657 that he had been shot "through the breeches by an arrow which did come over the College yard dike."[24] This was doubly heinous because students were denied use of weapons.

Football was permitted, and billiards were played in a tower of the college. Upperclassmen occasionally dared to "rag" their master in class. A few acquired a taste for disputation, which required each student periodically to defend or "propugn" a thesis before an audience of principal, masters, and students convened to "conpugn" it. Blair's native quickness was sharpened by these experiences.

Rivalry between Marischal and King's College, a Roman Catholic institution built in 1450 in the older section of the town, frequently erupted before the institutions merged in 1860 to become the University of Aberdeen. Feeling between Catholic highlanders and Protestant lowlanders was bitter, and it was heightened by Stuart efforts to force compliance with their ecclesiastical policies. Masters from each college were accused of proselyting the other's students. Scholars seeking to increase their tuition receipts were charged with scouring the countryside during vacation, "enticing the scholars of one college to the other." To end the practice, an offending professor was required to return a deserter's fee to his original school.[25]

Young James applied himself well to the study of Latin and Greek, acquiring such proficiency that he could write and speak both fluently. This would enable him to read the classical writers of antiquity, whose works were the basis of the liberal arts curriculum. Years later, as an old man, he took pleasure in composing Latin verses for ceremonial events in Virginia.[26]

Of Blair's schooling at Marischal little record remains. Nevertheless, the effects of his arduous studies showed themselves throughout his life in his logic, his breadth of knowledge, and his eloquence.

Completing his preparatory schooling at Marischal, young Blair was admitted to Edinburgh University, a much larger institution 160 miles south of Alvah in Scotland's capital. This was contrary to family tradition, for both his father and his older brother had been educated in Aberdeen. However, there were advantages to be found in the larger university. Probably the serious young man chose to be in Scotland's intellectual center, where he could also more advantageously pursue theological studies.

Whatever the reason, James Blair in the autumn of 1669 went southward to the newest and largest of Scotland's four universities. Founded in 1583, the University of Edinburgh had reached an enrollment of some three hundred students in 1669, divided among undergraduate and divinity students. Like Marischal, it was strongly ecclesiastical in outlook: most of its graduates would become clerics, teachers, or scholars. The university's first medical chair was not to be established until 1685[27]—twelve years after Blair left it. Even farther in the future were its faculties of law, music, and the fine arts.

Together with its port of Leith, Edinburgh by 1669 had become Scotland's chief metropolis, with a population of 35,000. Begun in the eleventh century on the slope of Castle Rock, it had survived English assaults in the Border Wars to become Scotland's capital in 1437. James IV of Scotland had settled his court there, and Holyrood Palace remained one of the nation's shrines, even after James VI had moved on to London in 1603. Despite a loss of prestige after the court's departure, Edinburgh remained the center of Scotland's ecclesiastical and judicial hierarchy.

The pinnacle of its intellectual life was the university, a rectangular block of stone buildings on Castle Rock, close to a remnant of the medieval city's Flodden Wall. From the entrance to its square, the College Wynd led like a narrow alley to a thoroughfare known as the Cowgate. Nearby was the city's main thoroughfare, the High Street where John Knox had lived and not far beyond was St. Giles' Cathedral, since the Reformation the heart of the Church of Scotland.

At Edinburgh, Blair entered a class under the mastership of James Pillans, who had become a regent at the university in 1644. Apparently discipline was less severe than at Aberdeen, for students lived outside the college and were required only to attend Sunday morning service in one of the town's churches. In addition to the one-month August vacation, they also enjoyed a holiday the week between Christmas and New Year's day.

Discipline was nevertheless severe. Lectures began at 6 A.M. in winter and 5 A.M. in summer. Each afternoon from 2:00 to 4:00 the students marched to the playing fields near the city's gallows to exercise under supervision of their masters. After this break, they marched back and resumed lectures, recitations, and oral examinations until late in the evening.

The university had not yet achieved the golden fame it acquired a century later. In local literature of the time, it was patronized as "the Town College." Its emergent role in educating ministers, physicians, and other professional men was beginning to stir resentment among older practitioners. Nevertheless, Edinburgh was stimulating for a youth of Blair's capacity. There were congregated many of the ablest men in Scotland, engaged in the intellectual discipline in which the Scottish mind exults.

At the laureation exercises on July 21, 1673, after four years in the university, James Blair became a master of arts.[28] Describing these exercises, D. B. Horn has written:

"All cloathed in black gowns after the fashion of their professor," the successful magistrands, who had been carefully coached for weeks beforehand in their parts, paraded in one of the town's churches or in their own common hall. The town's ministers were there in force, accompanied not only by the Provost, bailies, and members of the council, but by a distinguished gathering which included lords of session and prime advocates and even one or two of the great officers of state. The regent whose students were to be laureated had prepared a long list of theses, ethical, philosophical, mathematical, and so on, which had been printed with the names of the graduands attached.[29]

At the conclusion of the exercises the fifty-five graduating students signed their names to the oath, written in Latin, to which university graduates subscribed: "We, the youths whose names are undersigned, graduates of Edinburgh University, having been properly educated . . . and now about to be given the title of masters, promise in the face of God that we shall remain in loyalty to the King's Majesty and shall remain grateful towards the university to the ends of our lives. . . ."

Beneath the inscription, *"E Disciplina Magrl. Jacobi Pilani manumissa. Anno 1673,"* ("Released from the discipline of Master James Pillans, Year 1673"), Blair signed "Jacobus Blair." He was now entering his eighteenth year and was a youth of unusual promise. Not only had he survived a course that commonly disqualified half the matriculants,[30] but he had been accepted for theological training.

Young as he was, James Blair had a maturity and firmness that marked him as a leader. His skill of speech and pen was evident. He had a tough and logical mind, unflagging in pursuit of its ends. He was patient and untiring, with a tenacity rare even among Scots. He had the intellectual precision of an experienced advocate, coupled with a self-confidence that enabled him to speak with cool conviction in the most heated debates. These were qualities that would move monarchs and topple royal governors.

At the same time, James could be an agreeable companion. One chronicler described him as "hale, hearty, [and] red-faced . . . lively . . . though grave at times."[31] Beyond this, he was mildly handsome, as later portraits attest. Not a bad combination for an ambitious youth with no fortune.

Blair's theological studies were probably directed by the professor of divinity at Edinburgh University. These required four or five years' readings in theology, biblical languages, and literature, together with the dissection of religious controversies and endless disputations and practice sermons.[32] The professor during his first year was the Reverend William Keith, described by a contemporary as being "a great Master of Languages, being very well skilled in Hebrew and Rabbinical learning."[33]

When Keith died in 1674, he was succeeded as professor of theology by the Reverend Laurence Charteris, who was to affect Blair's life more than any other man had up to this point. In an age of bitter dogmatism, Charteris was a tolerant Christian who influenced many students with his broad churchmanship. Scotsman Gilbert Burnet, who emigrated to England and became bishop of Salisbury, described him as:

A man of composed and serene gravity, but without affectation or sourness. He scarce ever spoke in company, but was open and free in private. He made true judgment of things and of men's tempers, and had a peculiar talent for managing such as he thought deserved his pains. . . . He had great tenderness, and was a perfect friend, and a most sublime Christian. He lived in constant contempt of the world, and a neglect of his person. There was a gravity in his conversation that raised an attention and begot a composedness in all about him, without frightening them; for he made religion appear amiable in his whole deportment. . . . He was a great enemy to large confessions of faith, chiefly when they were imposed in the lump as tests: for he was positive in very few things. He had gone through the chief parts of learning, but was then most conversant with history.[34]

Six years after receiving his master of arts, Blair completed theological studies and passed the severe "tryalls" required by the presbytery. In late June or early July 1679, he was ordained a minister of the Church of Scotland, upon presentation of Robert Macgill, Viscount Oxfourd.

In accordance with the dictate of James I, renewed by Charles II in 1661, James Blair was ordained into the ministry of the Church of Scotland by a bishop appointed by the king. The officiant was John Paterson, Bishop of the Diocese of Edinburgh and brother of a master at Marischal College, the Reverend Robert Paterson. The certificate of ordination, signed "Jo:

Edinburgh," was later to become crucial evidence of Blair's episcopal ordination, when his authority to serve as commissary to the bishop of London in Virginia was questioned.

On July 11, 1679, Blair was "admitted and instituted" into his first parish in the Presbytery of Dalkeith ten miles southeast of Edinburgh. The parish of Cranston was within the patronage of the Macgills, the dominant family in the area. Not surprisingly in a nation oversupplied with clergy, it was a thinly-settled rural area, whose twelfth-century church was beyond the reach of most parishioners. It was indeed a modest beginning—too modest for a man of Blair's ambition.

The times were difficult for Scottish clergymen, at best. The revival by Charles II of prelacy in the Church of Scotland had redivided the church into presbyterian and episcopal factions. Again bishops were being appointed and installed against the will of most Church of Scotland adherents. "What existed at the time," wrote Gordon Donaldson, "was a kind of beheaded and imperfect remnant of presbyterianism, a system in which the general assembly had been in abeyance since 1653 and in which synods and presbyteries had been operating under the limitations imposed by the Cromwellian government. . . . Now, synods and presbyteries were retained, but for the general assembly there were substituted bishops under conciliar and parliamentary control and without any real independence in shaping policy."[35]

Recalling Scotland at this tragic time, Gilbert Burnet pictured a nation in chaos. "I had left Scotland [in 1673] under an universal discontent," he wrote after emigrating to England. "The whole administration there was both violent and corrupt . . . these things provoked the body of the people . . . [and] raised a very high discontent all over the nation. The affairs of the church were altogether neglected: so that in all respects we were quite out of joint."[36]

At such a time James Blair began his ministry. The revival of bishops' rule by Charles II did not in itself disturb him, for the Blairs, along with many other Scots of Banff and Aberdeen, favored episcopacy; Bishop Paterson affirmed that Blair served Cranston Parish for three years at this period "with exemplary diligence, care and gravity, and did in the course of his Ministry, behave himself Loyally, Peaceably, and Canonically.''[37]

However, Stuart efforts to disarm Scottish opposition to the accession of the Roman Catholic James II struck Blair quite differently. Here, he felt, was the beginning of an effort to re-institute the Roman Catholicism that lowland Scotland had largely discarded in the Reformation. Unacceptable to Blair and many others was James's requirement that all Scottish administrators, soldiers, scholars, and churchmen sign a test oath that in effect would have placed the Catholic James, upon his accession, at the head of the Scottish church.

Though the Scottish Privy Council issued an act permitting signers of the test oath to reject some clauses, Scottish clergymen of Protestant view could not readily accept it. About eighty ministers judged by Burnet to be "of the most learned and pious" in Scotland as well as "the best preachers and most zealous enemies of Popery" therefore refused to sign James's test oath.[38] Among these was James Blair.

Suddenly, at twenty-six, the career for which Blair had so carefully prepared himself was ended. His rejection was soon official. On December 22, 1681, the Privy Council of Scotland noted "that severall ministers doe undutifully refuse to swear and subscribe the Test." It ordered patrons of churches held by nonsigners to "present fitt and qualified persons to the said churches immediately after the first of January next."[39] On January 12, 1682, Viscount Oxfourd was asked to present a new minister to fill the vacated parish of Cranston.[40]

Blair's behavior at this point showed the courage he was often to show in resisting what he felt to be oppression. An example had been set for him by Laurence Charteris, who had already resigned his professorship rather than sign the oath. Now, to aid Blair and other ejected ministers who had "been formed by Charteris" in what Gilbert Burnet considered "an excellent temper and to a set of very good principles," the theologian wrote to Burnet in England to find places for them.[41]

Burnet had risen to be preacher of the Rolls Chapel in London, a prestigious post within the gift of the master of the rolls, Sir Harbottle Grimston, former speaker of the House of Commons and, like Burnet and Blair, an antipapist.[42] Having himself fled Scotland "under an universal discontent," Burnet sympathized with those who refused to sign the test oath. He replied to Charteris by inviting them to England and promising assistance in finding them places.

The decision was difficult for many, but it was easy for James Blair, who welcomed new enterprises. Moreover, he was twenty-seven and unmarried. On November 10, 1682, he designated his brother John, the apothecary in Edinburgh, to be his agent and prepared to take the high road to London. This document, the earliest existing example of Blair's script, was his farewell to Scotland. He wrote:

I, Mr. James Blair, lait minester of Cranstoune, being to remove out of the kingdome of Scotland, do now appoint my brother german,[43] John Blair, apothecarie of Edinburgh, my factor, with full power to him to have in all debts, sumess of money, house rents, give discharges, dispose of them as he judges fittest for my use and to raise proces and doe all and sundre other things as accords of the law, after the same maner that I, my self, may doe if I were present. And for the more securitie I consent that thir presents be registrat in the books of any judge competent within this kingdome and for that effect constitute Mr. Robert Deanes, advocat, my procurator. Writin and subscrivit with my hand, at Edinburgh, this tenth of November lm, vic, and eightie two. Sic subscribitur: —

James Blair[44]

By this instrument, Blair empowered John to collect for him any unpaid benefices and tuitions that might have been due from the laird or parishioners of Cranston Parish. Moreover, he allowed thereby for the settlement of his father's estate. As his father had ceased to serve Alvah Parish in 1679, it is probable that he was approaching death in 1682, if not already dead.

Scotsmen remained few enough in the London of 1682 to be conspicuous, as they had been to the acerbic authors of *Eastward Ho* at the beginning of the Stuart era in 1603. Their rustic manners remained as common a target for ridicule in the time of Charles II as they had been seventy-seven years earlier in James I's reign. Samuel Johnson was to express classic English condescension: "The noblest prospect which a Scotchman sees is the high-road that leads to England." But if Blair sensed hostility in London or later in Virginia, it was only to spur him on. He was impervious to criticism through his long life.

As preacher of the Rolls Chapel, Gilbert Burnet "esteemed it no small happiness" that he could "get most of [Charteris' protégés] well settled in England; where they behaved themselves worthily." Through Burnet's effort, Blair became an under clerk of the master of the rolls, in Chancery Lane near Fleet Street in London. For clerkships such as Blair's, Burnet thought the nation could "get so many good men, who suffered for their consciences, to be again well employed, and well provided for."[45]

The employment of clergymen as law clerks had become common since the middle ages. Indeed, the Anglo-Saxon "clerc" meant clergyman, arising from the earlier function of priests as dispensers of the law. At a time when few men except clerics were sufficiently literate to record laws, it was understandable that Scottish ministers deprived of pulpits should have found such employment in English record offices.

Like London's Inns of Court, the establishment of the master of the rolls lay close to the Thames. It included the Rolls Office, wherein Blair and other clerks wrote out records in "a fair hand;" the Rolls House, which accommodated Sir Harbottle Grimston's family and servants; and the Rolls Chapel, a house of Anglican worship built in the reign of Henry III as the Chapel of the House of Converts for christianized Jews but used since the sixteenth century by the family and staff of the master of the rolls.[46]

Townspeople attended Rolls Chapel services, along with Blair and his fellow scriveners. During the tenure there of the handsome Edward Stillingfleet, known as "The Beauty of Holiness," Samuel Pepys recorded in his diary: ". . . walked to the Rolls' Chapel, expecting to hear the great Stillingfleet preach, but he did not; but a very sorry fellow, which vexed me."[47]

Blair found London in 1683 an invigorating place, growing as the hub of an expanding empire. A handsome city had risen from the ashes of the fire of 1666. Since Milton's death, John Dryden was the reigning poet. Isaac Newton and John Locke beckoned the oncoming scientific age. The reopening of theaters with the restoration of the monarchy in 1660 had brought an outburst of wit and lyric charm, tainted though it was with the immorality of Charles II's reign. Playwrights like William Wycherley and William Congreve held the stage, while Samuel Pepys recorded London's scandals. Whatever puritanism Blair had brought from Scotland diminished during his two years in London.

Blair's association with Burnet in the Rolls Office acquainted him with other Church of England leaders who congregated at Lambeth Palace, seat of the Archbishop of Canterbury across the Thames from the city. Chief among these were Stillingfleet, who had preceded Burnet in the Rolls Chapel and who was to be bishop of Worcester; William Lloyd, who would serve successively as bishop of St. Asaph, of Lichfield, and of Worcester; and John Tillotson, who was to become archbishop of Canterbury in 1691.

Even more fortunate was Blair's acquaintance with Henry Compton, bishop of London, whose seat was nearby Fulham Palace. When Blair arrived in England, Compton was fifty years old and had been seven years in office. After Oxford he had essayed a military career before returning to Cambridge for his degree, entering the priesthood, and in twelve years winning a bishopric. Though derogated as a political bishop whose career had been advanced by his noble family—the ancient Comptons of Compton Wynyates in Warwickshire—Bishop Compton was to prove a dedicated and effective agent of Christianity.

Since England had first successfully settled a colony in the New World at Jamestown in 1607, spiritual care of English plantations overseas had been presumed to be the responsibility of the bishop of London. However, few of Compton's predecessors had attempted to recruit and send clergymen to the increasing colonists. In the infancy of England's long career of world colonization, Henry Compton was the first churchman to make an orderly effort to extend the hand of the church to English settlers, soldiers, and traders. He has been described as "essentially a practical man, concerned with the vital religious and constitutional problems of his day."

When Blair arrived in England, Compton was seeking clergy-men to go as missionaries to North America and the West Indies. It was impossible to recruit a sufficient number of English clergy, so Compton widened his efforts to Protestant refugees who had fled Scotland, Ireland, and France to seek asylum in England.[48] During the year 1685, after nearly three years with the master of the rolls, James Blair accepted Bishop Compton's invitation to go to Virginia in the service of the church.

To satisfy Compton's desire that the missionary be ordained to the satisfaction of the Church of England, Blair received this endorsement from his former bishop, John Paterson, in Edinburgh, dated August 19, 1684:

> To ALL CONCERNED, these are to certify & declare, that the bearer hereof, Mr. Jas *Blair*, Presbyter, did officiate in the Service of the Holy Ministery as Rector in the Parish of Cranston, in my diocese of Edinburgh for several years preceding the year 1682, with exemplary diligence, care and gravity, & did in all the course of his Ministry, behave himself Loyally, Peaceably & Canonically, & that this is a truth I certify by these presents, written & Subscribed with my own hand, the 19th day of Augt, in the year 1684.
>
> JO. Edinburgh[49]

Blair's departure from the Rolls Office may have been hastened by Burnet's sudden discharge as preacher of the Rolls Chapel. Burnet's going was certainly the more dramatic of the two. At the service in the Rolls Chapel on Guy Fawkes' Day (November 5), 1684, Burnet chose as his text, "Save me from the lion's mouth, thou that hast heard me from the horns of the unicorns." The king interpreted Burnet's text and two-hour sermon against popery as an attack on the royal arms and promptly ordered the master of the rolls to dismiss his impudent preacher.

Duly accepted by Compton as a missionary and assigned to the Parish of Henrico in faraway Virginia, Blair took leave of his fellow clerks in the Rolls Office. In the summer of 1685 he packed books and clothes and boarded the ship *William*, John Bennet commander, bound for Jamaica, together with fifty-six other passengers who had permission to go to the colonies.[50] For his expenses, Blair was entitled to £20 from the king's bounty.

Like many an outbound passenger, the minister was doubt-less filled with nostalgia as he stood on deck and watched the spires of the city fade over the horizon. From London the *William* slid down the Thames with the tide to Gravesend. Once in the English Channel, she sailed southward to the Azores or to the Canary Islands. After the usual watering stop, she plunged again into the South Atlantic toward the English colony at Jamaica, where Blair would reembark for Virginia.

It was the course that English vessels had plied since the days of Captain John Smith in 1607. With favoring winds it could be navigated in two months, but the usual time was longer. All we know is that by late 1685 the serious young Scotsman was established in his faraway parish in Virginia.

CHAPTER II

Behold, Virginia!
1685-1691

❧ England held most of the Atlantic coast of North America when Blair arrived in Virginia. Beginning with a settlement at Jamestown in 1607, companies of pioneers had colonized from South Carolina northward to New Hampshire. Even an inland colony had been chartered for the first time, when the Crown in 1681 granted Pennsylvania to William Penn and his followers.

In the islands of the South Atlantic, Englishmen by 1685 had claimed Bermuda, St. Kitts, Nevis, Jamaica, Barbados, and other footholds with a total population of more than 150,000 souls.

Virginia was by far the largest and most populous of these colonies. Her settlers by 1685 numbered nearly 70,000—many more than Massachusetts' 48,000 or the 20,000 each in New York and Maryland. Virginia's boundaries, defined in the charter granted by James I to the Virginia Company of London in 1606, extended along the coast from the area that became South Carolina to what later became Massachusetts. These bounds were reduced by subsequent grants to other colonies, but toward the west Virginia continued to claim "from sea to sea," as the company's second charter had put it in 1609.

When Virginia proved slow to grow, James I in 1624 annulled her charter and declared her to be a royal province. Thereafter, her governing council was appointed by the king rather than the company. Thus Virginia grew up under more direct royal control than did such proprietary colonies as Pennsylvania. Her legislative assembly at Jamestown was the first to be authorized in the New World, and her trade with the mother country exceeded that of any other province.

The motto of the Virginia Company of London in 1620 proclaimed the colony to be "the fifth kingdom" after England, France, Scotland, and Ireland.

When Blair's ship entered the Virginia capes late in 1685, the colony's eight original shires that had been created in 1634 had grown to more than twice that number. These embraced tobacco lands along the lower Chesapeake and also up the green peninsulas between the tidal rivers. Stretching like fingers of the great bay into the hilly uplands, these rivers bore stout English names like James and York or exotic Indian ones like Rappahannock and Potomac.

As his ship entered Chesapeake Bay, Blair could smell the pine forests that lined Virginia's headlands. First came a stop at Fort Algernon on Point Comfort and at the adjoining village of Hampton. At the fort, a handful of men kept watch for smugglers from Dutch and French possessions in the Caribbean. Pirates also were a threat; about the time of Blair's arrival, the English buccaneer William Dampier was boldly fitting out a ship on Virginia's Eastern Shore for a voyage with John Cook and Edward Davis around Cape Horn to Chile, Peru, and the South Seas.[1]

Once in the enclosed bay, the ship bearing James Blair bore westward and entered the mouth of the James River at Newport News Point. Here the voyagers probably refilled their water casks at a spring that had refreshed Virginia's settlers since Captain Christopher Newport's voyage in 1607.[2] Then, subject to favoring winds, it slowly beat its way up the James to the village of Jamestown, situated on a wooded peninsula on the north shore of the mighty river and thirty miles inland.

To concentrate shipping and promote Jamestown's growth, Virginia's assembly in 1633 had decreed that ships entering or leaving the colony should put in at the capital. There, on a low-lying peninsula jutting into the James River channel, lived the governor and most colonial officials, and there the assembly met to make the colony's laws. Despite repeated efforts to heighten the importance of the settlement, however, Jamestown remained a rustic village of small houses centered around a church and marketplace.

Burned by the rebel Nathaniel Bacon only nine years earlier in 1676, its statehouse was still being rebuilt. The assembly meanwhile met irregularly in taverns and homes, uncertain whether to rebuild or to move the capital across the peninsula to Tyndall's Point on the York River. In the interim, householders like Mrs. Ann Macon and William Sherwood were paid to accommodate the lawmakers and furnish "fire, candles and attendance."[3]

When Blair reached Jamestown, its fortunes were at low ebb. The former governor, Thomas Culpeper, Baron Culpeper of Thoresway, who had come over to claim his over-generous grant from Charles II, had returned to England in May 1683, leaving Virginia angry at his cold exploitation.[4] Until the arrival of his successor, Francis Howard, Baron Howard of Effingham, on February 21, 1684, President Nicholas Spencer of the council had acted as governor.[5]

Ill-kept though Jamestown was, Blair found the colonists hopeful. England's long frustrated dream of empire was being realized, though slowly. Every plantation grew tobacco, aided by the importation since 1619 of Negroes from Africa and the West Indies. At first they had come slowly, half-feared for their strength and savage speech. After they proved useful in the tobacco fields, however, more colonists had bought them from Dutch and English trading ships. By 1685 about five thousand Negroes worked the rich black soil that stretched from Chesapeake Bay to the fall line of the rivers a hundred miles inland.

The chief threat to English aims, the Indians, had been forced upland from this plain after a succession of bloody massacres. Despairing of the Crown's early efforts to force the colonists to build towns—a convenience for shippers and a precaution against attack—Virginia now recognized their division into nineteen counties. Besides the eight shires created by the 1634 assembly—Accomack, Charles City, Charles River (renamed York), Elizabeth City, Henrico, James City, Warrosquyoake (renamed Isle of Wight), and Warwick River (renamed Warwick)—there were now eleven others.[6] Settlers were steadily inching westward toward the Indian frontier, creating a need for new counties to provide military protection, a few roads and ferries, and parish churches, which in Anglican Virginia were supported by taxes.

Opposing overoptimistic growth, His Majesty's government sought to limit tobacco shipments to a few official ports and discouraged settlement in Indian areas. Governor Culpeper, on his first visit, had brought word that King Charles II was "resolved as soon as storehouses and conveniences can be provided, to prohibit ships trading here [in Virginia] to load or unload but at fixed places." Culpeper named the ports, and the assembly obediently encouraged the building of towns there. However, little progress was evident when Blair reached Virginia. In 1685 Jamestown and Elizabeth City were still Virginia's only villages worthy of the name.

Henrico County, to which young Mr. Blair was assigned, was the westernmost frontier of Virginia's settlement. To reach it, Blair boarded ship after having presented himself to the colonial officials at Jamestown and set sail for Varina some fifty miles further up the James.

As the sloop headed upstream the Scotsman could begin to see the vastness of his adopted land. Unlike the narrow streams of Banffshire, the James River's lower reaches stretched a full five miles wide. At Jamestown it measured almost a mile, narrowing gradually as it wended westward past James City, Surry, and Charles City counties. Standing at the rail, the minister now and then could see a planter's lonely house, standing among the pines and cleared fields. Not far above Jamestown was

Argall's Gift. Upriver a few miles and on the opposite shore was Martin's Brandon, a settlement that had sent a burgess to the first assembly at Jamestown in 1619; it was later to become the home of Blair's brother-in-law, Nathaniel Harrison. Maneuvering up the winding channel, the vessel passed riverfront lands patented by such pioneers as the Byrds, the Cockes, the Epes, the Hills, and the Harrisons, their docks welcoming any passing ships that might bring news or cargo.

Nearing Henrico, Blair's vessel crossed the entrance to the Appomattox River and came upon the site of Bermuda Hundred, a settlement made in 1613 to carry on trade with the Indians. Negotiating a winding stretch known as The Curls, the sailing ship passed Curles' Neck, lately the home of the rebellious Nathaniel Bacon, who had led his frontiersmen against Governor Berkeley nine years before.

Though Virginians had not warmed to Oliver Cromwell's brief regime, it was evident to Blair from the time of his landing in Virginia that they were equally disappointed in the treatment they had received from Charles II. Instead of reopening the colony's open trading with ships from the Netherlands and other European ports, the king had renewed the hated Navigation Act of Cromwell's regime, ignoring Virginia's pleas to be permitted to ship in Dutch bottoms and to trade at will. After Berkeley failed to alter King Charles' mercantilist views, England tightened control over Virginia. Royal governors were sent to the colony under instructions to limit the assembly and strengthen the executive role.[7]

The chief affront had been the king's grant of all Virginia territory in 1673 to two of his favorites, Lords Arlington and Culpeper, for a period of thirty-one years.[8] To claim this windfall, Culpeper had become governor in 1677 and served briefly at Jamestown. Lord Howard of Effingham, succeeding Culpeper in 1684, had been in Virginia less than a year when James Blair arrived, but already His Lordship had clashed with the burgesses when he sought to undermine their powers. Such was the political turmoil in the colony when James Blair entered.

As the new minister's ship at length emerged from the curls of the James, a cluster of buildings on the north shore came into view. This was Varina, named for Venezuelan tobacco of the highly-prized varinas type that was successfully grown in the vicinity. Here, among a few farmhouses and tobacco storehouses, stood Henrico County's courthouse, a jail, Thomas Cocke's tavern, and Henrico Parish church.[9] To the east a narrow horse path led through the thick forest to riverfront plantations and to Jamestown. Many settlers came to court and church by boat. The river divided the county and was its chief thoroughfare.

The settlement of Varina stood on a neck of river-bottom land known for its richness. Tobacco, a heavy feeder, grew abundantly in its moist clay soil. For this reason, land at Varina and neighboring Turkey Island, Presque Ile, and Curle's Neck plantations had been cherished since Henrico's beginnings. So well-favored was Varina that the assembly in 1680 designated it a tobacco port, responding to the Crown's directions to Governor Culpeper.

Like all early Virginia parishes, Henrico Parish was widespread and thinly populated. As its minister, James Blair was responsible for the spiritual life of all who dwelt within it. In addition to services in the church, he must conduct others at chapels of ease in remote parts of the county. He was also required by Anglican discipline to perform many other functions: to bless or "church" mothers of newborn infants, to baptize children, to pronounce the banns on three successive Sundays for betrothed couples, to catechize youths on their understanding of their Christian duties, to solemnize weddings, and to bury the dead.

At the western end of Henrico Parish, between the falls of the James River and the foothills of the Blue Ridge Mountains, lay the lands of the Monacan or Manakin Indians. By 1685 these tribesmen led a peaceful life as farmers and traders, but they were occasionally attacked by war parties of Iroquois who came southward from their lands in New York and Pennsylvania into the Virginia uplands. Henrico planters lived with their guns loaded and ready for use when they worked their fields by day or sat before the warming hearthfire at night, the younger children learning the alphabet from a hornbook while their elders did domestic chores: spinning, weaving, or preparing food for winter storage.

Though the area was Virginia's westernmost frontier, it had been settled by the English since almost 1607. Near Varina, Deputy Governor Sir Thomas Dale in 1611 had attempted to plant a new capital of the colony to supplant Jamestown. There he had installed 350 settlers on a palisaded peninsula in the James, naming it Henrico in honor of King James I's son, Henry, Prince of Wales. The Reverend Alexander Whitaker had been the first minister there, instructing the Indian princess Pocahontas in the Christian faith in 1614.

When Governor Sir George Yeardley had been sent to Virginia in 1619, he was instructed by the Virginia Company of London to build a university at Henrico. However, the prospect of both town and university languished after Indians overran the river settlements in 1622 and killed nearly 350 of Virginia's 1,250 settlers.

Despite the setback, plantations spread steadily up the James after 1622. By the time James Blair landed at Varina, tobacco clearings almost lined the river as far as the fall line. By the time of the 1622 attack, William Ferrar, son of the London merchant Nicholas Ferrar, who was treasurer of the Virginia Company, had settled there. Richard Cocke, the first of a long line of Virginians to bear that surname, had patented Bremo in 1639. About 1673 Henrico attracted William Randolph, who settled at Turkey Island with his wife, Mary Isham of Bermuda Hundred, and generated a large landholding family.

By 1685 such English surnames as Archer, Byrd, Bullington, Bacon, Soane, Glover, Worsham, Branch, Goode, Kennon, Field, and Jefferson were familiarly known along the upper James.

A handful of these families controlled the Henrico County offices that were filled by the governor and the council. Such appointments were coveted, for their fees were often paid in sterling, and sterling was rare and cherished in Virginia's economy. "Between 1670 and 1691," wrote Philip Alexander Bruce in *Social Life of Virginia in The Seventeenth Century*, "every official position in Henrico County was occupied by a member of the Randolph, Cocke, or Ferrar family."[10] Blair was closely associated with these planters, who served as vestrymen of his parish and as justices of the county court.

By February 1, 1687, he was sufficiently established to buy a hundred acres of farmland close to the parish glebe farm, where he was evidently living. The contract, "Between the hon'l William Byrd Esqr of the County and Parish of Henrico of the one part, and the Reverend James Blair of the County and Parish aforesaid, minister, of the other part," called for Blair to pay Byrd £35.

The acreage was "on the north Side James River which was by the said William Byrd purchased of Robert Sharp . . . April 2, 1683 . . . commonly known by the name of Varina and containing by estimation about one hundred acres . . . ." Byrd's wife, Mary Horsmanden, was represented by attorneys William Randolph and William Glover, and the deed was witnessed by Henry Randolph, clerk of Henrico Court and uncle to William Randolph.[11]

Not often did so much currency change hands in Virginia, where tobacco had become the medium of exchange in the absence of bank notes and coins. Blair's cash may have come from his savings or from collections of debts sent by his brother John from Edinburgh.

The hundred acres were the first of many which the Scotsman was to acquire in Virginia. As a result, James Blair was to amass an estate of more than £10,000 before his death, much of it farmland in New Kent, James City, and York counties and the town of Williamsburg. Like most Virginia fortunes built up in colonial times, Blair's was invested chiefly in real estate.

Henrico's minister found himself in demand in other parishes besides his own. Within Virginia, forty-eight parishes had been organized by 1680, but only thirty-four had clergymen.[12] One that lacked a minister was Charles City, adjoining Henrico, which Edmund Jenings, secretary of the colony, reported had "[lay] Readers Only" in 1680. Blair's visitations in his parish and in others nearby required him to be often away from home, on horseback or in boats that were rowed or sailed across the

Broader religious toleration was permitted in England and her colonies after the Glorious Revolution of 1688 and the accession of King William and Queen Mary. A toleration act was passed by Parliament, and strong effort was made to end divisive religious issues.

Courtesy of the British Museum

James. He was steadily called to attend the newborn, the dying, or the bereaved.

A parish minister's life can be seen from a report that the Reverend Anthony Gavin sent from Goochland County, formerly part of Henrico, to the Bishop of London in 1728. He wrote: "I have 3 churches, 23 and 24 miles from the glebe, in which I officiate every third Sunday, and besides these three I have seven places of service up in the mountains where the clerks read prayers, 4 clerks in the seven places. I go twice a year to preach in 12 places which I reckon better than 400 miles backwards and forwards, and ford 19 times the North and South Rivers. . . . In my first Journey I baptized White people, 229; Blacks, 172; Quakers, 15; Annabaptists, 2."[13]

Blair's duties frequently took him across the James aboard sail- or row-ferries at Varina, Westover, and later at Bermuda Hundred.[14] For a fare of from threepence to a shilling a foot-traveler could cross; horsemen paid double. The river was often rough (Alexander Whitaker, Henrico's first minister, drowned near Varina in 1617), but ferrymen were compelled by law to serve passengers in fair weather.

The young cleric had not been long in Henrico when he met seventeen-year-old Sarah Harrison, daughter of Benjamin Harrison II of Wakefield in Surry County.[15] Though he was about thirty, he and Sarah fell in love. She was a pretty girl with bright, almond-shaped eyes and a quick wit.[16] Moreover, she had an independent streak and an iron will that appealed to tough-minded James. The only obstacle was that she was already engaged to William Roscow of Warwick County, for whom she had jilted a previous fiance. Francis Nicholson later produced her marriage contract with Roscow, which read:

These are to certifye all persons in ye World, that I, Sarah Harrison, Daughter of Mr. Benja. Harrison, do & am fully resolved & by these presents do oblige myself (& cordially promise) to Wm. Roscow never to marry or to contract Marriage with any Man (during his life) only himself [.] to confirm these presents, I the above said Sarah Harrison do call the Almighty God to witness & so help me God. Amen.

SARAH HARRISON[17]

This document was sworn to on April 28, 1687. Yet despite it and her parents' entreaties, the determined Scotsman persuaded Sarah to marry him, though she was in Nicholson's words "a woman already contracted for." They were married June 2, 1687,[18] five weeks after she had pledged to marry Roscow.

Perhaps young William deserved no better treatment, for Nicholson ungallantly wrote later that "it is reported of this *Sarah Harrison*, that she was promised to two or three others; particularly to one Captain *Cox*; and her Father writ to the Gentleman that then granted Licence of Marriages, for one to the said Captain *Cox*, it being so nigh, that he kept the Wedding-Dinner."[19]

No penalty was specified in the breach between Sarah and William Roscow, but substantial payment was usual in such cases. A Harrison family marriage contract dated 1760, for example, carried an indemnity of £50 in case of forfeit. Benjamin Harrison doubtless paid a price for his daughter's fickleness.

The circumstances of James Blair's marriage reveal a more human side of the young man than any of the few records of his earlier life. Behind that mild countenance lurked a granite will —a will that was to make Blair one of the most influential colonists in America. To marry the teen-age Sarah, he defied propriety and Benjamin Harrison's goodwill, though he soon won acceptance by her family and friends. Moreover, the alliance brought him into the small circle which controlled Virginia. Whatever motivated his ardor—love, ambition, or a mixture of the two—James Blair became a member of the ruling class.

The Harrisons of Surry were among the leaders of the emerging planter society. "Of all the ancient families in the colony," wrote historian Hugh Blair Grigsby, "that of Harrison, if not the oldest, is one of the oldest." Backed by his Harrison in-laws, the ambitious Blair was to become one of the leading men in Virginia. This was the more remarkable in a colony that usually objected to clergymen in political office.

No record survives of the wedding. It was probably solemnized in the Harrison house, Wakefield, which was burned a century later by Benedict Arnold in his Revolutionary sweep through Virginia. The house would have been more convenient than the chapel that stood on land given by Harrison at Cabin Point, several miles away.[20] One unusual incident was later alleged by the hostile Francis Nicholson. "When Mr. *James Blair* was married to Mrs. [Miss] *Sarah Harrison*," Nicholson wrote in 1727, "it was done by one Mr. *Smith*.[21] When she was to say, Obey, She said No obey, upon wch he refused to proceed & the second time she said No Obey & then he refused again to proceed. The third time she said No Obey; yet the sd Mr. Smith went on with the rest of the ceremony."[22]

Had Blair scoured Virginia, he could not have found a more fortuitous connection than the Harrisons, however difficult Sarah proved. They were gregarious and enterprising people, with a knack for marrying well. Their emigrant English ancestor, the first Benjamin, became a burgess in 1646, a few years after his arrival. In his brief lifetime he acquired five hundred acres in Surry, married, and in 1645 sired a son also named Benjamin. Thus began the dynasty.

Benjamin Harrison II served for eighteen years in the House of Burgesses at Jamestown before being named to the council. He enlarged his estate by raising tobacco and by trading aboard his river boats and at his dockside store near Cabin Point. Adhering to Governor Berkeley in Bacon's Rebellion, he developed ties to the Green Spring faction which reinforced his influence. Six children born to him and his wife, Hannah, lived to marry offspring of other large landholders.

The eldest son, the third Benjamin (1673–1710), married Elizabeth, daughter of Colonel Lewis Burwell, a member of the council from Gloucester County, and built a large house at Berkeley Hundred on the James below Varina. He served as attorney general of Virginia, speaker of the House of Burgesses, treasurer, and, in the view of Governor Nicholson, was one of the two ablest attorneys in Virginia before his death at thirty-seven, two years before his father's.

Nathaniel (1677–1727), second son of Benjamin II, inherited Martin's Brandon near his father's Wakefield plantation and married Mary Cary Young, daughter of John Cary, merchant, of England and Virginia; like his father and brothers-in-law, he became a member of the council. To the third son, Henry (1682–1732), who followed his father to the House of Burgesses, went Wakefield and adjoining acres at Cabin Point in Surry. He married Elizabeth Smith of Gloucester.

Of the three Harrison sisters, the youngest, Elizabeth, married the second William Edwards of James City and Surry, whose father had been clerk of the general court and later of the council. Their home was at Pleasant Point near Scotland Wharf and across the river from Jamestown. Elizabeth Harrison Edwards evidently predeceased her father, for he did not mention her in his 1711 will. She was buried with other Harrisons and Edwardses in the Jamestown churchyard.[23]

Of Sarah Blair's sisters, Hannah (1678–1731) married the most brilliantly. She was the family beauty, described as "very pretty" and as "pious, charitable, and hospitable." A portrait painted of her in London by the fashionable Sir Godfrey Kneller depicts her delicate features and serenity. Like other belles, she lived "an exemplary life in chearful innocence."[24] She married Philip Ludwell II, a well-favored young man whose father in 1680 had taken as his second wife Frances, widow of Governor Sir William Berkeley and cousin to Lord Culpeper, erstwhile protégé of Charles II. Ludwell plantations at Greenspring and Richneck in James City and at Chippokes in Surry were among the colony's finest.

Even more valuable allies than the Harrisons were the Ludwells, father and son. Like James Blair, they were men of independent mind and were to help underwrite several of his reformist missions to England: a later governor, Alexander Spotswood, declared that the Ludwells were antagonistic to all governors in an effort to maintain their wrongful possession of Greenspring. Philip Ludwell II became one of Blair's two closest allies. The other was to be his brother Archibald Blair who came to Virginia from Edinburgh before 1690, bringing with him his young son John.

Returning to Varina with his bride in June 1687, James Blair resumed the duties of the rural parson. He was also occasionally in court, as Henrico records show. In October 1688 attorney

William Randolph represented a carpenter, William Stacy, who sued Blair for failing to pay for work done.[25] At the December session of court, judgment was rendered for Stacy after a committee of "viewers" had examined the job and the accounts. Blair was required to pay 422 pounds of tobacco and cask.

The minister was doubtless the speaker at Henrico ceremonies in the spring of 1689 to celebrate the accession of King William and Queen Mary. Virginians generally welcomed the deposition of the Roman Catholic James II and the belated news of the new reign. The assembly at Jamestown hailed William and Mary as "blessed Instruments" who had risked their necks to save England's parliamentary government and established church "from the Dangers and feares wee were ready to Sinke under."

In December 1689 Blair, Jeremiah Brown, and Nicholas Bullington appeared before Henrico's justices of the peace and offered to clear "a much shorter and more convenient" road to church and court, forty feet in width, provided they had permission to enclose their adjoining land. The request was granted.[26]

Blair added to his holdings on April 20, 1690, when Nathaniel Bacon the elder, president of council and uncle of Bacon the rebel,[27] deeded to Blair, Brown, and Bullington "130 acres of sunken swamp and marsh land lying and bounding their several plantations." The grant was made by the colony "for the importation of three persons." Below the entry of the patent is noted, "James Urwin 3 severall times,"[28] indicating that the grant was in payment for bringing a settler into the colony three times and claiming the fifty acres allowed for each such importation.

In August 1690 Blair testified in court for Captain William Soane, who sued Robert Napier for £10 "won at a horse race at Varina" on October 10, 1689: "After the swearing of ye Jury, Mr. Ja. Blair minister (being brought into ye Court as an Evidence for ye plt) did request that without an Oath he might (on ye word of a Priest) declare his Evidence, which was granted, and he did then affirm the same deposed by Capt. Wm. Randolph, adding farther his knowledge of ye def't's fetching his horse away some small time before ye Race; of which affirmacon the Jury was directed to take notice. . . ."

Judgment was rendered the same day: "We the Jury find for the plaintiff ten pounds in silver (the defend't's earnest understood to be returned) with costs of suit." The court upheld the finding and the defendant noted an appeal.[29]

The marriage of the Blairs began uneventfully. There is no record of any children, which was presumably a disappointment. A childless marriage in Virginia, where families often numbered a dozen, was a rarity. There is reason to believe that Sarah was in frail health, for she was to die in 1713 at forty-three. William Byrd II also intimated to his diary in 1709 that she was fond of strong drink. Describing a call on the Blairs, he noted: "I was very much surprised to find Mrs. Blair drunk, which is growing pretty common with her, and her relations disguise it under the name of consolation."[30]

In June 1690 a new lieutenant governor arrived in Virginia, bearing news that was to alter the Blairs' quiet life. He was the high-mettled soldier, Captain Francis Nicholson, who came as a deputy to replace Lord Howard of Effingham.[31] Nicholson brought instructions "to take care that drunkenness and debauchery, Swearing and blasphemy be Severely punished, and that none be admitted to public trust and Employment whose ill fame and conversation may bring scandal thereupon."[32] He also bore a commission from the bishop of London, dated December 15, 1689, naming James Blair as his commissary or deputy in Virginia. It read:

HENRY, by Divine permission Bishop of London, to all the faithful in Christ to whom this present Writing may come. Greeting eternal in the Lord.

Know ye that we, the Bishop of London aforesaid, to whom every ecclesiastical jurisdiction, and in every way, under Virginia situated in America, by Royal Constitutions is generally recognized to pertain, (except the power of granting licenses for celebrating marriages, probating wills of deceased persons and conferring benefices), have named, made and constituted, and by these presents do name, make and constitute, James Blaire, Clerk, our Commissary in and throughout all Virginia aforesaid, trusting very greatly his learning, probity

and industry, with all and every power of carrying out and perform-
ing, (previous exceptions excepted) , whatever pertains and belongs,
or ought to pertain and belong, to the office of our Commissary
aforesaid, by law or custom according to the laws, canons and constitutions followed and observed, in the Church of England; with
power moreover to set one or more clerk or clerks as substitute or
substitutes in his place.

In confidence and in testimony of all and singular of which
premises we have caused our Episcopal Seal to be placed upon these
presents.

Given on the fifteenth day of the month of December in the year
of our Lord, 1689, and in the twenty-fourth year of our Translation.
                                                    H. London[33]

The usual role of a commissary was to represent a bishop in
a part of his diocese. Though previously unknown in the American colonies, the office was common in England. It was a half-
step between absentee administration by the bishop of London
and the creation of a new bishopric. The Virginia commissary's
authority was limited, however, because the bishop of London
had only informal jurisdiction over the American colonies—an
anomalous situation that was never corrected.

Blair's appointment was concrete evidence of the new interest
taken in the colonies by William and Mary. Nicholson's arrival
was also welcome after the frustrations created by Culpeper and
Effingham. The new executive was young, friendly, and enthusiastic about his assignment. Though trained as a soldier, he
showed ardent interest in the economic and spiritual well-being
of the colonists. It seems likely that Bishop Compton had a hand
in his selection, as a member of the Privy Council's Committee
on Trade and Plantations. Certainly Compton had Nicholson's
support in inaugurating the position of commissary in Virginia.

Disembarking at Jamestown, Nicholson was sworn on June 3,
1690, and Blair's commission was then read to the council. It
was well received, for the Scotsman had shown diligence and
sobriety in his five years in Virginia. The council recorded that
"the Lt Govr is by this Board requested, to . . . returne his Lordsp
[the Bishop of London] the humble thanks of this Board, for
his pious care in this affaire, and the reposeing the trust in one
soe well deserveing thereof as the said Mr Blair is."[34]

The new commissary lost no time in calling Virginia's clergy to meet at Jamestown. Of the two dozen ministers in Virginia, it is probable that the majority attended, traveling by boat from remote points and by horse from nearby. Gathering on July 23, 1690, in the brick church on the river, the clergy were directed by Blair to form four regional groups, or convocations, and to meet twice a year before coming together with him each September at Jamestown.

As his "Substitute and Surrogate" in the counties south of the James River, Blair named the Reverend Patrick Smith of Southwark Parish, Surry, who had officiated at his wedding. The Reverend Samuel Eburne of Bruton Parish at Middle Plantation, later named Williamsburg, was designated for the peninsula parishes between the James and the York, together with the Eastern Shore. The Reverend Duell Pead of Christ Church in Middlesex County was responsible for the peninsula embracing Gloucester, Middlesex, and part of New Kent. Finally, the Reverend John Farnifold of Fairfield Parish in Northumberland was placed in charge of the northern neck, between the Rappahannock and the Potomac.

To these convocations Blair assigned the enforcement of ecclesiastical laws, which he mistakenly believed he had been authorized to oversee. The zealous minister apparently made the mistake in good conscience, but it served to turn many of the easy-going clergy against him. Though ecclesiastical laws had been enforced by bishops' courts in England and Scotland, they were alien to Virginia. To attempt so suddenly to punish swearing, fornication, and other violations of the Ten Commandments created an uproar. The Virginia clergy's mounting resistance to Bishop Compton's "Scots hireling" (as he was later called) began with Blair's attempt to reform the colony's morality.

The commissary issued a proclamation after the meeting, setting forth his aim:

... Whereas the Right Revd Father in God Lord Bp of London taking into his consideration the great contempt of Religion and dissoluteness of life & manners which are too visible, within this

Colony of Virginia to the dishonour of **God**, reproach of the **Church** & the Scandal of all good men,

And being willing & desirous as far as lyes within his power to make use of his Episcopal Authority for remedy and redress of the same, has commanded the Ecclesiastical Jurisdiction to be impartially executed in order to a speedy Reformation of the lives of both Clergy and Laity within this Colony; and for this end has by a publick instrument under his hand and Episcopal Seal nominated and appointed me James Blair his Commissary within the Dominion and colony forsd, as the sd instrument bearing date the 15th day of Decr in the year of our Lord 1689 doth more largely contain and express:

Now know ye yt I the sd James Blair by virtue of the forsd Commission do in the name of the Right Revd Father in God Henry Lord Bishop of London and with the Advice of the Clergy of this Colony at their General Meeting forsd, Certify to all persons Concerned yt I intend to revive and put in execution the Ecclesiastical laws against all cursers, Swearers & blasphemers, all whoremongers, fornicators and Adulterers, all drunkards ranters and profaners of the Lords day and Contemners of the Sacraments, and agt all other Scandalous Persons, whether of the Clergy or Laity within this dominion and Colony of Virginia. . . .

And for the more convenient execution of the sd design, according to another part of the power and authority comitted to me by an express article in the foresd Commission for nominating of Substitutes in the several precincts of the sd Colony, to the end yt due Information may be had of the sevll Scandals, and yt more convenient proofs may be brought, and yt the great burden of the work may be lightened by being divided among several persons with the consent and advice of the Clergy at their General meeting I have nominated and appointed . . . the persons following [,] Ministers of the gospel in the several precincts hereafter mentioned my Substituts and Surrogats. . . .[35]

While Virginia urgently needed higher moral standards, Blair's words had an objectionably puritanical ring. They smacked of kirk sessions in lowland Scotland, where John Knox had decreed that drunkenness and other misconduct "properly appertain to the Church of God, to punish the same as God's word commandeth." In the years since Sir George Yeardley had brought to Virginia the Great Charter of 1618, terminating "those cruel and unusual laws" imposed by Sir Thomas Dale in his *Lawes Divine, Morall and Martiall*, the colony had developed a hedonistic character.

True to this character, the Virginia Assembly in 1642 had forced several Puritan ministers to return to Massachusetts by requiring that all clergy in the colony must conform to the Church of England or depart. Again, during England's civil wars from 1642 to 1659, Virginia's sympathies had strongly supported cavaliers against Puritans; on his enthronement in 1660, King Charles II—the very embodiment of the cavalier spirit—recognized Virginia as his "Old Dominion." Such was the colony which Blair dared try to change.

In his 1690 proclamation, the new commissary put ministers and vestries on notice that he intended to establish a new severity. Clergy meetings should begin with prayers and a sermon "explaining some of the articles of our holy faith . . . or against the prevailing Sins of the time and place." It was the duty of his four clergy leaders to administer the churchwarden's oath in his convocation. Should a warden refuse, he should expect "ecclesiastical discipline." Wardens were "to make true presentment of all such Scandals and enormities as shall be comitted within their jurisdiction." If an offense proved "too difficult and intricat" to be adjudged at a regional meeting, it should be referred to the commissary's convocation at Jamestown in September.[36]

Despite clergy resistance, Blair's efforts provoked favorable action by the council. Meeting at Jamestown the day after the first clergy gathering, the councilors asked Nicholson to condemn the evils that the commissary proposed to overcome.[37] Nicholson did so, warning county sheriffs that they should expect an annual visit from the commissary to assure compliance. "I have spoke with ye Reverend Mr Blair," the Governor wrote, "who is appointed by ye Rt Reverend Father in God Henry Lord Bishop of London Commissary of this their Majties Territory and Dominion of Virga who intends God willing in ye Spring to make a Genll Visitacon, and hope your County will be found in Such order yt he will have no reason to punish any

"And to that End I have herein sent you their Majties Lere [letter] to ye Rt Reverend Father in God ye Bp of London, and do order that you cause ye Same to be published at every other Court, and once in two months in each Church in your County, that all people encouraged by so good Example may demean themselves accordingly."[38]

Lacking the letter referred to, we can only assume that King William and Queen Mary had authorized the bishop of London to appoint a commissary to Virginia and empower him to act. No doubt Compton then conferred with Virginia's titular governor, Lord Howard of Effingham, before dispatching Blair's commission to Virginia in care of Effingham's lieutenant governor, Francis Nicholson.

Blair's proposals for ecclesiastical courts died quietly, apparently of official consent, ten months after he announced them. An entry in the Journal of the House of Burgesses intimates that Nicholson and the burgesses were ready to forget the matter: "A Message from the Councill . . . acquainted the House from the Rt honble the Lt Governour That Mr Eburne Minister who lately issued out a precept for *Ralph Flowers* clerk of *York* parish to answer before him Severall allegations complaintes & misdemeanors, and Mr Sclater Minister[39] who procured the Same had before his Honr acknowledged their Errors, and that his honr had sent to the House to know, if they desired any further proceedings against them, to which the House returned answer, that being well satisfied of his Honrs care in that affaire they humbly Submitted it to his honr prudence."[40]

Blair had learned his lesson. During his years as commissary he would never again resort to such severe means to correct ungodly behavior. If anything, the commissary seemed to lose heart for the disciplinary aspect of his work. Only twice in his fifty-three years as commissary did he suspend a minister, explaining that the limited number of replacements made it impractical.[41] Nevertheless, Blair's very presence after 1690 was a sobering influence on clergy and laity. Little escaped his watchful eye.

Another move emanating from Blair's first convocation also died aborning. This was the clergy's request that the colony stabilize the money value of their salaries. Being paid in tobacco, these were subject to the yearly rise or fall of the market. "The Petition of *James Blayre* minister on behalfe of himselfe & the rest of ye Clergy of this Dominion abt the better paymt of their Salaries" went first to the governor and council, who referred it to the burgesses at their meeting in April 1691.[42] There it too died.

The most fruitful proposals by the commissary were "Several Propositions" for a college in Virginia. Living at Varina, James Blair had often heard the story of the first English college undertaken in the New World. This had been proposed by the Virginia Company of London in 1618, and an endowment of ten thousand acres of land had been set aside in Henrico. To this was added the sum of £155 collected after the Reverend Patrick Copeland, a Marischal College graduate, had solicited from passengers aboard the *Royal James* in 1621, en route from the East Indies to England. The next year Copeland had been appointed rector of the proposed college, but news of the Virginia Indian massacre of 1622 reached England before he could sail for Henrico. Among the victims was George Thorpe, the governor's deputy on the college lands.

Although the college lands were abandoned as colonists withdrew towards the safety of Jamestown, the idea persisted. Now, with the benevolent William and Mary in power, the time seemed ripe for a college in England's oldest colony.[43]

The new commissary was the logical advocate, and Virginia's first gathering of ministers was the appropriate occasion. James Blair's "Several Propositions," approved by the clergy, suggested an institution to consist of a grammar school teaching Latin and Greek, an undergraduate college, and a divinity school. The enthusiastic clergymen authorized a petition to the assembly and an appeal for donations in the colony and from English merchants trading in Virginia.[44]

When Blair's proposal came to the council, it was presented by Colonel John Page of Middle Plantation. An educated man and the donor of the land for Middle Plantation's church, Page gathered a few leading men and spread the idea. He was later credited for his efforts, at the college's first recorded May Day exercises in 1699. "The first publick consultation about it," declared a student orator, "was at a meeting of some private gentlemen at James City" in February 1691. "The person that had the chief honour to be the first mover in procureing such a meeting was the Honorable Colonell [John] Page; to whom and his family this great work has been exceedingly beholding."[45]

When the assembly met in April 1691, nine months after Blair had publicly proposed the idea, a joint committee of the council and burgesses was named to petition the King and Queen to charter a college. Recognizing Blair's ability and his contacts in England, the assembly then and there chose the commissary to prepare a petition to their Majesties and go to England with it. Meanwhile a committee of leading men from the council, the House of Burgesses, and the clergy was named to gather subscriptions.

In May or June 1691 James Blair said goodbye to Sarah and sailed for England. In his sea chest lay the assembly's petition and an impressive list of Virginia subscribers. As his ship nosed into the blue water of Chesapeake Bay, he exulted in God's providence. Only six years before, he had come to Virginia as a friendless missionary. Now he was the bishop's commissary and the spokesman chosen over all Virginia's settlers to go to England and petition their Majesties for a college and theological school.

The winds filled the sails, and the little ship was borne swiftly out into the dark Atlantic. Virginia lay behind him. Before him loomed opportunity and a great adventure.

CHAPTER III

The Church and the Empire
1607-1691

⋘ The English church that was planted in America at Jamestown had a history of trial and triumph.

When Martin Luther nailed his ninety-five theses to the door of the Wittenberg castle church in 1517, most of Europe was part of the medieval Latin Church. Then, for the next 150 years, the schism resulting from piecemeal reform along various lines swept much of the continent. Among the peoples of the Mediterranean basin, the lustre of Rome remained largely undimmed. However, the fires of more radical reform spread ravenously from Germany to the North Sea and Scandinavia.

Led by such reformers as Luther in Germany, John Hüss in Bohemia, John Calvin in France, Ulrich Zwingli in Switzerland, and John Knox in Scotland, national reformed churches arose —Lutheran, Anabaptist, Presbyterian, and others.

England, divided from the mainland by the English Channel, escaped the worst severities of religious conflict. There the Reformation was primarily a contest between church and state. No great reformer like Luther or Knox revolutionized its religious life. Rejecting both the Church of Rome and Protestant reformers, Henry VIII in 1534 pushed through Parliament the Act of Supremacy, which disclaimed papal control and made the Church of England answerable to the king instead of the pope.

Like the Byzantine emperors of Constantinople, Henry imposed the majesty of the crown over that of the church.[1] Thus, like the Orthodox Eastern Church in Constantinople, the Church of England claimed a common heritage with Rome, without giving allegiance to Rome's pope. The *Book of Common Prayer* in 1549 offered the plea, "From the tyranny of the Bishop of Rome and all his detestable enormities . . . Good Lord, deliver us." Instead, English ecclesiastics regarded themselves as part of a "catholic and universal church" whose authority extended through medieval bishops to Christ's apostles.

Two centuries were to pass before most of England was reconciled to Henry's Act of Supremacy. Throughout the reign of his daughter Elizabeth and the Stuarts who followed her, the island kingdom was torn by dissension. In the uplands of northern England, unreformed Catholicism or Romanism remained powerful and rebellious.

Conversely, in industrial cities like London, Bristol, and Plymouth, the rising middle class was imbued with the Calvinist zeal of northern Europe. These burghers regarded Anglican ritual as "popish" and demanded a simpler worship—a direct communication between man and God. England's larger towns remained strongholds of dissenters and Puritans and of the Quakers and Methodists who followed them.

Unlike ascetic Puritans and Presbyterians, Anglicans enjoyed worldly pleasures without guilt. Their theme was one of triumph—the triumph of God over death—and of man's entitlement to the enjoyment of earthly diversions such as dancing, gaming, the theater, and other pastimes. In liturgy and music, they proclaimed Christ's power to redeem sin, evoking visions of an orderly universe, presided over by a just and merciful God. Standing between the ceremonialism of Rome and the austerity of Geneva, Anglicanism sought the best of both.

Assailed from both sides, the Church of England hardened gradually after 1543. Slowly and painfully, it groped toward a *via media* that conceivably might accommodate both Catholic and Puritan, savant and peasant. Yet try as it might to be "catholic and universal," the English church exerted its strongest appeal to the educated class. Its clergy, often the younger sons of noble families, had been schooled at Oxford and Cambridge. Its bishops, selected by the king, were usually chosen for learning or diplomacy—sometimes for family connections. Its theology was the product of solid scholarship, its liturgy the creation of gifted poets.

Embattled as the Church of England was, its faith was a vital one to the people of England. When the Virginia Company of London was chartered in 1606, King James I directed that the "word and service of God be preached, planted, and used as well in the said colonies and also as much as might be among the savages bordering them." Among the 105 settlers who sailed from London on December 20 of that year was the Reverend Robert Hunt, a graduate of Oxford, who died at Jamestown in 1608. Prayers were offered daily, and God's help was asked whenever troops were mustered or colonists sat down to eat.[2]

Unlike the Church of Rome, which in the fifteenth century established its Congregatio de Propaganda Fide to send missionaries to Spanish and Portuguese settlements, the Church of England took no step until 1701 to provide for the orderly spread of the faith abroad when the Society for the Propagation of the Gospel in Foreign Parts was formed. Because Virginia was planted primarily as a private venture, the Church of England was not officially involved. However, the bishop of London and other churchmen were among early investors in the corporation.[3] As London was the heart of England's imperial ambitions, the Virginia Company looked to London's bishop as the colonies' own.

The church's concern for overseas work quickened when William Laud became bishop of London in 1628.[4] By this time, Virginia had become a royal colony and Charles I in 1625 had succeeded James I. When Charles named Laud as archbishop of Canterbury in 1633, Laud vowed to establish the royal ecclesiastical supremacy in every corner of the English dominions.[5]

The king was no less determined. "The Company of Merchant Adventurers should not hereafter receive any minister into their churches or foreign parts without his Majesty's approbation of the person," Charles ordered on October 1, 1633. "The Liturgy and discipline used in the Church of England should be received there, and in all things concerning their church government they should be under the jurisdiction of the Bishop of London."[6]

However determined Laud may have been that English colonists should adhere to the established church, it proved impossible to control their religious life from faraway England.

Caught up in domestic dissension, the Church of England for eighty years left Virginia to find her own way. Countless enactments by the Virginia Assembly evidence the colony's interest in spiritual matters.

At their first session, held in the wooden church at Jamestown from July 30 to August 4, 1619, Virginia's legislators ordered that "All persons whatsoever upon the Sabboath daye shall frequente divine service and sermons both forenoon and afternoon; and all suche as beare armes, shall bring their pieces, swordes, poulder, and shotte."[7] Thereafter, the duties and forms of Christianity were considered at nearly every session.

In 1623, the assembly ordered every plantation to set apart a place for compulsory Church of England worship. Settlers were to pay ministers "out of the first and best tobacco and corn," and clergymen were to be diligent in their duties.[8]

The young colony at first had no landholders capable of bestowing parochial livings, as England and Scotland had had since feudal times. Instead, settlers banded together to attract priests on the promise of a glebe, or church-owned farm, of a hundred acres plus a benefice supported collectively by the tithables, or adult communicants. For lack of currency, most trade in Virginia was in tobacco. So early did this system develop that Captain John Smith could write in 1630, "they have builded many pretty Villages, faire houses and Chapels, which are growne good Benefices of 120. pounds a yeare, besides their owne mundall [mundane] Industry."[9]

Bit by bit, the church planted at Jamestown spread. When an area attracted enough settlers to support a church, the assembly decreed a new parish. At first, parish lines coincided with those of the counties, but as settlement grew denser, parishes were divided. As a result, a chapel of ease, originally served once a month by the rector of a large parish, often grew in time into a full-fledged parish church with a rector of its own.

So great were the hardships of clerical life, however, that few ministers came. Some who did returned to England with such scandalous reports that other clergy dared not come over. John Hammond wrote in his *Leah and Rachel*,[10] published in London in 1656, "*Virginia* savouring not handsomely in *England*, very few of good conversation would adventur thither, (as thinking it a place wherein surely the fear of God was not) ." Under such a cloud, Virginia often attracted clerics of doubtful or irregular ordination.[11]

It is not surprising that several Church of Scotland ministers, reared in a poor and exploited land, were among those who came to Virginia as chaplains. Such was William Wickham, who assisted Alexander Whitaker in Henrico and Charles City during 1616 and 1617 and was thereafter serving in Henrico Parish and was a member of the council in 1619. Although permitted to officiate at other services, he could not administer communion.[12] In a report to London, Virginia was said in 1619 to have had "three ministers with orders and two without," the latter possibly Church of Scotland clergy lacking episcopal ordination.[13] Lay readers and Presbyterians continued to serve some Anglican churches.

Despite the Anglican spirit of Virginia, a few clergymen of Puritan persuasion came in. Alexander Whitaker was perhaps one of these, for he was the son of a well-known Puritan cleric and wrote from Virginia: "I marvaile much—that so few of our English ministers that were so hot against the surplis and subscription come hither where neither are spoken of."[14] In 1642 three Puritan divines came from Massachusetts at the invitation of settlers on the south side of the James River, prompting the Virginia Assembly in 1643 to require that all ministers conform to the "orders and constitutions" of the Church of England and that "all nonconformists . . . be compelled to depart the collony with all conveniencie."[15]

So badly needed were clergymen that this measure was rarely invoked. Puritans, Presbyterians, and Quakers continued to come. However, one instance occurred in 1645 when the Reverend Thomas Harrison, rector of Elizabeth River Parish on the later site of Norfolk, was haled before the county court "For not reading the Book of Common Prayer, and not administering the sacrament of baptism according to the canons and order prescribed, and for not catechizing on Sunday in the afternoon, according to the Act of Assembly."[16] The puritanical Harrison was banished to Massachusetts in 1648, where he preached for two years before returning to England.

During England's civil wars and Cromwellian protectorate, which ended in 1660 with the triumph of the cavaliers and restoration of the monarchy, Virginia also became a haven for Quakers, a pietistic sect originated in England which opposed military service and oath-taking. Still attempting to preserve Anglican dominance, the Virginia Assembly in 1660 passed an "Act for Suppressing the Quakers," but this too proved ineffective. Virginians were not easily coerced.

Virginia churches continued to use the *Book of Common Prayer* despite the Puritans' refusal to acknowledge the Church of England and disavowal of the book in 1645. The Virginia Assembly in 1647 blithely specified that each parish use the *Prayer Book* as before. Should a minister disobey, his parishioners were not to pay his salary.[17] Later, the assembly retreated slightly by voting to discontinue prayers for the king and royal family in public services, but it left to each parish vestry the decision on use of the *Prayer Book*.[18]

Virginia rejoiced in the restoration of the monarchy in 1660, having remained Royalist in sympathy. Besides, its tobacco economy had suffered wartime loss of sales, and Virginia was impatient to revive this essential trade. Soon after Parliament adopted the Act of Uniformity in 1662, which reinstated the

Book of Common Prayer and other Anglican usages, Virginia's Assembly strengthened its laws that defined parishes and duties of their clergy and vestries.

This call for a stronger ministry in Virginia was prompted by the king's instructions that were brought by Governor Berkeley to Jamestown in 1662:

And that God almighty may be more inclined to bestow his blessing upon us and you in the improvement of that our Colony, you shall take especiall care He may be devoutly and duly served in all the government; the Booke of Common Prayer, as it is now establisht, read each Sunday and Holy Day, and the Blessed Sacrament administered according to the Rites of the Church of England; You shall be carefull that the Churches already built there shall be well and orderly kept, and more built as the Colony shall, by God's blessing, be improved; And that besides a competent maintenance to be assigned to the Minister of each Church, a convenient house be built, at the common charge, for each Minister, and one hundred acres of land assigned him for a Glebe and exercise of his industry.

And our will and pleasure is that no Minister to be preferred by you to any Ecclesiastical Benefice in that our Colony, without a certificate from the Lord Bishop of London of his being conformable to the doctrine and discipline of the Church of England. And also our pleasure is, that in the direction of all Church affairs, the Ministers be admitted into the respective Vestrys.

... And because Wee are willing to give all possible encouragement to persons of different persuasions in matters of Religion to transport themselves thither with their stocks, You are not to suffer any man to be molested or disquieted in the exercise of his Religion, so he be content with a quiet and peaceable enjoying it, not giving offence or scandall to the Government; But Wee oblige you in your own house and family to the profession of the Protestant Religion, according as it is now established in our Kingdome of England, and the recommending it to all others under your government, as farre as it may consist with the peace and quiet of our said Colony. —You are to take care that drunkenese and debauchery, swearing and blasphemy, be discountenanced and punished; And that none be admitted to publick trust and employment, whose ill fame and conversation may bring scandall thereupon.[19]

The church laws enacted by the assembly in 1662 were in effect when Blair reached Virginia a quarter of a century later. They made the church in Virginia largely self-governing, answerable in some matters to the governor and assembly but in

Books were few and rare in seventeenth-century Virginia. In parish churches, psalm-singing was led by the clerk and followed line by line by the congregation. In common use in the Church of England was the 1662 edition of the Book of Common Prayer, *printed by His Majesty's Printers.*

Courtesy of the British Museum

most to local vestries. It was a scheme that compelled Virginians to act for themselves. Service on the vestry, with its mixed governmental and ecclesiastical responsibility, was to acquaint men like Washington, Mason, and Patrick Henry with public life.

The Virginia parish ranged from thirty to four hundred square miles.[20] Ideally, it should have been of such size as could be governed by a vestry of twelve, representing resident freeholders, but new and thinly settled frontier counties like Henrico usually began with one parish. The vestry's duties included "makeing and proportioning the levyes and assessments for building and repayring the churches, and chappells, provision for the poore, maintenance of the minister, and such other necessary duties for the more orderly manageing all parociall affaires. . . ."[21] Beyond their maintenance of church, glebe house, and lands, vestrymen were also responsible for the indigent, orphaned, and mentally incompetent.[22]

Two vestrymen were chosen yearly as churchwardens. These were responsible for collecting from each tithable his tenth of tobacco or corn for the minister's support, for keeping the church and glebe house in repair, and for presenting to the court any conspicuous offenders against morals and religion. Proscribed offenses were: "Swearing, profaneing Gods holy name, or sabbath abuseing [,] or contemning his holy word or sacraments or absenting themselves from the exercises thereof, As alsoe of those foule and abominable sins of drunkennesse [,] fornication [,] and adultery, and of all malitious and envious slandering and backbiting."[23]

Once a parish was formed, its vestry undertook to provide a church. "For the advancement of God's glory, and the more decent celebration of His divine ordinances," the 1662 code specified a church should be built unless, "by reason of fewnes or poverty of the inhabitants," it proved necessary for the parish to attach itself to another. Where a parish was too large to be served by one church, smaller chapels of ease were built in outlying areas for services once or twice a month. Such was Benjamin Harrison's chapel at Cabin Point in Surry.

The vestry's chief difficulty was in keeping a suitable minister.

Virginia's remoteness and her reputation for godlessness were not the only problems. Because of the uncertain quality of clergymen who came out to Virginia, vestries were reluctant to guarantee tenure until the cleric had proved himself, although church law directed that the parish formally "induct" its rector and let him serve at will, unless removed by an ecclesiastical superior. Not many English clergymen were willing to emigrate on such terms.

The 3,750 miles of ocean that separated Virginia from England delayed communication six months or more. When a parish sought a rector, one of its vestrymen first had to write an acquaintance in England to find a suitable applicant. Despite the offer of £20 from the king's bounty to transport clergy to the colonies, the move usually was expensive. Sailings were few, and arrival uncertain. A year's lapse between ministers was common.

The difficulty of attracting clergy was the greater because they were a privileged group in English life. In England and Scotland they ranked as gentlemen, enjoying the prestige of that class. Younger sons of noblemen usually entered the church or the army, enhancing clerical status. Unlike dissenting sects, the Church of England supported clergy from public funds and forbade them to demean themselves with physical labor or trade. Only preaching, teaching, and scholarly pursuits were appropriate to their calling.

Comfortable benefices were available in England through the gift of nobles, trade guilds, and church endowments accumulated since early Christian times. Many university graduates entered the ministry on promise of a landholder of his advowson, or presentation, to the benefice that he controlled. This was a relic of feudal years when noblemen provided a church for their tenants. Such a benefice was that to which Robert Macgill, Viscount Oxfourd, had named James Blair at Cranston in 1679. The income was predictable and paid partly in currency—not tobacco. English livings often included a fine house, garden, and other perquisites. Ambitious clergy might simultaneously hold several livings.

Lacking a missionary tradition, it is no wonder so few Anglican ministers emigrated to early Virginia. Without roads and often without a glebe house or church, they were expected to organize a parish. The cleric must be constantly on horseback or aboard ferries crossing the rivers. The tobacco that paid his salary fluctuated in value.

To improve the clergy's lot, the assembly of 1662 followed the king's recommendation and directed that glebe farms be set aside "for the better encouragement and accomodation of the ministery."[24] The minister was required to "preach constantly every sunday (viz.) one sunday in a month at each chappell of ease in his parish (if there be any in it) and the other sundays at his parish church."[25] He was also to keep a register of births, marriages, and burials, as in England.[26]

A primary responsibility was to insure that children grew up knowing the Bible and *Prayer Book* and could recite the catechism. Wrote Alexander Whitaker during his 1611–17 ministry at Varina: "Every Sabbath day wee preach in the forenoone, and chatechize in the afternoone. Every Saturday at night I exercise in Sir Thomas Dales house."[27]

In churches without a minister, vestries could appoint laymen to lead the service and to read a written sermon or homily from the *Book of Homilies*. Funerals and Sunday worship services were sometimes conducted in this fashion. However, the church requirement that the eucharist be celebrated by an episcopally ordained priest at Christmas, Easter, and Whitsunday was often disregarded for lack of such minister. The rites of marriage and of baptism of infants were frequently delayed for the same reason. And without a bishop, there could be no confirmations in the colony.

Despite clerical laxity in some English practices, services in Virginia roughly followed the Church of England forms. These were set forth in church canons and *The Book of Common Prayer*, produced in the reign of Edward VI in 1549, chiefly by Thomas Cranmer, archbishop of Canterbury. Suppressed by Cromwell and the Puritans from 1645 to 1660, the *Prayer Book* was restored and designated by the Act of Uniformity of 1662 as the only legal service book for use in England.[28]

Until 1689, when James Blair became commissary to the

bishop of London in Virginia, the *Prayer Book* was the chief unifying force in Virginia's churches. Though episcopal in name, these churches were in large measure independent in policy. The laxity that they developed was to create problems for Blair and for his successors as commissary throughout colonial times.

Hymns had been abandoned by the English church in the Reformation as too popish. In lieu of them, the Psalms were rendered in verse and set to simple tunes, which were sung by the congregation. They were of poor quality. Elizabeth I called them "Geneva jigs," and Thomas Fuller complained that blacksmiths at an anvil could make better music.

As in England, it was the duty of the clerk or lay reader of the parish to read the prescribed lessons from the Old and New Testaments at each service. He also raised the tune for the metrical psalms, singing each line first for the guidance of the congregation, which had few prayer books or psalm books but which responded lustily, in unison. No church had a pipe organ, and most church singing was unaccompanied.[29]

In general use was *The whole Book of Psalmes, Collected into English Meeter, by Thomas Sternhold, John Hopkins, and others . . . with apt notes to sing them withall*, first published in 1562. After 1696 a better psalm book by Nicholas Brady and Nahum Tate, the poet laureate, slowly supplanted the "Old Version" except with the rank and file.

The most popular Psalm in the old psalm book, sung to a tune known as "Old Hundredth," was the 100th:

All people that on earth do dwell, sing to the Lord with chearful voice:
    him serve with feare, his praise forth tell, come ye before him & rejoice.

The Lord, ye know, is God indeed, without our aid he did us make:
    we are his flock, he doth us feed, and for his sheep he doth us take.

O enter then his gates with praise, approach with joy his courts unto:
    praise, laud, and blesse his Name alwayes, for it is seemly so to doe.

For why? the Lord our God is good, his mercy is for ever sure:
    his truth at all times firmly stood, and shall from age to age endure.

The 42nd Psalm began thus:

Like as the Hart doth breath and bray, the wel-spring to obtaine:
so doth my soul desire alway, with thee Lord to remaine.

My soule doth thirst, and would draw neere the living God of might:
oh, when shall I come and appeare in presence of his sight?

The 23rd Psalm took this form:

The Lord is only my support, and he that me doth feed:
how can I then lacke any thing, whereof I stand in need?

He doth me fold in coats most safe, the tender grasse fast by:
and after drives me to the streames which run most pleasantly.

And when I feele my selfe neere lost, then doth he me home take:
conducting me in his right paths, even for his owne names sake.

And though I were even at death's doore, yet would I feare none ill:
for with thy rod and Shepheard's crooke, I am comforted still.

Thou hast my table richly deckt, in despight of my foe.
thou hast my head with balme refresh'd, my cup doth overflow.

And finally while breath doth last, thy grace shall me defend:
and in the house of God will I my life for ever spend.[30]

The earliest Virginia churches were simple wooden structures. William Byrd II wrote a century after the Jamestown settlement: "Like true Englishmen, they built a church that cost no more than Fifty Pounds, and a Tavern that cost Five hundred."[31] When Blair arrived in the colony, James City and Bruton parishes had brick churches, but most other Virginia churches were of clapboard. From a simple rectangular form, some churches were made cruciform by the addition of transepts or were lengthened by the extension of their chancel or nave. Bell towers were usually added last, if and when funds permitted.

Churches were so oriented that worshippers faced eastward, toward the rising sun, from whence theologians had surmised that Christ would appear on His second coming. In Virginia's earliest years the arms of the reigning monarch were displayed against the wall behind the communion table. In the nave of the church, near the communion table, stood the lectern, where the clerk read the Bible lessons. Above and behind the lectern towered the pulpit, whose height symbolized the sublimity of God. Often an hourglass was used to time the sermon, set in the Eucharist or in ante-Communion, which followed morning prayer and the litany from the *Prayer Book*.

The influence of John Calvin was evident despite Virginia's rejection of puritanism. Services were simple and unadorned. Early Virginia churches were austere and barely decorated; they did not become elaborate until the Georgian era of 1714–1820, when box pews, rounded windows and doorways, and wineglass pulpits replaced simpler features. Lighter and more elaborate Communion silver in the same era succeeded the massive chalice and paten from which James Blair served wine and bread to communicants at Henrico Church in 1686.

A clergyman was commonly referred to as "minister" rather than as "priest." In person, he was addressed as "mister" rather than by the later title, "father." The eucharistic service was called "Holy Communion" rather than "mass," and services were said in English, as they generally were in English churches since Edward VI, even though Anglican (and Scottish) ordination required that a cleric know Latin, as well as Greek and Hebrew.

Although the English church observed many holy days, few of these were celebrated in rural Virginia unless they fell on Sundays; it was too difficult for parishioners to get to church on weekdays. Saint George's Day, honoring England's patron saint, was celebrated on April 23, and All Saints' Day on November 1. King Charles The Martyr was commemorated on January 30. After more Scotsmen came into Virginia in the late seventeenth century, the observance of Saint Andrew's Day on November 30, honoring Scotland's patron, became popular.[32]

As Englishmen, Virginians continued to enjoy feast days and holidays of medieval Christianity's ecclesiastical year, even if they could not always get to church. That year began in late November or early December with Advent, presaging the birth of Christ, followed by Christmas and culminating on Twelfth Night. On January 6, called Epiphany, the arrival of the Magi at the manger in Bethlehem was celebrated.

Then, forty days before Easter, Anglicans put aside worldly

pleasures to observe Lent, commemorating Jesus' fast in the wilderness before His crucifixion. Then came Easter, the Queen of Feasts, on which every Anglican was obliged to receive Holy Communion. Fifty days after Easter came Pentecost or Whitsunday, commemorating the descent of the Holy Spirit on the Apostles.

Rector and vestry were by law responsible for the well-being of all people, of whatever race or creed. The introduction of Negroes into the colony in 1619 created an unprecedented problem that the church never faced or resolved. The situation became acute after Virginia's commerce revived with the Restoration in 1660. As shipments began to move in and out of Chesapeake Bay after two decades of disruption, farm labor came to be in great demand. Large-scale importation of slaves from Africa and the West Indies then began. From fewer than a thousand Negroes in 1660, the black population increased by an average of five hundred a year.

How could the church minister to these primitive people? Because slavery seemed irreconcilable with Christianity, the Society of Friends in England preached that the baptism of a slave made him free in the eyes of God. This view was never accepted in Virginia, but it continued to agitate the colony. Many owners deferred baptizing servants for fear of arousing hopes for freedom. At its session in 1667, the Virginia Assembly declared: "Whereas some doubts have risen whether children that are slaves by birth, and by the charity and piety of their owners made partakers of the blessed sacrament of baptisme, should by virtue of their baptisme be made free; *It is enacted and declared by this Grand Assembly and the authority thereof,* that the conferring of baptisme doth not alter the condition of the person as to his bondage or freedom; that diverse masters, freed from this doubt, may more carefully endeavour the propagation of Christianity by permitting children, though slaves, or those of greater growth if capable to be admitted to that sacrament."[33]

The subject of the education and Christianization of slaves was to become increasingly pressing during Blair's lifetime.

With the restoration of the Church of England by Charles

II, so many clergymen were needed in England that few could be spared to go overseas. Seven thousand had been deprived of their livings when Cromwell had come to power in 1653, and those who survived could easily find pulpits and classrooms after 1660. The Virginia Assembly in 1661 requested Governor Berkeley and the Reverend Philip Mallory to seek ministers in England. A pamphlet urged that a bishop be sent to ordain Virginia's lay readers as deacons, that fellowships be established at Oxford and Cambridge for men who would serve in Virginia, and that the colony become a diocese with a bishop of its own.

The old hope of a college and theological seminary in Virginia revived briefly in 1660 and 1661. Governor Berkeley, the councilors, and the burgesses subscribed funds for it and petitioned Charles II for permission to solicit in England. However, other demands on the king were more urgent. The collapse in tobacco prices occasioned by the Navigation Act and Dutch hostilities again delayed Virginia's hoped-for university.

Churchmen were encouraged by Charles II in 1670 to prepare a charter for a diocese in Virginia with a bishop and cathedral at Jamestown. The Reverend Alexander Moray, or Murray, a Scottish royalist who had fled England in 1652 for Ware Parish in Gloucester County, Virginia, after defeat of the king's forces at Worcester, was selected by the king to become bishop. However, the charter never received the Great Seal of England. Thus another effort of English ecclesiastics to reinforce the church in Virginia went awry.[34]

So concerned was Virginia's Assembly in 1668 at the "Many sins of this Country" that they appointed August 27 as a day of fasting and enjoined all people to repair to church "with Fasting and Prayer, to implore God's Mercy and deprecate the Evils justly impending over us."[35]

Such was the Church of England in Virginia in 1675, when Henry Compton was named Bishop of London. Compton first planned to go out to the colonies and reform the church in person, but domestic problems prevented it. Instead, he presented his recommendations to the Committee on Trade and Plantations, an arm of the Privy Council to which he was appointed in 1676.

Foremost among Virginia's problems, Compton felt, was the failure of colonial governors to maintain "the King's Right of patronage and presenting to all Benefices and Cures of Souls which happen to be void." He regretted that accumulated ministerial salaries in vacant parishes were "for the most part converted by Ye People to Their oun use" and that clergymen were "hired" year-to-year and paid in the worst tobacco. Even so, he believed Church of England clergy to be better off in Virginia than in any other English colony.[36]

To heal Virginia, Compton sent instructions by Colonel Herbert Jeffreys, the lieutenant governor who succeeded Berkeley at Jamestown in 1677. Jeffreys began by "causing a strict Inquiry to be made into the lives, licence, abilities and qualifications, of the Clergy here, and by reporting home the same to the Rt. Reverend Father in God, Henry Lord Bishop of London (within whose Diocese Virginia is)." This inquiry, he explained, was in obedience to the bishop's "express and pious admonition and charge in this behalf for suspending & removing such scandalous, unworthy Ministers and Pastors as, do now exercise and officiate in any of the parishes, or precincts of this Colony."[37]

Compton followed this inquiry with instructions to Lord Culpeper during his governorship in 1680 that no minister be installed without certification from the bishop of London that he was properly ordained.[38] Four years later, when Lord Howard of Effingham went to Virginia as governor, he was authorized to remove any cleric who gave "Scandal either by his Doctrine or manners." Royal instructions drawn up by the Committee on Trade and Plantations for Charles II's approval prescribed this division of authority between bishop and governor, giving rise to inevitable conflict between secular and ecclesiastical administrators: "And to the end the Ecclesiastical Jurisdiction of the said Bishop of London may take place in that our Colony as far as Conveniently may be, we do think it fit that you give all Countenance and Encouragement in the exercise of the same Except only the Collating to benefices [,] granting licenses for Marriage [,] and probate of Wills [,] which we have restored to you our Governor and Commander in Chief for the Time being."[39]

With refreshing promptness, Compton moved to fill vacant parishes in Virginia, Maryland, and other English colonies. Since these grew faster than England's supply of ministers, the bishop turned to Huguenot clergymen who were fleeing France to escape persecution by Louis XIV, and to episcopally ordained Scotsmen like Blair who had refused to take the test oath in 1681.[40]

With the flight of unpopular James II and the accession of King William and Queen Mary in 1689, Virginia and the other English colonies sensed a new spirit in England's empire. The tone was one of greater tolerance, concern for overseas colonists, and encouragement of education. Once again England chose the *via media*, which never again was to be seriously challenged. The year 1688—the year of the "Glorious Revolution"—was a turning point for England, for Virginia, and for the growth of religious toleration within the expanding empire.

CHAPTER IV

Virginians Have Souls
1691-1693

❧ The ship bearing Blair to England left Lynnhaven Bay, Virginia, in June 1691[1] and reached Bristol late in the summer. On September 1 the commissary arrived in London. It had been six years since he had departed that city in the twilight of Charles II's dissolute reign. Since then, resentment against James II had forced him from the throne and replaced him with his Protestant daughter, Mary II, and her husband, William III of Orange, who was James II's nephew. The political climate of England had greatly changed since 1685.

In the Glorious Revolution of 1688 which toppled James, a new consensus of political and religious forces had swept into power. A heterogeneous group known as Whigs[2] had coalesced to defeat the Court or Tory party and to give greater power to Parliament. In a sense, the Whigs were political heirs of Oliver Cromwell's Roundheads and the Country Party, which had for a century struggled to limit the power of capricious kings and assume popular control of affairs. Among the Whigs were most of the Church of England party plus rural squires and dissenters. In the new political atmosphere James Blair was to find sympathetic support for Virginia's "good design."

After the Revolutionary Settlement of 1688, no monarch of England would ever again be able to levy taxes or declare war; those powers were now Parliament's. A Bill of Rights enacted in 1689 confirmed the role of the Anglican church and asserted the powers of Parliament and the rights of the people. Restrictions against all dissenting religionists except Romanists and Unitarians were removed. On these terms "the Whig monarchs" had ascended the throne.

William and Mary set for their subjects a heartening example of toleration and concern for education. The pious Queen showed special interest in her people's religious life and welfare. Henry Compton, who had given religious instruction to Mary and her sister Anne, pronounced them conscientious Anglicans.

No sooner had William and Mary come to power, however, than England joined Spain in a war to prevent Louis XIV of France from extending his boundaries. Impatient James Blair found that King William spent most of his time with English forces in Flanders. He soon saw that the war took precedence over domestic and colonial affairs.

"When I first came to London," Blair wrote on December 3 to Governor Nicholson,[3] "there were many things concurred to hinder my sudden presenting of the address about the College, for Mr. Jeoffreys[4] was in Wales, & did not come to Town to present the address upon their majesties' accession to the crown; the Bishop of London thought it not so proper to present an address about business; then the King was in Flanders; my friend the Bishop of Salisbury[5] was at Salisbury; the Bishop of St. Asaph[6] at his diocese in Wales, and before Mr. Jeoffreys came to Town the Bishop of London was taken very sick, so that for a month's time he was not able to stir abroad. . . ."

Finding so few expected allies in London, Blair was forced to change tactics. Compton, whom he had counted on as his mentor, had been passed over by the king in filling the archbishoprics of Canterbury and York and was, in Blair's words, "under a great cloud and mighty unwilling to meddle in any court business." Furthermore, Blair doubted the wisdom of Compton's advice to make Virginia's request of the king in presence of the Privy Council. Since money was needed, Blair felt it would fare better in ecclesiastical hands. Bishops could emphasize the spiritual values of higher education more than the council was likely to do.

Edward Stillingfleet, bishop of Worcester and described by Blair as "much in favour with the Queen," proved more helpful. He urged Blair to make his request to the monarchs jointly, the queen being "a very great encourager of all works of charity." Stillingfleet acquainted the queen with the plan and commended it. "The business of the College," as Blair called it, could have had no better ally than the handsome Stillingfleet, then fifty-six and at the height of his influence.

She "seemed to like it extraordinarily," Blair wrote, and "promised to assist in recommending it to the King, but ordered that the address should not be presented till the King came himself."

Gilbert Burnet, now bishop of Salisbury, also offered advice. "He told me I must have patience," the commissary wrote Nicholson, "for the King at his first coming would be full of his Parliament business but if I would leave it to him he would tell me when was the proper time to deliver the address & would before hand prepare his majesty."

Blair filled the tedious months by soliciting London merchants who traded in Virginia for gifts to the proposed college endowment. He used "three quires" of stationery writing letters to churchmen in support of his "Nursery of Religion." He was occasionally at Lambeth and Fulham palaces seeking advice of ecclesiastics. Meanwhile, he kept up with events in Virginia through the infrequent arrivals of tobacco ships in London as well as the outports. To departing ship captains he entrusted letters for Sarah Blair and for Governor Nicholson, informing them of his activities.

John Tillotson, archbishop of Canterbury, at length reached King William's ear with Virginia's request. The king was pleased, and the archbishop told Blair he had never seen King William "take anything better than he did the very first proposal on our college."

Queen Mary's endorsement was apparently decisive. As Burnet wrote, "The King had left the matters of the church wholly in the Queen's hands. He found that he could not resist importunities, which were not only vexatious to him, but had drawn preferments from him, which he came soon to see were ill bestowed. . . ."[7]

At length, on November 12, the king and queen were ready to receive the commissary from Virginia. Accompanied by Lord Howard of Effingham, who had returned from Virginia in 1689 but continued as governor,[8] Blair was presented by the archbishop and Lord Howard to their Majesties, who were enthroned in the Privy Council Chamber in the handsome palace at Whitehall adjoining the Thames. Blair wrote that "the Bishop of London should have been there but was that day taken again with a fit of the stone."

Blair knelt before the king and queen. Then, petition in hand, he addressed the King:

"Please, your majesty here is an humble supplication from the Government of Virginia for your majesty's charter to erect a free school & college for the education of their youth."

"Sir," King William replied, "I am glad that that colony is upon so good a design & I will promote it to the best of my power."

Blair noted with relief that "The King gave it to the principal Secretary, my Lord Nottingham, at whose office within two days, I had it again. . . ." The king sent directions that Blair present his detailed request for financing the college to the bishop of London. If agreeable to him and the archbishop of Canterbury, it would then go before the Lords of Trade, a committee of the Privy Council.

"The parliament sits so close that it is an hard matter to find anybody at leasure," Blair wrote Nicholson, "yet I persuaded the Bishop of London . . . to come for half an hour to his chamber at Whitehall, where I presented and read to him a Memorial I had prepared for his Maties. use, and the Archbishop and he are to wait an opportunity to speak to the King about it. Every one thinks it is in so good a way that it cannot well miscarry. I make it my whole business to wait upon it, and if I hear further before the ships go your honour may expect another line about it. . . ."[9] Blair spent the winter pursuing his charter. Among those whose help he sought was the Reverend James Kirkwood, a Scot who had attended Edinburgh with him and who had likewise emigrated to England after refusing to take the test oath. Kirkwood arranged for Blair to meet influential friends, probably including the scientist Robert Boyle, who was supporting Kirkwood's distribution of the Bible in Gaelic to Scottish highlanders.[10]

Nearly three months later, Blair wrote Nicholson that little had happened since his last letter. Blair continued to find the court absorbed in war plans, while the archbishop was "for five weeks frozen up at Lambeth and unable to get to Whitehall. Since that time my patience has been sufficiently exercised," he complained, "for our College business (as indeed all business whatsoever) has bin at a stand, the King being so wholly taken up with the thoughts of the war and the transportation of the household and the Army, that for a long time he allowed not the Lords of the Treasury to lay any other business before him till all affairs of that kind were dispatched."[11]

Not only warfare but Privy Council apathy frustrated Blair. The operations of the committee known as the Lords of Trade that had been created under the council to supervise England's growing empire had been disrupted by the revolution of 1688 and the war with France. Colonists and merchants complained bitterly of the neglect of colonial matters.[12]

Blair's contact with Virginia grew less frequent as tobacco ships were diverted to war. To assure delivery of letters, he sent identical copies by several vessels. Although about 150 merchant ships were normally engaged in Virginia tobacco trade, the Crown in 1690 decreed that only 400 seaman could be spared to this commerce.[13]

Blair fumed impatiently as his memorial made its way from the treasury to William Blathwayt, surveyer and auditor general of His Majesty's Plantations in America,[14] who was asked to judge its effect on colonial revenues. The proposal by the Virginia Assembly that its quitrents (taxes paid by landowners in lieu of once-required feudal services to the king) be granted to the college met with no objection from Blathwayt.

These unappropriated funds amounted to £2,000, Blair estimated, "and both King Charles and King James by their letters have promised the Country, that the Quit-rents shall be employed for the Country's Service."[15] Blathwayt concurred in this, but he opposed the suggested diversion of the penny-per-pound tax on tobacco shipped from Virginia and Maryland to other American ports. Since the tax was the responsibility of the customs commissioners, he commented, they must be consulted. Besides, he pointed out, the tax was not primarily for revenue but for control of exports.

But the commissary was not to stand idly by. Robert Boyle, the scientist, who had originated the theorem in chemistry known as Boyle's law, died on December 30, 1691, and left £5,400 in his will to be invested and its income distributed for "pious and charitable uses." Blair was quick to obtain an audience with Boyle's executor, aided by his old friend Gilbert Burnet. The executor decided to invest Boyle's legacy in Brafferton Manor in Yorkshire and pay to the college for a school for Indians all manor profits except a £45 bequest to Harvard College and another to the Society for the Propagation of the Gospel in New England.[16] Blair underestimated the college's total proceeds at £500; instead, the college realized £90 from the Boyle bequest each year until the American Revolution.

A more novel endowment was the £300 that Blair obtained from three pirates who had been captured in 1688 in the James River in Virginia and sent to England for trial. The three—Edward Davis, Lionel Delawafer, and John Hinson—argued that when captured they were on their way to surrender and claim amnesty under a royal proclamation granting pardon to pirates who renounced their trade. Their plea for pardon and restitution of their booty was skeptically received until Blair suggested they give a fourth of their loot, or £300, to the college. This compromise was adopted after conferences between the

Lords of Trade, Blair, and Micajah Perry, a London merchant who acted as agent for Virginia.[17]

Blair assured Nicholson that "tho my main business is not yet finished, yet I make use of my time for something else than mere waiting. But I confess the trouble of managing the affair is so vastly great beyond expectation, that I doubt, could I have foreseen it, I should never have had the courage to have undertaken it."[18]

Nearly eight months elapsed before the Lords of the Treasury reported back to the king. Their reaction was in part favorable. Quitrents should not be given the college but should be held in reserve "for fortifications or other unforeseen circumstances." They questioned the legality of granting escheats and felt that transfer of the office of surveyor general to the college would be unwise. More acceptable was the proposed grant to the college of unoccupied lands south of the James near Blackwater Swamp and on Pamunkey Neck in the upper York River. They were also amenable to transfer of the penny-a-pound tobacco export tax to the college provided arrangements were made with the commissioners of the customs.[19]

Blair immediately wrote a rebuttal, arguing the merit of devoting the quitrents to the college. Despite the promises of Charles II and James II, he said, these funds had been diverted to uses other than the good of the colony. As to their need in war, he submitted that Virginia had built adequate defenses by public levy. There was "no Custome more generally to be observed among ye young Virginians than that they all learn to keep & use a gun, with a Marvelous dexterity as soon as they have strength enough to lift it to their heads."[20]

Should Virginia require further defenses, Blair argued, the tax on liquors could be increased. Governor and Council were also empowered to raise a defense force when needed. Blair conceded that these expedients were temporary, but he felt this to be advantageous since the assembly could thus serve as a check on the governor. Advancing the Whig doctrine that executive power should remain subject to parliamentary check, Blair observed: "Frequent Assemblies . . . are Esteemed as necessary there as parliaments in England, and they reckon that if they gave away ye power of Levying & maintaining at the Countrey's charge, such an Arbitrary Armed Force with out any limitation of time, there would be no more Occation for Assemblys, because the Governor might do what he pleased without them."[21]

It is doubtful that Nicholson would have sanctioned Blair's views on the adequacy of Virginia's defenses had he known Blair was advancing them. At that moment in Virginia, Indians were menacing the frontiers, and the lieutenant governor informed the Committee on Plantations by letter of July 16, 1692, that border settlers were leaving their homes for fear of attack.[22]

Despite Blair's rebuttal, the Treasury Lords continued to oppose diversion of quitrents. With England at war, they feared Virginia might be threatened. Furthermore, if Virginia built a college with quitrents, others "will be for building Colledges out of the King's Revenue."[23] Three Treasury Lords signed a hostile document, specifically opposing Blair's efforts to gain quitrent money for the salary of Virginia's commissary and clergy.[24]

Not all of this opposition to the college plan was disinterested. Some imperialists believed the colonies should be kept in subjection lest they become too demanding. Shipping men and merchants who had profited from colonial trade were reluctant to encourage an independent spirit in Virginia. Burnet thought them fearful that a college "would take the planters off from their mechanical employments and make them grow too knowing to be obedient and submissive."[25]

This sentiment was substantiated by the reaction that Benjamin Franklin in later years imputed to Sir Edward Seymour, one of the Lords of the Treasury. Seymour's reaction was described thus:

The Reverend Commissary Blair, who projected the College . . . relates, that the Queen, in the King's Absence, having ordered Seymour to draw up the Charter, which was to be given, with £2000 in Money, he oppos'd the Grant; saying that the Nation was engag'd in an expensive War, that the Money was wanted [for] better purposes, and he did not see the least Occasion for a College in Virginia. Blair represented to him, that its Intention was to educate and

qualify young Men to be Ministers of the Gospel, much wanted
there; and begged Mr. Attorney would consider, that the People of
Virginia had souls to be saved, as well as the People of England.
"*Souls!*" says he, "damn your Souls. Make Tobacco!"[26]

This tale no doubt had some basis, but it contained a significant error. Seymour was not attorney general, as the story im-
plies. That office was held by Sir John Somers, a friend of Burnet
and of John Tillotson, archbishop of Canterbury—both Blair's
friends. As ᴏne of the Treasury Lords, however, Seymour would
have had opportunity to express opposition during the months
of negotiations that kept Blair so long in England.[27]

Despite some selfish opposition, "the business of the College"
received a generally sympathetic hearing by churchmen and
adherents of the House of Orange. It was a timely and sound
plan. Thus, when Blair's memorials and the appended com-
ments of the Lords of the Treasury finally reached the Privy
Council on July 28, 1692, Blair's hopes were finally vindicated.[28]
Authorization was withheld only until an opinion could be received from the attorney general confirming the legality of
granting escheats before they accrued.

This in hand, Queen Mary approved the grants at a meeting
of the Privy Council on September 1, 1692, ten months after the
first audience. By her direction, the college received nearly
£2,000 in Virginia's quitrent tax receipts, accumulated to the
credit of the royal treasury; twenty thousand acres of Virginia
land, half of it known as Pamunkey Neck, in what is now King
William County, and the rest, Blackwater Swamp, in the present
Isle of Wight and Southampton counties; the penny-per-pound
tax on tobacco exported from Virginia and Maryland to des-
tinations other than England, Scotland, or Wales; and the office
of surveyor with "all its Issues, Fees, Profits," and other perquisites. It was a considerable endowment, especially when
joined with the pirates' booty and funds pledged by planters
and the colonial government in Virginia.

Blair now turned to the drawing of a charter. For guidance
he studied those of English and Scottish universities. He employed the services of lawyers for assistance in the final drafting.
Nicholson had urged him to consult "Mr. Robert Sawyer and

Mr. Finch, because they were great Lawyers and Church of England men & were every way qualify'd for him to make use of."[29]

As finally granted by the monarchs on February 8, 1693, the charter for the College of William and Mary in Virginia closely followed the recommendations which Blair had submitted. It began:

> Forasmuch as our well-beloved and trusty Subjects, constituting the General Assembly of our Colony of *Virginia*, have had it in their Minds, and have proposed to themselves, to the end that the Church of *Virginia* may be furnish'd with a Seminary of Ministers of the Gospel, and that the Youth may be piously educated in good Letters and Manners, and that the Christian Faith may be propagated amongst the Western *Indians*, to the Glory of Almighty God, to make, found, and establish a certain Place of universal Study, or perpetual College of Divinity, Philosophy, Languages, and other good Arts and Sciences, consisting of one President, six Masters or Professors, and an hundred Scholars, more or less, according to the Ability of the said College, and the Statutes of the same, to be made, encreased, diminished, or changed upon the Place, by certain Trustees nominated and elected by the General Assembly aforesaid. . . .[30]

The phrase, "that the Christian Faith may be propagated amongst the Western *Indians*," which enabled the college to qualify for the Boyle bequest, had been mentioned in the 1690 proposals of the Virginia clergy to the House of Burgesses. It was to have strong appeal to British churchmen during the evangelical "Great Awakening" that was to come. The college's other purposes had been set forth in the "humble supplication," which the assembly had formulated at Jamestown and Blair had presented to the King and Queen: ". . . ye urgent necessities of this yor Ma[jes]ties Dominion, where our youth is deprived of the benefitt of a liberal & vertuous Education, and many of our Parishes of that instruction & comfort which might be expected from a pious & learned ministry. . . ."[31]

Following the scheme recommended by Nicholson and Blair in 1691 in Virginia, the charter provided for from eighteen to twenty trustees to "erect, found, and establish" the college and to become, after the college had been erected, in compliance with the charter, a board of visitors and governors. One of these was to be chosen annually as rector. Named as trustees were

Governor Nicholson, four clergymen, four councillors, and nine burgesses.[32] The councillors were William Cole II of Warwick, Ralph Wormeley of Middlesex,[33] William Byrd I of Henrico, and John Lear of Nansemond. The clergymen were Blair, John Farnifold of Northumberland, Stephen Fouace of York, and Samuel Gray of Middlesex. The burgesses were Thomas Milner of Nansemond, Christopher Robinson of Middlesex, Charles Scarborough of Accomack, John Smith of Gloucester, Blair's father-in-law Benjamin Harrison II of Surry, Miles Cary of Elizabeth City, Henry Hartwell of Jamestown, William Randolph of Henrico, and Matthew Page of Gloucester.

All except Matthew Page, William Randolph, and the Reverend Samuel Gray had been suggested by the assembly in 1691 to serve as trustees. These replaced three of the 1691 nominees who had died: John Page, father of Matthew; Nathaniel Bacon Sr. of York, and the Reverend John Banister of Charles City.

Once the college was in full operation, control of its properties and revenues was to be transferred by the trustees to the president and six masters provided for in the charter. From the context, it was evident that the need for trustees was expected to be brief, for no provision was made for replacement. The charter referred to the transfer being made by "the major part" of the eighteen trustees or "the longest livers of them"—a phrase that was to have bearing on the future of the college.

The visitors and governors continued in perpetuity as the policy-making body of the college. As the original visitors died or moved away, they were to be replaced by election among surviving members. They were the "true, sole, and undoubted visitors and governors of the said college forever," with "full and absolute liberty, power and authority of making, enacting, framing and establishing such and so many rules, laws statutes, orders and injunctions for the good and wholesome government" of the institution. In their hands was the selection of "other apt, fit and able persons" to replace the president and masters.

To the post of chancellor—an honorary office that English and Scottish universities awarded to a distinguished public man —the charter named Henry Compton, bishop of London. Following his seven-year term, the visitors and governors were to elect another "eminent and discreet Person." The chancellor was expected to obtain benefits, but Blair was to be disappointed in the tangible results. "The imperfect notion we had of him, was this," Blair wrote of the chancellor's role in 1702, "that he was to be a Great man at the Court of England."[34]

The college administration, centering in the board of visitors and governors, followed Scottish rather than English practice. Named to preside was a rector, a "fit and discreet person," to be chosen annually from the board, as was done at Marischal College and the University of Edinburgh. To this office, which had not been envisioned in the commissary's original instructions from Virginia, the charter named Blair himself.

The document was issued at Westminster on February 8, 1693, with the notation, "By a Writ of the Privy Seal. PIGOTT." The principal and most difficult object of the journey was accomplished, but more remained to be done.

Blair's successful mission was commended by Gilbert Burnet in his lengthy *History of His Own Time.* Describing advances made in the reign of William and Mary, he wrote:

Another effect of the Queen's pious care of the souls of her people was finished this year [1693], after it had been much opposed and long stopped. Mr. Blair, a very worthy man, came over from Virginia, with a proposition for erecting a college there. In order to which, he had set on foot a voluntary subscription, which arose to a great sum; and he found out some branches of revenue there, that went all into private hands, without being brought into public account, with which a free school and college might be well endowed. The English born there were, as he said, capable of every thing, if they were provided with the means of a good education; and a foundation of this kind in Virginia, that lay in the middle, between our southern and northern plantations, might be a common nursery to them all; and put the people born there in a way of further improvement. Those concerned in the management of the plantations, had made such advantages of these particulars, out of which the endowment was to be raised, that all possible objections were made to the project, as a design that would take our planters off from their mechanical employments, and make them grow too knowing to be obedient and submissive. The Queen was so well pleased with the design, as apprehending the very good effects it might have, that no objection against it would move her: she hoped it might be a means of improving her own people, and of preparing some to propagate the gospel among the natives; and therefore, as she espoused the matter with a particular zeal, so the King did very readily concur with her in it. The endowment was fixed, and the patent was passed for the college, called from the founders, the William and Mary college.[35]

During his twenty-seven months in London, Blair had also given thought to teachers for his college-to-be. He concluded that only a grammar school master and usher would be needed until the college was built. This master would teach the subjects normally required of English and Scottish grammar schools. Additionally, Blair now concluded that the college would require a full-time president.

Shortly after reaching England, Blair had written Nicholson:

There was one thing that was forgot in my Instructions (& 'twas my fault, for I was not sensible of the necessity of it at this time), that is, that I should have been ordered to provide a President of the College at the same time with the School Master & Usher. I thought that at first a Grammar school being the only thing we could go upon, a good school Master & Usher were enough to manage that. But the Bishop of London & some other Bishops & a great many other skillful men whom I have consulted, have undeceived me & perswaded me that the President of the College ought to be the first man of all the Masters we provide for it. . . .

[Blair cited these reasons:] . . . 1. That the good success of ye whole business depends upon the setting up & executing of a good discipline at first both among the Masters & Scholars, which if it be left wholey to the School Master he will be sure to make it easy enough for himself & will contrive to lead the scholars in such a method as will keep them a great deal longer at school than they needed to be kept, only for his own advantage; most of the Masters here in England keep their scholars seven years at the Latin which might be as well taught in four if they pleased. 2. It may so happen that the School Master & Ushur may want as much to be inspected as the scholars themselves. . . .[36]

But where to find a president? If the assembly thought one should be brought from abroad, Blair blandly offered to try to find one, though it would be difficult. Then he offered a modest suggestion:

But if it be thought that I or any other person there can be fitt to supply such a place, they [the assemblymen] may save themselves the trouble of writing, together with the 50 £ for Transportation. To use all freedom with your Honr now that I see that not only the design of a College in Virga but yt this particular draught & scheme of it has passed the strictest examination of the best Judges here & has mett with a general approbation, I am more desirous than ever to see it brought to perfection, & tho I never sought a place in my whole life time, I could find in my heart to seek this, being well assured that tho (if we could perswade them to go to Virga) there are many men in England much fitter for it upon the account of Learning, prudence & authority, yet perhaps there is none to be found that has a greater zeal for the Country, or that is more concerned in point of honour to see this work prosper than I am.[37]

This written, Blair seemed to recoil from his boldness. He hoped indeed that the lieutenant governor would not think ill of him. After all, the idea had originated with the bishops of Salisbury and Worcester. Only when he realized how different Virginia's college would be from England's had he agreed that: . . . "if we take a man from either of the Universitys who never saw any such Institution, but has been accustomed to a much more easy & idle way, that he will never bear it & will not at all be fitt for such a small College as ours will be."[38]

Replying from Virginia, Nicholson approved. A president would be needed to push the projects, and Blair was the man. Nicholson thereupon persuaded the General Assembly to supplement its instructions and nominate Blair. No mention of Blair's election appears in assembly records, but on April 27 and 28 it was ordered that a letter be written to him, together with letters of appreciation to the bishops who had aided him. No doubt it carried word of Blair's election as president.

Thus, in accordance with Blair's own proposal, the charter named him president of the college, to serve "during his natural life." This was done, the document affirmed, because the "General Assembly of our colony of Virginia, has named, elected or appointed the said James Blair, clerk, as a fit person to be President of the said college."

As to professors, Blair wrote in the same letter in which he suggested himself as president that he was searching for men qualified to teach and willing to go to Virginia: "I find there will be a great deal of difficulty in finding of able Masters & yet I am sensible the life of the business lies in this. In England their Masters of their Colleges have a much easier life than is designed for the Masters & Professors of our College in Virginia. I can have severall young men that are fitt enough to be Ushers but can't perswade any of the Eminent Experienced Masters to go over. I have two in my eye that are very fitt for it, if I can prevail with them to undertake it."[39]

As he sailed from Portsmouth for Virginia in the spring of 1693,[40] Blair could justly feel a sense of triumph. He had achieved his object. Moreover, he had strengthened his ties with leaders of England's church and state, placing him in position to influence Virginia's affairs in increasing measure. Queen Mary had ordered him paid £100 from the royal bounty,[41] while the Virginia Assembly was to vote him an honorarium of £250[42] in addition to the £600 that he claimed for expenses. Of this sum, Blair showed that £322 was spent on fees and gratuities, leaving £279 for his travel and living expenses for the twenty-seven months he had been away.

The expenses were approved without objection,[43] but Nicholson years later assailed it as a "very extraordinary & extrava'gt account and may be an unjust one."[44] By this time Blair and Nicholson had become mortal enemies, but Nicholson's change of heart came too late to be used against Blair.

On September 1, 1693, Commissary Blair presented the charter to the governor and council at Jamestown. The commissary was honored as a hero. When the General Assembly convened, they sent their "most hearty thanks" to their Majesties for "such a signall Testimony of yor Majts pious & Christian care of yor Subjects in this part of the world." Blair himself no doubt compiled the memorial, which rejoiced that Virginia children might now be educated in the duties of "piety towards God and Loyalty to yor Sacred Majesties."

Supplementing the royal endowment, the assembly levied a tax on raw and tanned skins and furs that were exported from Virginia. Duty paid on such pelts as elk, deer, beaver, otter, wildcat, mink, fox, raccoon, and muskrat thus went to help build the college. However, a proposal in the assembly to tax liquors for the college's benefit was voted down.

The location of the College of William and Mary was long

debated by the councillors and burgesses. Although the charter reflected sentiment for a site near the port of York on the York River, which had prevailed when Blair had sailed in 1691, further reflection led in 1693 to the selection of an inland site roughly midway between the James and the York. The location finally chosen in 1693 was "as neare the church now standing in Middle Plantation old fields as convenience will permitt."[45] For the sum of £170, about 330 acres of land were purchased from Captain Thomas Ballard[46] adjoining the remains of the palisade once erected athwart the peninsula to protect settlers against the Indians. It adjoined extensive lands of Colonel John Page and of Philip Ludwell.

From the viewpoint of Virginia in 1693, it was an excellent location. Accessible to the James River by Archer's Hope Creek (later called College Creek) and to the York by Queen's Creek, the crossroads was convenient to many of the seventy thousand inhabitants of the tidewater coast. It lay along the cart path that extended from Jamestown to Greenspring and thence eastward to York and Kecoughtan. Westward, a path led from Middle Plantation to New Kent Courthouse. Sloops could reach the village from Chesapeake Bay and numerous rivers. Soon a small sail vessel would begin operating from Queen Mary's Port, as the Queen's Creek landing was to be called, to Claybank in Gloucester across the York.[47]

The settlement had grown up since 1633, when the palisade was first erected there by settlers from Jamestown. Several houses now stood along the horse path that followed the broad ridge extending laterally down the peninsula, drained on the north by creeks flowing into the York and on the south into the James. In 1693 the crossroads had an ordinary, two mills, a blacksmith's shop, several stores, and the gabled-end brick church of Bruton Parish, completed in 1683 on land given by John Page.

With the growth of county roads, colonists by 1693 were depending more on horseback than on river transport. Middle Plantation was more centrally located than Jamestown or the two proposed sites on the York. Still, rumblings of disapproval were heard. Some subscribers were "angry at the place where the College is situated," wrote Mungo Inglis, first master of the grammar school, though he himself thought the site was "absolutely the best of the whole Country."[48]

The college thus seemed well begun. While it had lost powerful support with the transfer of Francis Nicholson to Maryland in September 1692, Nicholson would remain a member of the board of trustees. As for the new governor, Sir Edmund Andros, he seemed in the beginning disposed to cooperate. When Edward Randolph, surveyor general of customs in America, passed through Jamestown in 1693, he wrote that Virginia alone of all the colonies he visited, showed the "face of peace" and enjoyed good government.[49]

It was the lull before a terrible storm.

CHAPTER V

Lion versus Unicorn
1693-1697

❧ Blair's appointment as president of the college changed the tenor of his life. Until his return to Virginia from London in the summer of 1693, his career had advanced with quiet regularity. The record of his life in Scotland, in London, or in Henrico had evinced no unquenchable thirst for power. Except for his refusal to sign the test oath, he had displayed no combativeness. Ecclesiastical superiors had found him cooperative, and the Virginia Assembly in 1690 had thought him a worthy choice as commissary.

Yet Blair had a ruthless ambition and contentiousness that now began to show. Time after time he disgraced his high office with violent outbursts. From the administration of Andros through that of Alexander Spotswood, ending in 1722, he was embroiled with royal governors as well as clergy and schoolmasters. The result was to impede the progress of the college and to impair the commissary's leadership in the church.

Yet despite Blair's shortcomings, he served as a brake on the exercise of authority by royal governors. He became for a brief period the most articulate spokesman in Virginia against the tightening web of English control. Unexcelled in debate or diatribe, he seldom hesitated when aroused to hurl himself recklessly against the king's representative.

In an era of unguarded rhetoric, he was a vicious combatant, seizing on any scandal or mischance to discredit an opponent. Such fearlessness was to give the commissary power that led to wealth, but it detracted seriously from his effect as a spiritual leader. He might well have asked himself, as Christ asked his disciples: "For what shall it profit a man, if he shall gain the whole world, and lose his own soul?"

It was Blair's thirst for money that showed first. It appeared at the session of the council in 1690, when Nicholson had presented Compton's appointment of Blair as commissary. The council had asked Nicholson then to thank the bishop for appointing "one soe well deserveing" but to call to his attention the lack of a salary.[1] Blair had pressed the matter the next year when in England to obtain the charter for the college. He presented a petition from Nicholson and the council, asking that unappropriated quitrents paid by Virginia landowners, amounting to about £800, be granted to the commissary and clergy. These would be used to defray "the great charges Such a Person must be at, in travelling all over the Country for making Visitations of Churches, and sending messengers from time to time,"[2] and to augment ministerial pay.

The grant was made by Queen Mary for a three-year period but soon recalled by King William, who promised to reconsider the matter in three years.[3] Blair apparently was not paid as commissary until 1695, though meanwhile drawing his parochial benefits and the expense account and honorarium appropriated by the assembly and augmented by Queen Mary for his services in England for the college. At last the royal treasury authorized that Blair, in 1695, be paid £100 as commissary from quitrent receipts out of the royal bounty, and Bishop Compton asked that the arrangement be continued thereafter,[4] which was done.

Failing initially while in England to obtain a salary as commissary and higher pay for the clergy, Blair renewed his efforts in 1693 in Virginia. Had Nicholson remained in office, Blair might have had an ally, but Sir Edmund Andros was not to be one. Taking office as governor on September 20, 1692, after arriving from New York, Andros learned with displeasure of Blair's attempted inroads into the royal funds. If Blair should succeed in diverting surplus quitrents to ecclesiastical uses, Andros realized, the governor would become dependent on assembly appropriations.[5]

Andros had come to Virginia heralded as a "Church of England man," as a result of efforts to promote that church in Puritan New England. However, defense against Indians and French warships claimed his first attention in Virginia, and he ordered expensive fortifications built on Jamestown's shore. When the Virginia Assembly met in 1693, Andros felt unable to recommend better pay for the clergy, as London had instructed him. In Blair's view, Andros did nothing to push the proposed revision of laws that contained such provision, and he dissolved the assembly without obtaining the relief for ministers that Nicholson had promised.[6]

Blair wrote Nicholson from Virginia that Andros "thought it not fit in any of his Speeches, to recommend the business of the College, nor the clergy . . . he has had very bad success in managing of Assemblies."[7] Relations between Andros and Blair worsened.

As a veteran administrator, Andros recognized Blair as a threat. Like most of England's colonial governors, Sir Edmund had been trained as a soldier. He held the rigid royalist views of King James II, who before being forced from the throne had named Andros governor of New York and then of the Dominion of New England. Citizens of Boston revolted against Andros' Jacobite rule in 1689, resulting in his transfer to Virginia. Unlike Nicholson, Sir Edmund held himself aloof from the whiggish Virginians. As one historian has written, "He was quite conscious that he represented the authority and prerogative of the Crown, and he seemed unable to comprehend, or to sympathize with, the democratic aspirations of the people he governed. He was on occasion dictatorial and arbitrary. His manner with those who opposed him was brusque rather than conciliatory, and he was subject to fits of violent temper when his policies were questioned."[8]

Compared to the young and personable Nicholson, Andros was dull and unappealing. He was also to reveal himself as slow-witted and narrow, unable to comprehend the impetus that the Glorious Revolution had given to colonial affairs.

Feeling as he did, Sir Edmund was dismayed to receive instructions from London in 1694 to swear in Blair as a member of the twelve-man council. He had been asked earlier to suggest names, and he had written on July 22, 1693, to propose twelve "noted Inhabitants or planters of the best Estates," not including Blair, to replace members of the council who died or moved from Virginia.

At that point Henry Compton had proposed Blair's name at a meeting of the Lords of Trade,[9] which recommended the diligent clergyman for the king's appointment.

Blair was partly indebted for his appointment to Nicholson, who had asked Blair when he went to England in 1691 to urge the bishop of London to place an ecclesiastic on the council. Nicholson thereby had hoped to allay "the miserable condition the clergy will be in as they increase[,] having no Vote in the Governm't." Lacking such a vote, Nicholson thought, they came near being "debarred from any Ecclesiastical Discipline" by the 1691 session of the Virginia Assembly because they had no representative in either house."[10] Nicholson obviously saw the council as parallel to England's House of Lords, in which bishops sat as lords spiritual.

Nicholson had suggested that the commissary and the president of the college, not at that time chosen, would be the "fittest" councillors, having "the best Salarys & the greatest authority." He followed up his suggestion with letters to Compton and other of the Lords of Trade.

The council that Blair joined was Virginia's political Olympus, advising the governor and sitting as the colony's upper legislative house and court. Meeting at times on the ground floor of the State House, which had been rebuilt since Bacon's rebels

In response to Blair's request, the College of Heralds in London
granted a coat of arms to the college on May 14, 1694. The arms
were described as "Vert a College or edifice ar, masoned ppr., in
chief the rising sun or the hemisphere of the third." These
colors prescribed that the college building be painted in silver
on a green field, with a golden sun at half orb against a blue
sky.

Courtesy of the College of William and Mary

had burned Jamestown in 1676, and at other times at the house of a member, the council assisted the governor in carrying out royal instructions and in choosing county lieutenants and other officers to serve under him. Councillors also suggested recipients for county offices and other coveted appointments—taking care, of course, to keep some for themselves.

When the General Assembly was in session, the governor and council sat as an upper house to review, amend, or on occasion to reject bills passed by the burgesses. When sitting as the general court, the council had final jurisdiction in all cases save those involving £300 or more and capital crimes, which could be appealed to England.

Blair's appointment surprised others besides Andros. Councillors had all previously been wealthy planters, who were theoretically less apt to profit from office than poor men. A large estate was thought to be assurance of a councillor's business acumen and a guarantee in case his default in any transaction should entail a loss for the colony. Except for Sarah's potential share of her father's estate, the Blairs had no claim to membership in the great planter group. It was an unprecedented appointment.

Beyond power and patronage, membership on the council bestowed social distinction of the highest order. "They were and knew themselves to be the envied of every aspiring planter family," wrote a recent author of the council.[11] And such indeed were the men with whom Commissary Blair took his place around the council table in June 1694.

Foremost on the council was the aged Ralph Wormeley of Rosegill in Middlesex, who was senior member. Others were Richard Lee II of Westmoreland; John Lear of Nansemond; William Byrd I of Henrico and Charles City; Christopher Wormeley II of Middlesex; Henry Whiting of Gloucester; Edward Hill of Shirley in Charles City; and Edmund Jenings of York. Although he took his seat to replace William Cole on June 23, 1692, to serve until his election by the council was confirmed by the Crown, Henry Hartwell of James City was sworn in at the same time Blair was, July 18, 1694. All these were men of substance and standing.

Blair was now within the inner circle of Virginia's leaders, and the time had come to move to the center of power. This he did in 1695, when he was chosen as rector of James City, the oldest and most desirable parish in the colony. Perhaps this was through the efforts of Philip Ludwell, who was a vestryman. The church was at Jamestown, but the rector ministered every third Sunday at Mulberry Island, eight miles down the James in Warwick County.

Blair's move was also in response to the direction of college trustees that he open the grammar school and oversee the college's construction. Here again he came into conflict with Andros, who occupied the Middle Plantation house of "Madam Page"—probably the widow of Colonel John Page—which Blair had hoped to rent. Though Blair had arranged to occupy the house before Christmas 1694, Andros stayed on until May and then demanded the house for one of his employes. Tired of waiting, President Blair " (being very desirous to make a beginning of teaching at ye grammer school wch could not be done till he had yt house in Middleplantation) Brought down his goods in a sloop. . . ."[12]

Blair had by that time arranged with the Ludwells to occupy a house they owned at Richneck, adjoining Middle Plantation. Although it placed him six or seven miles from Jamestown, it was only a mile and a half from the college. Furthermore, Blair could probably foresee that the capital must sooner or later be relocated. Middle Plantation, which had been considered since 1676, was the likeliest alternative. With houses there so few, Richneck was probably as close to the village as the Blairs could hope to get.[13]

Thus James and Sarah in 1695 had their household goods loaded aboard a sailing sloop, bade goodbye to their Henrico neighbors, and descended the James forty miles to Archer's Hope Creek. Then, proceeding up that winding rivulet almost to Middle Plantation, they disembarked and moved into their new home, which was on the plantation owned earlier by Thomas Ludwell, secretary of the colony, and bequeathed by him to his brother Philip.

Colonel Ludwell first rented the property to Blair and in 1699 sold him one hundred acres of it, immediately adjoining Williamsburg, for "fifty pounds good and lawfull money of England."[14] Here, close to the palisade that Middle Plantation's settlers had erected in 1633, James and Sarah were to make their home until Sarah's death.[15]

Watered by streams that became known as Paper Mill Creek and Raccoon Chase, draining from Middle Plantation ridge, Richneck in James City County offered the same good bottom lands as had Varina in Henrico. Employing an overseer and using slave labor, Blair grew tobacco, as nearly all other tidewater landholders did. After the college was built in 1699 he also had an apartment in it. Evidently he thereafter divided his time between the two abodes until he moved into the president's house at the college many years later.

Blair's move led him in 1697 to sell his plantation in Henrico. By a deed of August 2 of that year one Allenson Clark, as his agent and attorney, sold to Bartholomew Fowler the one-hundred-acre Varina farm that Blair had bought from William Byrd I on February 1, 1687. In the same transaction he sold a tract of 230 acres that he had purchased from Thomas Taylor on Roundabout Swamp, near Varina, for £100 of "good and lawfull money of England." He also sold to Fowler at the same time the tract of 130 acres of Sunken Swamp and marshlands that he had been granted on April 20, 1690, along with Jeremiah Brown and Nicholas Bullington, receiving £20 therefor.

The texts of the deeds suggest that buyer and seller had come to terms on April 24, 1697, before Blair left for England, leaving his attorney to work out details. The deeds were witnessed by William Randolph and James Cocke.[16]

The years 1694 and 1695 were frustrating ones for the commissary. The building of the college proved more difficult than obtaining the charter had been. For one thing, settlers had begun to claim tracts within the college lands on Blackwater Swamp and the Pamunkey River, reducing income from that source. In addition, revenues from duty on tobacco shipped to non-English ports declined as shipping dwindled in the war with France.[17] Finally, since Surveyor General Alexander Culpeper had refused to surrender that lucrative office, fees from land surveys intended for the college did not begin to come in until after Culpeper died in 1695.[18]

The assembly of 1695 showed no disposition to help. Asked to enact further revenue provisions, it declared "the Colledge to be under no Circumstances of want at present & that Likewise the Countrey is in no Capacity of giveing it assistance at this time."[19] Blair blamed Andros' influence. Obviously, he wrote Nicholson, the college had no friend in Sir Edmund.[20]

The college had other problems. Now that the Crown had endowed it, colonists were backing away from pledges they had made in their first burst of enthusiasm. Nearly £3,000 had been promised in the subscription authorized by the 1691 assembly and undertaken by forty-two planters and clergymen, but only some £500 had been paid by 1697.[21] Court records of Henrico County in this period list several suits brought by Blair and others to force payment of pledges, but many proved uncollectible.

Who was to blame? Blair pointed to the governor. "The Persons that stand out are the Council and Great men who have places of profit and preferment under Sir Edmund," he charged.[22] But the governor's friends blamed Blair. It was wrong for the commissary to pocket the £150 salary as president of a college when only its grammar school was in operation, they said. William Byrd II was among those to voice this sentiment.[23]

Both Blair and Andros could have done more for the college had they been less concerned for their own advantage, but fault also lay in the apathy of the colonists toward intellectual and ecclesiastical matters. Not until 1695 was the college's cornerstone laid, and two years later the building was still unfinished. In addition, some persons had subscribed "that they might not be thought singular or enemies to so good a worke" but "hoping & supposing it would come to nothing," wrote Mungo Inglis, first master of the grammar school.[24] Other 1691 subscribers had done so "to oblige and curry favor with his Excell'y [Nicholson], the principall promotor of it," Inglis opined, and Nicholson was no longer in Virginia.

The site cleared for the college was close to Bruton Parish Church, facing eastward along the cart path that followed the central ridge of the peninsula, between the James and the York. On August 8, 1695, the laying of "the Foundation" was celebrated by the governor, council, and trustees "with the best Solemnity we were capable," wrote Councillor Ralph Wormeley, who was present. Lacking workmen, he feared the job would not be finished "in the tyme was hoped and desired," he informed William Blathwayt,[25] surveyor and auditor general of His Majesty's Plantations in America.

Blair was more outspoken. In 1695 he wrote Nicholson, then governor of Maryland, that: "we have been taken up three days at James Town abt ye College business wch now looks wth as bad an appearance as ever; Collo. Ludwell [Philip Ludwell I] seeing how matters are like to be governed, will not be perswaded on any Acc't to undertake the work. The reason he gives out Publickly is his age & unwillingness to leave his son entangled; But he sticks not to say among his Friends, that he sees no possibility of carrying it on in this Governrs time."[26]

Once the work began, it appeared to Blair that the governor was covertly delaying it. One account called Sir Edmund Andros "an enemy to the College of W & M in Virginia," noting among reasons for the accusation the following: "By seducing some of the workmen that were gone from England to Virginia upon ye account of the College: Money was given to Pocock to relinquish the work of ye College, & [he] was afterwards entertained & work given him by Sir. E. A. [Edmund Andros]. Mr. [Daniel] Park[e] wn agreed wth, to burn the bricks for ye College was desired by the Governour to make & burn some 30,000 for him."[27]

From his pulpit at Jamestown, Blair chastised those who had failed the college. From Annapolis, Nicholson reported that one Clarke told him that he had heard Andros disparage the college. The reason "Sir Edmond was angry with Mr. Blaire was for his preaching a Sermon wherein he did say, that they who withdrew back & did not put forward their helping hand towards the Building of the College would be Damned."[28] Another informed Nicholson that Andros had said of the college, "Pish, it will come to nothing."[29]

When the elder Ludwell refused to undertake the work of overseeing construction, Councillor Edmund Jenings was urged

Sir Edmund Andros was governor of Virginia from 1692 to 1698, during which time he incurred the bitter opposition of Blair and other councillors. He was recalled to England after hearings by the Board of Trade in London, at which James Blair was chief spokesman against the soldier.

Courtesy of the Virginia State Library

to do it. However, the job finally fell to a committee headed by Miles Cary of Warwick, an experienced builder who had succeeded Blair as rector of the college, and five or six trustees. Thomas Hadley came over from England at Blair's behest to act as surveyor, with responsibility for design and construction, and workmen were recruited from England and among slaves and indentured servants. Two of the carpenters were Blair's servants from Richneck plantation.[30]

The design of the college evidently was sent from England. Clearly it was the work of a skilled hand. Twenty-five years later, a master at the college, who had returned to London during Wren's lifetime, credited it to Christopher Wren, prolific genius of English churches and schools. "The Building is beautiful and commodious," wrote the Reverend Hugh Jones in *The Present State of Virginia*, "being first modelled by Sir Christopher Wren, adapted to the nature of the country by the gentlemen there . . . and is not altogether unlike Chelsea Hospital."[31] Wren, as surveyor general of their Majesties' Public Works, would have had supervision of a college erected by royal grant and charter.

The college was designed to a scale beyond that of any public building previously built in Virginia. Despite its church-like severity, its rhythm of windows and textured brick gave it a pleasing effect. It loomed awesomely above the muddy cart paths from Jamestown and New Kent which converged before it.

Like many English colleges, William and Mary's structure was conceived as a quadrangle, though only two sides were completed between 1695 and 1699 because funds ran out. These were the front, or eastern facade, and the part of the north side which included the great hall. The structure included an English basement and three full stories, with a half-story roof. Five or six steps led from the yard up to the entrance threshhold, and thirteen bays of casement windows or doors were evenly spaced across the front on the basement and three above-ground floor levels. The shingle roof was pierced by dormer windows, a cupola, and six chimneys issuing from fireplaces scattered throughout the building.[32]

So large a structure taxed the ingenuity of Virginia artisans, who up to that time had undertaken little more than two-story row houses at Jamestown. Timber was cut from the college land, while oyster shells for lime came from nearby waters. Brick were burned from clay at nearby Queens Creek Plantation by Councillor Daniel Parke, who received 14 shillings per thousand. Blair accused Andros of failing to make good a promise to give bricks for the chapel wing, but the governor denied it.[33] Philip Ludwell I provided roof shingles on credit, probably made at Greenspring. Through divers efforts, constantly pushed by its impatient president, the college rose.

Smoldering relations between Andros and Blair finally burst into flame in April 1695. At a meeting of the council, the governor read a speech he had drafted to open the session of the burgesses. Councillor Blair, listening, was indignant to hear only one reference in support of his clergy and one other to the needs of his college.[34] He chided Andros vigorously. Older members were shocked, reproving Blair and defending the governor. They stated in Blair's presence that "Itt is the Unanimouse Opinion of the Councill that to discourage all such proceedings for the future wch tend so greatly to the Diminution and Contempt of their Majties Authority placed in their Govr Mr Blair ought not to sitt att the Councill Board till directions therin."[35]

When the council reconvened a week later, Blair blithely took his seat. The ouster was accordingly read again, and Andros recited other complaints. He said that during Blair's illness and absence from his parish, James City's churchwardens had asked him to appoint a supply priest. He had agreed and promised to pay the cost, but Blair had told the wardens that neither "the Govr nor the King had Authority to Appoint a Minister to preach; and might be of ill Consequence as in King James Tyme."[36]

By Andros' account, Blair had also denied to the wardens that the governor could demand to see a minister's credentials; this, he said, was his concern as commissary.

Blair disputed the governor's charges and demanded to see his accusers, but when two ministers were brought in to confirm them, Blair for once seemed nonplussed. According to the

Executive Journals of the Council,[37] "Mr Blair Not shewing any reason for any his Unjust reflections nor so much as Extenuating the same," the council reiterated its position and Andros suspended Blair from the council.[38]

Thus began Blair's first contest with royal authority in Virginia. Though the cards seemed stacked against him, he had not blundered blindly into his position. Instead, he was looking for a fight with Andros. Blair sensed that he could solidify the same antigovernmental forces that had been active against Berkeley, Culpeper, and Howard of Effingham, for popular sentiment was apt to favor any colonist bold enough to stand up against a governor. Nathaniel Bacon the younger had organized such sentiment, and Philip Ludwell I had prospered while defying two governors. Confident of the support of Compton and other Lords Commissioners of Trade and Plantations in any effort to better the church, Blair proceeded to antagonize Andros.

Both men then took counsel with friends. Andros wrote to England to give his account to the Lords Commissioners[39] and to the Duke of Shrewsbury, principal secretary of state.[40] Blair wrote Francis Nicholson, who was having his own problems as governor of Maryland.

The commissary was urged by friends to go to London and seek reinstatement, he told Nicholson, but he thought he would be blamed if the college suffered in his absence. He might also lose his parish. Should he leave without permission of the college trustees, he would risk suspension. He also felt "it would not be Decent for one of my Function to be so impatient, Ambitious or Pragmatical as to run home to complain of such a small injury."[41] However, if Andros did not first obtain official confirmation from London of the ouster, "I hope I may be called home," he broadly hinted, which "will look a great deal better."[42]

The commissioners pondered Blair's ouster, and nearly a year later they instructed the governor and council to restore the commissary "until it shall appear that he has justly forfeited the King's good opinion of his abilities and conduct." On September 25, 1696, Blair took his seat again. If anything, his position had been strengthened in the interim by the assembly's provision of 16,000 pounds of tobacco annually for clergy salaries at the 1696 session, fulfilling the clergy's petition to Andros and the Lords Commissioners' urgent instructions to Andros.[43]

Nicholson and Blair remained in contact by letter and at meetings of the board of the college. The commissary wrote Nicholson from Richneck on February 12, 1697, that Nicholson should supplant Andros as Virginia's lieutenant governor "even if it be necessary to launch out any money" for that end. He also advised Nicholson "to try to gain [William Blathwayt] by money, as no doubt Gov. A[ndros] doth."[44]

Early in 1697 the two conspirators concluded that Blair should return to England. Funds for the college had been overspent by £170, and money was needed. Privately, they intended to displace Andros and have Nicholson named governor. As a result of Nicholson's efforts, the majority of the college trustees authorized Blair to sail with the spring fleet to England for more funds.

Before Blair sailed, however, a new contest split the council. By incoming ship, governor and council were informed of a parliamentary fiat that "all places of trust in the Courts of law or what related to the Treasury of the plantations shall from the making of the said Act be in the hands of native-born subjects of England."[45] Mindful of his stigma as a "Scots hireling," Blair made an issue of it. When the law was read, the commissary "of his motion, declaring himself a native of Scotland," asked if he were disabled from sitting in the general court[46] or in the council itself, since it was responsible for colonial moneys.[47]

After weighing both sides, eight of the councillors concluded that Blair was debarred from serving on the Council[48] and asked that he absent himself until his status could be clarified. He declared this a device to keep the public accounts from him, and he refused to leave unless forced to.[49]

Andros faced an impossible choice: should he adhere to Parliament's will and remove the Scotsman, or should he follow the king's instructions and retain him? Blair's fellow Councillors concluded that the parliamentary act should take precedence, but Blair insisted that Andros himself make the decision. According to Blair, the harassed governor avoided a decision by

stating that Blair was "going for England" shortly and requesting him to absent himself from council for the few days that
remained.[50]

Carefully collecting evidence for use in England, the commissary sailed. He could ill afford to be away from Virginia
at a time of such momentous intrigues, but the future of Blair,
Nicholson, and the college hung in the balance. Again Sarah
stayed behind, but this time she had the anticipation of her
sister Hannah's wedding to handsome Philip Ludwell II to occupy her. That union, on November 11, 1697, strengthened the
ties between the Blairs and the equally strong-willed Ludwells.[51]
Young Ludwell would soon become a member of council, in
1702, as his father had been a few years earlier.

The marriage also reinforced the Harrison family's connections with the wealthy and well-connected Burwells of Gloucester. The younger Ludwell's mother, Lucy Higginson, had
wed Lewis Burwell (died 1653) of Carter's Creek in Gloucester,
and Colonel William Bernard before marrying Philip Ludwell
I; after Lucy died in 1675, Ludwell married, in 1677, Frances
Culpeper Lady Berkeley, widow of Sir William Berkeley of
Greenspring. The Burwells were already connected with the
Harrisons through the union of Benjamin Harrison III, who
acquired Berkeley Hundred in Charles City, with Elizabeth
Burwell, daughter of Lewis and Lucy Higginson Burwell.
Through such interrelationships, the Blair-Harrison coalition
gained strength.[52]

The "college faction" was beginning to form. Sir Edmund
Andros would need all the friends he could command.

CHAPTER VI

Exit Sir Edmund Andros
1697-1698

❧ England was finally at peace with France when Blair returned to London in the summer of 1697. The commissary was safely settled by August at the Surgeon's Arms, a public house in St. Martin's Street, near the church of St. Martin's-in-the-Fields.

Crucial as the college's needs were, it was Andros' recall that moved Blair to make the trip. His mission was one of defamation rather than affirmation. From Maryland, Nicholson had connived with him to obtain the Virginia governorship, agreeing to pay the expense of his trip. From Micajah Perry and Company, merchants of London, Blair drew sums totaling £510 17s 6d, submitting to Nicholson in 1698 an itemized statement that Nicholson later printed. It indicates that Blair spent £50 on his sea passage and £200 for living expenses and "solliciting business" in England.[1] Nicholson later alleged that Blair had expected a large reward and that Blair turned against the governor when he did not offer it.

Blair pointed out to Nicholson by letter from England that the governor's commission had been obtained "in the most honourable manner that ever Government was obtained, that is, that directly nor indirectly it does not cost you one Farthing to any Favourite."[2] He rebuked Nicholson later by saying he had saved him many hundreds of pounds by gaining the favor of English bishops in "place of a purchased interest."[3]

In their own minds, Nicholson and Blair thought their activities a justifiable effort to restore an administration favorable to the church and college. Indeed, such lobbying for office was common in their day. Sir Harbottle Grimston, for example, was rumored to have paid the Earl of Clarendon £8,000 for the office of master of the rolls. Nevertheless, Blair's secrecy indicated a consciousness of wrongdoing.

Nicholson's service in Maryland, which partly salved his pride on being displaced by Andros in Virginia, had not been happy. The colony was less than half Virginia's size, and the governor was paid less. When he arrived there as lieutenant governor, he had been resented by Governor Lionel Copley, whose death in 1698 made the full governorship available.[4] His strong support of the Anglican establishment gained Maryland its own commissary and increased its Church of England clergy from three to eleven, but it was resented by Roman Catholics and dissenters. A faction headed by renegade clergyman John Goode opposed him and sent accusations against him to England. To the Lords Commissioners, Nicholson groaned that he had "a continual very troublesome and chargeable Government in all Respects."[5]

In contrast, Nicholson's administration in Virginia had been popular and her colonists had been cooperative. It was understandable that the thirty-eight-year-old career officer would want to finish his work there, especially when he had the support of so vigorous a champion as the commissary.

James Blair arrived in London in July 1697, after having sailed with the spring fleet from Chesapeake Bay. He found England rejoicing over its triumph over Louis XIV in King William's War. In place of the old Lords of Trade, Blair found England's foreign commerce was now in the hands of a new Board of

Trade—formally titled the Lords Commissioners of Trade and Plantations—named by King William the year before.[6] It was a powerful body, described by the English historian Peter Laslett as "made up of ten Stuart noblemen and gentlemen sitting in their silken knee breeches in front of pewter sandboxes and goose quill pens."[7]

At an early meeting the board had resolved to distribute "the business of Virginia and Maryland to Sir Philip Meadows; that of Barbados, Jamaica and the Leeward Islands to Mr. Blathwayt, or in his absence to Mr. Locke; that of Proprietary and Charter colonies and of Bermuda to Mr. Pollexfen; that of New England, Newfoundland to Mr. Hill."

The most eminent member of the board was John Locke, who had been appointed by the king to advise the political and civil servants of the board, at a stipend of £1,000 yearly. Locke had strong notions of how England's possessions should be governed, and he seized on Blair's presence to question the commissary about Virginia. In August or early September he invited Blair to his rooms in Mr. Pawling's house, in Little Lincoln's Inn Fields, and there quizzed him at length about the colony.

To sum up Blair's criticism of Virginia's laissez-faire administration, Locke had him write a paper titled "Some of the Cheif Greivances of the present Constitution of Virginia with an Essay towards the Remedies thereof." With this as a guide, the philosopher dictated a list of questions about Virginia, in the presence of the commissary. Locke then persuaded the Board of Trade to put these questions to Blair and two other Virginians then in London to provide basis for changes in the colony's government which Locke felt desirable.[8]

The questions were sent out by the board on September 9, 1697, to Blair and his colleagues: Henry Hartwell, a trustee of the college who had been named to the Virginia Council in June 1692, and Edward Chilton, a former Virginia attorney general.[9] The board invited the three to appear before it to answer them, but when Hartwell had to decline because of severe gout,[10] it asked them to write their answers instead.[11]

The three men worked for six weeks, and on October 20, 1697, handed their report to William Popple, secretary of the

Board of Trade, at Whitehall, styling it "An Account of the Present State and Government of Virginia." In a covering note, they termed it "a large and true account" and added that there were "some few things which were known only by one or two of us, that remained longer in the Countrey."[12] These were marked with the initials of the cognizant writer or writers.

"The Present State of Virginia" is the fullest statement in existence of Blair's views on government, especially of Virginia's. His probing mind is evident on every page, pointing out defects here and suggesting corrections there. Not only paragraphs marked "B" but those by all three show Blair's desire to restrict the broad privileges of governor and council and to correct abuses of power by those in high places.[13]

In exercising so many functions, the governor enjoyed excessive authority without being subject to control, the authors wrote. Councillors were "Men devoted to the Governor's Service," they observed, "and not in the least any Check or Restraint upon him." By holding several offices, they too went unchecked, as "when Their Collectors Office obliges them to inform their Judges Office against an unfree Bottom," or when in different capacities they "do both sell and buy the King's Quit-Rents."

The power of vestries was also attacked by the writers, who attributed church abuses to their autocracy. By refusing to hire ministers for more than a year, vestries kept the clergy "in more Subjection and Dependence" or, when a parish was vacant, saved "all the Minister's Dues in their own Pockets."

Of the treatment given the college, "The Present State of Virginia" was particularly critical. The "Governor and his Favourites" had saddled the institution with "as many Enemies as ever they had had friends." The college was "honestly and zealously carry'd on by the Trustees" but it was threatened by the "Backwardness of the Government." As to the college's finances, Blair submitted that "The Gentlemen of the Council, who had been the forwardest to subscribe, were the backwardest to pay; then every one was for finding Shifts to evade and elude their Subscriptions; and the meaner People were so influenced by their Countenance and Example, (Men being easily persuaded to keep their Money) that there was not one Penny got out of new Subscriptions, nor paid of the old 2500 but about 500."[14]

The report cited salaries and perquisites, and it implied that the governor and high officials were well rewarded. In an account of "All publick Money and Tobacco," it listed payments from the "two Shillings per Hogshead" revenue, by the governor's warrant:

To the Governor for Salary,	2000 £.
To Him also for House-Rent,	150 £.
To the Council,	350 £.
To the Clerk of the Council,	50 £.
To the Attorney General,	40 £.
To *William Blaithwaite*, Esq;	100 £.
To Mr. *John Povey*,	100 £.
To a Messenger	25 £.
To two Gunners, about	25 £.

The contrast between the Governor's £2,150 stipend and the commissary's £100 was presented without comment. The report read: "Concerning the Church and Religion: In *Virginia* the Lord Bishop of *London* deputes a Commissary for this Part of his Jurisdiction, whose Business is to make Visitations of Churches, and to take the Inspection of the Clergy. The present Commissary is Mr. *James Blair*, he hath no Salary nor Perquisites, but the King makes it up by his Royal Bounty, having been graciously pleas'd, for two Years, to order him 100 £. a Year, out of the Quit-Rents of Virginia, which we suppose his Majesty intends to continue."[16]

The tone of "The Present State of Virginia" was idealistic and constructive. As a recent editor of the work has observed, "All three authors represented somewhat the same point of view, that of English or Scottish born officials residing in the colonies. No one of them being Virginian born, their outlook naturally differed in numerous respects from that of those who had spent all their lives in the colony and whose ancestors in many instances had for several generations dwelt there. All three had held important commissions under the crown and were consequently favorably disposed to the exercise of the royal authority in the colony and zealous in promoting the policies favored by the crown. . . ."[17]

At the same time, the report was severely critical of procedures of appointment, taxation, and administration. It depicted excessive power in the hands of the governor ("Lieutenant General, Vice-Admiral, Lord Treasurer, Lord Keeper [of the seal], Chief Judge in all Courts, President of the Council, Bishop") and of his favorites, at the expense of the people. With the dry detachment of a legal brief, the two lawyers and the scholar-churchman confirmed complaints that Blair had already detailed in his "Memorial." "The Present State of Virginia" paved the way for the removal of Andros and determined the instructions that would be sent to his successor, Francis Nicholson.

After his early conversations with Locke and the Board of Trade,[18] Blair individually presented his charges against Andros to the board in a separate "memorial." This, indeed, was the chief objective of his trip. The lengthy document listed numerous offenses, ranging from personal insults to Andros' alleged effort to undermine the college. The commissary began by describing mistreatment of the clergy.[19] Unlike Nicholson, Andros was depicted as unconcerned about empty parishes, with the result that only twenty-two of the fifty in Virginia had ministers. The governor "hates every thing that looks like an imitation of Governor Nicholson," Blair asserted.[20] Andros had also disregarded royal instructions to obtain higher clergy stipends, and the assembly's tardy provision in 1696 of 16,000 pounds of tobacco per parish was inadequate.[21]

Blair charged that Andros had failed to provide glebe farms and had not compelled vestries to induct ministers for lifetime service. He had tried to "feed & foment a Jealousy" against the ecclesiastical discipline that Compton had directed Blair to enforce. "He makes the County Courts try incestuous marriages and all other spiritual causes," Blair objected. "If any parish upon occasion of scandal in their minister makes application to My Lord Bishop of London's Commissary for a visitation, the Churchwardens (instead of being commended for their diligence) are sure to be frowned upon and chid for it. Such of the

Clergy as are most refractory against that authority are upon that account received i..o favor. And it is a common maxim among his friends that we have nothing to do with the Bishop of London nor no church power."[22]

A black picture was presented of clerical life in Virginia. The "servitude" of underpaid clergy "hinders all good ministers from coming in or staying amongst us," he declared. ". . . it hinders all women of the better sort from matching with the Clergy while their circumstances are so precarious and uncertain. It exposes the ministers to great poverty and contempt, and makes them base, mean and mercenary . . . that they dare not so much as preach against the vices that the great men of their vestry are Guilty of, for if they do, they must expect a faction will be prepared in the vestry to be against renewing the agreement with them for another year."[23]

Impugning Andros' honesty, Blair noted that "unusual supplies were ordered out of the Treasury of Virginia for the Province of New York (which Orders I suppose were procured by him and his friends) [;] this did not serve, but he supplied them with about 1000 [pounds sterling] over and above all his Orders."[24]

Arguing that Virginia's funds, properly expended, were adequate for its ecclesiastical and educational outlay, Blair said that Andros

has thrown away a great deal of money in raising an old fort at Jamestown, & in building a powder house, and in making a platform for 16 great guns there, and another platform at Tindal's point in York river. I never heard one man that pretended to understand anything of Fortification, that, upon sight of these works, did not ridicule & condemn them as good for nothing but to spend money. The Guns at Jamestown, are so placed that they are no defence to the town, which being much lower in the river, might be taken by the Enemies' shipping, without receiving any the least assistance from those Guns. The powder House stands all alone without any Garrison to defend it, and is a ready prey for any foreign or domestic Enemy.[25]

Blair also listed grievances suffered by the college, which were similar to his criticisms in "The Present State of Virginia." Not only had the governor contributed nothing, but he had influenced his friends not to give, Blair wrote. Enemies of the college were promoted by the governor while friends were slighted. The college had encountered opposition in taking possession of lands granted on Blackwater Swamp and the Pamunkey River, and Andros' faction had defeated efforts in the 1696 assembly to force payment of pledges to the college.

"All the common people . . . do observe, that Sir Edmund Andros chooses his friends and favorites only out of such as are Enemies to the College," Blair wrote, adding:[26] "And it is observed that in Elections of Burgesses for the General Assembly, or in the choosing of a speaker for the House of Burgesses, all the Governor's friends employ their utmost interest to keep out any one that is a friend to the College, and do commonly prevail by this very argument: 'if you choose such a one,' say they, 'he is a Collegian, and we shall have a tax for the College.' "[27] Blair no doubt referred here to circumstances attending the election of Philip Ludwell I as speaker of the House of Burgesses in 1695.

The college also suffered from the decline in the colony's revenue from the penny-per-pound exported out of Virginia and Maryland to other English plantations, Blair reported. He attributed this to ". . . the Governor's permitting the collectors to make up their accounts clandestinely with the auditor, without appointing a day for a public audit as used to be yearly appointed formerly. By this means both the collectors have better opportunity to cheat the College of the said Revenue, and the Governors of the College incur the displeasure of the Honorable the Commissioners of his Majesty's customs, who expect from them a copy of all the accounts of the penny per pound fairly audited."[28]

The most interesting passage in Blair's memorial describes affronts by Andros and his supporter, Colonel Daniel Parke, to Nicholson on his visits to Virginia for college meetings. "At first Sir Edmund tried to make him [Nicholson] weary by dryness, and frowns, and asking uncivil questions—demanding the reason how he came to leave his Government, or what he had to do in Virginia to amuse the people? But when this would not discourage him from coming, a very strange method was used. . . ."

His Excellency Governour Nicholson,
To Cash laid out about his Business, (viz.) D^{tor.}

	l.	*s.*	*d.*
To Mr. *Shelton,* to engage him of his Side when he was accused by Captain *Sly,* Five Guineas,	5	10	0
To Fees and Gratuities about his Commission and Instructions,	15	5	0
To Fees for Instructions at the Treasury,	3	11	0
Given there in Gratuities, Ten Guineas,	11	0	0
To the Door-Keepers,	3	6	0
Gratuities to four Clerks at the Council of Trade,	11	0	0
Fees at the Secretaries Office,	7	19	0
To the Messengers there,	2	4	0
Fees expended by *B. Harrison, junior,* about the two Commissions when I was in *Scotland,* of which *Frank* gave an Account,	178	15	0
Paid for Copying Memorials,	4	5	0
Paid for Passage of Letters,	2	2	6
	244	17	6
To all my Expences living in *London* and folliciting Business,	200	0	0
To my Passage at Sea and Travelling by Land,	50	00	0
To Mr. *Robinson's* Passage 6 *l.* and advancing him 10 *l.*	16	00	0
	510	17	6

James Blair's accounting of his expenses in going to England in 1697–98 included £50 for his voyage and £200 for living expenses. His list of receipts, headed "Per Contra," follows. The two were presented by the Commissary to Francis Nicholson and were published by Nicholson in 1727 in his Papers Relating to an Affidavit *to contravert Blair's claim that he suffered financial hardship in his trip to obtain the governorship for Nicholson.*

Courtesy of the College of William and Mary

"There is an handsome young man of that country, one Mr. Daniel Park," Blair continued, "who to all the other accomplishments that make a complete sparkish Gentleman, has added one upon which he infinitely values himself, that is, a quick resentment of every the least thing that looks like an affront or Injury. He has learned they say the art of fencing and is as ready at giving of a challenge especially before Company, as the greatest Hector in the Town. This Mr. Park as being a proper tool for his designs, Sir Edmund Andros gained to his interest, advanced him into the Council, made him a Colonel, and received him into his particular favour."

Upon a slight pretense of affront, Parke sought out Nicholson at Blair's house at Richneck in September 1695, Blair recounted.

Finding the Company at Breakfast he said nothing of what he came for till they had risen from the table. After Grace, he addressed himself thus to the Governor of Maryland. "Captn Nicholson" said he, "did you receive a letter that I sent you from New York?" "Yes, I received it" said the Govr of Maryland. "And was it done like a Gentleman," said Col. Park, "to send that letter by the hand of a common post to be read by every body in Virginia? I look upon it as an affront and expect satisfaction." "You must go to Pennsylvania then," said the Govr of Maryland, "my hands are tied up in Virginia. But if you go hither you shall have the satisfaction you desire." Says Park, "Come out here," and so, putting his hand upon his sword, went towards the Door. "What" says the Governor of Maryland "is this your way, Mr. Park, of giving challenges before so much Company? If you have anything to say to me you know always where to find me. I am often in these parts, and you shall never find that I fly the road for you. I am going this very afternoon to Sir Edmund Andros's. But you shall not catch me making any appointments in Virginia."[29]

When Nicholson paid a courtesy call on Andros the same day,

Sir Edmund took occasion to quarrel with him, alleging that he reflected on him in Maryland and the sheriff of James City being present, he ordered the Governor of Maryland into custody. The Govr of Maryland told Sir Edmund Andros that he knew what was their design in all this; that they thought to scare him from coming into Virginia to wait upon the business of the College, but that it should not at all do. He would still come and perform his duty in that trust. After he had been about half an hour in the Sherriff's custody (tho' not out of the room all the while), Sir Edmund being afraid of the consequence of imprisoning and detaining one of the King's Governor's, ordered that he should have his liberty.[30]

According to Blair's memorial, Colonel Parke persisted in his effort to provoke a fight with Nicholson. At a meeting of the college board in February 1697, the commissary said he had been urged by trustees—probably Nicholson chiefly—to return to England to obtain payment of funds from the estate of Robert Boyle, which he had been promised in 1692. But Parke, "who was utterly against Mr. Blair's going for England, . . ." argued that Nicholson was already going, which was sufficient. When others expressed ignorance of Nicholson's intention, Parke insisted: "Yes, I can tell you that the Governor of Maryland is going for England, for he has promised to meet me there this shipping." Blair continued:

Upon this the Govr of Maryland made answer, "Sir," says he "you are mistaken. I promised to ask the King's leave to go for England. But for meeting you, I'll meet you where you will, except in Virginia and Maryland." Upon which Col. Park, with an high and angry tone, replied, "No sir," said he, "you positively promised to meet me in England." "It is a lie," said the Govr of Maryland "and it is not the first you have told." "A lie!" says Col. Park, and, having a horsewhip in his hand, runs to the Govr of Maryland, who was sitting bareheaded, & gave him a slash with the horsewhip over the head. The Govr of Maryland at this time happened to have no sword or other weapon about him, for he had left his sword in an house where he dined at Jamestown . . . but presently flew to Col. Park with his naked fist. There being Company enough in the room, they were immediately parted. Upon this the Governor of Maryland (as was afterwards known) sent Col. Park a private challenge to fight him in Carolina. . . . but Col. Park for all his huffing and hectoring in company, was extremely nettled at this, and contrived to have the matter discovered to Sir Edmund Andros, who, by putting him under confinement, took care to keep his skin whole.[31]

The most outrageous incident Blair described was Parke's assault on Sarah Blair in 1696 one Sunday in Bruton Parish Church. As Blair told it,

Mistress Blair having no pew of her own in the Church of that Parish . . . was obliged to her good neighbours for their Courtesy in allowing her a seat in the church along with them. Among the rest my Lady

Berkeley, who was then married to Col. Philip Ludwell,[32] generally invited her to sit in Col. Ludwell's pew. This had continued to be her ordinary station in the Parish Church for about two years, there being a very entire friendship between Col. Ludwell & Mr. Blair. Col. Park was this Col. Ludwell's Son-in-Law, and by Col. Ludwell's permission had used to sit in the same pew with his Lady and children from the time he had married his daughter, but had now for above a year left the Church upon a prejudice he took up against the Minister,—one Mr. Samuel Eburne for preaching a little too home against adultery, in several sermons wherein he took himself to be reflected on; for he did at that time, & still doth, entertain a Gentleman's Lady, one Mistress Berry, whom he had conveyed away from her husband in London in the year 1692, and carried to Virginia along with him, calling her by the name of his cousin Brown.

But, to have a blow at Mr. Blair, he resolved for one day to lay aside his resentments against Mr. Eburne and to come to Church to pull Mistress Blair out of that pew, which for that time (and to give some color of right to that action) he was pleased to lay claim to as his own; tho' no such pretension was ever heard of before. Accordingly about the month of January in the year 1695–6 he came one Sunday suddenly to Church & rushing in with a mighty violence with which he frightened the poor Gentlewomen who were in the pew (without any man to defend them as fearing no attacks in such a sanctuary), he seized Mistress Blair by the wrist, and with great fury and violence pulled her out of the Pew in presence of the Minister and the Congregation, who had begun divine Service, all the people being extremely scandalized at this ruffianly & profane action. Mr. Blair (tho' as things then stood, he expected no redress) thought it his duty to represent this to the Governor, who together with his council considering the matter, as they could not justify Col. Park in a thing upon which all the country cried out shame, so was resolved to give Mr. Blair no satisfaction, and therefore upon hearing of both parties gave their opinions in these words: "That it did not lie before them." At the same time Col. Ludwell having presented a Petition complaining of Col. Park for invading the right and disturbing of Mistress Blair who sat there at his desire & permission, had the same answer.[33]

No other reference to this incident has been found in records of the time, but presumably Blair's charges had some basis.

Blair praised Nicholson's patience under provocation. "[He] has (as I am told) desired my Lord Duke of Baltimore to intercede with his Majesty, for leave for him to come home. But I hope the King will find a better way to keep up the honor of his Governors, than by suffering them to be thus exposed to the insults of every rude and unmannerly subject."[34]

Toward him, the commissary concluded, Andros' faction had directed constant harassment. They had misrepresented him to the bishop of London, persecuted his friends and relatives, conspired to deprive him of the college presidency, and tried to deny him his benefice at Jamestown "with no less offers to the vestry, than that if they would do it, a Minister should be found for them gratis." Finally, he had been twice suspended from the council without "any process or trial." "Why," he asked, had Andros "been so eager to have him out, that the King's express Warrant . . . could not preserve him"?

The commissary finally presented charges against Andros at a hearing at Lambeth Palace on December 27, 1697, before the archbishop of Canterbury, Thomas Tenison,[35] and the bishop of London, Henry Compton. Present as representative of the Privy Council was John Povey, a clerk of that body. Blair had with him his brother-in-law, twenty-four-year-old Benjamin Harrison III, recently trained in the law at the Middle Temple, who took little part in the hearing. Present for Andros were Ralph Marshall, probably an English attorney,[36] and William Byrd II, the son of Blair's former neighbor from Westover plantation on the James River near Varina.

The proceedings were held without Andros, a colonial governor being required to remain at his post unless ordered home. He had designated as his representative the twenty-three-year-old Byrd, who had recently been admitted to the English bar after studies at the Middle Temple. However, Byrd had spent most of his youth out of Virginia and had made only one prior appearance before a court of law.[37] The hearing was to be the slaughter of the innocents.

Byrd began by proposing that Blair repeat his accusations so that they might be answered serially. Archbishop Tenison, presiding, rejected this and directed that certain accusations against Blair be answered. What of the charge that Blair had "filled the church with Scotchmen and endeavored to make a national faction by the name of the Scottish party?"[38] Byrd attempted to support the statement, but Blair and Compton quickly showed that most of the alleged "Scotchmen" were English and, in any case, had come to Virginia before Blair's day. Compton accepted responsibility, explaining that not enough English priests would go to the colonies and that needy clerics who had fled Scotland were available.[39]

The other charge mentioned by the archbishop was that Blair had "misapplied and squandered away the money that should have gone to the building of the college."[40] Byrd replied that Blair had received £150 yearly as president, contrary to the charter. When the wording of the instrument was disputed and Byrd asked that the pertinent provision be read, the archbishop said time did not permit it. Was it not true, he asked Byrd instead, that the trustees had asked Blair to move nearer the college to superintend its building? After Blair had detailed his sacrifices, the archbishop agreed that he would probably have taken the salary, too. When Byrd blamed Blair's taking his salary for the refusal of subscribers to pay up, Harrison and Blair argued that some of the great men did not pay up, and they were responsible.[41]

Blair also testified that funds from the royal grant had been kept separate from the public subscription, his salary coming solely from the first.[42]

With a fresh show of spirit, Byrd next asked Blair to state his accusations against Andros. This was what the commissary was waiting for. He plunged into an account of the governor's misuse of clergy and college. When Povey observed that Blair's second suspension from the council, on grounds that he had not been born in England, was of his own choosing, the commissary replied that Andros' purpose had been to keep him from seeing the wasteful revenue accounts.[43]

When Byrd tried to stem Blair's torrent, he was brushed aside. Occasionally Tenison or Compton put in a question, but it merely brought new grievances to Blair's mind. The sympathies of the two churchmen were clearly on the side of the commissary.

Bringing Blair's two-hour tirade to an end, Archbishop Tenison adjourned the hearing. Blair had made his case, as the surviving transcript reveals. Though the Archbishop tried to save Byrd's face by saying "we must take a time to consider what is fit to be done in all this," the outcome was clear. "Never was vindication more complete than that of the Commissary," wrote the church historian, William Stevens Perry; "never was indictment more fully sustained than that in which in full detail and with logical precision he assailed the character and conduct of the royal governor."[44]

As for the crestfallen Byrd, he remained awhile in England to learn more of the laws. Although he had prepared a lengthy brief listing Blair's offenses against Andros, he had no opportunity to deliver it.[45] In the words of his biographer, "the Lambeth affair had rather thoroughly demonstrated that he knew very little about them [the laws]."[46]

Blair continued to find in Locke a receptive mind. Despite the disparity in their eminence and age—Locke was sixty-five and Blair forty-one—they became friends. The philosopher had some knowledge of colonial affairs, for he had served as secretary to the Lords Proprietors of Carolina from 1668 to 1675 and had drafted "The Fundamental Constitutions for the Government of Carolina." For his part, Blair had read and approved Locke's two *Treatises on Government*, written in 1685, which became the basis of Whig policy in the reign of William and Mary. He was not surprised to find the author of the *Essay Concerning Human Understanding* and of *Some Thoughts on Education* sympathetic to the colonists of Virginia.

Locke recommended steps to be taken, but before the board could hear Blair's complaints, Locke was forced to leave London to escape the winter chimney smoke that aggravated his lung ailment. When January 1698 arrived, Blair was still waiting to be heard. On the advice of Archbishop Tenison, Blair thus wrote to Locke at his home in Essex:

> Jan. 20, 1697/8
> London at the Surgeons
> Arms in St. Martins Street.
>
> Sir
> I hope your goodness will pardon the abruptness of this Address, which makes bold to intrude upon you in your retirement. The extraordinary countenance and assistance wherewith you favoured me while you was in the City, encourages me to enquire, with a most

particular concern after your health in the Country. I have not
offered, since you went, to stirre in any business at the Councill of
Trade and Plantations; fearing less in your absence I should have
marred and mismanaged it, by an untimely forcing it into other
hands, and other methods than you had contrived. But I can not
but flatter my self with the hopes, that God, who made you such an
eminent instrument of detecting the Constitution and Government
of Virginia, will likewise furnish you with health and opportunities
to redress the Errours and abuses of it. It is expected that the business
of the Plantations will shortly be taken into consideration; and my
Lord of Canterbury a few days ago expressed himself with abundance
of concern for your being out of the way. He told me he had wrote
to you, but had no answer; which made him apprehend the bad state
of your health: & perhaps his letter might not be right addressed. I
promised his grace to write to you, and to acquaint him with what
I should learn of your health or resolutions to come to London:
which I think my self obliged to acquaint you with, as a further
apology for my giving you this trouble, and for the request I must
conclude with, that by your Amanuensis you'l let me know, what
to say to his grace on this occasion. I pray God to restore you to your
health, and am

> Sir
> Your most obliged, humble servant.
> James Blair[47]

The commissary's activities after the hearing at Lambeth were
largely in behalf of Nicholson's appointment. Having discredited
Andros, he now aided John Locke in his efforts to reform Virginia's government along lines proposed in "The Present State
of Virginia" and to send out a new governor, empowered to
correct abuses.

He also faced the necessity of regaining his seat on the Council
of Virginia, and this he set out to do. The matter had been referred by the Board of Trade to the attorney and solicitor
general, who ruled that neither the act of Parliament "nor any
other Law that We know of does disable Mr. Blair from being
of the Council of Virginia, because being born in Scotland he
is by construction of Law a Native born Subject of England."[48]

The decision came a little too late for Blair's purposes, unfortunately. Acting on recommendations of Hartwell, Blair, and
Chilton, the Board of Trade had drawn up instructions to ac-

company the next governor of Virginia, and Blair's name was not included among council members. The commissary vainly appeared before the board and recited the circumstances of his now invalidated ouster, but the board would not amend its instructions. Presumably it had been concerned by testimony against Blair which Daniel Parke had meanwhile given it. In any event, their Lordships "resolved to leave the names unaltered."[49]

Perhaps William Blathwayt, a partisan of Andros, persuaded the board that Blair had been too contentious, or perhaps the board concluded that a cooling-off period would be welcome. Not even the efforts of Blair's loyal bishop could persuade the board to reinstate him. "It gives him more consideration [among the people of Virginia]," Compton wrote, "who are too apt upon the smallest occasion to condemn his Slender Authority. He is a discreet man, and will I am sure give no Offence, but do what good he can."[50] But the board knew Blair better than his bishop did.

Early in 1698, Blair was told that Andros would be recalled and Nicholson sent to Virginia as governor. The commissary wrote Nicholson by the next sailing,[51] and on May 26 Nicholson returned his thanks to John Locke for promoting his appointment. "Gratitude obliges me to pay you the best of my acknowledgement for your having been pleased not only to speak favourably of me, but to recommend me to some of his most sacred Majesty's great ministers of state, which the Reverend Mr. Blair give me an account of. . . ." A few months later Nicholson wrote Locke again, this time from Virginia: "The Rev. Mr. President Blair has acquainted me how very zealous you were in using your great interest for my being so very advantageously removed hither. And I shall endeavor (God Willing) to so behave myself in my station here that you may never have cause to be concerned that you were so very instrumental in accomplishing that affair. . . ."[52]

On May 31, 1698, it was announced at Whitehall that Sir Edmund Andros had asked "leave of the King to resign his Government of Virginia, that he may return unto England about his own affairs." King William was willing to comply,[53] though his Majesty did not immediately name a successor. Thus Andros' pride was spared.

At this point Blair wrote Nicholson:

London, June 2, 1698

May it please Your Excellency,

After many Letters that I have sent Your Excellency, giving You an Account only of tedious Attendance and Dependance, this comes at last, with the good News that Sir *Edmond Andros* is called home, and his Majesty on *Sunday* last named Your self Governour of *Virginia*, of which all your Friends here wish You great Joy, and I am sure none more than my self: I am further to acquaint You, that you have not only gotten the Government, but have obtained it in the most honourable manner that ever Government was obtained, that is, that directly nor indirectly it does not cost you one Farthing to any Favourite; that You have been recommended to it by Persons of the greatest Worth and Reputation, such as are far above the Suspicion of dealing in any dishonourable Way, and that it is purely the Strength of Your own good Character, that hath prevailed over the Suggestions of all Your Enemies.

To give to the perfect History of it, would require a Volume; but in short, the Persons You have been most obliged to, and to whom I hope You will return Your Thanks with the first Opportunity, are my Lord Arch-Bishop of *Canterbury*, my Lord Chancellor, my Lord Bishop of *London*, my Lord Bishop of *Salisbury*, the Earl of *Bridgwater*, and Doctor Lock.

Sir, Your Excellency's most Humble
and Obliged Servant,
James Blair[54]

When Nicholson's commission was announced on July 20,[55] Andros' return was attributed to illness. As evidence of his good standing in the colonial service, the old soldier in 1704 was named lieutenant governor of the Isle of Guernsey.

Along with Nicholson's commission, the Board of Trade sent to Virginia instructions to correct abuses. The governor was ordered to communicate regularly with his council, "such and so many of thos Instructions wherein their Advice and Consent is mentioned to be requisite." Councillors were not to be suspended without "good and sufficient cause," in which case the record must be forwarded to England for review. The governor was also required to have all orders purporting to be from him and the council properly approved by the council. The governor's power to remove judges and officials was restricted, and he was required to appoint for stated terms.

An effort was also made to end abuses of trust by councillors. Henceforth they must take oaths to impartially administer justice before serving on the general court. No longer would they be exempt from civil suit. Tobacco paid to the king's quitrent account was not to be sold privately to councillors but at a fully-publicized public auction at county courthouses, "by inch of Candle to the highest bidder."[56] As its predecessor body had done, the board instructed the governor to encourage growth of towns as trading centers, to discourage the patenting of large tracts of idle land, and to prevent illegal claiming of lands. All were needed reforms.

Having done his best for Nicholson, Blair returned in the fall of 1698 to Virginia. On arrival, the commissary received no public acclaim, for this time he brought no college charter or new funds to show for his efforts. At Jamestown he found greater hostility against the governor. After convening a turbulent session of the House of Burgesses beginning September 28, Andros dissolved the assembly on October 6, 1698, and soon departed for England.

Nicholson's arrival in December brought a change in Virginia's mood. Several years' absence in Maryland had not diminished his popularity. Blair painted an idyllic picture to Locke:

Virginia Feb. 8 1698/9

Sir

The tranquility we begin to enjoy in this Country by the happy change of our Governour, and Government is so great that I who have the happiness to know by whose assent these workings were provided have all the reason in the world to take all occasions of expressing my gratitude for them, and to pray to God to reward those noble publick souls that bestow so many of their thoughts, in contriving the relief of the oppressed, and the happiness of mankind.

Dear Sir think not that I speak this from any other principle or design I have, and only from a sense how much this whole Country in general and my self in particular are beholding to you for the thoughts you was pleased to bestow on our late unhappy circumstances, and the methods you contrived to relieve us. You are to look for your reward from a better hand. Only give me grace to say that I think no sort of good works are preferable to these, that have such an universal good influence on whole Countries to make all the people happy.

This Country is so barren of action that it affords nothing to satisfy your curiosity. Our new Governor Coll. Nicholson is very greatly welcomed to this place. Sir Edmund Andros is gone home mighty angry not only for the loss of such a good Government but for being succeeded by such a person, whom of all others he had the least kindness for. I doubt not if he or his great friend at your board,[57] can get him to be put into any post wherein he can reach this Country we shall feel the effects of his resentment and revenge to the utmost of his power. . . .[58]

Locke's reply indicates his interest in the civilization that Englishmen were planting in North America:

London, 16 Octr, '99

SR,

You that know my bad health, some part of my business in town: will I doubt not pardon the slowness of my return to your letter of February last, especially since it contained no thing of business to be done but grateful reflections on what had been done with an overgreat opinion expressed of that service which you imagine you had from my hand in the doing of it. I shall not undertake to answer all the great compliments you make me on this occasion. I take them as I ought, to be the language of your civility. But this give me leave to say, that if I have been any way instrumentall in procuring any good to the Country you are in, I am as much pleased with it as you can be. The flourishing of the plantations under their due & just regulations being that which I do & shall always aim at whilst I have the honour to sit at the board I now do.

I hope the College grows & flourishes under your care. I would be glad to know whether you carried over with you a Baroscope & Thermoscope[59] from hence when you went over last, for I think a constant registar of the air kept there would not be only of general use to the improvement of natural philosophy but might be of particular advantage of the plantation itself by observations to be made on the changes of the air.

I know your country has many natural curiosities. Such of them as come in your way & are of no difficult transportation I should receive as an obligation from you more particularly all seeds of all strange & curious plants, with an account of the soils they grow in & best seasons you observe there for sowing of them: amongst other things you will do me a favor to send me a plentifull stock of peach stones of your best sorts of peaches.

I am Sir, &c., &c.,
JOHN LOCKE[60]

Blair probably sent the "plentifull stock of peach stones" and the "seeds of all strange & curious plants," though there is no record of it. In any event, the ailing Locke resigned his post on the Board of Trade a few months later and retired to Oates Manor to devote himself to biblical study. He died in 1704 and was buried in the local churchyard. The epitaph which he wrote in Latin translates thus:

Near this place lies John Locke. If you wonder what kind of man he was, the answer is that he was one contented with his modest lot. A scholar by training, he devoted his studies wholly to the pursuit of truth. Such you may learn from his writings, which will also tell you whatever else there is to be said about him more faithfully than the dubious eulogies of an epitaph. His virtues, if he had any, were too slight to serve either to his own credit or as an example to you. Let his vices be interred with him. An example of virtue, you have already in the Gospels; an example of vice is something one could wish did not exist; and example of mortality (and may you learn from it) you have assuredly here and everywhere. That he was born on August 29, 1632, and died on October 28, 1704, this tablet, which itself will quickly perish, is a record.

In Locke's death the colonies lost a friend. Had he lived longer he might have helped avoid some of the mistakes in British policy that finally brought on the American Revolution. Even so, he was instrumental in placing colonial government on a sounder footing. He could have done an equal service had he been able to direct the commissary "wholly to the pursuit of truth." Blair, however, had begun to suffer the corrupting effects of power, and worse was to come.

CHAPTER VII

Building the College
1698-1703

☙ On October 21, 1698, the state house at Jamestown burned, changing the life of the colony. The little village had fared poorly since 1607, and some burgesses had favored building a new town after Bacon had burned it in 1676. For nearly a decade, while the assembly met irregularly in taverns and houses, members had talked of moving to Tyndall's Point or Middle Plantation. In 1680 the vote for Tyndall's had risen to eighteen against twenty-one for Jamestown. Only after Charles II refused to sanction removal had the state house been rebuilt on its old footings. Blair wrote the Lords of Trade in 1697 that there were only "twenty or thirty houses at Jamestown."

When Nicholson arrived from Maryland six weeks after the 1698 fire, he found agitation again strong for removal. The marshy Jamestown peninsula afforded few well-drained acres for building sites. Even before the fire the state house had been woefully inadequate, so crowded that the House of Burgesses had had to meet in a house nearby. Built in the old-fashioned cross shape of Queen Elizabeth's time, its rooms were dark and narrow. Because it adjoined a row of residential tenements,[1] it was vulnerable to fire.

In the charred debris of the 1698 blaze, Nicholson and Blair now saw their chance to move the capital to Middle Plantation. It would strengthen the college to have the governor nearby, and it would be more accessible to newer settlements along the York, the Rappahannock, and the Potomac. The prospect appealed especially to Nicholson, who was a planner and builder. During his governorship of Maryland, he had moved its seat of government from St. Mary's to the new Annapolis, which he had designed with splendid circles and diagonal streets reminiscent of the Italian Renaissance. He hoped to do the same for Virginia.

Nicholson introduced the subject at the opening of the assembly on April 27, 1699, crowded into a house that John Tullitt had prepared for its use for £50. Nearby, in the great hall of Mrs. William Sherwood's brick house, met the council and general court. "I do recommend to you to have such a Pile of Buildings erected so soon as possible," His Excellency told the lawmakers, "as may not be only larger, but more conveniently serve the public uses than that which was unfortunately burnt the last fall."

Once the opening formalities were done, Nicholson announced a "public day of rejoicing" on May Day for blessings that the colony owed to "the great goodness of Almighty God" and to "his most gracious Majesty King William." He invited the assembly to "his Majesty's Royal College of Wm and Mary, where they might be Eye Witnesses to one of His Majesty's Royal bounties and favors to this, his most ancient and great Colony and Dominion of Virginia." There they could sit as "Judges and Ear Witnesses of the great improvement of our youth in Learning and Education."[2]

On the appointed day, councillors and burgesses gathered for the "Scholastick Exercises."[3] The college had been erected, and several dozen youths from twelve years of age upwards now learned Latin and Greek there from Mungo Inglis, the grammar school master. The high point was to be oratory by five of the aptest scholars, who no doubt entered the proceedings in academic robes with Governor Nicholson, President Blair, Master Inglis, and the college trustees.

The occasion had been well planned. The governor and the commissary desired to show not only that Middle Plantation would be the best location for the capital but that the college was functioning to the colony's benefit. To judge from the speeches, the young men had been well coached by Blair or Inglis, for they several times spoke of having been "commanded" or "directed" to deal with particular matters.[4] Their remarks indicate Nicholson's and Blair's plans for improving Virginia.

The first speaker declared learning to be essential to the public good. Without it, he asked, how "can lawes be made, Justice be distributed, Differences be Composed, publick speeches be begun or concluded, Embassys be managed & whate is fittest and best to be done on all Occasions bee Discovered?" Plato had written that nations would be happy only when governed by philosophers. Learning was not only essential to church and state, however; it was man's only solace in a world where "all things are perrishable except the Goods of the Mind."

With the benefit of learning, he concluded: ". . . wee may Converse with the most Excelent men of all ages, with the Sublime Philosopher Plato, with the Prince of Philosophers Aristotle, with the most Christian Philosopher Seneca, with Tully the Master of Rethorick, & unexhausted Fountaine of Eloquence, with Livy that Notable Historian, & with Tacitus the polititian in accord with the Muses. . . . Learning makes us not only more knowing but more Vertuous . . . excites in our Minds those Generous Instincts of our Natures after Glory, & by Showing us virtue in its Comeliness, & Vice in its deformity, makes us ever after Admire the first, & Abominate the Last."[5]

The second speaker explained the advantages of being educated in Virginia rather than abroad. Not only was English schooling twice as expensive but it was less suited to Virginians' needs. The voyager was liable to be captured and enslaved. Once in England the student must become acclimatized, sometimes falling ill in the process. Money spent in the colony supported Virginia's trade balance, and creation of the college had already brought funds from abroad. The "vulgar error wch has been Industriously spread among the Common people that the College will Ruin the Country" should be discounted by thinking people.

An even more pertinent note was struck by the third speaker, who may have been Orlando Jones, grandfather of Martha Washington.[6] His theme was "By What Means a Virginia Education May Be Most Easily Promoted." He told the assemblymen:

This I am commanded to make the subject of my discourse but with this express injunction, that I shall strictly observe the modesty and bashfulness of the Muses, and howsoever pressing our wants may be, that I shall offer [no argument] which may seem to beg . . . either from the country in general, or private benefactors in particular. After I have given you my promise punctually to observe this injunction, I hope you won't be offended if I hint at any method of promoting our college without taking anything out of your pocket, or putting you to any other public or private charge. . . . [The earnest orator thought a college environment required:] the convenience of good company and conversation; For in such a retired Corner of the world, far from business, and action, if we make scholars, they are in danger of proving meer scholars, which make a very ridiculous figure: made up of Pedantry, disputatiousness, positiveness, and a great many other ill qualities which render them [unfit for participation in public affairs.] Now there is one way of procuring for us [this convenience,] and that is by contriving a good town in this place, and filling it with all the selectest and best company that is to be had within the government. Providence has put into your hands a way of compassing this without charge. I mean without any more charge than you will necessarily be at on another account, namely the building of the statehouse, which alone will be attended with the seat of the government, offices, markets, good company, and all the rest. [In short] the Colledge will be a great help towards the making of a Town, and the Town towards the improving of the Colledge.

By this time, even the dullest burgess must have realized that Governor Nicholson and President Blair had stage-managed the performance.

Young Jones proceeded to list reasons why Middle Plantation was well placed "for making a pleasant, strong and wealthy city": (1) It was healthfully elevated and supplied with freshwater springs; (2) It was easily reached by land as well as by Queen's Creek and Archer's Hope Creek; (3) It was secure from enemies by sea and from Indian attack by land, thanks to its location; (4) Its ridge offered situations for windmills to supplement the usual watermills; (5) Its soil would offer firm ground for house sites and provide clay for brick; (6) It was centrally situated for a market town; and (7) "Here are great helps and advances made already towards the beginning of a town: a Church, an ordinary, several stores, two Mills, a smith's shop a Grammar School, and above all, the Colledge."

These were persuasive arguments, but the speaker returned to economics for his climax:

The colledge will help to make the town, the chief difficulty in making a town being in the bringing a considerable number of inhabitants to it, especially so considerable a number of mouths as may give vent to a weekly market. The very numbers of the colledge who will be obliged to reside at this place—viz. the president and masters with all their servants and attendants, the scholars with such servants as will be necessary for kitchen, buttery, gardens, wooding, and all other uses, will make up above 100 persons to be constantly supplied at this market. And these, it is like will encourage tradesmen to come and live here for their relief and supply. Besides, the colledge, being not yet finished, will employ in builders and laborers a very considerable number; and it is easy to be foreseen that the prime youth of the country being here, it will occasion a great resort hither of parents and other friends to see their children and relations. . . . Experience (as well as the reason of the thing) shows us that there never was a colledge anywhere but that alone made something of a town. . . . By this method we have an opportunity not only of making a town, but such a town as may equal if not outdo Boston, New York, Philadelphia, Charlestown, and Annapolis. . . ."

The last reference was adroit, for Nicholson had been chiefly responsible for creating Annapolis, and the town in a few years had surpassed Jamestown. The speaker concluded: "And thus now having, I think, sufficiently recommended this place, as well on the account of the colledge's being already here, as the other great natural advantages and conveniences of it . . . I hope there are no such men as out of pure spite to the colledge will endeavor to deprive it of the blessing we have been pleading for, unless they can show any other situation in the country that has the like or greater conveniences for answering the ends of the government in general, or of a noble City in particular."

The fourth speaker traced the origins of the college, giving praise to the late John Page and other unnamed benefactors, who included many men present from the council and House of Burgesses. The implication was clear: the college was the creation and responsibility of others besides its president.

Finally, a concluding orator urged the lawmakers to cherish the College of William and Mary and promote its growth. Appealing to their pride, he reminded them of the universities of England and asked:

Shall we that are descended of English progenitors be against haveing so much as one? Shall we not rather with one consent & accord, with one heart and mind & will welcome the Muses into our Countrey? That the nations of America takeing example from us, may be excited to the Study and exercise of Learning and virtue, and may confess and acknowledge that the Colledge of William and Mary in Virginia is the Mansion house of virtue, the Parnassus of the Muses, and a Seminary of excellent men. . . . [With a flourish, he concluded:] Methinks we already see that happy time when we shall surpass the Asiaticians in civility, the Jews in Religion, the Greeks in Philosophy, the Egyptians in Geometry, the Phenicians in Arithmetick, and the Caldeans in Astrology. O happy Virginia!

When the assembly resumed session at Jamestown, the burgesses acknowledged Nicholson's opening address and proceeded to consider a new state house. The assembly at the same time received from James Blair an address from "the President, Masters and Scholars of the Royal College of William and Mary in Virginia," expressing pleasure in their visit and hope for their continued support.

Nicholson then made an important proposal. He recommended to the assembly "the placing your publick building (which God willing you are designed to have) somewhere at Middle Plantation nigh his Majesty's Royal College of William and Mary, which I think will tend to God's glory, his Majesty's service, and the welfare and prosperity of your country in general and of the college in particular, and will be a greater kindness than if you had given two thousand pounds of the use of it." With his message he sent a copy of the third student's May Day oration, which was read again to the burgesses.

Nicholson and Blair had made their case with the finesse of a Madison Avenue public relations firm. Constituting themselves as a committee of the whole, the burgesses now resolved that "the said statehouse be built at the Middle Plantation." They ordered a committee to wait on council for its concurrence, which was unanimously given next day. The statute enacted called for a "Capitol" to be built at Middle Plantation, which the assembly decreed should be forever "called and known by the name of the city of Williamsburg, in honor of our most gracious and glorious King William."

Prospects for the college thus took a better turn. Blair wrote Archbishop Tenison on February 12, 1700, that subscriptions were being paid and other circumstances improved.[7] Late in 1700 Master Inglis and his students completed their move into the building. King William had recommended the college's care to Nicholson,[8] and the governor helped in several ways. He believed the enrollment suffered because students completing grammar school had as yet no master to teach them in college. Nicholson accordingly wrote Tenison on May 27, 1700, asking him to send a scholar to teach mathematics and philosophy.[9]

The grammar school, which had functioned in a small building since 1694, now occupied a severe white-walled room in the completed college. Besides intensive study of Latin and Greek, its young men learned writing, arithmetic, and other subjects. This qualified them at fifteen or sixteen to face oral examination for acceptance into the college, as in the universities of England and Scotland.

The classical niceties of the classroom contrasted oddly with the rough simplicity of early Williamsburg, which was yet a far cry from "the Parnassus of the Muses" envisioned by one May Day speaker in 1699. A Swiss visitor in 1701, Francis Louis Michel, sketched and described it in his journal: "There are at present, besides the Church, College and State House, together with the residence of the Bishop [Commissary Blair], some stores, and houses of gentlemen, and also eight ordinaries or inns. . . . The youth is instructed in the higher branches in the College there. But, because most of the people live far away, only the more well-to-do . . . can secure boarding for their sons there, which costs yearly twenty guineas. There are about forty students there now. Before this it was customary for wealthy parents, because of the lack of preceptors or teachers, to send their sons to England to study there. . . ."[10]

Despite Nicholson's efforts, the first philosophy school master did not arrive from England until 1711, and he was dismissed in less than a year. Master LeFevre, who had been recommended by William Blathwayt,[11] proved indifferent to work and moral standards. Apparently "most of his irregularities were owing to an idle hussy he brought over with him."[12] The position was not filled again until Hugh Jones arrived in 1716.

The London Post Boy proclaimed in its issue of March 19–21, 1700: "Some letters from Virginia tell us, that the University which has been lately founded there by the Government of that Province, is so crowded with Students, that they begin to think of enlarging the College." This was an exaggeration, though enrollment was slowly growing. In June or July 1700 the first grammar school commencement was held. English historian John Oldmixon wrote of it a few years later: ". . . there was a Commencement there in the Year 1700, at which there was a great Concourse of People; several Planters came thither in their Coaches, and several in Sloops from *New-York, Pennsylvania* and *Maryland*. It being a new thing in *America* to hear Graduates perform their Academical Exercises, the *Indians* themselves had the Curiosity to come to Williamsburg . . . and the whole Country rejoiced as if they had some Relish of Learning."[13]

The transfer of the government from Jamestown now began. By proclamation of October 27, 1699, the governor and the council had ordered all sessions of the assembly and general court to be held after May 10, 1700, in Williamsburg. The following April, trustees of the college offered use of its building to the government until a capitol could be erected. The council accordingly held its first session there on October 17, 1700, and the House of Burgesses on December 5, meeting in the great hall. In such fashion was the assembly housed until the Capitol was completed, a mile away from the college, in 1703.

Nicholson enthusiastically set about designing streets and buildings for the forest clearing. According to architectural historian Marcus Whiffen,[14] he "proposed a plan which employed Baroque diagonals to produce something with rather the character of a sixteenth-century 'conceit,' " reminiscent of his plan for Annapolis. It remained for a later governor, Alexander Spotswood, to amend it by substituting a gridiron of intersecting streets in more usual form.

Nicholson's plans did not please everyone. Robert Beverley in his *History and Present State of Virginia*, published in 1705, complained that he had caused the government "to be removed from Jamestown, where there were good accommodations for people, to Middle Plantation, where there were none. There he flattered himself with the fond imagination of being the Founder of a new City. He marked out the streets in many places, so that they might represent the Figure of a W, in memory of . . . King William." (Beverley's view may have been colored by the fact that he owned three acres at Jamestown.) Hugh Jones, on the other hand, reported that the streets were "in the Form of a Cypher, made of *W*. and *M*." In either case, such eccentricities of design were fortunately eliminated.

The assembly acquired from the Page family and others a total of 283 acres for Williamsburg's site, consisting of a rectangle along the principal ridge and narrow rights-of-way to merchant ship landings that were built on Queen's Creek and Archer's Hope Creek to allow for the expected shipments to and from the British Isles. The town site bestrode the boundary between York and James City counties, and it attracted trade and settlers from both.

Near the center of Nicholson's "city," a square was reserved as a market, as was the custom in villages of England and Scotland. The wide central avenue was named by the assembly for the king's nephew, the Duke of Gloucester, who was heir presumptive to the throne. It was ninety-nine feet wide and seven-eighths of a mile long, with a five-acre Capitol Square at the

English merchants trading in Virginia were asked to give funds to build the college in Virginia. A popular gathering place for eighteenth-century traders was the Virginia and Maryland Coffee House in London.

Courtesy of the British Museum

end farthest from the college. "There," Beverley wrote, Nicholson "procur'd a stately Fabrick to be erected . . . and graced it with the magnificent Name of the Capitol."[15]

Williamsburg's plan interestingly resembled early Edinburgh, whose Royal Mile extended from Holyrood Palace at one end to St. Giles' Cathedral at the other. The similarity, which might suggest that James Blair had a hand in it, has been pointed out by Professor Thomas E. Thorne.

The commissary's fourteen-year-old nephew, John Blair, was chosen to lay the cornerstone when the Capitol was begun in 1701. The eldest child of Dr. Archibald Blair, he had been born in Scotland before the physician followed his elder brother James to Virginia before 1690. Young John was a favorite of his uncle James and was admitted as one of the first students of the college's grammar school. Bright and industrious, he was to become president of the council; in that capacity, he laid the cornerstone also for the second Capitol in 1754 to replace its burned predecessor.

By Nicholson's plan Williamsburg was divided into half-acre lots along three major thoroughfares, two of which the proud governor named for himself. Builders were required to set their structures back a uniform distance from the street to enhance its grandeur. Unlike Jamestown's ill-assorted mixture of row houses and cottages, Francis Nicholson's design afforded not only beauty but also ventilation, elementary sanitation, and some precaution against the spread of fire. Householders had space for a kitchen house, necessary or privy, stable, a garden, and fruit trees in the long rectangle behind their dwellings. Flanking Duke of Gloucester Street were Nicholson Street on the north and Francis Street on the south.

West of the village, near Archer's Hope landing, lived James and Sarah Blair at Richneck plantation.

Into this new-found Eden named Williamsburg a serpent soon appeared. The Scottish commissary had hardly returned from England before he and the governor began to disagree. The two had differed before, though not to this extent; privately, Blair had used his influence to have Nicholson transferred from Virginia to Maryland in 1693, though he later regretted it and worked to have him brought back. At that time, he had written to an English official—evidently the Earl of Nottingham, secretary of state—as he awaited passage from England after obtaining the college charter:

Thinking the peace of the Colony wherein my lot is cast to be endangered by Col. Nicholson's temper, I wrote to Mr. Blathwayt about it, who communicated the letter to you; and accordingly I find that Colonel Nicholson is stopped. I think this [assignment to Maryland] much better than to send him to Virginia, unless some care had been taken first to modify his mind by bettering his circumstances; but I hasten to add that I know nothing worse against him than I have written, and that I do not believe he has any design of exciting any commotion. . . . I should be sorry if what I formerly wrote should give a worse character of him than is true and just, or should hinder encouragement or reward to one who deserves it as well as any Governor that ever was in America.[16]

Hardly had James Blair returned from his second successful mission to England than he and Nicholson were completely at odds. It began when the commissary handed the governor a letter from the archbishop of Canterbury which warned the hot-tempered Nicholson to control the anger he had exhibited in Maryland. The governor was furious.

"What the Devil do they mean to recommend moderation to me?" he stormed.

"Your friends are all of the opinion that it's the best advice you could have," Blair replied.

"God," roared Nicholson, "I know better how to Govern Virginia and Maryland than all the Bishops in England. If I hadn't 'hampered' the people in Maryland and kept them under, I should never have been able to govern them."

Blair, who recounted the incident, said he replied: "Sir, I don't pretend to understand Maryland but if I know anything of Virginia they are as good natured tractable people as any is in the world and you may do what you will with them by the way of civility but you will never be able to manage them . . . by hampering and keeping them under."[17]

Despite the archbishop's warning, Blair reported that Nicholson assailed him again when Blair warned against losing control of the assembly. The governor roared that he could govern without an assembly. Wrote Blair, "In a great passion he commanded me never to speak to him more in any matters relating to ye Government but to let him alone and to meddle with my own business."

The commissary drew Nicholson's wrath again for a funeral oration he preached when news of King William's death reached Virginia in March 1702. Blair's praise of "the mildness and gentleness of the King's reign" struck the governor as criticism of him, and he lit into Blair when the service ended.[18]

Was this the mild-mannered Nicholson whom Virginians remembered, or had his disposition soured? The commissary thought him now "so furious, imperious and menacing" when angered that he was a "mad man." He called planters "the vile names of rogues, rascals, villains & cowards" and threatened to cut their throats. Blair had been reluctant to judge the governor, "recollecting his charitys, his constancy in publick prayers, his vigour & diligence in stirring about & driving on the business of his Government,"[19] but Nicholson was a changed man.

Blair's judgment of governors might by this time have been properly suspect, but others like Robert Beverley confirmed his opinion. Nicholson had not returned to Virginia, Beverley wrote, "with that Smoothness on his Brow, he had carry'd with him, when he was appointed Lieutenant-Governour. . . . He likewise gave himself Airs of encouraging the College: But he used this Pretext for so many By-Ends, that at last the Promoters of that good Work, grew weary of the Mockery. They perceiv'd his Views was to gain himself a Character, and if he cou'd but raise that, the College might sink. And in Truth he has been so far from advancing it, that now after the Six Years of his Government, the Scholars are fewer than on his Arrival."[20]

After a year or two, Nicholson had stirred up as much opposition as Andros had done, though a few defended him. Mungo Inglis, who felt Blair's £150 salary was unfair to the college and himself, saw the college president rather than the governor as the cause of Virginia's strife: "Mr. Blair was never quiete nor easy until wee had our present good Governor . . . and yett he is now doing all he can to gett him removed, from which reason the Master [Inglis] . . . is resolved that he will have noe more to do with the College whenever his Excellency leaves the country. . . . I am resolved to have noe more to do with such a man and will not longer bee a member of the Body or Corporation of which he is the head. Besides I am none of Mr. Blaire's party and can never expect to live easy in his society. . . . I am resolved to quitt the college if his Excellency, the great patron of it was removed by Mr. Blaire's meanes and I am not one that will give myself the lie."[21]

In a tract that Inglis wrote against Blair in 1703, he declared: "Wee have had the name of a College now these ten years in Virginia, a College which should have consisted of a President & Six Masters to bring up our youth in the learn'd languages & Liberall Arts & Sciences . . . but instead of such a college we have only a Grammar School . . . yet all this while we have a President (which makes our College a College without a President)— who pockets yearly £150 of the College money. . . . And we must never expect to have those other Masters so long as things continue as they are, for no Master will serve without a salary. . . ."[22]

On August 8, 1705, the exasperated Inglis wrote Nicholson that he was quitting: "The intended College . . . will never arrive at any greater Perfection than a Grammar School, while Mr. Blair demands & takes his salary yearly as President . . . & while there remains no more money behind than will barely pay the Usher & Writing Master & myself . . . For these reasons, I am resolved to quit the School . . . & to have no more to do with it, while Mr. Blair is concerned in it."[23]

Beverley blamed the college's troubles more on Nicholson than on Blair. Many fathers, he wrote, "chose to send their Sons to *England*, and others to keep theirs at Home, rather than put them to the hazard of being harassed, and living in the Combustion which that Gentleman [Nicholson] makes among them." But he also felt instruction was "very much impair'd by the chief Masters [Blair's] minding his Country Affairs: For by this means he is obliged to live several Miles from the College, upon his own Plantation; so that he cannot give that Attendance and Application, which was design'd, by appointing so good a Salary, as 100 £ *per Annum* besides Perquisites."[24]

Blair justified his salary on the ground that he had been named by the charter as president for life. At the trustees' first meeting, he asked if they thought a president was needed immediately. He had, he reminded them, "a good plantation and a good living" at Varina, which had been his for life. However, he said the trustees had urged him to move to Middle Plantation to oversee the building and staffing. "Upon this . . . I gave up my Induction and as soon as I could get an house to live in, I removed to the place appointed for the building of the College and have ever since given all due attendance upon the business of it and . . . as before I had the right so now I thought I had likewise Equity and good conscience on my side for taking my Salary."[25]

This legalistic position, which Tenison had endorsed in the hearing at Lambeth Palace, had been more defensible in 1695 than it was after the college was erected. Blair's duties in an institution of so few students could not have been many. If college income had been inadequate to hire a professor for the college, Blair himself might well have undertaken such instruction or returned enough of his salary to engage one. Instead, as one historian has rightly observed, "Year after year, he continued to take the lion's share of the revenue available for salaries and, consequently, no professors could be added to make possible a Philosophy or Divinity School. Even when the funds became so depleted that such teachers as there were could not be paid the full amount due them, he suggested that reductions be made on a proportionate basis, which he, having three other salaries, could afford better than they."[26] The three other salaries, of course, were Blair's £100 per year as commissary, an equivalent amount in tobacco as minister of James City Parish, and his share of the £350 which was yearly divided among the twelve members of the council, based on the number of meetings that each had attended. No wonder he was regarded by his adversaries as grasping.

The split between Blair and Nicholson was deepened by changes in the fortunes of both men when they met again at Jamestown in 1699 after six years of separation. While Nicholson was being bombarded with criticism as governor of Maryland, James Blair as councillor and president of the college had risen rapidly in influence. No longer need he defer to a man no older than he and less well endowed in intellect and knowledge.

But Blair's chief grievance against the governor was his ingratitude. Pleased to have obtained Andros' recall and Nicholson's appointment, the commissary had returned to Virginia in 1698 expecting congratulations. Instead, Nicholson had not expressed "so much as thanks, far less any other consideration for that service," Blair wrote Archbishop Tenison in 1702.[27]

Although the governor later published his account stating that he had paid James Blair the generous total of £510 17s. 6d. to go to London to obtain the Virginia governorship, Blair felt inadequately rewarded. The commissary said he had saved Nicholson "at least many hundreds of pounds" by lobbying for his appointment, though meanwhile losing a year's salary in Virginia, "besides all other losses & inconveniences by leaving my family and business."[28] Nicholson claimed that Blair had expected to be paid £500 plus expenses instead of the £250 plus expenses that the governor paid him.[29]

His Excellency was guilty of even baser sins than ingratitude, Blair declared. He would not specify them in writing, but the bachelor soldier had committed the "vilest & grossest sorts of Lewdness," which revealed him as "a man of the blackest soul & conscience" he had ever known: "It had almost broke my heart with sorrow . . . I could never Induce myself after this to have any good thoughts of his sincerity in religion but look't upon him from that hour as a great monster of Immorality & my opinion received daily confirmation by the new discoverys I made upon enquiry into the particulars of his life & conversation."[30] What monstrous offenses, if any, called forth this charge? In a period of loose sex morality, they were presumably more heinous than a casual liaison. He gave no clues though Nicholson as he grew older did indeed exhibit indecent ardor in his pursuit of the opposite sex. It is possible that Blair exaggerated, for he could stoop to strike an enemy.

In their embittered state, Nicholson was in no haste to have Blair restored to the council. Though he drafted a letter to the bishop of London on February 4, 1699, terming Blair's absence therefrom "a very great blow to ye clergy" and expressing hope that the commissaries of Virginia and Maryland would serve on their respective councils, it is uncertain that he sent the letter.[31] Royal warrant for Blair's readmission was not issued in England until late in 1700, and he was not reseated until June 1701.[32] It was an irritating wait.

The growth of the "college faction" in the council gave Blair new strength and simultaneously weakened Nicholson's dominance. When the commissary took his seat among the "Great men" again after a five-year absence, only three of the eight councillors who had favored Blair's suspension in 1697 remained: Edmund Jenings of York, John Lightfoot of New Kent, and the elder William Byrd of Westover. Replacing the others he found Benjamin Harrison II, his father-in-law; Philip Ludwell II, his brother-in-law; the powerful Robert "King" Carter of Lancaster, Matthew Page of Gloucester, and William Bassett of New Kent. Besides Harrison and Ludwell, two others were potential allies, for Bassett was linked with the Harrisons through the Burwells, and Carter's daughter Elizabeth was to marry Nathaniel Burwell, another connection.

Though once a modest churchmouse on the council, James Blair was now one of the oldest and most experienced members. The erstwhile critic of the planter group which monopolized Virginia's offices and honors was now very much a member of that elite. However, his unprincipled inconsistency was not known to many people, for "The Present State of Virginia," which he had written with Henry Hartwell and Edward Chilton, had been filed in 1701 with records of the Board of Trade in London and would not be published until 1727.[33]

Clearly, Blair's new powers were corroding the idealism that had brought him to Virginia. The erstwhile reformer was beginning to lose his zeal, and this was equally true of Francis Nicholson. Now that their principles were giving way to self-interest, the two former friends engaged in the bitterest vendetta that Virginia had ever witnessed.

Beyond personalities, however, the Blair-Nicholson battle bared an important question of principle: was Virginia to be dominated by England, or was the maturing colony entitled to increased self-determination? Colonists resented capricious controls imposed by the Board of Trade, and this was to grow as the years passed. Robert Beverley in 1705 criticized Nicholson for the exploitative policy he personified:

He talked then [when first in Virginia in 1690–92] of improving of Manufactures, Towns, and Trade. Neither was he pleased to make the Acts of Assembly the Rule of his Judgments, as formerly. But his own All-sufficient Will and Pleasure. Instead of encouraging the Manufactures, he sent over inhuman Memorials against them, which were so opposite to all Reason, that they refuted themselves. In one of these, he remonstrates, *That the Tobacco of the Country often bears so low a Price, that it will not yield Cloaths to the People that make it*; and yet presently after, in the same Memorial, he recommends it to the Parliament, *to pass an Act, forbidding the Plantations to make their own Cloathing*; which, in other words, *is desiring a charitable Law, that the Planters shall go naked.*

Beverley also attacked Nicholson's proposal that all of England's North American colonies be placed under one governor and provided with a standing army. This, ". . . in plain English, [is] imploring Her Majesty, to put the plantations under Martial Law, and in the Consequence, to give the Vice-Roy a fair Opportunity of shaking off his Dependance upon *England*."[34] Nicholson represented the imperialistic view, while Blair and Beverley expressed the colonies' interest. In time, these positions would solidify as Tory versus Patriot.

Nicholson encountered council opposition even before Blair had been reseated. He wrote the Board of Trade on July 1, 1699, that he was correcting land-grant abuses, as it had directed after the Hartwell, Blair, and Chilton report was made.[35] Among the worst land-grabbers were the Harrisons,[36] he noted. He provoked a new outcry when he attempted to redistribute colonial appointments and end the council's monopoly of the best jobs. To this move the councillors petitioned that if they were to lose other fee-paying duties, then their council pay should be raised.[37]

This was a just complaint, and Nicholson promised to comply with it. However, his letter to the Board of Trade was so weakly stated that the board took no action. Robert Quary, a former Virginia councillor who was rewarded for his loyalty to Nicholson by appointment as surveyor general of customs in America, defended his patron before the board and attributed Nicholson's growing difficulties in Virginia to the council's arrogance: "they expected yt. the Governor would be governed by them, yt. all places of honours and profitts should be in their hands and disposing, and yt. now they should be able to crush and ruin ye other [pro-Nicholson] party."[38]

At the height of his conflict with the council, Colonel Nicholson foolishly played into their hands: he fell in love and completely lost his head. The forty-six-year-old bachelor sought the hand of eighteen-year-old Lucy Burwell, the winsome daughter of Colonel Lewis Burwell, who was allied with the Harrisons and Ludwells. Lucy's charms stirred William Byrd II to write, "Her eyes have enough fire to inflame the coldest saint; and her virtue is pure enough to chill the warmest sinner." Throwing discretion to the winds, Nicholson penned ardent love letters and besought Lucy with gifts and poetry:

> Virtuous pretty charming Innocent Dove
> The only Center of my Constant Love.[39]

When Lucy disdained him, Nicholson grew violent. He swore that if he could not have her, none other should. He threatened that if she married he would cut the throats of her bridegroom, the officer issuing the license, and the clergyman.[40] He harassed Lewis Burwell for not compelling his daughter to marry and threatened Blair's widowed brother Archibald, whom he mistook as a rival for fair Lucy's favors.[41] Several others, including John Monro, Jr., whose daughter had married Archibald's son, also felt Nicholson's indignities.[42]

Bishop Compton counseled the commissary to make peace with Nicholson. He understood that the governor had recovered from "his Love-Fit," he wrote, but that the commissary kept up the "Feud." Blair should lay aside "all Prejudice and Passion" and promote reconciliation. Compton had heard that his commissary involved himself too deeply "in the politick Affairs at Council," and he urged him to be "tender in that Point" and let "Meekness and Modesty" guide him.[48] This was asking the lion to make friends with the tiger, however; bitterness between the governor and the commissary had now gone too far to be reconciled.

Hostility had reached such intensity by the spring of 1703 that the college faction in council determined Nicholson must go. After all his work to have the pious colonel returned to Virginia, Blair was now at odds with him in the council, the college, and in the administration of Virginia's churches. Other councillors had also fallen afoul of his vile temper.

Accordingly, six councillors on May 20, 1703, drew up a petition to Queen Anne to recall the governor. Besides Blair it was signed by Robert Carter, John Lightfoot, Matthew Page, Benjamin Harrison II, and Philip Ludwell II. They complained of "the many great grievances & pressures" suffered "by reason of the unusuall, insolent, & arbitrary methods of Government" and of their revulsion at Nicholson's "wicked & scandalous examples of life."[44]

Reluctant to offend the queen's ears, the petitioners promised Her Majesty to send detailed complaints to "some noted friends of this country," who could testify when called upon.[45] The "particular instances of the Mal-administration" were so many that the "very enumeration of the several sorts of them" would presume upon Her Majesty's time.

If Blair were embarrassed by his change of heart toward Nicholson, he did not show it. The text of the petition and memorials against the governor were clearly his. The unshakeable commissary was the leader of the campaign to unseat Nicholson, just as he had been in the case of Sir Edmund Andros.

CHAPTER VIII

God's Angry Apostle
1694-1703

❧ Had you been a planter living along the Great Road from Middle Plantation to Jamestown at the end of the seventeenth century, you would have seen a darkly clad figure riding his horse to church each Sunday morning toward Jamestown. Such was James Blair's Sabbath routine from the time he became minister of James City parish in 1694 until he accepted a call to Bruton Parish in Williamsburg in 1710.

This was Blair the country clergyman, a man of stout faith and dedication. It was the unworldly and stoical Blair of Cranston and Henrico parishes, braving the heat of summer and the cold of winter to keep his "appointments" at chapels of ease and to bring the gospel and the sacraments to country dwellers, cut off from every other source of enlightenment except the written word. It was in sharp contrast to the Blair who fought for position and power on the Council. Yet it was another side of the same complex man.

Mounting his horse at Richneck early on Sunday, Blair skirted Ludwell's mill, which spanned Raccoon Chase, and followed the cart path that led past Great Neck, Jockey's Neck, Drinking Swamp (later dammed to become Powell's Lake), and Fowler's Neck to a cluster of dwellings at Archer's Hope, near the James River. Then, turning westward, he crossed the parish glebe farm, Neck of Land, and wound his way through a settlement of small farm-houses that clustered close to the isthmus approaching Jamestown's peninsula. In his pocket he carried the homily he had written to deliver at the Sunday service.

When Blair became minister of James City, the congregation at Jamestown numbered the governor and several of the colony's "Great men" among its parishioners. There on Sunday gathered families from as far away as Mulberry Island, eight miles downriver in Warwick County. On foot, by horse, or on sail- or row-galleys the faithful came, expectantly awaiting the solace of the Psalms and the Bible readings from the church clerk. The high point of the two-hour service approached when the minister mounted the pulpit and launched into his examination of the day's biblical text.

The fact that James Blair was a strong preacher is indicated by the loyalty of his parishes and the demands for his services. It is further documented by the texts of 117 of his sermons, which were printed in 1722 in England and sold for decades throughout the English-speaking world.[2] These reflect his simplicity of manner and his down-to-earth approach to living. Seldom was he guilty of the literary mannerisms that marred so much of the writing in his day. He avoided ecclesiastical subtleties and displays of classical learning, as profound as his knowledge was. He knew his congregation wanted the simple gospel.

The commissary's sermons also show him to have been a tolerant clergyman, who was broad in his views. Some of this may be attributed to his association with Laurence Charteris, Gilbert Burnet, and Henry Compton, who preached a conciliatory Protestantism, willing to tolerate nearly every dogma except those that were peculiar to Roman Catholicism and Unitarianism. But some of Blair's permissiveness was absorbed from the bland

and easy-going Virginians, who had escaped the worst excesses of religious dogmatism. In an age of superstition, early Virginia afforded only one example of witch-hunting.[3]

Into the Jamestown church on Sundays came such residents as the Jaquelins, Amblers, Travises, Sherwoods, and Beverleys. The families of Henry Hartwell and Edward Chilton, who with Blair wrote "The Present State of Virginia," were also among its parishioners. From nearby Greenspring came the Ludwells, and from settlements at Archer's Hope and on the mainland adjoining the Jamestown isthmus came other worshippers.

The church, measuring 28 feet wide and 56 feet long,[4] seated about 150 people on simple benches. Near the small chancel at the east end of the church, the governor sat in a chair of state. The clerk's lectern and Blair's pulpit were nearby. In a narrow gallery, which was entered from a stairway in the brick church tower, indentured servants and an occasional Negro servant sat. No church organ graced the structure. Instead, psalms were sung unaccompanied, led by the clerk.

Standing today on the threshold of the brick church that has been reconstructed upon the foundations of the 1617 and 1639 structures,[5] one can almost visualize Blair and Nicholson facing the congregation from their seats in the chancel. Clothed in white surplice and bathed in the sunlight that streamed through the tall, diamond-paned windows of greenish glass, the commissary must have seemed the very picture of benevolence. With a hearty voice, he joined with his congregation as it intoned a psalm, line by line, following the clerk:

The Lord is only my support, and he that me doth feed:
  how can I then lacke any thing, whereof I stand in need?

He doth me fold in coats most safe, the tender grasse fast by:
  and after drives me to the streames which run most pleasantly.

And when I feele my selfe neere lost, then doth he me home take:
  conducting me in his right paths, even for his owne names sake.

And though I were even at death's doore, yet would I feare none ill:
  for with thy rod and Shepheards crooke, I am comforted still.

Thou hast my table richly deckt, in despight of my foe:
  thou hast my head with balm refresh'd, my cup doth overflow.

And finally while breath doth last, thy grace shall me defend:
   and in the house of God will I my life for ever spend.[6]

During Blair's ministry, Jamestown's church still showed signs of the fire set by Bacon's rebels in 1676, which had destroyed all but the brickwork. Though rebuilt along with most of the town in the next ten years, it remained a barren structure. Red bricks paved its aisle, and paving tiles covered the chancel floor surrounding the holy table, where Communion was celebrated several times yearly.

The church was the fourth to have been built at Jamestown and the second to stand on the same site. The first two had been rude structures, probably of wattle-and-daub, erected at the center of the acre-and-a-half James Fort, where the settlers had huddled for several years after their arrival from England. The third was a clapboard rectangle built between 1617 and 1619 close to the vacated fort, within the four acres of the expanded palisaded town. It stood on high ground, near the area that had served as a burial ground for earlier settlers.[7] Around this church, whose dimensions were "50 by 20 foote,"[8] a later generation built between 1639 and 1647 a brick church and tower, evidently retaining the clapboard structure inside,[9] at least during construction.

Wrote Governor Sir John Harvey in 1639: "Such hath bene our Indeavour herein, that out of our owne purses wee have largely contributed to the building of a brick church, and both Masters of Shipps and others of the ablest Planters have liberally by our persuation underwritt to this worke."[10]

When Blair became Jamestown's minister, the little church stood at the apex of the religious and official life of the colony. Within its walls or nearby were buried many pioneers of Virginia's first eighty-seven years. Under one black ironstone tablet, inlaid with brasses, lay the remains of a knight, probably Governor Sir George Yeardley, who died at Jamestown on November 12, 1627. Beneath the chancel nearby was the crude tombstone of the Reverend John Clough, an erstwhile rector, who had survived sentence of death by the rebel Bacon to die peacefully in 1684.

Within the burial ground, which had been consecrated about

1617 as God's Acre, lay other worthies. Most of them were in unmarked graves, but handsome tombstones covered the remains of Ludwells, Beverleys, Edwardses, Amblers, and a few others. Of the eroded and broken gravestones that survive, all have now been rendered illegible. One of these covers the grave of William Sherwood, attorney general of the colony, whose widow rented the great hall of her house in 1699 for sessions of the council and general court. Sherwood's epitaph originally read:

> Here Lyeth WILLIAM SHERWOOD
> That was Born in the parish
> of White Chappell near
> London. A Great sinner
> Waiting for a joyfull
> Resurrection[11]

Another fragment nearby recorded the burial of Frances Culpeper Ludwell, the erstwhile Lady Berkeley,[12] who died in Virginia before her husband, the elder Philip, returned to his native Somerset in England about 1700 to spend his last years.[13]

Occasionally Blair invited visiting ministers to his pulpit. On April 25, 1703, the Reverend George Keith, a graduate of Marischal College and an evangelist for the Society for the Propagation of the Gospel in Foreign Parts recorded in his journal: "I preached at Jamestown on John I, 3, ['All things were made by Him and without Him was not anything made that was made.'] at the request of Reverend Mr. Blair, minister there, and commissary, who very kindly and hospitably entertained us at his house."[14]

Despite such hospitality, Blair lost the support of most Virginia clergy during his years of conflict with Nicholson. As more than one Virginian had written to Bishop Compton, the commissary had become too deeply involved in secular affairs to do justice to churchly duties. After his first clergy conference in July of 1690, he made no mention of further ministerial meetings, for he avoided them.

Nicholson shared with the commissary responsibility for the church's functioning, and the personable governor gradually allied most of the clergy with him in his bitter dispute with the commissary.

Nicholson convened the clergy at Jamestown early in his administration. In a letter to the sheriff of each county, in March 1700, he directed that ministers ". . . do not fail of meeting me here & that they bring with them their priest's & Deacon's Orders, as likewise the Rt Reverend Father in God the Lord Bishop of London, his License for their preaching or what other License they have, & withal a copy out of the Vestry Books of the agreement they have made with the parish or parishes where they officiate."

Evidencing his determination to fill vacant parishes, he added: "If there be any parish or parishes within your County who have no minister, I do hereby in his majesty's name command that the vestry of the said parish or parishes do by the said 10th of April return me an account how long they have been without a minister, & ye reasons thereof, as also if they have any person that reads the common prayers on Sundays at their Church."[15]

At the meeting, held in the church at Jamestown on April 10, 1700, Blair and twenty-seven of the colony's three dozen clergy were present. Nicholson first asked them to present evidence of their ordination. Then he gave them a fatherly lecture before turning the meeting over to the commissary. He urged the ministers to make their lives "answerable to the holy religion you profess, and the doctrine you teach the people," since colonists were influenced "more by example than by precept." He hoped ". . . that those of you who have not heretofore been as exemplary in your lives, as orthodox in your preaching; will for the future be more careful as to your morals & diligent in your several Parochial duties; or else you must expect that I will have you prosecuted with the utmost severity & rigor of the Law. . . ."[16]

Before their deliberations ended next day, the clergy wrote a fulsome address of thanks to the governor. Blair did not sign it, although his allies, Stephen Fouace of York County and John Monro, Jr., of King William County, did. The ministers praised "Your Excellency's Zeal for the Church of Engld," and promised obedience to his will: "Our obligations to comply . . . are so great & so many, & we hope so well understood by all of us, that

we do all unanimously & sincerely declare our resolutions . . .
not only to avoid the lash of the law, & (if possible) that of
censorious tongues, but chiefly what is infinitely more terrible
to us, the displeasure of our heavenly Master. . . ."[17]

The commissary's loss of his clergy's loyalty developed after
the Assembly of 1699 at Jamestown failed to enact an ambitious
program that Blair had put forward to improve the lot of Virginia's clergy. These were to have been part of a revision of the
colony's laws, which was put off until 1705. Even then, however,
the reforms were not enacted. Perhaps they stirred up the latent
anticlericalism of Virginia, or perhaps they were ahead of their
time. In any case, the failure of Blair's efforts played into
Nicholson's hands.

Blair's proposals are preserved in "A PROPOSITION for supplying the country of Virginia with a sufficient number of much
better Clergymen than have usually come into it," a copy of
which he sent the archbishop of Canterbury.[18] He first lists
hardships common to Virginia: the thin population of parishes,
the failure of vestries to fill pulpits, the slimness of clerical in-
comes, the uncertain tenure of ministers, the lack of towns, the
inferiority of tobacco with which clergy were paid, the scarcity
of books, and the need for an ecclesiastical court to discipline
clerics.

Blair then suggested means of correction. He would merge
small parishes to achieve a minimum of four hundred titheables.
To prevent delay in filling cures, he would require a parish to
continually pay a ministerial salary, using the money for other
parish purposes when the cure or benefice was vacant. Instead
of permitting a year's lapse in a parish ministry before em-
powering the king to fill it, he urged that a three-and-a-half-year
lapse be permitted: two and a half years for the vestry to act and
another for the bishop of London or his commissary.

"I do not mean that the parish should be so long without a
minister," Blair explained, "but that 18 months time be allowed
for procuring of one and then a years time of Trial of him before
they be obliged to present," meaning to signify to the ecclesiastical authority that the vestry was satisfied with its minister
and willing to guarantee him life tenure.

To increase clergy salaries, Blair proposed that instead of the 16,000 pounds of tobacco payment, fixed by the 1696 assembly, the allowance be made 40 pounds for each parish resident. "Now this 40 per poll when the parishes are so divided . . . in the smallest Parishes will come to 16,000," he explained, "but as much as the number of Titheables shall happen to be above 400 will be proportionately more, so that in some parishes it will be 20,000, in some perhaps 24,000 at present, and its possible in time in some parishes it may amount to 32,000 which is a very considerable encouragement for an able Divine. . . ."

Of all the clergy's hardships, Blair thought uncertain tenure was the worst. "I humbly propose," he wrote, "that within the space of two years & a half after the vacancy, the vestry be obliged to present [recommend to the commissary] a minister in order to induction [assurance to the minister of life tenure in the parish]." By failing to act, the vestry would forfeit its right of presentation and induction to the governor.

The provision of a glebe farm and house for each parish was required by law, Blair noted. The commissary now proposed that the farm be large enough to require "5 or 6 hands to work upon." He recommended that the type of glebe house also be specified, "such as that it be a framed house, that it have brick chimneys and Glass windows with casements, that the walls within be plaistered and the roof shingled, that it have at least one clear storey 10 foot pitch with two rooms and a large closet, besides cellars and Garrets; that care likewise be taken to have a kitchen and whatever other outhouses shall be judged necessary."

From unexpended ministerial salaries, Blair recommended to the assembly and the archbishop that each glebe "be stocked with 4 or 5 negroes under an overseer & with a stock of cattle of 7 or 8 milch cows and calves for the use of the minister, and for keeping these houses in due repair & keeping the negroes in their full number between the ages of 15 & 45 and the Cattle as to number & age as shall be directed, let each vestry have power to oblige the incumbent to do it. . . ."

If any other unexpended salary funds remained, Blair proposed that a parish "be provided with a Library of well chosen books for the use of the minister to the value of 50 pounds sterling;" that the incoming cleric receive £30 for his transport from England; that clergymen's widows and orphans be aided; and that "poor scholars of that parish" be maintained at grammar school or college.

These proposals were similar to reforms that John Knox had wrought in Scotland a century earlier, but they were untimely in the primitive Virginia of 1699. Few settlers had achieved the comforts that Blair recommended for clergymen. To hardworking Virginia farmers who were clearing pine lands and contending with Indian threats, the proposal for lifetime tenure plus moving costs, a house, library, and four or five slaves was absurd.

The commissary made other proposals that were equally objectionable to the clergy. He called for an examination of each incoming cleric, to be administered by himself and "the Learnedest ministers of the country." The ministers in each convocation should gather quarterly and "exercise their Talents by set discourses of every man in his turn, against popery, Quakerism, or any other prevailing heresey, as also in the explication of Scripture." At these meetings, he envisioned the clergy as "resolving of Cases of Conscience, explaining the several parts of the ministerial function . . . and exhorting and admonishing one another that so by fraternal admonitions they may prevent the complaints of the Parishes and vestries. . . ." Obviously, Blair was courting trouble from his obstreperous ministers.

As he had done at his first clergy meeting in 1690, he repeated his proposal for an annual gathering of ministers with their commissary, to be held at "the seat of the Government."

Blair's worst mistake was to revive the possibility of ecclesiastical courts, which he had introduced in 1690. He recommended that: "Whatsoever Minister shall be found guilty of fornication, adultery, Blasphemy, ridiculing of the Holy Scriptures or maintaining by preaching, writing or in any open public discourse any Doctrine contrary to the 39 Articles shall upon Trial and conviction thereof loose his living and be suspended from all exercise of the ministerial function in this country for three years. And whosoever shall be found guilty of cursing, swearing, Drunkeness, or fighting (except in his own defence), shall for the first offence be suspended from his office for one whole year. . . ."

Worse was to come. The zealous commissary went on to recommend a test to determine whether a minister were drunk. First, he decreed, "let the signs of Drunkenness be proved such as sitting an hour or longer in the Company where they were a drinking strong drink and in the meantime drinking of healths or otherwise taking his cups as they came round like the rest of the company; striking, challenging, threatening to fight, or laying aside any of his Garments for that purpose; staggering, reeling, vomiting, incoherent, impertinent, obscene or rude talking. Let the proof of these signs proceed so far till the Judges conclude that the minister's behaviour at such a time was scandalous, indecent and unbecoming the Gravity of a minister."

If these tests should be inconclusive, the commissary suggested, two or three other persons in company of the tipsy minister "and not drunk themselves" could swear to the offense. He admitted such judgment was not simple, "for vomiting may happen to a sober person from an accidental sickness or weakness of stomach, & reeling and staggering from a sudden disease occasioning a giddiness in the head. . . ."

On and on went his catalogue of offenses and punishments. For neglecting his "preaching, catechising, visiting the sick & administering the sacraments," an errant divine should first be admonished at the quarterly meeting of his convocation. A second offense would be reproved at the annual clergy conference, while a third would warrant a year's suspension from his cure. Should the miscreant stray again, he would "loose his living" and forfeit the glory of serving God in Virginia.

The commissary next attacked the evil of pluralism—the simultaneous enjoyment by one minister of several benefices. Though he himself was being paid more than £330 yearly plus perquisites from three sources, he blithely proposed to "prevent the great abuse of pluralities." To ferret these out, he would appoint two clergymen in each area to serve with him. These watchdogs would visit each parish every three years "to see

Henry Compton, bishop of London, sent Blair as missionary to Virginia in 1685 and in 1689 named him commissary. Son of a noble family of Warwickshire, Compton recruited Scottish and Huguenot clergy for the colonies. He was chancellor of the college in Virginia from 1693 to 1700 and from 1707 to 1713.

Gilbert Burnet, preacher of the Rolls Chapel, provided a clerkship for James Blair in London in 1682. Burnet, who had himself emigrated from Scotland nine years earlier, rose to be bishop of Salisbury. He greatly assisted Blair in his quest for a charter for a college.

A Swiss visitor to Virginia, Francis Louis Michel, drew a sketch in 1702, labeling it "The College Standing in Williamsburg in Which the Governor [Nicholson] Has His Residence." It is the only likeness of the original building, burned in 1705 and rebuilt by 1716.

Courtesy of Colonial Williamsburg

The Virginia Assembly, after 1660, met spasmodically in a state house attached to the group of row houses that Thomas Ludwell, colonial secretary of state, had built and left to his brother, Philip Ludwell I. The cross-shaped third state house is shown at the right.

Painted by Sidney King, courtesy of the
Association for the Preservation of Virginia Antiquities

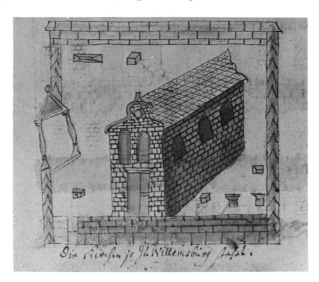

The Swiss diarist Francis Louis Michel sketched in 1702 the little church that had been completed in 1683 at Middle Plantation. James Blair assumed the ministry of this Bruton Parish Church in 1710, joining with the vestry and Governor Spotswood in undertaking construction of a larger church, completed in 1715.

Courtesy of Colonial Williamsburg

Francis Nicholson befriended Blair as lieutenant governor of Virginia from 1690 to 1692. However, the two became bitter enemies after Blair had maneuvered Nicholson's return to Virginia as governor from 1698 to 1705.

John Locke, philosopher and political scientist, befriended Blair and Virginia as a member of England's Board of Trade beginning in 1696. His questions concerning the colony led Blair, Hartwell, and Chilton to write "The Present State of Virginia" in 1697.

Courtesy of the Virginia Museum of Fine Arts

Daniel Parke II of York County supported Andros in his conflict with Blair and the college faction of the council. Parke allegedly attempted to pull Sarah Blair from her pew in Bruton Church in 1696.

Courtesy of the Virginia State Library

William Byrd II of Westover was a colleague of Blair's on the Council of Virginia and in the affairs of the college. As a twenty-three-year-old lawyer, he unsuccessfully defended Sir Edmund Andros against Blair before some of the Privy Council in London in 1697. The two lived to become friends, sharing an enthusiasm for literature and learning.

Sarah Harrison Blair was thirty-five when her portrait was painted in 1705 in England by J. Hargreaves. It shows her fashionably attired in a red dress with lace collar, with a matching armlet and brooch of black beads. She died in 1713 at the age of forty-three.

Courtesy of the College of William and Mary

The second church of Bruton Parish, built during 1711–15, occupied much of Blair's attention for the last thirty-three years of his life. The bell tower was added after Blair's death.

Courtesy of Colonial Williamsburg

Designed by Alexander Spotswood, the 1715 Bruton Parish Church contained a pew for the governor and council and galleries for students of the College of William and Mary. It was later enlarged by extension of the chancel and the addition of two more galleries. The pipe organ was installed in 1752.

Courtesy of Colonial Williamsburg

*First completed in 1697 and burned in 1705, the College of William
and Mary was rebuilt by 1716. President Blair and the masters
had living chambers there, and students roomed on the third floor.*

*Archibald Blair, brother of the commissary, built this house on
Williamsburg's Courthouse Green shortly after 1716. He lived and
practiced medicine there until his death in 1733.*

The third Virginia Governor to be unseated by Blair and his
supporters was Alexander Spotswood, who served as lieutenant
governor of the colony from 1710 to 1722. This portrait hangs in
the family dining room of the Governor's Palace in Williamsburg,
whose building he supervised.

Blair moved into the new president's house in 1733, where he lived as a widower the last ten years of his life and died on April 18, 1743, after a lingering illness of gangrene.

Courtesy of the College of William and Mary

James Blair and the eleven other members of the council met after 1704 in a paneled chamber on the second floor of the Capitol in Williamsburg. The room's furnishings were specified by the assembly. At the left is a portrait of the monarch and at the right is the royal coat of arms.

Courtesy of Colonial Williamsburg

Blair was writing the sermons that were to be printed in 1722 as Our Saviour's Divine Sermon on the Mount *when this portrait was painted of the sixty-year-old cleric. The painting was owned by Elizabeth Blair, the commissary's niece, before it came to the College of William and Mary. Painter and date are unknown.*

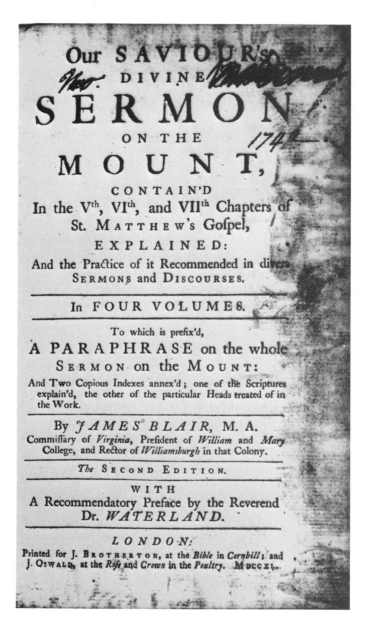

The title page of the second edition of the sermons, published in 1740, listed several features added since the 1722 edition. Distributed by the Society for Promoting Christian Knowledge, Blair's work defended the Church of England against skeptics and deists. It opposed the beliefs of Quakers and other "Enthusiastic" sects.

Courtesy of the College of William and Mary

Blair was nearly eighty when this likeness was painted, probably by the visiting Englishman Charles Bridges. The portrait depicts a New Testament in Greek at Blair's elbow, open to the passage in St. Matthew which provided the texts for Our Saviour's Divine Sermon on the Mount. *The college and a phoenix rising from the ashes are also visible.*

The tombs of Sarah and James Blair in the Jamestown Churchyard were separated a century ago by a sycamore tree that grew between them. This photograph, taken by Huestis Cook of Richmond after the Civil War, shows the inscription tablet on Sarah Blair's tomb, which was subsequently broken.

Courtesy of the Association for the Preservation of Virginia Antiquities to the Execution of all the laws of this country, concerning churches, churchyards, Church registers, church books, utensils and ornaments, Glebes, mansion houses, parish Libraries, negroes and stocks of cattle, church wardens, ministers' assistants, vestries and parish clerks."

Appended to this outline, Blair made his most constructive proposal. This was "A PROPOSITION for encouraging the Christian Education of Indians, Negroes and Mulatto Children." Coming at a time when Negro slaves were treated as soulless savages, it shows Blair to have been a humane man, whatever his other faults. Like Colonel John Page before him, Blair in his proposal recognized the unchristian treatment of African and West Indian slaves in the colonies. Wrote Blair:

It being a duty of Christianity, very much neglected by masters and mistresses of this country to endeavour the good instruction and Education of their Heathen Slaves, in the Christian faith, the said duty being likewise earnestly recommended by his Majesty's Instructions for the facilitating thereof amongst the young slaves that are born among us (the old ones that are imported into the country by reason of their not understanding the Language being much more indocile). It is therefore humbly proposed that every Indian, negro or mulatto child that shall be baptized and afterwards brought to church and publicly catechised by the minister and in church before the 14th year of his or her age, shall give a distinct account of the [Apostle's] Creed, Lord's Prayer and Ten Commandments and whose master or mistress shall receive a Certificate from the minister that he or she hath so done, such Indian, negro or mullatto child shall be exempted from paying all levies till the age of 18 years, but whatsoever Indian, negro or mulatto child shall not be baptized nor give such public account of his or her faith, nor whose master or mistress receives no such certificate as aforesaid shall pay levies at the age of 14 years for it is humbly supposed the advantage of 4 years' difference in levies will have great effects to this purpose.[19]

It is easy to see why Blair's 1699 clergy reforms were not accepted: Virginia's hard-working settlers thought their clergymen were already paid enough. The council had so informed the Board of Trade in 1697, after the burgesses had increased their salaries to 16,000 pounds of tobacco.[20] This amount yielded an income of between £80 and £100 and exceeded "most of their [the Burgesses'] own circumstances and of ye Country in Generall," the council wrote. Such was also the view of Robert Beverley, the colony's first native historian. "The Labour of a dozen Negroes, does but answer this Salary," he wrote, "and seldom yields a greater Crop of sweet-sented Tobacco, than is allowed to each of their Ministers."[21]

A few of Blair's proposals seem to have been acceptable to the burgesses, but the program was pigeonholed—probably intentionally—when the 1699 assembly abandoned its contemplated revisal of Virginia's laws.[22] By the time the statutes were rewritten in 1705, Blair was locked in deadly combat with Nicholson. By that time other issues had become more compelling, and Blair's idealistic reforms were permanently buried. The revised 1705 laws barely mentioned the clergy.

In the Blair-Nicholson feud, nearly all of Virginia's ministers took the governor's side. Some stiff-necked Oxford and Cambridge graduates disdained Blair as a "Scots hireling." Others resented his thirst for power. In a succession of testimonials from 1699 to 1705, they praised Nicholson as governor and as patron of the church—endorsements that the governor promoted by convening the clergy now and again and haranguing them. Councilor Philip Ludwell II correctly observed that Nicholson curried favor with churchmen.[23]

In England, Archbishop Tenison and the Anglican hierarchy were disturbed by letters from Virginia assailing both Blair and Nicholson. The Reverend Nicholas Moreau wrote from St. Peter's parish in New Kent that Blair had "cast an odium upon himself by his great worldly concerns." Virginians "resent an high affront made to their nation, because his Lordship [the Bishop of London] has sent here Mr. Blair a Scotchman." Leading planters had asked Moreau, "Don't you think, there may be in England amongst the English, a clergyman fit to be Commissary and Counsellor and President of our College?" Moreau thought "An eminent Bishop . . . being sent over here with him, [Nicholson] will make Hell tremble and settle the church of England in these parts forever. . . ."[24]

Nicholson also wrote the archbishop of Canterbury and the bishop of London to complain of Blair. He warned the bishop that the Blair faction had sent Stephen Fouace as its agent to England, a "proud, haughty, Insolent, covetuous, Ungratefull Frenchman." (Fouace was actually a Walloon.) Nicholson said he had told Blair to his face that he was "one of the worst Clergymen that ever I was acquainted with, and that if I was guilty of those things which he is, I should think my self hardly Capable of Salvation."

He reported that the commissary had forced his own wife to keep store in his house, without shoes or stockings.

He added that Sarah Blair's brother "hath often Complained to me what a Scandal it was and [that it is] now supposed that he is principal trader but Clokes it under the name of [his] brother who Came over hether about 2 Years ago with his plaster box." He accused Blair of "Defyling [his] Wife's Sister both before and after marriage."[25] This was the most serious charge Nicholson was to make against Blair, and it is significant that he did not repeat it in his compendium of complaints published in 1727 in a final effort to disgrace Blair.

Nicholson paid the expenses of seven clergymen from several colonies to meet in New York in 1702 to consider measures for strengthening the Anglican church. The group concluded its week-long meeting by praising Nicholson and requesting that a suffragan be sent to the colonies by the bishop of London.[26]

Twenty Virginia clergymen in 1703 protested to the bishop of London that Blair "hath invested himselfe with many condemning powers without any protecting or relieving one." He was accused of removing two ministers from their parishes in violation of canons of the church and of instilling fear in others. "We think it hard that we all are Subject to be sent a begging at the arbitrary Decision of one Man and Lying at his mercy," they wrote.[27]

Six clergymen, acting as spokesmen for the "English" clerics in Virginia, depicted Blair as a tyrant and recited "the Bigg words he trys to scare us with; as Schism, Canonical, obedience, the *Omnia* and *Omnimoda potestas Ecclesiastica* in ye Instrument for his commissary's place." They complained to Compton of the commissary's "Constant practise of stealing into our addresses to his Excellency Nicholson some odd kind of two-fac'd

Expressions, and shy Reflections; and the Tricks he uses, by wheeling us abt. with his slow, circling harangues, & putting us upon significant debates about words and syllables to cast a mist before our eyes, and blind us from observing them. By w'ch guile we have been caught by him more than once."[28]

The chief charge against Blair was that he no longer supported the clergy's desire for permanent tenure. Once the leading advocate of lifetime induction to improve the lot of the ministers, Blair by 1703 had reversed himself and had accepted the Virginia practice of "hiring" them from year to year. In their petition in 1703, twenty ministers endorsed Nicholson and assailed the commissary: "But we are not ignorant that Mr. Commissary hath given too much encouragement to Vestrys by siding with them against the opinion of the govern's in asserting the uncontroulableness of their power in admitting receiving & entertaining of Ministers and in giveing his opinion in various ways at distant places, that he might curry favour with the great men of the Country to Support his owne Interest which hath been ye principal occasion why no Induction is now to be obtained."[29]

To Blair's discredit, the record supports the clergy's charge of his duplicity. Time after time he wrote to London that the insecurity of Virginia livings could only be corrected by induction. In "The Present State of Virginia" he had blamed Andros for failing to correct it, and in his 1697 memorial against that unfortunate governor he had recommended security of tenure to protect men of the cloth against "great poverty and contempt." Now he had changed.

Was Blair's reversal in 1703 an effort to harass Nicholson and avenge himself on his clergy? Had he become so allied with the landholding class that produced the vestrymen that he now saw only the planters' viewpoint? No doubt selfish considerations played a part, but Blair's years in Virginia may have demonstrated to him the disciplinary value of vestry control over ministerial tenure. Lacking powers to direct the clerical establishment and frustrated by the division of authority between himself and the governor, Blair may have concluded that life tenure was too great a risk for the church to take. Whatever the explanation, Blair's record on induction raises a question of his truthfulness and sincerity.

The induction issue came to a head in 1703, hastening the clash between Nicholson and his clergy versus Blair and his faction in the council. In that year the Queen's attorney general, Sir Edward Northey, wrote Nicholson that the vestry's right to present a minister for induction into a vacant ministry devolved upon the governor after a six months' vacancy within a parish.[30] Offensive as this ruling was to vestries, it greatly pleased Nicholson. He ordered copies sent to churchwardens and instructed them to convene their vestries to "offer to his Excellency what they think proper thereupon."[31]

Thus the vestries were arrayed against Nicholson. It was not long before Blair was advising vestrymen to uphold their rights and defy the governor. Accordingly, some did not respond to Nicholson's instructions, while others replied in terms intended to discourage him. His Excellency was forced to renew his request by proclamation a year later.[32]

Relations between Blair and Nicholson were at a breaking point. Battling each other in meetings of the clergy, the college trustees, and the council, they divided Virginia into two camps: the Blair faction and the governor's. In the spring of 1703, the Scotsman thought the time had come to act, for Nicholson had become more obstructive than Andros had ever been.

In May or June, James Blair packed his sea chest and sailed from Virginia on his third mission to England. Two of his loyal friends, Philip Ludwell I and the Reverend Stephen Fouace, were waiting for him there. This time Sarah Blair went with him, and both their portraits were painted there by London artist J. Hargreaves. The details of Blair's voyage are obscure, but the purpose of his mission was clear: he was going to seek the recall of his once dear friend, Francis Nicholson.

CHAPTER IX

The Fight
with
Francis Nicholson
1703-1705

❦ Nicholson's six years as governor, from 1698 until he was replaced by Edward Nott in 1705, were the most hectic of the commissary's life. Each convoy that sailed from Chesapeake Bay carried news of strife in Virginia. The governor, the council, and the clergy showered the Board of Trade and the bishops with their complaints and advice. The commissary was in the thick of it, first in Virginia and after July 1703 in England.

It was a long and bitter battle, but Blair won.

Francis Nicholson came to Virginia with a fine record. He efficiently carried out policy for the Board of Trade, and he was admired by churchmen for his support of religion and education. He was normally an attractive man of good humor and polished manners, but he had a violent temper, which grew worse with age. In this respect he resembled Sir William Berkeley, who was eminently successful as Virginia's governor from 1642 to 1652, but who became an ill-tempered autocrat when returned to office from 1660 to 1677. An Indian who saw Nicholson in a fit of rage thought he had been "born drunk."

Nicholson was the son of obscure parents on the Duke of Bolton's estate in Yorkshire, born in 1655 about the same time as Blair. According to one tradition he was a son of the duke, but more probably he was son or grandson of one Francis Nicholson, who had befriended an earlier owner of the estate. Young Francis had served as a page to the Duchess of Bolton and entered the army at twenty-four, spending time in Tangier as aide to the governor. In 1686 he came to North America as captain of an infantry company under Sir Edmund Andros, who then served as governor of the Dominion of New England. Ambitious and efficient, he was named lieutenant governor two years later.[1]

Like Andros and most other career soldiers of his era, Nicholson was a Tory in his loyalties. When he received word that the absolutist Stuarts had been succeeded by William and Mary in the Glorious Revolution of 1688, Nicholson indignantly declined to proclaim the accession of the new monarchs and returned to England.[2] Here is partial explanation of his differences with Blair, for the commissary sympathized with Whig policies and approved the moderate relaxation of autocracy under "the Whig monarchs," William and Mary.

Nicholson's early popularity in Virginia owed something to his contrast with Andros. Their careers had brought them into contact with each other in New England, New York, and Virginia, but the two men had never been friends. Where Sir Edmund was stiffly military, Nicholson had at first been warm and affable. Such was true, at least, until he had returned to Jamestown from Maryland in 1698. Then, as Robert Beverley had noted, "he went not . . . with that Smoothness on his Brow, he had carry'd with him, when he was appointed Lieutenant-

Governour. . . ."[3] From that time onward Virginians observed his progressively worse temper, which in 1703 impelled Blair and five other councillors to seek his removal.

For some reason, Blair delayed six months after arriving in England before formally bringing his fellow councillors' charges in March 1704 before the Lords Commissioners of Trade and Plantations. John Locke by this time had resigned as a commissioner and had retired to his home at Oates Manor in Essex, where he died the following October. Blair besought advice in the meantime from other friends in high office, including Archbishop Tenison and Bishop Compton.

On March 30, 1704, the petition from the six Virginia councillors to Queen Anne, asking Nicholson's removal, was submitted to the Board of Trade. Affidavits supporting the request were signed by Blair, Philip Ludwell I, and Fouace. Others came from the Reverend James Wallace of Elizabeth City County, one of Blair's Scottish supporters; Robert Beverley, historian and secretary of the colony; George Luke, a collector of customs in Virginia; and Captain James Moody,[4] of H.M.S. *Southampton*, who had run afoul of the governor while in Virginia waters. Beverley, Luke, and Wallace were called before the board in person to present their complaints.

Nicholson charged later that the filing of accusations was delayed until after the sailing of the winter convoy of merchant ships for Virginia, in order that he could be kept ignorant of charges against him.[5] Whether this was Blair's strategy or not, it greatly disadvantaged Nicholson.

The long controversy showed Nicholson to be over confident and childishly naïve. He was no match for Blair. The proceedings followed the same form as the hearings against Andros had followed, seven years earlier. Again the governor was not permitted to come home to England to defend himself. As a result, by the time Nicholson had received copies of charges and had replied to them, Blair's arrows had done him much damage.

Instead of being represented by William Byrd II, as Andros had been, Nicholson was defended by John Thrale, agent for the colony in England. Thrale's arguments show him to have been a more experienced advocate than Byrd had been, but he was largely ignorant of the matter and lacked witnesses to sustain him. He portrayed Nicholson as a faithful servant of Queen Anne, who deserved the right to see accusations against him and answer them. The affidavits supporting the councillors' petition showed a misunderstanding of the governor's duties, Thrale argued, and many charges reflected upon Nicholson's person rather than upon his discharge of his duties.

Thrale's opposition to the proceedings was interrupted after one appearance, on May 4, 1704, by his illness, followed by his death. As Nicholson had no one else in London to defend him, the Board of Trade sent the affidavits against him to Virginia so that the governor and his supporters on the council could reply.[6] The papers were dispatched in June 1704, but the ship did not leave England until July, and its arrival in Virginia was delayed by a stop at New York.[7]

When the affidavits reached the governor in Williamsburg in December 1704, he unwisely decided to hold them and refer charges concerning his dealings with the House of Burgesses to that body when it met in April. Thus, while Blair in London was lobbying steadily for Nicholson's recall, the governor took his time making his defense. So confident was Nicholson that he invited his critics to make affidavits and offered assistance in taking them.[8] He even expressed satisfaction to the council that the Board of Trade "had been pleased to give such a favourable determination"[9] to Blair's charges.

To the board, Nicholson acknowledged receipt of his opponents' affidavits and promised his rebuttal. Unfortunately for him, the vessel bearing his letter was captured by the French, and the English captain threw it overboard, but the Board of Trade did not learn this until February 8, 1705.[10] Blair meanwhile spread the impression that the governor's silence implied his guilt.

Blair's first affidavit against Nicholson was dated April 25, 1704, and the second followed six days later.[11] Together they run to twenty-six printed pages. The first he divided into four chapters, dealing in turn with the offenses alleged in the memorial of the six councillors in 1703 and with "His Behaviour in the Upper House of Assembly," "His Behaviour in General

Courts," and "Some Other Publick Abuses in his Government."
At its conclusion he signed the traditional oath in Latin,[12] followed by the endorsement "Coram me jo: Edisbury," or "In
my presence, John Edisbury." The witness was master of chancery in London.

Blair's complaints were many: the governor altered county
courts without advising council, appointed sheriffs without advice of council, chose county militia commanders from other
than councillors, avoided a "fair audit" of revenue in council,
convened the burgesses when spring planting required them to
be on their farms, refused to make college lands available for
sale, and kept from council the instructions sent over by the
Board of Trade to guide Virginia's government.

"I have heard him often debase & vilify the Gentlemen of the
Council," he wrote, "using to them the opprobrious names of
Rogue, Rascal, Cheat, Dog, villain, & Coward. I have heard him
say they got their estates by cheating the people & swear that
he valued them no more than the dirt under his feet & that he
would reduce them to their primitive nothing. . . ."

Among his other offenses against the council, Blair cited Nicholson's dictatorial bearing, his "high, haughty, passionate &
abusive way of browbeating, discouraging & threatening all that
do not speak & vote as he would have them," his threats to
"ruin" a councillor and "cut his throat," and his "very rash
extempore Speeches, threatning & abusing the whole assembly."

Of Nicholson's behavior in general court, Blair reported that
he had "very often been witness to his gross & visible siding
with some & running down of others upon the account of
friendship or enmity to themselves or their relations or their
lawyers or the part he thought they acted in the publick unhappy
differences. . . ." He further described him as "a Gentleman
that accustomes himself to very irregular hours of Eating, Sleeping & doing business, by which the morning is often lost, & he
obliges the Court to sit often till 12 at night sometimes two or
three in the morning. . . ."

Under the heading of "Publick Abuses," the commissary depicted Nicholson as a tyrant who called people from church
"in the King or Queen's name" and fetched them pell-mell to

Williamsburg, only to "scold at & abuse them after he had put them to the trouble & charge of their Journey." He accused Nicholson of constantly stirring up trouble between individuals, creating factions, spreading rumors, and belittling colonists:

I have seen a great number of instances of his haughty, furious & insolent behaviour to the Gentlemen of the Country, particularly I heard him in a very menacing manner tell 8 or 9 of them that he knew how to govern the Moors & would beat them into good manners. . . . He sent a message to his mistress [Lucy Burwell][13] that he would be the death of her Father and Brother & all her nearest relations. . . .

I have heard him say of the Gentlemen of the Country that they were all a parcel of Rogues, Villains, Newgate Birds,[14] Beggers, Cheats & Cowards, and of the Gentlewomen that they were all a parcel of ** Jades, & Jilts . . . I saw him run after one Gentleman to cane him who fled from him having no weapon to defend himself.

He revived an earlier charge in reporting "many pranks of wicked Lewdness & rudeness to Gentlewomen in several parts of the Country[,] several of them from the persons themselves whom he has so attacked & some of his debauched attempts so abominably gross that I never heard of the like. . . ."

So picayune were a few of Blair's charges that they weakened his whole testimony. In demonstrating Nicholson's penury, for example, Blair reported that "he lives in a very sorry house not worth above £10 or 12 a year (tho' the Queen pays him £150 per ann. for house rent), that his furniture & attendance are miserably mean, having but two servants both within doors & without (besides his Chaplain) . . . ."

The fact was that Nicholson had rented from a tavern-keeper, John Young, one of the few houses available in Williamsburg, for lack of a governor's mansion. Even if the bachelor Nicholson did entertain poorly, this was hardly argument for his removal.

General dissatisfaction with British rule is intimated in one complaint. Blair quoted Nicholson as accusing colonists "very unjustly & disadvantageously as being grown rich & haughty, tainted with republican notions & principles, uneasy under every Governmt, & to the best of my remembrance ready to shake off their obedience to England, & in the same letter he advised a military force to keep the Continent to their duty. . . ." In 1704

Nicholson anticipated the shape of colonial resistance to come.

Beyond his other faults, Blair said Nicholson was unfaithful to England's parliamentary principles. "I have heard him . . . speak in the most contemptible terms of the English Laws & even use that Expression Magna Charta, Magna F---a & commend some body that said he would hang them with Magna Charta about their Necks." He also expressed concern, as Robert Beverley also did, at Nicholson's military ambitions and his expansion of the county militia.

Blair's second affidavit dealt with "the Clergy, the College & Himself [Nicholson]." Like the first, it was a mixture of the serious and the trivial. The governor had called the clergy "a Pack of Scandalous fellows," praised the Quakers, wished Virginia's clergy were dead, and abused them with such epithets as "Dog, Rogue, Rascal, Villin, Jesuit." He ignored the College of William and Mary and was "the forwardest to throw abuses on the College, particularly he railed against the building, tho' extraordinary good for that country."

Blair especially resented Nicholson's monopolization of the college as a temporary state house, even though Blair in happier days had invited him to use it until the new Capitol could be completed. "I have heard him swear that he would seize the College for the King's use & he crowded into it, the Secretary's office, the Clerk of the Council's office, the Clerk of the House of Burgesses' office & all their lodgings, with himself & all the Committees, & had all his public treats in their hall to the great disturbance of the College business. . . ."

"As to the finishing part of the College," Blair reported, "he did so excessively hurry it on for those several uses, that partly by the Plank & timber being green & unseasoned & partly by employing a great number of unskillful workmen to comply with his haste, it was shamefully spoilt. . . ." Although Nicholson had enjoyed public applause for advancing £200 for the college, he later demanded its repayment, Blair said.

Nicholson's groundless suspicions that Blair's brother Archibald was courting Lucy Burwell were also recited for the Lords Commissioners. As the commissary described it, the governor had flown at him in a rage: " 'Sir, your brother is a villian & you have betrayed me,' then with hands & eyes lifted up to heaven, he added these strange words (thundering out as loud as he could roar them on the high way), & 'Mr. Blair,' said he, 'take notice, I vow to the Eternal G--, that I will be revenged on you and all your family. . . .' "

The commissary darkly implied that Nicholson was behind the attempt of students to "bar him out," a traditional antic of English schoolboys to assure their Christmas holidays. "I will not say he [Nicholson] has had any design upon my life," Blair conceded, "though I will give your Lordships an Acct of two Strange passages that have an ill aspect that way."

As Blair described the first of these incidents:

about a fortnight before Christmas 1702 while I lodged in the College, I heard the School boys about 12 o'clock at night, a driving of great nails, to fasten & barracade the doors of the Grammar School. I was mightily surprised at it for we had banished this custom & it was quite left off for some years. I made haste to get up & with the assistance of 2 servant men, I had in the College, I had almost forced open one of the doors before they sufficiently secured it, but while I was breaking in, they presently fired off 3 or 4 Pistols & hurt one of my servants in the eye with the wadd as I suppose of one of the Pistols, while I press'd forward, some of the Boys, having a great kindness for me, call'd out, "for God's sake sir don't offer to come in, for we have shot, & shall certainly fire at any one that first enters." Upon the hearing of this, I began to think there was something more than ordinary in the matter & desired a parley with them, thinking to find out upon what acct it was that they had provided fire arms, Powder & Shot, which they had never used to do formerly, but that night they would not discover it, tho' I confess, I had some suspicion, of the designs of my malicious neighbour; & resolved to let them alone till morning, & then getting all the other masters together & calling for workmen to break open the doors; Before we began, we offered them a pardon, if they would open, of their own accord & tell us the truth, who it was that set them on, tho' by that time we had more than a suspicion of it, for I had seen one of his excellency's servants that morning a handing of them in, some more Powder, upon this, the Boys, sent out at a Window by a ladder. One of the Chief confederates that knew the whole plot with orders to discover it. The Short of his story was . . . that while they had no thoughts of any such thing, the Govr Sent for him, & put him upon it, gave them money to buy victuals & drink & Candles, & Powder, & Shot, & lent them 6 of his own Pistols. Upon hearing that the Governor, was the Author & the contriver of this business, we sent the boys to him, leaving it to his excellency to determine the time when he would have them dismiss'd, for it was then about a week before the usual time. His excellency being out of humor, to the great disappointment of the Boys, ordered that they should continue at their books till the usual time & then be dismiss'd, this decision made them very angry & they said they wondered what he had made all that to do for, when they were not to be dismiss'd one day sooner than ordinary for their pains. . . .[15]

On entering the grammar school quarters, Blair said he found the governor's three pairs of pistols, plus swords and other weapons. "It was God's great mercy to me that the boys gave me warning of the Shot & so saved me from the danger," he wrote.

Blair described another odd exchange with Nicholson six weeks later. "As I was asleep in bed with my wife in my Chamber, in the College, between one & two in the morning," he wrote, "a maid who lay in the Closet just by, heard somebody a opening the door of the outer room & after he had turned the lock of it, come quite thro' to our chamber door. . . ." The violent effort to open the locked door waked James and Sarah Blair, and they cried out, "Who's There?" The intruder departed.

On inquiry, Blair learned that Nicholson on that January night "had appeared to be in so bad a humor that every body was afraid to speak to him. And the person of good credit tole me, he was seen between one & two of the Clock in the morning, to go directly from his own house toward the college without a light. . . ." Nobody other than Nicholson, Blair thought, would try to break into his bedroom at 2 A.M. of a dark winter's night, "when he could not be a walking for pleasure." Strange indeed were the moods of Francis Nicholson.

Stephen Fouace submitted an equally damaging affidavit against the terrible-tempered colonel.[16] Fouace, who had come to Virginia in 1685 and served Yorkhampton parish in York County, had returned to England in 1702 after a clash with Nicholson. He had been one of four clergymen among the eighteen charter trustees of the college, serving as rector of its board in 1697. He remained loyal to Blair all his life and was to die a few years before the commissary.

After a supper party at Blair's Richneck house, Fouace wrote,

Nicholson accompanied Councillor Edmund Jenings into the garden and excoriated him. Fouace recalled "the vile names of pitifull rogue, Rascall, Thief, &c.," and the governor's threat to kick the old councillor. When Fouace intervened, Nicholson offered no apology but continued his threats.

On another occasion, when the governor had stopped at Fouace's glebe house in York County while enroute to Kecoughtan, he detained the cleric from 5:00 P.M. until nearly 11:00 P.M. with threats against Lucy Burwell's father and brother for discouraging his pursuit of her. When Fouace had attempted to "pacify his mind," Nicholson ignored him.

On another occasion Fouace heard the governor assail St. John Shropshire, a Blair supporter who had been dismissed by the vestry of one parish and had besought the governor's presentation to another. "What do you talk to me of this and the other minister being dead?" Fouace heard Nicholson roar. "I wish there were forty of you dead. The Quakers are in the right, you are all hirelings." Fouace said he and Shropshire had fled, "wondering betwixt our selves how we & the world had been imposed upon by his pretended zeal for the church & clergy."

Fouace's worst affront was received from Nicholson in May 1702, on the way from Williamsburg to Gloucester County, where Lewis and Martha Burwell lived with their four sons and seven daughters, including the beguiling Lucy. Fouace wrote:

When we came near one another he accosted me with a very angry look, very abruptly in these very words (raising his voice to a perfect vociferation) "I command you in the King's name & upon your Canonical obedience as I am your Bishop not to go to that house (pointing to Major Burwell's house) except you be sent for, nor to speak to the young Lady." "Why Sr" said I, being frightened & much amazed "what is the matter? Does your excy take me for your rival? I can assure you Sr I have not that foolish presumption to think to be preferred to your Excellency. I never spoke or acted anything that could justly give you any such jealousy." "Hold your prate Sirrah," said he to me, "I have taken good notice of you, you are an impudent Rogue, a Villain, a Rascal, you are now insolent and proud, but I'll humble you & bring down your haughtiness. When you came hither you had more rags than bags." I answered something to this purpose that if I had been formerly as poor as he was pleased to say, it was no shame to have been poor & that it was nothing to his ill usage to me. . . . Upon this he renewed his opprobrious names of impudent rascall, scoundrell, &c., and as we were riding along together he turned short upon me laid hold of my hat & pulled it off my head & asked me how I had the impudence to ride with him having my hat on. . . .

The embarrassed Fouace finally got his hat back with the warning that henceforth he obey Nicholson's commands. "Sir," he had replied, "I must obey your Excellency; but I think your Excellency would do better to turn me out of the parish & indeed out of your Government than to command me not to do that which is my duty to do, viz: to visit the sick of my parish. . . ." After telling the governor he would leave Virginia on the next ship, Fouace retreated under verbal attack and "ran away from him as fast as my horse would carry me."

When Fouace paid his farewell call on the governor, Nicholson threatened to prevent his sailing for England. However, Fouace told him he had complied with the law, had received a pass from the secretary to sail, and could not lawfully be detained. Angrily, the governor summoned to his office Blair, Benjamin Harrison III, the Reverend Peregrine Cony, and William Robertson, clerk of the council. Nicholson demanded to know whether Fouace had received the bishop of London's permission to return. Blair said it had never been required.

"Sir," Nicholson retorted, "I will not argue the thing with you now, I desire you only at present to take notice as you are Comissy & you Mr. Harrison as you officiate in the place of the Queen's attorney [as attorney general of Virginia] & you Mr. Cony as you are my chaplain & you Mr. Robertson as you are Clerk of the Council, that I do not give leave to Mr. Fouace as he is a clergyman to leave this Country. . . ."

Fouace had had enough. On July 30, 1702, the aggrieved cleric sailed with the tobacco fleet from Chesapeake Bay. Before it cleared the Virginia capes, however, he received word to report to the governor on board H.M.S. *Southampton*, which would convoy the merchantmen to the British Isles. "But I," wrote Fouace, "fearing & suspecting his design of stopping my voyage under one pretence or other . . . went some days before into another ship & continued hid there till the South Hampton man of War had left the Fleet."

Anticipating Fouace's accusations, Nicholson sent letters by the *Southampton* to the archbishop of Canterbury and bishop of London, charging him and Blair with misconduct.

One of the strongest witnesses against Nicholson was Robert Beverley, the historian, who had been dismissed by Nicholson as clerk of King and Queen County for criticizing the governor. Beverley said Nicholson habitually bullied witnesses and lawyers in court. Once he so abused attorney Benjamin Harrison III that Blair as a judge of the court rose and objected. "If Mr. Harrison has done any ill thing . . . I hope your Excellency will find another time to call him to an account of it," Blair had said. "I am sorry to see so much of the court's time taken up . . . by reason of your Excellency's prejudice against him."

"Sir, I deny the prejudice, put it down in writing," Nicholson shouted.

"I hope I have liberty to speak my opinion," Blair replied.

"Who hinders you?" the Governor barked.

"I am ashamed to sit here and see people so used," Blair said.

"Get you gone then," Nicholson roared. "It had been good for the country if they had never seen your face."[17]

After nine months elapsed without bringing Nicholson's reply, Blair attempted to bring the matter to a head. In January 1705 he and Fouace and Philip Ludwell I appeared before the board and argued that Nicholson had had adequate time to answer his accusers. In "an abstract of ye late advices from Virga concerning Govr. Nicholson,"[18] they wrote the Board of Trade that letters dated as recently as November had been received from Virginia. They also reported that instead of growing milder since the councillors had brought charges, Nicholson had become more tyrannical, setting up "Inquisition Courts" to try critics and intimidating colonists to render favorable judgments. His critics on the council were still being abused, Blair said; pressure was exerted by the governor to force them to make affidavits favorable to him.

A note of humor was injected with publication in London in

1704 of an anonymous ballad lampooning seventeen of Nicholson's friends among the Virginia clergy who had gathered at Mann's Ordinary in Williamsburg, near the Capitol, and signed an affidavit against Blair. The talented versifier, who may have been Robert Beverley, thus described the gathering:

> Bless us what dismal times are these,
>   What stars are in conjunction,
> When Priests turn Sycophants to please,
> And Hair brained Passion to appease,
>   Dare Prostitute their Function.
>
> Sure all the Furies must combine
>   To Sway the Convocation,
> When 17 Clergymen should join
> Without one word of Proof to Sign,
>   So false an accusation.

After a stanza implying that Nicholson had subverted several clergymen by promising to make them commissary after turning Blair out, the poet continued:

> First Whatley heads the Revd Tribe,
>   Amongst the Chiefest Actors,
> A Tool no pencil can describe
> Who sells his conscience for a bribe
>   And slights his benefactors.

The benefaction alluded to was a gift of £30 to the Reverend Solomon Whateley of Williamsburg by Benjamin Harrison III and Robert Beverley, after Whateley had been "affronted and abused by the Govr & not suffered to preach."

> Portlock the Cotqueen of the Age,
> Deserves the Second Station,
> A Doubty Clerk & Revd Sage,
> Who turns his Pulpit to a Stage
> And banters reformation.

> Rude to his wife, false to his friend,
>   A Clown in Conversation,
> Who rather, than he'd be confined
> To either to be just or kind,
>   Would sign his own damnation.

The Reverend Edward Portlock was minister of Stratton-Major Parish in King and Queen County. The ballad identified him in a footnote: "He preached a Sermon against women, upon the Serpent's beguiling Eve, Wherein he laid out his wife, to the best advantage, for hanging his Cat, called Alice, whom he more dearly lov'd. He is his own Brewer, Baker, Butcher & Cook."

> Corah comes next, that Sturdy Swain,
>   A bawling Pulpit hector,
> A Preacher of Hugh Peters'[19] vein
> That Sacred writ can twist & strain,
>   To flatter his Protector.

> A sot abandoned to his Paunch,
>   Prophane without temptation,
> Who, flames of jealousy to quench,
> Creeps in a Corner with his wench,
>   And makes retaliation.

A footnote identified "Corah" as Ralph Bowker, who was minister of St. Stephen's in King and Queen, and "his Protector" as Nicholson. "When he [Bowker] goes abroad a drinking," the author observed in an aside, "he makes his wife sit, with him, amongst the men, tho' perhaps there are several women at the same house of her acquaintance."

> Then in comes Ware with fudling school,
>   Well warm'd & fit for action,
> A mongrell, party color'd, tool
> Equally mix'd of Knave & fool,
>   By nature prone to Faction.

This was Jacob Ware of St. Peter's Parish in New Kent.

> Fainthearted Smith like Aesop's bat,
>> Both Birds & Beasts reject him,
> With his blue vest & Cock'd up hat,
> He signed & threatened God knows what
> But now pleads *non est factum.*

This was Guy Smith of Abingdon Parish in Gloucester.

> The Tavern was the place they chose,
>> To hold their consultation,
> Where each one drank a lusty dose,
> His Stupid Coxcombe to dispose
>> To form the accusation.

> Good Store of Bristol Beer & Stout
>> By dozens was expended
> The Glass went merrily about
> Some Sung & others swore & fought,
>> And so the farce was ended.

> Blest state to which the orders sunk,
>> A happy reformation,
> Now without fear they may be drunk,
> And fight & swear & keep a Punk
>> And laugh at deprivation.[20]

After a prolonged and unexplained silence, the word reached London on February 2, 1705, that Nicholson's reply to the charges had first been delayed in New York and had later been thrown overboard at sea to prevent capture by the French. Almost two years had elapsed since the six councillors had asked for Nicholson's removal. Concerned about conditions in Virginia and weary of delay, the Board of Trade concluded that the impasse must end. On April 5 it commissioned Edward Nott as Virginia's governor. Its notification to Nicholson probably crossed in transit his delayed affidavits, sent from Williamsburg for the second time in March.[21]

The board's recall of Nicholson found no fault with him, but deemed a change for the good of England's service. Nicholson was told that the decision was based not "upon account of any information against you, or of any displeasure H.M. has taken against you."[22] Nevertheless, his indignation was great and never to be forgotten; after having been assured of opportunity for rebuttal, he had been judged by the board without their waiting for it.

Nicholson obtained some measure of revenge against Blair with his publication in London in 1727 of the affidavits and exhibits that he had vainly sent the Board of Trade twenty years earlier, issued under the title *Papers Relating to an Affidavit made by His Reverence James Blair, Clerk, pretended President of William and Mary College, and Supposed Commissary to the Bishop of London in Virginia, against Francis Nicholson, Esq.* This publication provides the most intimate view of Blair and his times which has survived from those crucial years.

In four letters written on March 1, 2, 3, and 6, 1705, the governor admitted to a few of the six councillors' charges but argued they were consequent to his instructions from the Board of Trade. The rest he blamed on the animus of a small group of men who wished to dominate. Unwilling to be "guided and governed by them and turne Secretarys, Auditors, Collectors, Naval Officers, and others out of their places, and put them and their friends in," Nicholson declared that those who had besought him to come to Virginia now sought to turn him out. Blair's connections among the councillors were angry simply because Nicholson would not add others of their kin to that body. They regarded Virginia as their own fiefdom.[23]

"Mr. Blair and his little faction have set up to have the power and interest of turning out and putting in Governors, and affect the title that the great Earl of Warwick had." (The title was "King Maker.") To remove him, they would "stick at nothing," but their "artful trickeries, malicious insinuations and many notorious falsities" would be disproved by the records he was sending.[24]

The chief trouble-maker, James Blair, had "not only sworne through deal boards and brick walls, but even to my very thoughts and imaginations."[25] Nicholson thought he had erred in naming so many members of the Blair-Harrison-Ludwell connection, but he would not make that error again. And one of the family, Councillor William Bassett of New Kent, had indeed remained loyal to him.[26]

Nicholson wrote that Blair was known in Virginia for his disregard for truth, which dismayed even his friends. "I hear his own brother said that his memory failed him about what he swore concerning his scholars barring out, etc."[27] The governor defied his accusers to prove his "ruining people" who opposed his views. If he were called home to answer his accusers, he would bring suit under English law for malicious slander and perjury.[28]

Nicholson also sent the Board of Trade an affidavit signed by Councillors John Custis of Northampton, John Smith and John I. Lewis of Gloucester, and Henry Duke of James City, refuting the allegations of the six other councillors. The House of Burgesses in May 1705 also came to Nicholson's defense and adopted a resolution, twenty-seven to eighteen, denying that Virginia was dissatisfied or desired his recall. That body refused to admit the anti-Nicholson Councillors Robert Carter, Philip Ludwell II, and John Lightfoot to its debates.[29] The burgesses remained loyal to Nicholson, despite the calumnies of Blair and his faction.

Though too late to save him, Nicholson's affidavits made a spirited case. Rather than be the tyrant that Blair's faction depicted him to be, the governor said he would be jailed on a diet of bread and water. He insisted that the mass of Virginians supported him and that he would resign if as many as 5 percent were opposed. However, Nicholson could not explain away many instances of his intemperance cited by his accusers.

Nicholson had been outmaneuvered by Blair, and he knew it. "My accusers have had all the advantage of me both here and in England," he protested to the Board of Trade, "for the Petition and Memorial I find was signed May 20, 1703, a little after the Assembly and General Court[,] and Mr. Blair used privately to invite these gentlemen and some of the Burgesses and others to his lodgings in the Colledge to drink chocolate in the morning, and may be sometimes in the afternoon a glass of wine. . . ."[30]

Nicholson's affidavits accused Blair in turn of improprieties and indiscretions. He recounted Sarah Harrison's breach of her contract to marry William Roscow, her refusal to say "obey," and other irrevelancies. Much of it was unworthy of a man in his position. At the same time, the recital of his proposals for defense measures reveal his foresight in anticipating need for a British military force in North America. Similarly, his recognition of the need for more effective governance of the church in the colonies impelled many ministers to write to England in support of him. In many respects Francis Nicholson was a man ahead of his time.

We can well imagine the old soldier's fury when his recall reached him. For a man of his towering pride, it was a mortal affront. For the rest of his life he obsessively hated Blair and all his works. His hostility was long an obstacle to the transfer of the college from its trustees, who included Nicholson, to its president and faculty. Not until after Nicholson died in 1728 could this be accomplished.

Nicholson's published *Papers Relating to an Affidavit* contained many allegations of James Blair's perfidies. Among others, the governor printed a deposition from Katherine Young, who with her husband John—later the keeper of a Williamsburg tavern—had "Charge of Dieting the Scholars in the College" in 1701. When Blair one day met her in the hall and upbraided her for feeding students after they had barred him out, she replied that they had paid for their board. "Upon which words," she deposed, "he called me Impudent Hussey, and said, he would make me know he was Governor of the College." Mrs. Young said she had reminded Blair that Nicholson was above him. Thereupon Blair, "taking up his Cane, push'd me in the Breast with it, being at that time standing at the head of the Stairs . . . and had not my Cook-Maid been just at my Back . . . he had pushed me down the Stairs. . . ."[31]

Nicholson listed his gifts to the college from 1699 to 1702 at £2,652 6s. 11d. while arguing that Blair had taken advantage of his position to profit at every turn. "Col. Ludwell, Major Burwell, Mr. [Benjamin] Harrison [II], Mr. Fouace and himself [Blair], had a great deal of Money, while the College was building, for Labourers, Cart-Horses, Victuals, &c and by Their Stores, and got more of it by their paying Workmen and Labourers, in furnishing Them with Goods &c, and may be, by their Ways, they had a Third, or a Quarter, of the Money which the College cost. . . ."[32]

Nicholson also wrote that some of the money that Blair had charged to expenses on his first trip to England, 1691–93, probably went for goods for his private resale in Virginia. Here was perhaps the genesis of the store that Archibald and James Blair began to operate with Philip Ludwell II about this time. Asked Nicholson: "How could the Necessity of [Blair's] Condition bring him very considerably in Debt since he came last for *England*, when by his Account made up with the Assembly, he had received Eight Pounds, Nine Shillings, and Eight Pence more than he had charged in his very extraordinary and extravagant Account, and may be, an unjust one. . . . Sure he will not say, that he run himself in Debt upon the Account of not charging the Articles of *ad purgandos renes* [for purging the kidneys], but he might be in Debt for a Cargo or two for Himself and Wife to Keep Store with, at *Virginia*, as they use to do."[33]

From England, Blair gave his friends advance notice that Edward Nott would replace Nicholson. Writing from London to Philip Ludwell II at Greenspring in January 1705, he said the governor-designate had "as good a character in all respects as we can wish." The Scottish king-maker may even have had a hand in selecting him. A few months later the commissary returned to Williamsburg, and on August 12 the amiable Colonel Nott arrived and assumed the reins of government.

The change of governors did not bring immediate peace, for Nicholson had to remain several weeks in Williamsburg to await departure of the autumn tobacco fleet. As a result when the commissary convened his clergy two weeks after Nott took office, hostilities broke out anew. Though Blair tried to let bygones be bygones and offered to forget the affidavits that most of the clergy had signed against him, they refused his olive branch and took counsel with Nicholson in an effort to achieve revenge.

The 1705 clergy convocation opened in the small, gable-end church of Bruton Parish, completed in 1683. First the commissary preached a conciliatory sermon from Matthew XI:29. "Take my yoke upon you, and learn of me," he exhorted his fellow ministers, "for I am meek and lowly in heart: and ye shall find rest unto your souls." After the sermon the commissary introduced Governor Nott, who brought a message from the bishop of London deploring censures of Blair and the "indecent and irregular methods" by which Francis Nicholson had drawn the clergy into the feud. The bishop therefore proposed to wipe the slate clean. "I shall be perfectly deaf to all that is passed," Compton wrote, "& expect to hear from you in the future, as if you had never seen or known one another before."[34]

Blair then made a placatory address endorsing Compton's message. He promised to live in peace with the clergy.

But [he warned] if any are still desirous to blow up the coals of contention, I am afraid I must tell you, they themselves may have occasion to repent it, when it is too late. The case is much altered now from what it was some time ago. God be thanked we have now a Govr who is as studious of union & quiet as some others have been of Party & faction & notwithstanding the Idle stories which are industriously spread all over the Country to the contrary; we who have been near the fountain head of business know that he is a gentleman of that established good character & that firm interest, that we are like to be long happy under his Govt and they will find, that they do but kick against the Pricks who go about directly or indirectly to undermine him or make him uneasy. . . .[35]

At this point, the indignant clergy could contain themselves no longer. Up stood the Reverend Emanuel Jones of Petsworth Parish in Gloucester County and approached Blair's lectern with a paper that he said several clergy wished him to read. The commissary asked when and where the paper had been written. Jones replied "at a separate meeting held at the house of Mr. Jno. Young, where Govr Nicholson lives."

The commissary refused to let Jones read. He explained that the meeting in Nicholson's quarters was not a regular clergy session, having been called without authority and "without the Privity, Presence or Assistance of himself as being my Lord Bp of London's Commisy without whom no ecclesiastical meeting . . . ought to be held. . . ." He termed Nicholson's meeting "very unfair" and designed to preclude free deliberation at the general meeting. However, he offered to consider the same subjects if they were now submitted.

At this, the dissidents arose and walked out of Bruton to confer in the churchyard. When they returned, their spokesman withdrew their request to read their protest but asked Blair instead to accept it informally, "directed to himself in private for the resolution of a Case of Conscience. . . ." The commissary temporarily adjourned the meeting to read this paper, in which twenty-three of the clergy repudiated him and described his allegations against Nicholson as "frivolous, Scandalous, false, and malicious." They accused him of perjury and disclaimed his authority until he had cleared himself. They also charged him with having left England to avoid answering Nicholson's affidavits and contrary to instructions from the queen.[36]

Blair at last quieted the hubbub and replied that the bishop of London had fully approved his movements, had not withdrawn his power, and had known of his departure for Virginia. As to instructions from the queen, Blair said he had made answer "which I shall be very willing to shew any of you in private." He warned against their petitioning Her Majesty's government, which "would be construed, as a medling with things not within your province."[37]

When the clergy agreed that the commissary's answer satisfied their material complaints, Blair suggested they withdraw "some gross reflections upon himself, which were interspersed in their paper." A debate followed, some of the ministers arguing for a new document and others for a revision. After night fell, the angry meeting was adjourned, to reconvene next morning.

When the convocation was again deadlocked next day, most of the anti-Blair clerics again walked out and closeted themselves in Nicholson's house nearby. After a half hour, the Reverend Edward Portlock was sent by the twenty-three objectors back to church, where Blair remained with six clerics loyal to him: John Monro, Jr., of King William Parish,[38] James Wallace of Kecoughtan Parish in Elizabeth City, St. John Shropshire of Washington Parish in Westmoreland County, George Robertson of Bristol Parish in Prince George, Charles Anderson of Westover Parish in Charles City, and James Brechin of St. Paul's Parish in Hanover.[39]

Portlock handed Blair a letter from twelve of the twenty-three anti-Blair men, proposing that the clergy adjourn and that Blair submit his objections to the written record of the proceedings after adjournment to Solomon Whateley, who would distribute them to all the clergy. Blair's supporters agreed, and the commissary's account was duly written. It concluded with this observation: "Mr. Commry . . . had the minutes of the proceedings fairly drawn up & attested & being sensible of their [his critics'] frequent recourse to Govr Nicholson's lodging & their former subscriptions & obligations to him, that there was little appearance of their being persuaded into a good temper while he [Nicholson] was in the Country & they so much under his influence [, Blair] resolved to trouble them no further at this time, especially being assured from some of themselves, that a little time & patience after his absence would set all things right. . . ."[40]

Along with Blair's minutes of the chaotic convocation, Solomon Whateley distributed his own, which he completed on September 21 in time for Nicholson to take to England when he sailed. These portrayed Blair as a bully and a liar, soon to be recalled to England. "To have an whole body of English Clergy thus Cow'd & aw'd, Abused, Bespattered & Bely'd to their very faces by one Scot hireling & yet to turn nothing but a deaf ear," Whateley wrote, is "a tryal of our Patience, out of which we hope God will . . . deliver us."[41]

Whateley mocked Blair by satirizing his exaggerated charges of plots against him:

Plain it is that here's a plot! A Plot as deep as Hell itself. A Plot against both Church and State; a Plot for the subversion not only of the Ecclesiastical, but also the civil government of this Country, a Plot to turn out Edwd Nott, Esqr, our present Govr. A Plot to reinthrone the late Govr Nicholson. . . . To lay a bridge over the

Bay & let in the Accomackians; To make the Mouth of the Potomac Fordable for the New York-kians; to set all the Slaves & negroes free & arm them against their masters. To murder President Blair in his bed, fit all the Schoolboys with Firelocks & turn the College into an Arsenal. In a word, a plot to cast off the Yoke of Engld, to erect a fifth Monarchy on this northern Continent of America & make Govr Nicholson Emperor of the West, & who should have been at the bottom of this plot, but the English Clergy of the Colony of Virginia. . . .[42]

Blair no doubt rested easier after the fleet had sailed through the capes, bearing the angry Nicholson. But many years would pass before Blair's clergy forgot his treatment of that unhappy governor.

CHAPTER X

A Time to Sow
1705-1715

❧ As Williamsburg grew from crossroads to capital, it was a village of crude simplicity. At one end stood the college and at the other the Capitol, occupied by the assembly for the first time in 1704. Sprinkled between them, on the muddy lane that became Duke of Gloucester Street, stood tradesmen's shops, a public munitions magazine, Bruton Parish Church, and a few small dwellings, including the public houses of Mr. Young, Mann, and other innkeepers.

The first draft of the "city," made in 1699 by surveyor Theodorick Bland and sent to England,[1] shows the location of the college, the town boundaries, and the rights-of-way to the intended docks on Archer's Hope and Queen's Creeks. To make way for the Duke of Gloucester Street, which Nicholson planned, four houses and an oven owned by the late Colonel John Page had been torn down. On half-acre lots that had been sold for 20 shillings apiece, brick and clapboard houses began to dot the landscape.

A few planters built houses in Williamsburg to which they could resort in the dreary winter months. On Duke of Gloucester Street, Philip Ludwell II of Greenspring erected a handsome house not far from the Capitol. Nearby, on Francis Street, John Custis began to create a plantation. By official decree, colonists were permitted to remove brick from Jamestown's burned state house and haul it to Williamsburg for new buildings.

One of the earliest businesses to be planted in Williamsburg was the store established by Dr. Archibald Blair with his brother James and James's brother-in-law, young Philip Ludwell. Francis Nicholson in 1705 called it "one of the principal stores in the Country, which hath been kept about three years," and Alexander Spotswood described it in 1718 as "one of the most considerable Trading Stores in this Country."[2] The commissary's silent partnership in Doctor Blair's Store was to be a source of considerable wealth, as well as of whispered criticism that a clergyman should engage in trade.[3]

Records of the early Blair-Ludwell store are few, but they increased as the business grew. Archibald was its storekeeper, dispensing a variety of goods besides the remedies he prescribed for his patients. Mercantile establishments were few in Virginia, and they dealt in a profusion of goods. No doubt Dr. Blair's store inventory was similar to that of the Hubbard store in York County, which in 1667

contained lockram, canvas, dowlas, Scotch cloth, blue linen, oznaburg, cotton, holland, serge, kersey, and flannel in bales, full suits for adults and youths, bodices, bonnets, and laces for women, shoes . . . gloves, hose, cloaks, cravats, handkerchiefs, hats, and other articles of dress . . . hammers, hatchets, chisels, augers, locks, staples, nails, sickles, bellows, froes, saw, axes, files, bed-cords, dishes, knives, flesh forks, porringers, sauce-pans, frying-pans, gridirons, tongs, shovels, hoes, iron posts, tables, physic, wool-cards, gimlets, compasses, needles, stirrups, looking-glasses, candlesticks, candles, funnels, twenty-five pounds of raisins, 100 gallons of brandy, 20 gallons of wine, and 10 gallons of aquavitae.[4]

As James Blair's fortunes increased, so did those of his younger brother. Little is recorded of the early years of Archibald Blair, who was overshadowed all his life by James. Nevertheless, relations between them were close, and Archibald became a man of influence and standing. In 1705 he was named one of the directors for building the city of Williamsburg. From 1718 until his death he represented James City or Jamestown in the House of Burgesses, and in 1722 he was named an alderman of Williamsburg in the charter incorporating the city.

After Archibald's Scottish wife died, leaving him to rear their son, John, the physician married Sarah Archer Fowler, widow of Bartholomew Fowler, the onetime attorney general who had bought James Blair's Henrico holdings in 1697. When she too died about 1703, Archibald took as his third wife Mary Wilson Cary, widow of Colonel Miles Cary of Celey's plantation in Elizabeth City County. Four attractive daughters and a son, James, who died young, were born to Archibald's second and third wives. After Mary Wilson Blair's death in 1710, the physician remained a widower.[5]

So few were mercantile businesses in early Virginia that Doctor Blair's store prospered. There, as at Benjamin Harrison's store at Cabin Point, planters traded tobacco they had raised for other needed goods—sugar, salt, spices, wines, and English-made clothing and furniture. The store in turn stamped its tobacco casks with its merchants' mark, "AB," and sent them to England in exchange for other goods.

After Ludwell's death in 1727 and Archibald Blair's in 1733, the business was valued at £7,000 current money of Virginia. By that time it included two lots on Duke of Gloucester Street with "Store houses" valued together at £150, plus a large stock.[6] Upon Archibald's death, his only surviving son, John, and three daughters inherited his interests. After 1733 the firm was reorganized as a stock company with James Blair retaining a half interest. The other half was divided between Archibald's widowed daughter, Anne Blair Whiting; his son-in-law, Colonel Wilson Cary, who married Archibald's daughter Sarah; and an employe named William Prentis, who for the sum of £900 bought the share that Archibald had left to his daughter Elizabeth,[7] at that time married to John Bolling, Jr.

Like his brother, Archibald Blair moved from Jamestown to

Williamsburg as the new capital grew. In 1716 he bought lots on Nicholson Street, where he built a fine house.[8] The two-story frame structure, still standing with its wide central hall and two rooms on each side, is typical of dwellings of tradesmen and merchants in Williamsburg.

Though small, Williamsburg was not without its pleasures. Royal governors entertained frequently, and the annual Public Times and Saint George's Day on the Market Square afforded the rustic gaiety of an English county fair. During sittings of the general court, lawyers rode to town and enjoyed the nightly merriment of the taverns and ordinaries. To these diversions others were gradually added: balls at the governor's palace, quarterhorse racing on a track east of town, and theatricals by visiting troupes. A playhouse was built in 1716 on the Palace Green.

An impression of the little town was provided by the Swiss diarist, Francis Louis Michel, when he viewed the public cere-monies at the college in May 1702 on arrival in Virginia of news of King William's death and of Queen Anne's enthronement. After describing elaborate preparations for the approaching night's fireworks, Michel wrote:

The armed contingents, on foot as well as on horse, were drawn up in line. Two batteries were also mounted and a tent was pitched, where the bishop [Commissary Blair] delivered an oration on the King's death. . . . On the uppermost [of the college balconies] were the buglers from the warships, on the second, oboes and on the lowest violinists, so that when the ones stopped the others began. Sometimes they all played together. When the proclamation of the King's death was to be made they played very movingly and mourn-fully. Then the constable appeared with the scepter. It was like the English standards, which were woven with gold, covered with crape. Likewise those who carried them were dressed in mourning. Then followed the Governor [Nicholson] in mourning as also his white horse, whose harness was draped with black. . . .

After Secretary Robert Beverley had proclaimed King Wil-liam's death, the governor ordered the assembled county militia-men to reverse muskets underarm and watched them march, "with mournful music," to a tent pitched in the college yard, where Commissary Blair delivered "a touching oration . . . which caused many people to shed tears."

At noon, Michel wrote:

The musicians began to play a lively tune. Then the constable appeared in a green suit, the scepter no longer draped. The Governor, who had retired, appeared in blue uniform, covered with braid. He had also exchanged his horse. The Secretary then read publicly, while heads were uncovered everywhere, the royal letter and edict, that the second daughter of the departed and late King James had been chosen and crowned Queen . . . Then everybody shouted three times Hurrah! . . . Then the Governor caused most of those present, i.e., the most prominent people, to be entertained right royally; the ordinary persons received each a glass of rum or brandy with sugar. . . .[9]

Blair by this time was no longer receiving his original £150 yearly from the college, though he continued to hold the position of president. During his two-year absence in England, Nicholson and three other surviving trustees—William Randolph, Miles Cary, and the Reverend Samuel Gray—had decided he was not entitled to his pay in absentia. Relations between Blair and these trustees were therefore strained on his return to Williamsburg from London in 1705. Although they had been Henrico neighbors, Randolph had aroused Blair's resentment in 1697, when he as attorney general had advocated that "my Lord Bishop of London's authority should be suspended by law, and no Commissary of his suffered to act."[10]

While he was in London, Blair had lent his college chambers to his brother-in-law, Benjamin Harrison III, who was speaker of the House of Burgesses, and he had in turn lent them to Colonel Edward Hill II of Charles City. They were occupied by Hill when the assembly convened by Governor Nott gathered in the new Capitol on October 23, 1705.

Six nights after the assembly opened, the sleeping village was waked by a blaze that illuminated the nearby countryside. The college was on fire!

Blair was away, but his overseer saw the blaze from Richneck plantation, a mile and a half distant. According to the overseer: "after he was gone to bed he heard ye dogs bark in his corn field, and his wife getting up to see what was ye matter, and telling him there were horses in his corn field, he made a shift to get up, tho' he was very lame and as he comes out he perceived a light in ye air and a great smoke, and ye light encreasing he perceived the College was on fire and could see clearly the chimneys and the cupulo, and it seemed to him that the fire was on ye north side of ye cupulo, between ye two chimneys on the back part of ye college over the piazzas, but the Deponent being very lame could not go to ye college. . . ."[11]

Colonel Hill, clad only in his breeches, and other occupants of the building safely fled, though some had close calls. Among these were the Reverend Solomon Whateley, who had been reading before a fire in his room; Henry Randolph and two other young students, who fled down a stairway from the top floor; and Henry Lightfoot, who helped Colonel Hill save his clothes chest. Some burgesses were waked at John Young's ordinary and ran up Duke of Gloucester Street to witness the disaster.

Arson was first suspected. Mungo Inglis, the grammar school-master, pointedly mentioned "the singular and Notorious blackness"[12] of the exterior of the chimney of Blair's chamber. Inglis thought the blame must "unavoidably fall upon Mr Blair for his letting his Chamber to Collo Hill and his Brother [-in-law]," Harrison. However, construction defects had been recognized in the college from the beginning. Nicholson had found fault with the shallow fireplaces and exposed joists close to hearths in a "Memorandum of Several faults in the Building of William & Mary Colledge which have proved dangerous & prejudicial to the said Building."[13] Clearly the calamity was the result of inherent defects of the building, whose hearth fires exposed it to hazard in cold weather.

Whatever the building's faults, its loss was a great blow to the college and to Blair. Valuable books and scientific equipment—no doubt including the baroscope and thermoscope mentioned by John Locke—were destroyed. The sturdy labors of many men were undone overnight. Eleven years and much money would be needed to restore the institution to the state that it had achieved after such effort in its first ten years.

Blair seems to have shown uncharacteristic forbearance during the suspension of the college and of his salary. After the fire he wrote Archbishop Tenison, saying that money previously paid by the college to masters was being accumulated to rebuild. "I have freely parted with my salary for that use," he wrote, "though I had an undoubted Title to it, being named President under the Great Seal of England and that during my natural life."[14]

Though he continued to be president, his salary was not restored until 1721. In that year the college trustees sent a petition to the archbishop pointing out that "some Disputes have arisen among the Visitors and Governors, touching the Rights of Mr. Blair the president, to a Salary of one hundred and fifty pounds pr. annum which he formerly received for Several years."[15] The trustees did not wish to misapply college revenues, but they were "very desirous Mr. Blair should have justice done him." Could the lord chancellor please advise them?

That official decided that Blair was not president in 1721, since the institution had not been activated as the charter had directed. However, because James Blair had been "usefully employed in fitting up the College, and looking after the Children," he ought "in Equity and Justice to have a reasonable Salary paid to him from 1718 until the College be founded," in accordance with its charter provisions.[16] Lord Chancellor Macclesfield set the sum of £100 as fair, and this was paid until 1729, when the college was at last legally founded and Blair qualified for the full £150 salary.

Four years after the 1705 fire, rebuilding finally began. In response to a request from the trustees, Queen Anne granted £500 to it from the colony's quitrents. On August 4, 1709, William Byrd II recorded in his diary that he rode with William Randolph from Charles City to Williamsburg to a meeting of trustees, held in the building where the grammar school was temporarily taught. There, he wrote, "we at last determined to build the college on the old walls and appointed workmen to view them and [determine] the charge."[17] At a meeting six weeks later, "after some debate the majority were for building on the old wall," though Byrd "was against this and was for a new one for several reasons."[18] On October 31, John Tullitt offered to do the work for £2,000, "provided he might wood off the College land and all assistants from England to come at the College's risk."[19] The agreement was concluded on December 8.[20]

After the queen had been informed in April 1710 that "Workmen have been employed to clear the Foundation and prepare Lyme and Timber for such Building, [and] that more will be laid out than the Governours have a present in Cash before they can expect Our further Supply and that they depend very much thereupon," Her Majesty authorized another £500 gift for the building. As it approached completion in 1716, the trustees sent to England for "Standing furniture for the Colledge Kitchen, Brewhouse, and Laundry, & . . . a bell of 18 inches Diameter at the Brimms for the use of the Colledge." They also requested "1 Ingine for Quenching Fire" and "2 Doz: leather [fire] Bucketts with the Colledge Cypher thereon."[21]

The rebuilt college differed from the original. While it used the same foundations and rear wall, its east facade was changed by Spotswood to make the former second story its main level, with an outdoor stairway leading up to it. To this end, the ground level of the college yard was raised, hiding most of the original ground floor. The main facade was broken by a bay, which projected to frame the entrance, while the cupola was diminished. Safety was enhanced by repositioning a stairwell and enlarging the fireplaces.

In the basement beneath the ground floor was placed the kitchen, while the main floor was divided into rooms for mathematics, writing, grammar, and philosophy. On the second and third floors were a "convocation room," library, and quarters for president, masters, and a few students. However, most students, except for scholarship holders, roomed in town, as Blair had done at Edinburgh.

A master's quarters were described in a letter from Virginia to England:

You have two rooms—by no means elegant tho' equal in goodness to any in the College—unfurnished, and will salute your eyes on your entrance with bare plaister walls. However Mr. Small assures me they are what the rest of the Professors have, and are very well satisfied with the homeliness of their appearance tho' at first sight rather disgusting. He thinks you will not chuse to lay out any money on them.

You may buy Furniture there [in Virginia], all except bedding and blankets, which you must carry over; chairs and tables rather cheaper than in England. He says his Furniture consists of 6 chairs, a Table, grate Bed and Bedstead, and that is as much as you'll want.[22]

Among students enrolled in the early years were a few of the Indians whom Robert Boyle, the English scientist, had hoped to educate and Christianize at the college. Boyle's settlement, which Blair signed in England in 1697, specified that the benefaction be used to "keep att the said Colledge soe many Indian Children in Sicknesse and health in Meat drink Washing Lodgeing Cloathes Medicines bookes and Educacon from the first beginning of Letters till they are ready to receive Orders and be thought Sufficient to be sent abroad to preach and Convert the Indians at the rate of fourteen pounds per Annum for every such Child."[23]

This idealistic program had been heartily pushed by Nicholson, who in 1700 had engaged two Indian traders to persuade the chiefs to send their sons there. They were to tell the Indians "that a great & good man who lately died in England . . . having a great love for the Indians, hath left money enough to the College here in Virginia, to keep 9 or 10 Indian children at it, & to teach them to read, write & all other arts & sciences, that the best Englishmen's sons do learn." The governor suggested that the boys enrolled should be seven or eight years old, and he invited the chiefs to visit the college.[24]

In the same effort, Governor Alexander Spotswood in 1711 invited the queen of the Pamunkeys and the "great men" of the Chickahominies to send sons to the college as "Hostages for their fidelity," and the queen accepted. When Christopher Smith became master of the Indian school in 1716,[25] the trustees agreed to his request that the grammar school be partitioned to separate his red heathens from young Virginians. By 1723 the Boyle funds permitted the building of "a good house and apartments for the Indian master and his scholars,"[26] and this was called the Brafferton building for the Yorkshire estate in which Boyle's bequest had been invested. Housed in the Brafferton, it was hoped young braves would escape disease and homesickness, which had hitherto beset the Indian school, but this hope proved vain.[27]

Life at the college was not all work. Virginia's country-bred youths were devotees of horse and hound, and their high spirits burst forth on weekends and at Market Square frolics during Public Times. In 1716 the college permitted William Levingston to use a classroom "for teaching the Scholars and others to dance untill his own dancing school in Williamsburg be finished."[28] Showing a visitor the great hall, President Blair called it the most useful room he had. "Here," he said, "we sometimes preach and pray, and sometimes we fiddle and dance; the one to edify, and the other to divert us."[29] Blair's statement typified Anglican acceptance of worldly pleasures.

But Blair was Scotsman enough to insist on discipline. College rules decreed that "the masters of the Colledge allow no more play days to the scholars at the Request of any person whatever than one afternoon in a month, except onely upon the comeing of a new scholar, when they may allow one afternoon extraordinary upon every such occasion and no more."[30] Another rule compelled students to be examined by ministers who preached before the general court.

Once Nicholson left Virginia, Blair seems to have determined at last to live in peace and harmony with his fellow men. He remained on good terms with Governor Nott, praising him in letters and in person. Whether this amity would have long survived will never be known, for the popular Nott contracted fever during his second summer in Virginia and died on August 23, 1706.[31]

Blair's inconsistency plagued him on one occasion during Nott's tenure despite his effort to avoid trouble. With the majority of the council, he requested the governor to petition the Board of Trade to permit councillors to serve again as naval officers,[32] although Nott, like Nicholson, had come to Virginia under instruction to limit conciliar privileges. When reminded that he had signed a petition in Andros' time against such practices, Blair was excused from signing.[33] Colonel Robert Quary, surveyor general of the colonies, warned Blair that if he signed he must explain his former position or admit that he had unjustly abused Sir Edmund Andros. The commissary lamely explained that he had previously signed "by order or direction from Coll. Nicholson."[34]

But Blair could not avoid controversy. A few months after Nicholson's departure he was again engaged in unseemly public dispute with Mungo Inglis, the outspoken Scottish master of the grammar school, whom he had brought to Virginia as the institution's first teacher.[35]

Inglis was determined not to let Nicholson be forgot, and he wrote bitterly of Blair's political activities and self-interest. He accused Blair of using the college to enrich himself and to undermine Nicholson. To avenge himself against the governor, Inglis charged, Blair had taken his nephew John out of the grammar school and encouraged his in-laws to do likewise. As a result, seven boys—a third of his class—had left school. This, of course, reduced Inglis' income from tuition that he received in addition to his salary.

With Nicholson's recall to England, Inglis made good his threat and resigned. After a period of three years, in which he suffered the death of his wife and three of his children, however, Inglis accepted Blair's invitation to return to his former post at the college in 1716. He continued to teach there until he died in 1719.

After Nott's term, Virginia went nearly four years without a royal governor. Aging and absent-minded Edmund Jenings, president of the council, acted as chief executive while Great Britain engaged in a second conflict against Louis XIV, Queen Anne's War. Fought on the seas and in several continents, the conflict threatened several times to reach Virginia. It came close in 1707 when Colonel Robert Hunter, who had been sent from England to govern the colony, was captured at sea and interned as a prisoner of war in Paris.

Hunter's capture occurred at a time when the Society for the Propagation of the Gospel in Foreign Parts was making a new effort to establish an Anglican bishopric in Virginia, as Archbishop Laud had contemplated in 1638 and as Henry Compton had hoped to do fifty years later. Churchmen in England and North America argued that an indigenous ministry would strengthen the American clergy, enforce morality, and promote the church. Colonel Hunter was a friend of Jonathan Swift, the Irish cleric who was to win fame for *Gulliver's Travels*, and the two had discussed the possibility of making Swift bishop of Virginia. The idea appealed to some English Whigs as a means of ridding them of Swift's fearful pen; how much less dangerous would the satirist be in faraway Virginia!

Thus, while governor-designate Hunter was enjoying his amicable internment in Paris, he received a letter from Swift, dated January 12, 1709: "*Vous savez que Monsieur d'Addison, notre bon ami, est fait secrétaire d'etat d'Irlande*; and unless you make haste over and get my Virginia bishopric, he will persuade me to go with him. . . ."[36]

Though Swift was a talented preacher and later became dean of St. Patrick's Cathedral at Dublin, the hierarchy concluded that the colonies were still unready for a bishop. In Virginia, colonists suffered from the wartime loss of foreign markets, which glutted warehouses and barns with tobacco awaiting shipment. Moreover, those who knew the colonies realized that most colonists opposed a larger clerical establishment. "Lord Bishop" did not come easily to American tongues. As Hugh Jones was to write in his *Present State of Virginia* in 1724, the people "hate almost the very name" of the ecclesiastical court.[37] The death of Queen Anne and the accession of George I in 1714 put an end to the discussion.

England's triumph in Queen Anne's War was reflected in a return of prosperity to Virginia and the other colonies. The Board of Trade extended British control to Nova Scotia, Newfoundland, and the Hudson Bay country, which were taken from France. Tobacco shipments began to move again each fall and spring from Chesapeake Bay, and the spirits of the planters rose. Riding the crest of this wave of change came Colonel Alexander Spotswood, who arrived in Williamsburg in June 1710 to replace the captured Colonel Hunter.

Emboldened by the Act of Union that Parliament had passed in 1707, Scottish traders now swarmed into Virginia's tobacco ports and took over much of the profitable shipping that London had formerly controlled. The triumph over France brought a burst of unprecedented growth to Virginia, the population rising from 78,000 in 1710 to 114,000 in 1730.

If Francis Nicholson is considered the architect of Williamsburg, Spotswood was to be its builder. Imbued with a military sense of order and experienced, like Nicholson, in public administration, Spotswood pushed plans for the college, a governor's residence, and a larger church to serve townspeople and legislators.

Sir William Keith, who served as governor of Pennsylvania while Spotswood governed Virginia, wrote of the handsome colonel: "He was well acquainted with Figures, and so good a Mathematician, that his Skill in Architecture, and in the laying out of Ground to the best Advantage, is yet to be seen in *Virginia,* by the Building of an elegant safe Magazine, in the Centre of *Williamsburgh,* and in the considerable Improvements which he made to the Governor's House and Gardens."[38]

Construction of a governor's mansion had begun in 1706, but it had progressed slowly during the war for lack of funds and materials. Though the central structure was outwardly complete when Spotswood arrived, its courtyard, kitchen, and stables were still to be built. The elaborate plan proved costlier than anticipated, but Spotswood so successfully squeezed funds from assemblies that it was handsomely concluded during his term. He also had built a debtors' prison adjoining Capitol Square, a new magazine to house the colony's munitions, and a new house of worship.

In building the second and still used Bruton Parish Church from 1711 to 1715, Spotswood found himself closely associated with the commissary. Blair had been minister of James City since 1694; by 1710 he was fifty-five years old and could not easily make the six-mile trip by horse from Richneck to Jamestown and back each Sunday. Though he took care to hide the knowledge from everyone except one friend, he was suffering from a hernia that was frequently painful.

Thus, when Bruton's ministry was vacated in 1710 by the death of Solomon Whateley, offering an opportunity for Blair to preach again to Virginia's officialdom, he quickly offered himself and was elected.[39] This was partly through the influence of William Byrd, according to Byrd's diary, and probably also through

Philip Ludwell II, a vestryman of Bruton. Blair accepted in a letter to the Bruton Parish vestry on December 4, 1710: "It is true, I have soe many obligations to ye Parish of James City, that nothing but the urgent Necessity of health, often impaired by such long Winter Journeys, and a fear that as age and Infirmities increase, I shall not be able to attend that Service (being at such a distance) so punctually as I have hitherto done, could have induced me to entertain anything as of leaving them. If ye Shall think fitt to approve of this My proposal, I hope ye shall have noe occasion to repent your choice. . . ."[40]

The first Bruton church, where Blair had often preached on state occasions, stood at the intersection of Duke of Gloucester Street and the Palace Green, slightly north of the present church. A sketch of the church and its churchyard wall, drawn by the Swiss traveler Francis Louis Michel in 1702, shows it as a brick structure with gabled ends and arched windows, similar in proportions to the church at Jamestown. The interior was sixty feet long and twenty-four feet wide, and five buttresses were added after 1702 to support each side wall. Completed in 1684 when Middle Plantation was a mere crossroads, the church by 1706 was inadequate for Williamsburg's congregation. The vestry decided to build a new one and levied a charge of 20,000 pounds of tobacco against parishioners.

Because many worshippers were transients, drawn to the capital during Public Times by the meeting of the assembly and the courts, the vestry in November 1710 decided also to ask the assembly "for their Generous Contribution" toward the church, assuring that they would "consider of such a building as in their [the assembly's] wisdoms shall be thought proper for the said Occasions, & to give directions that a Draught thereof be laid before your Honours dureing this Assembly: the Vestry on their part being willing to advance towards the same, what may be thought necessary for the building of a Suitable Church for their Parish."[41]

The vestry thought " 'tis very Apparent the Parishionrs are very much straightened & often outed of their places & seats, by dispencing with & allowing room for the frequent resort of Strangers, & more particularly at the meetings of the General Assemblies: Courts: Councells: & other public Occasions." Unless much money were expended, "wch their abilities will not admit of," Bruton's vestry could not "Appropriate decent & fitting places or Pews in the intended Church for the reception of the Genll Assembly, and such as have Occasion to attend the Publick services of the Country."

Spotswood saw the justice of this request, and on his recommendation the burgesses appropriated £200 to the church from the duty on liquors and slaves. The governor accepted the burgesses' request to draw up a design. Blair as minister reported to Bruton's vestry on March 1, 1711, that "He had received from the Honble. Alexr. Spotswood, a platt or draught of a Church, (whose length is 75 foot, and bredth 28 foot in the clear, with two wings on each side, whose width is 22 foot) which he Laid before the Vestry for approbation—Adding further, that the Honble. the Governor proposed to the Vestry to build only 53 of the 75 foot, and that he would take care of the remaining part."[42]

The vestry approved the "commodiousness and conveniency" of Spotswood's design, and the building was completed in 1715, after the usual delays in receipt of materials from the British Isles. The structure was a handsome one. Even the Reverend Hugh Jones, whose tongue was sharp, averred that "the Church . . . is a large strong piece of brickwork in the form of a cross, nicely regular and convenient, and adorned as the best churches in London. . . ."[43]

Although most early Bruton records have been lost, much more is recorded of Blair's ministry there than at the Jamestown Church, built seventy-five years earlier. Virginians had grown more affluent and society more polished in the interim. The Bruton Parish vestry book for January 1716, for example, prescribed congregational seating in the new church, so greatly admired by parishioners and visitors:

Ordered that the Men sitt on the North side of the Church, and the Women on the left.

Ordered that Mr. Commissary Blair sitt in the head pew in the Church and that he may Carry any Minister into the same.

Ordered that the Parishioners be seated in the Church, [that is, the nave rather than the transepts] and none others.

Ordered that the Vacant room in the west end of the Church be made into three convenient pews, and that the Church Wardens agree with some workmen to do the same.[44]

The church built during Blair's ministry was enlarged and refined over the years. The chancel was lengthened, a church-tower and vestry room added, and two galleries were added to the original one to accommodate students and servants. Never in Blair's time, however, did Bruton lose the simplicity that lingered in the Anglican worship of colonial Virginia. There were no altar flowers, no brass altar ornaments, no crucifers, and no processional. The minister stood in the rector's pew to change from gown to surplice and to don his wig.

Describing a service in Blair's years, the Reverend W. A. R. Goodwin, a later rector of Bruton, imagined such circumstances as these:

The governor's coach sweeps down the driveway from the Palace and draws up before the gate. . . . We go into the church with those who have been loitering without, and are embarrassed by the noise our steps make on the flagstone floor. Passing into one of the large square pews we close the door and wait. It is difficult to see those in front of us; the high pews were built to encourage reverence rather than observation. There are some things which we can see, however, in spite of the pews. We notice that the men sit on the north side of the aisle, and the women on the south; we know that in accordance with custom, this is the ruling of the vestry. . . .

The door at the west end of the church opens, the minister enters passing down the aisle into the chancel at the east end; for this church, as were all colonial churches in Virginia, was exactly ori-entated. The clerk takes his place at the desk below the pulpit, which stands at the southeast corner of the crossing.

Again the west door opens, and . . . his Excellency the Governor passes down the aisle to his pew in the choir of the church. The silk canopy which hangs over the pew carries his name in letters of gilt. The Council of State, members of the House, and the Surveyor General take the pews officially assigned them. The service begins; the minister reads, the responses are led by the clerk, the congregation saying them just a word or two behind, for prayer books were not as easily had then as now and many people had to depend on the clerk's reading from his large book. The beadle keeps his eyes upon the college youth in particular, and upon the whole congregation in general. . . .

The service is ended, the minister passes down the chancel into the high overhanging pulpit, and announces his text. Those in the congregation who have braziers with them to warm their pews listen with comfort, if not always with patience. Others grow cold and restive, if it be a wintry day. . . .

The sermon is followed by the benediction, the minister and officials leave as they entered, then the congregation disperses, gathering into groups in the churchyard to exchange greetings, collect news, and discuss the sermon before going home with any guests whom they may have persuaded to accompany them. . . .[45]

Whatever Blair's other conflicts may have been, he had no serious dispute with the vestry or parishioners of Bruton in his thirty long years there. The Scotsman was growing older, and death struck frequently in his family. Within three years he buried his brother-in-law, Benjamin Harrison III, his father-in-law, and his wife. Sarah's death at forty-three in 1713 especially saddened him.[46] As he had done at Jamestown, he held Bruton's ministry without the security of lifetime induction. Consistent with Bruton's practice—and with Blair's own change of view during the administration of Nicholson—he was content simply to be hired as rector from one year to the next.

Viewing the middle-aged minister in the early years of Spotswood's governorship, one might conclude that James Blair was a changed man, determined to work in peace for church, college, and kingdom. Such may indeed have been his intention, but by 1716 another battle with a governor was in the making, and James Blair did not shrink from it.

The Struggle
with
Spotswood
1714-1721

❧ Alexander Spotswood was probably the best governor in Virginia's colonial years. Certainly he would vie with William Gooch and Francis Nicholson for that position. Yet like Nicholson and Sir Edmund Andros before him, his term was to end in discord and frustration. What happened to so promising a beginning?

The fault was not all Spotswood's. Like other royal governors who sought to enforce the will of the king, he found Virginians not always amenable to royal authority—or to any authority whatsoever. It was easy enough for him to say that "justice is to be done here to the King as well as to the Subjects; that the Rights of the Sovereign are not to be parted w'th merely because an humoursome people thinks they would be more conveniently Lodged in their hands."[1] The trouble was that king and colonists disagreed on what was just.

Like Andros and Nicholson, Alexander Spotswood came to Virginia dedicated to the concept of England as the center of a growing empire. He accepted the imperialist view that colonies existed for the benefit of the mother country, receiving protection and finished goods in return for cheap raw materials. Was not the wealth of France proof that imperialism could enrich princes? The difference was, of course, that Virginians regarded themselves as full-fledged Englishmen and not as dependent colonials.

Spotswood's administration began well enough. "I have a fair prospect of a good Agreement with the People," he wrote "& believe I shall live very contentedly here; for if I have not the Diversions of London (which I do not in the least hancker after) neither have I the perplexitys of that Town." Society in Williamsburg was rustic but pleasant: "The life I am likely to lead here is a perfect retir'd Country life; for here is not in the whole Colony a place that may be compar'd to a Brittish village."[2]

Like Nicholson, Spotswood soon found James Blair the chief challenge to his authority. Yet Blair and Spotswood had much in common. Spotswood was an educated man and a supporter of the Church of England. He came of a Scottish family that had been conspicuous in national affairs for more than a hundred years. His great-great-grandfather had been an associate of John Knox, while his great-grandfather had been archbishop of St. Andrew's. He had himself been promoted for service in the wars between England and France.

Unfortunately for him, however, Spotswood had the simplistic attitude toward politics of the professional soldier of his day. Beneath his good manners was a little of the disdain for colonials that had toppled Andros and Nicholson. In his differences with Virginia planters, he was often the bureaucrat that Andros and

Nicholson had been. In outlook he was a Tory, whereas most Virginia leaders shared the Whiggish mistrust of centralized power which animated Blair.

To Spotswood's credit, he began to understand the colonial viewpoint during his twelve-year governorship and ended by marrying and settling in Virginia. His change came too late, however, to save him from the commissary's intrigue.

Spotswood's first relations with James Blair were good. The new governor was concerned for the welfare of Indians, and he took interest in building Brafferton Hall and in enrolling Indians at the college. He made use of Blair's abilities by naming him to committees of the council dealing with Indian affairs, importation rights for land, tobacco, and land-policy reforms. When Philip Ludwell II went to England in 1713, Spotswood named Blair as interim deputy auditor with substantial pay.[3]

The mild-mannered governor encountered his first serious difficulties three years after assuming office, when he criticized William Byrd and Philip Ludwell for their conduct as receiver and auditor of the revenue. When he removed Ludwell from office in 1714, Spotswood incurred the ill will of the Blair-Ludwell faction. The governor later attributed his troubles with Blair—"the constant Instrument of Faction against all former Governors"—to this act.[4]

To handle the accumulating criminal cases awaiting judgment by the general court, Spotswood in 1712 created a court of oyer and terminer to meet in June and December to supplement sessions of the general court held in April and October. The incumbent councillors assumed that they, who sat as the general court, would also serve on the new tribunal. Spotswood, however, planned to name additional judges. As he wrote the Board of Trade, seven of the twelve incumbent councillors were of "one particular family," the Blair-Harrison-Ludwell group, and should not sit in a case in which any one of them might be involved.[5]

The councillors referred to were Blair and Ludwell, of course; Benjamin Harrison II, Blair's father-in-law;[6] William Byrd II, who had married Ludwell's half-niece, Lucy Parke; and William

Bassett and Edmund Berkeley, who had married Joanna and
Lucy Burwell, nieces of Ludwell. Spotswood also included
Robert "King" Carter (whose daughter Elizabeth had married
Nathaniel Burwell) as the seventh member. The remaining
five councillors—Edmund Jenings of York, Dr. William Cocke
of Williamsburg, and Mann Page, John I. Lewis, and John
Smith of Gloucester—were not connected by blood or marriage
with the group.

Unable to depend on more than five of the twelve-member
council to sit in an important trial, Spotswood went outside
the council and named the speaker and two burgesses to the
court. It was this step that inflamed the council. "It would be
hard that men's lives should be try'd by more inferior Judges
than their Fortunes," they wrote. As councillors had been the
"last resort" in property cases, so should they be in criminal
matters, they submitted. If the governor insisted on naming
other men, council members asked to be excused from "attendance on such occasions in the future."[7]

Asked to rule on the matter, the Board of Trade upheld
Spotswood's right to appoint other than councillors. His commission so empowered him, and unless an act of assembly con-
travened, he could exercise his discretion, the board decided.
Some of the council felt Spotswood had misstated their position
to the board, and they sent a protest to England. As might be
expected, Blair was among the seven protestors.[8]

The same seven charged Spotswood with misconstruing their
motives in other cases. They felt he had made them appear in-
tent on depriving the governor of his rightful due when they
had joined with the burgesses in asking a larger share of quitrents for the use of Virginia. He had also reflected on them in
terming revenue collections "dark and confused" and in suspending Ludwell as the colony's auditor.

Although Colonel Spotswood had taken credit for reforms,
they told the Board of Trade that "whatever good laws or orders
have been made were either proposed by us or at least readily
assented to." They had paid "utmost deference" to the governor, but conscience now compelled them to object to his ill-

considered measures. They feared Spotswood would make other charges and even suspend councillors, and they requested a hearing by the board.[9]

This time William Byrd, instead of Blair, was chosen by the dissidents to bell the cat. Already in London, the worldly councillor appeared as spokesman for the seven and argued that Spotswood had violated precedent and royal instructions. A worse governor in future might name mere hacks to the court, he submitted.[10]

The Board of Trade referred the question to Solicitor General Edward Northey, who ruled that the right to name special judges inhered in the Crown. Spotswood was empowered to do so if he felt it necessary, but the Crown discouraged special commissions "except in Extraordinary Emergencies" for the "preventing of Inconveniencies, and Quieting the Minds of His Subjects there."[11] The board felt that any conciliar challenge to the royal prerogative should be discouraged, but, like Northey, it urged Spotswood to make discreet use of his power.[12]

Somewhat sobered, the governor agreed to name only councillors to the court if the council would acknowledge his larger powers,[13] but the seven intractable council members continued to find fault with him. When he asked the council to cite one instance in which he had asked them to endorse a law that would have had ill consequences, they failed to make satisfactory answer.[14] In a rebuttal to the Board of Trade, Spotswood disputed their allegations point by point. He accused councillors of making an issue of the judgeships "to make themselves Formidable & keep the Country in subjection to their Party." He attributed their other charges to disappointment at his rejection of their scheme to obtain for themselves salaries of £100 a year from quitrents.[15]

In the elections to the House of Burgesses in 1718, the dissident councillors encouraged Virginia's voters to elect only men opposed to Spotswood. The long honeymoon between governor and the Virginia "Creolians" was definitely over.

The burgesses were also smarting from disdainful remarks that Spotswood had made to them at an earlier session. At that time the council had upheld Spotswood against the burgesses, but now most of the twelve councillors had joined the anti-Spotswood forces. The governor cited Blair, Ludwell, Byrd, and their connections as "the very persons who infuse into the people jealousys of H. M. Prerogative, and of designs against their libertys."[16]

Writing to the Board of Trade, Spotswood also complained that the Blair faction portrayed him as "a publick enemy to the country," fanning "misunderstandings which otherwise would soon be removed and dissipated."[17] To George Hamilton, Lord Orkney, who remained in Great Britain as governor of Virginia while he served as deputy, Spotswood commented: "It is surprising to see how barefacedly these Councillors proceeded in their extravagant Measures."[18]

Anti-Spotswood activity reached its apogee when the 1718 assembly gathered in Williamsburg for one of the most turbulent sessions in the colony's history. Philip Ludwell's townhouse, midway between the Capitol and governor's palace,[19] was headquarters for dissident councillors and burgesses. Ludwell's mansion was the "common rendezvous of the disaffected Burgesses," Spotswood observed, and Blair was "continually in their consultations." No dissident was "more violent" than Blair's brother Archibald, then a burgess, whose "Billingsgate expressions" defied repetition. Equally hostile was Ludwell's son-in-law, John Grymes, a burgess from Middlesex.

Two disappointments angered Archibald Blair. First, he had been recommended by the Earl of Orkney for a seat on the council in 1713, but the Board of Trade instead had chosen Edmund Berkeley, a nominee of Spotswood's. Secondly, Spotswood had discouraged the assembly's enactment of a bill to lend Archibald's store £4,000 from the treasury surplus, to be retained without interest as long as Archibald desired. Spotswood opposed this outrageous proposal on grounds that it would be difficult to enforce repayment. The bill was nevertheless passed by burgesses and council, although it was never submitted for Spotswood's signature, in view of his known opposition.[20]

Spotswood's letters reflect his admirable restraint during these running attacks. When he was accused of misrepresenting his critics in England, he replied that even if he "took Mr. Commissary Blair for a very ill man, it was no more than what the generality of themselves had at times declared of him."[21] To soften his opponents, he said he fell into "a Merry way of talking, & endeavoured to laugh them out of their Sullen mood," but this had no effect. Even after he had invited his enemies to the governor's palace to share a bowl of arrack punch, they remained "strangely reserved" despite the ceremonial bonhomie of toasts. When some opponents showed signs of relenting, Blair and Ludwell, "the chief engines of faction," would whip them up again.[22]

Spotswood expected no improvement as long as the incumbent councillors held office. In Blair, he wrote Lord Orkney, the faction had "a Staunch Achitophel[23] in all Conspiracies against Governors and will take upon him the whole Drudgery of forming their Letters, Memorials, Remonstrances and whatever else they design shou'd be couch'd in Writing. Nay and they know he will not be overscrupulous of swearing to them when he has done."[24]

Blair's supporters counted on his important church connections to deter the Board of Trade in London from upholding Spotswood, the governor warned Lord Orkney. If this "powerful Knot of Relations" should "obtain another Victory in the turning out of a third Governor," Spotswood predicted, "the country will be persuaded that they hold their places for Life and the Governor his only during their pleasure." No governor would risk offending a "nest of Wasps" for fear of attack by the "whole swarm."

Spotswood accordingly suggested to Orkney that the council be purged. Why should "a Juncto of relations," he asked, be allowed to "grow to that height of power as to bear Uncontroulable Sway over both Govr and People"? He suggested removing the "most turbulent Spirits"—Blair, Ludwell, Byrd, and John Smith of Gloucester[25]—and replacing them with Peter Beverley, Cole Digges, John Robinson, and Edward Hill.

So hostile were the lawmakers to Spotswood, that they decided he must go.

When the assembly met in 1718, the burgesses at Blair and Ludwell's instigation[26] drew up instructions to Byrd in London to present charges against the governor and seek his recall.[27] They accused Spotswood of advocating retroactive penalties for nonpayment of quitrents, of exceeding appropriations for building the governor's house, of attempting to prevent collection of burgesses' salaries, and of abusing the burgesses in speeches.[28]

History was repeating itself, but this time William Byrd was to share the onus with Blair. Though Spotswood wrote that "everybody here concludes [the author of the request for his removal] to be the Commissary,"[29] Blair wisely recognized that he no longer had the powerful friends in England who had helped him to eject Andros and Nicholson, and he willingly let Byrd, a younger man, act as spokesman. Henry Compton had been succeeded as bishop of London by John Robinson, and Tenison had been followed as archbishop of Canterbury by William Wake. Blair could not claim close acquaintance with either, though Robinson was the uncle of Christopher Robinson of Middlesex, a trustee of the college. Gilbert Burnet and studious John Locke had also passed from the scene.

Spotswood offered to bet £1000 that he would be vindicated,[30] but he knew what had befallen Andros and Nicholson. Like Nicholson, he obtained testimonials from adherents: the clergy, college masters, and officials of twenty-one counties, all testifying to his wise governorship.[31] Though he talked confidently, however, he did not sleep soundly.

"Far from being possesst with a fondness of remaining longer among these People," Spotswood wrote Orkney, he wished to hold office only long enough to vindicate himself. As long as the Blair-Ludwell faction persisted, no Virginia governor would long endure. Already the "power Intrest and Reputation of the King's Governor" had been "reduced to a desperate Gasp." Should "present unrighteous attempts" succeed, then "the Haughtiness of a Carter, the Hypocrisy of a Blair, the Inveteracy of a Ludwell, ye Brutishness of a Smith, the Malice of a Byrd, the Conceitedness of a Grymes, and the Scurrility of a Corbin, with about a score of base disloyalists, & ungrateful Creolians for their adherents must for the future Rule this Province."[32]

Spotswood's patience and good humor were worn out.

Lord Orkney came to his lieutenant's defense before the Board of Trade in August 1718. He urged that before complaints against Spotswood were considered, the Lords Commissioners should contemplate removing the council dissidents.[33] When the complaints at last reached the board in 1719, Spotswood was upheld. Byrd's removal from the council was recommended instead, and two new councillors were proposed: Cole Digges to succeed Edmund Berkeley and Peter Beverley to succeed Byrd. Byrd barely saved his skin by promising to return posthaste to Virginia and to promote reconciliation with the governor. Instead of getting Spotswood's job, as he hoped to do, the master of Westover almost lost his own.

Spotswood thus survived the first major assault. When Byrd reached Virginia he proved as good as his word, and in May 1720 Spotswood could write that "a new revolution in the management of public affairs" had brought peace to the proceedings of the council and burgesses.[34] By conceding to land-hungry Virginians,[35] he had survived and—he failed to note—simultaneously assured himself of extensive lands for his retirement.

Spotswood's trials were not over, however. Blair and Ludwell were not easily appeased.

Being the man he was, James Blair was bound to collide sooner or later with the determined Spotswood. That collision occurred in 1719, when the governor inducted new ministers into Essex and James City parishes against their vestries' will. Spotswood held that, as king's deputy, only he could discharge that prerogative in Virginia. But Blair and the vestries, now firmly aligned, insisted that Virginia parishes had built their churches and therefore had the right to choose their own ministers.

The issue was fought out at a meeting of clergy that Blair convened in the great hall of the college in April 1719. The ostensible purpose was to satisfy John Robinson, bishop of London, that the Virginia clergy were properly ordained. Like other clergy gatherings, it ended in a pitched battle.

"I have information of some irregularities," Bishop Robinson had written, "which if practiced, will need very much to be redress'd. . . ." The question concerned the validity of the ordination of Virginia's ministers. However, when the commissary asked his brethren in God if any of their qualifications were doubtful, the only ordination to be questioned was his own. Twelve men expressed doubts about it, eleven were satisfied, and one suspended judgment. Some said they did not recognize the signature on Blair's certificate of ordination, "JO. EDINBURGEN." When Blair exhibited his license from Compton, others objected that his certificate was not in the English form.

Blair insisted that he had been ordained by a bishop, but he did not go into detail. The Reverend Hugh Jones observed that "most here . . . believe Mr. Commissary never had any but Presbyterian Ordination,"[36] while Blair, in a long account, told Robinson he had been ordained by a bishop and had shown Spotswood his license to officiate, which was given him by Compton in 1685. He failed to mention that the bishop who had ordained him was of the Church of Scotland, for he had no doubt learned that a Virginia statute of 1662 declared that "noe minister be admitted to officiate in this country but such as shall produce to the governour a testimoniall that he hath received his ordination from some Bishopp in England."[37]

Thus the dilemma: though Compton had accepted him to serve the church in Virginia, the law of Virginia did not. In these circumstances he had understandably held his tongue and trusted to Compton's successors to keep him in office.

While the clergy argued in the great hall, William Robertson, clerk of the council, entered and presented two messages from the governor. The first assailed the commissary:

. . . For none more eminently, than Mr. Commissary Blair; sets at nought those instructions which your Diocesan leaves you to be guided by. . . . He denying by his practice, as well as discourses, that the King's Govr has the right to collate ministers to ecclesiastical benefices wthin this Colony; for when the Church, he now supplys [Bruton Parish] became void by the death of the former incumbent, his solicitation for the same was solely to the Vestry, without his ever making the least application to me for my collation, notwithstanding it was my own parish Church; and I cannot but complain of his deserting the cause of the Church in genl, and striving to put it on such a foot, as must deprive the Clergy of that reasonable security, which, I think, they ought to have with regard to their livings.[38]

Spotswood accused Blair of sitting idle in Bruton while his clerk read the service. "I have also seen him present in the church-yard, while the same clerk has perform'd the funeral service at the grave," Spotswood noted. "And I remember when he was for having the church wardens provide lay-readers, who should on Sundays read to their congregations some printed sermons; and so far he declar'd in council his approbation thereof, that such practice had like to have had the sanction of the Government, had I not withstood it, as destructive of the establishment of the Church."[39]

Referring to Blair's ordination, the governor urged the convocation "diligently to enquire of the disorders which your Diocesan [the bishop of London] takes notice of, and earnestly to apply yourselves to proper means for redressing them."[40]

In Spotswood's second communication, which was a letter he had written to the vestry of St. Ann's Parish in Essex County, the governor explained why he alone, as the king's representative, held the right to institute ministers in Virginia's parishes:

Every minister sent hither is denominated one of ye King's chaplains . . . and as such receives £20 out of his treasury to defray ye charge of his passage. If any of the King's ships are coming hither these ministers have their passage & provision gratis. The Bishop of London recommends them to the Govr to be preferred to some ecclesiastical living. But they bring no recommendation to any vestry, as patrons of the Churches; nor doth either the King or the Bishop direct or desire the Governor to interceed with the patrons of the Church here to bestow on such ministers the vacant livings in their gifts. Now to what purpose is the King at so much expence to send over clergymen to the plantations, if they are to starve here till a lay-patron thinks fit to present them? to what purpose doth the Bishop recommend them to the Governr, if he has no preferment to bestow? To what purpose do they bring the Bishop's testimonial & licence to preach, if these qualifications are to be again tried by a vestry here; and they do depend on popular humour for their livings?[41]

Blair characterized Spotswood's first communication as "an Invective against Mr. Commissary" and said it "contributed very much to the ill Temper of the Convention." When it was first read, it provoked such an outcry that no one could be heard. But "when that confusion was a little over," Blair said he was sorry to be "under the frowns of the Governour" and would explain matters and clear himself. Hardly had he quieted the group when "another confused clamour arose, that they were not proper Judges of these things" and that Blair should make his reply to the governor's charges to the bishop of London instead.

At this point Hugh Jones questioned Blair's sermon of the preceding day, and several clergy asked that it be printed. Blair demurred that he had "never . . . appeared in Print," but he offered to defend it or send a copy to the bishop. This seemed to appease them.

The recalcitrant clergy then voted a laudatory address to Spotswood. The commissary urged that the Bishop's matters come first, but he was overruled and a drafting committee was named, from which he was pointedly excluded. When Blair suggested the group confine itself to church matters and "abstain from intermedling with those unhappy differences" between governor and burgesses, he was again overruled.[42] Finally, when the commissary and seven other clergy asked if they might enter in the record their reasons for opposing the address, they were again voted down.[43]

The controversial statement, drafted that night by the committee and presented to the clergy next day, expressed satisfaction with the episcopal orders of all "except Mr. Commissary, of whose Ordination a major part doubt, a true account of which he has promis'd to transmit to yr Lordship, together with the Journal of this Convention."[44]

The clergy further informed Bishop Robinson that conditions in Virginia differed so from England's that many church usages had to be altered: "Parishes are so large, the Inhabitants so dispersed, and so distant from the Church (some 20, 30, 40 miles and upward), that throughout the whole country we have Divine service but once every Sunday, and but one sermon; and for the same reason the people neglect and refuse to bring their dead to be buried in the church yards; and seldom send for the minister to perform the office. . . . Also that people observe no Holydays, except those of Christmas day and good Friday, being unwilling to loose their dayly labour. . . ."[45]

The majority also expressed the view that "The people in General are adverse to the Induction of the Clergy, the want of which exposes us to the great oppression of the Vestries; who act often arbitrarily, lessening & denying us our Lawful salaries. . . ."[46] Minutes of the meeting noted that the commissary had refused to sign the communications to Governor Spotswood and the bishop of London.

Blair concluded with an appeal for unity. After excoriating "Informers" who had disturbed the bishop concerning "Irregularities," he rebutted Spotswood's views. He reminded his flock that when Nicholson had asked Sir Edward Northey in 1703 who had the right to select and institute Virginia ministers, the attorney general of England had ruled that the parishes were first empowered to choose but that the right lapsed to the governor if not promptly exercised.

According to Blair and John Monro, Jr., at this point the Reverend Emanuel Jones of Petsworth Parish interrupted him, shouting that Blair was wrong: it was vestries and not parishioners to whom Northey assigned the right of induction. "I have reason to know it," he cried, "for I brought in that Opinion."

Blair asked for quiet. "I have Sr Edward Northey's opinion here," he told Jones, "and I'll show you presently, that it is right quoted," which he preceeded to do.[47]

Blair's persistent critic, Hugh Jones, then admitted to having sent the bishop of London reports of irregularities. Jones blamed Blair for some of these, and Mungo Inglis, now teaching at the college, for others. According to Blair's account, both he and Inglis proved themselves to be innocent. Some "small variation from the Rubrick" was conceded by Blair, but this was recognized by the assembled clergy as reasonable.[48]

Before adjournment, Hugh Jones moved that the governor be asked to suspend Blair and request another commissary. However, "This proposal was with a general voice exploded, and cryed out upon," Blair and Monro reported. "When no body backed his motion, he desired it might be entered . . . but the whole Convention rejected it with a great Indignation."[49] So the men of God turned homeward.

After the meeting, Blair and seven other clergy sent Spotswood a minority address,[50] explaining their inability to subscribe to portions of the laudatory message concerning "Persons & Things, which as we apprehended, were not properly under our cognizance, nor within our Province." When Blair went to the governor's palace to present this, however, Spotswood glanced at it, called it "a libell," and gave it back to the commissary.[51]

Blair concluded his defense with two papers that answered the governor's accusations against him.[52] These retraced the course of the historic dispute between governor and vestries over the right to appoint Virginia's ministers.

As in Governor Nicholson's time, the clergy clearly regarded their commissary as a spokesman for the vestries rather than for themselves. The meeting set off flurries of argument in taverns and courtyards. Laymen and ministers debated the rights of the vestries versus the governor as to the "presentation," "induction," and "collation" of ministers.[53] The issue reinforced the opposition of anti-Spotswood councillors and burgesses, for many of them were also vestrymen. Blair sent to London a complaint that the governor was attempting to "prepossess" the ministers, while the pro-Spotswood ministers sent the governor an address regretting "with the utmost indignation & resentment" that he had been "affronted and abused by a few prejudiced men."[54]

Along with Hugh Jones and other clergy who had gathered in William and Mary's great hall for the conference, Spotswood questioned part of Blair's sermon on the grounds of disloyalty to the Crown, and next day sent the clerk, William Robertson, to demand the text. Blair complied and the governor was apparently satisfied, for he said no more about it.[55] However, the sermon was never published for examination by the clergy, as they had asked.

The appeal to English authority in Spotswood's term closely followed Nicholson's appeal in 1703. The governor in August 1718 asked the Board of Trade to obtain the English attorney general's opinion as to his right to collate a minister of his choice in any Virginia parish.[56] In response, Solicitor General Sir William Thompson upheld the governor's contention that the king had delegated to that official the power to fill all benefices in Virginia.[57] Meanwhile Blair and Ludwell had quietly obtained from Attorney General Sir Robert Raymond the contrary opinion that each vestry held the right to select its own minister and present him to the governor for induction.

When Spotswood triumphantly presented the solicitor general's opinion to council on December 9, 1719,[58] Blair and Ludwell countered with Raymond's view, enraging the governor. After violent argument, it was agreed to bring the dispute before the general court in a suit by the vestry of Bruton Parish against the governor and then to appeal the decision to the king in council. Because Virginia's fifty vestries were vitally concerned in the outcome, the General Assembly employed an attorney at public expense to prosecute the case.[59]

Blair and Ludwell directed these maneuvers on behalf of the vestry of Bruton Parish. The fearless Scotsman had been minister of Bruton for nine years on a year-to-year basis, the vestry having voted in 1695 that "whoever shall be admitted to serve as Minister in this Parish, shall have no induction."[60] Indeed, Bruton's vestry had fought with Nicholson during the 1703–5 period over a similar issue, winning a moral victory by accepting Solomon Whateley as minister without inducting him.[61]

Now the planters saw an opportunity to settle once and for all their right to choose their ministers. It had become gospel with them that parishioners who paid the clergymen should also have the right to select them. Blair's leadership in this cause had the support of the mass of literate Virginians.

While the case awaited hearing, Blair in the spring of 1721 sailed again for England. He said he went on business for the college, but Spotswood thought otherwise. Writing the bishop of London, he doubted Blair's mission was " (as he gives out), about the college affairs."[62] When the commissary offered to perform any service for the governor, Spotswood privately hoped he would not do him "any Disservice."[63] Once in London, Blair worked behind the scenes. This time he accomplished his object without testimonials or affidavits.

It was not long before Colonel Hugh Drysdale, a friend of Prime Minister Sir Robert Walpole, was commissioned lieutenant governor of Virginia in place of Spotswood.[64] Blair reputedly capitalized on Spotswood's large acquisitions of lands on Virginia's frontier, though he never said so. Criticism that had grown during the governor's twelve-year tenure seemed to demand a change. The Board of Trade more probably wished to head off a confrontation between the governor and the vestries. Significantly, the British courts never ruled on the rights of Virginia's vestries versus her governor's.

Spotswood's downfall probably resulted from a combination of circumstances: misgivings on the part of the Board of Trade, Blair's opposition to him through Bishop Robinson, and Walpole's desire to place Drysdale in the governorship.

From England word reached Virginia that "Parson Blair was likely to act as Prime Minister" for Lieutenant Governor Hugh Drysdale, for they appeared together before the Board of Trade and sailed to Virginia on board the same ship.[65] Spotswood was in Albany to sign a treaty with the Indians when Blair reached Williamsburg with the new lieutenant governor. We can imagine the proud colonel's chagrin when he returned in October and found a successor had taken office a month earlier, under a commission dated April 3: "George, by the Grace of God King of Great Britain, France and Ireland, defender of the faith, etc., to our trusty and well beloved Hugh Drysdale, Esquire, greetings. We reposing especial trust and confidence in your loyalty, courage and prudence do by these presents constitute and appoint you in case of the death or absence of our right trusty and right well beloved cousin and councilor George, Earl of Orkney, our present Lieutenant and Governor General of our colony and dominion of Virginia in America, to be our Lieut. Governor there in the room of Alexander Spotswood, Esquire."[66]

Again Blair had had his way. This time, however, Virginia colonists were more sympathetic with the litigious old Scotsman. Though Spotswood had been a vigorous leader, he had become a threat to the rights of the native "Creolians," as he had called them. This time the "Great men" of the council were joined in opposition by lesser burgesses and vestrymen. No man had done more to instill this spirit of defiance than James Blair, the controversialist. Once again his cool courage had stiffened the spine of England's oldest daughter. It was an augury of future events.

As Drysdale took office, Commissary Blair stood at the pinnacle of his power. At sixty-seven he had outlived most of his enemies and was still strong in mind and body. Respected by his intimates and feared for his awesome influence, he was the most powerful man in Virginia next to the governor. William Byrd might be more accomplished, and King Carter wealthier, but the Scottish schoolmaster was the ablest strategist of all. King-maker, indeed!

Spotswood, licking his wounds as he retired to build a plantation on the Spotsylvania frontier, sputtered indignantly at "that old Combustion," the commissary. Once again the unshakeable Scotsman had unhorsed a veteran soldier.

CHAPTER XII

The College Grows
1721-1743

❧ Of all that James Blair did in Virginia, his creation of the
College of William and Mary was of highest value. Yet its life
hung in the balance for more than thirty years while Blair con-
tended with governors, clergymen, and querulous college masters. Not until Spotswood left the capital and Hugh Drysdale
became governor in 1722 did the college cease to be a pawn in
the politics of the Old Dominion.

Drysdale came at a fortunate moment in the sporadic growth
of Virginia's planter economy. It was a time of high hopes—a
breathing spell in Britain's endless wars to rule the seas. British
trade continued to rise in the wake of the victory over France,
and tobacco spread a golden glow over the Chesapeake region.
New settlers took up acreage on the colony's frontiers, which
had been opened up by Spotswood's far-sighted treaties with the
Indians. Trading in Negro slaves burgeoned as planters cleared
new fields for their Orinoco and Varina.

Along myriad creeks and rivers, new plantation houses arose, some in the elegant style introduced by Spotswood in the structure that Virginians wryly called "the Palace." It was a time of expansion, of the release of energies pent up during the interminable wars with Roman Catholic France.

In this boom, Blair turned his attention at last to hiring the six masters enumerated in the college charter as essential for its founding. Though this had once been expected to require only a year or so, it had been delayed for lack of funds and then by the fire that nearly killed the institution. By the time it had been rebuilt in 1716, Blair was at odds with Spotswood and had little time for the college.

Yet the fault was not all Blair's. The nature of Virginia life did not encourage intellectual or literary pursuits, and attendance at the Williamsburg college was disappointingly small. Because only a few classical scholars offered instruction in Virginia except at the college grammar school, few youths knew sufficient Latin or Greek to undertake a collegiate education.

Even the few boys who enrolled were not disposed to accept the discipline that Scottish and English masters expected. Unlike New England, whose colonists clustered in towns and grew up in the bookish Puritan tradition, Virginia's rural life did not fire many young men with the desire to become clergymen or schoolmasters. In the Chesapeake country, the almost universal ambition was instead to acquire tobacco land and create a great estate. For these reasons, William and Mary did not find as many matriculants as Harvard College had attracted when it opened in 1636.

The shortcomings of students were described by Hugh Jones, a master who came to the college in 1716. He found young Virginians had "good natural notions" and abilities, "quick apprehension," and "a sufficiency of knowledge, and fluency of tongue" but that their learning was superficial. The majority were "only desirous of learning what is absolutely necessary, in the shortest and best method," and they were "more inclinable to read men by business and conversation, than to dive into Books."[1]

It was in recognition of these traits that Blair directed his masters to "daily examine their Scholars, prescribe them tasks, hear them dispute, try them in all manner of exercises & wait upon them as punctually as a School Mastr."[2]

Attendance at the college increased somewhat after it was rebuilt, and President Blair persuaded the assembly of 1718 to devote the income from £1,000 to educate "ingenious scholars, natives of the colony," who otherwise would not be able to attend. Part of this capital was invested in a tract of two thousand acres of the Nottoway River in southern Virginia. Other money was invested in seventeen Negro slaves who were hired out when not needed at the college, and the remainder was loaned out at interest.[3]

In 1726 President Blair succeeded in obtaining from the assembly £200 a year for twenty-one years from a penny-per gallon tax on liquors. From 1734 till 1747 the college was allocated the entire liquor tax revenue, chiefly to build up its library. These grants showed new faith in the college, stimulated by the growth of scientific thought in France and England. The discoveries of Isaac Newton and the writings of Francis Bacon and John Locke were slowly opening the provincial mind.

Some individual gifts were also made to the college. After the advance subscriptions in 1693, these came slowly, however. John Mann of Gloucester made the college a contingent beneficiary in his will in 1695, as did Lewis Burwell of the same county in 1710. Henry Hartwell, a trustee, left a conditional gift of £50, and Mrs. Philarity Giles in 1717 left a reversionary interest in land on Blackwater River south of the James.[4] Colonel Edward Hill II of Shirley plantation, who had escaped from the burning college in 1706, left £50 on his death in 1720. But no other large gifts were recorded.

Donors of books were more numerous. Francis Nicholson, whom Mungo Inglis called "the Great Maecenas of the College," gave his library in 1698 when he returned to Virginia as lieutenant governor from Maryland. Others were Bishops Compton and Burnet; London merchant Sir Jeffrey Jeffreys; the Anglican society known as Dr. Bray's Associates; several ship captains who plied the Atlantic; William Wake, archbishop of Canterbury who served as chancellor of the college from 1721 to 1729 and again in 1736–37; the Reverend Emanuel Jones of Gloucester, who bequeathed most of his books in 1739;[5] and Alexander Spotswood, who left his library on his death in 1740.

President Blair made a great gain for the college in 1716 when he engaged the Reverend Hugh Jones, a graduate of Jesus College, Oxford, as master of philosophy and mathematics. For a brief period in 1716 the college had two masters simultaneously, the Reverend Arthur Blackamore having succeeded Mungo Inglis as head of the grammar school. However, Blackamore was dismissed after an alcoholic debauch, and the president renewed his pleas to the bishop of London to send another teacher.

Hugh Jones proved as prickly as Inglis, but he was an able pedagogue. It was Jones who led the opposition to Blair in the 1719 clergy convocation, and he was also one of the three masters who sent an unsigned paper to the governor the same year disparaging Blair.[6] In *The Present State of Virginia*, published in 1724, he struck at Blair by depicting the college as ill-run and poorly equipped.

. . . it is now a college without a chapel, without a scholarship, and without a statute.

There is a library without books, comparatively speaking, and a president without a fixed salary till of late: A burgess without certainty of electors; and in fine, there have been disputes and differences about these and the like affairs of the college hitherto without end.

These things greatly impede the progress of sciences and learned arts, and discourage those that may be inclined to contribute their assistance or bounty towards the good of the College.[7]

The book praised Spotswood for his reconstruction of the college, but its one reference to Blair was brusque: "The salary of the President, Mr. James Blair has been lately ordered to be reduced from 150 to £100 per annum."[8]

Another disparaging description was contained in a memorandum, probably written in 1722, by a new arrival in the colony. The college was said to have one master of grammar and writing, one usher or assistant master, twenty-two or twenty-three students, and no Indians. "In the whole," it concluded, "the Colledge is in all Respects in a very declineing condition," and "The People of Virginia are at Present in a kind of Lethargy in regard to so noble a Building As well as pious Design as no doubt it was Originally." The situation "argues no great dependance on [confidence in] the President."[9]

Such views probably reflected Spotswood's antipathy for Blair, for the governor by 1721 conspicuously absented himself from trustees' meetings in protest against Blair's demand for the president's salary and against his "general management of the college." Remembering the conflict between Nicholson and Blair, Spotswood wisely wished "to avoid contention . . . & meddle for ye future as little as possible with the concerns of that Foundation."[10]

All of this changed for the better when Lieutenant Governor Drysdale arrived in Williamsburg. No doubt at Blair's behest, he reminded the assembly of 1726 that the college was in a "Languishing condition" and must have funds to hire six masters in order to realize at last the noble conception of its founders. As a result of Drysdale's influence, the assembly appropriated £200 from the duty on imported liquors, and President Blair prepared for his last voyage to England to manage the proposal when it reached the Board of Trade. If only Francis Nicholson could now be persuaded to sign the transfer, the college might at last be set up as its charter of 1693 directed.

Word of the assembly's action meanwhile reached Nicholson, who had retired in 1725 as governor of South Carolina and returned in ill health to London. Still determined to have revenge on his former ally, the aging general appeared before the Board of Trade, to Blair's dismay, and argued that the proposed appropriation was contrary to the college's charter. However, the board saw no objection to Virginia's taxing imported liquors for the college's use and confirmed it. Once again James Blair triumphed over Francis Nicholson.

Even with money, President Blair had trouble finding scholars to teach in distant Virginia. Like ministers, English schoolmasters were unwilling to cross the Atlantic and plunge into the American wilderness. As Blair had written in 1691, when the college was still the mere dream of "a Small Remnant of Men of Better Spirit, who had either had the benefit of better Education themselves in their Mother-Country, or at least had heard of it from others,"[11] it was not easy to lure scholars away from the cloisters of Oxford and Cambridge: "I find there will be a great deal of difficulty in finding of able masters & yet I am sensible the life of the business lies in this. In England their masters of their colleges have a much easier life than is designed for the masters & professors of our college in Virginia. I can have several young men that are fit enough to be ushers but can not perswade any of the Eminent experienced masters to go over."[12]

Under the charter of 1693, control of the college was to pass from the charter trustees, or "the longest livers among them," as soon as a president and six masters were in office. When this condition was at last about to be met in 1728, the only survivors of the original eighteen trustees were Blair, Stephen Fouace, and Francis Nicholson. Fearing that Nicholson would refuse to sign the articles of transfer to spite him, Blair had Williamsburg attorney John Randolph, an alumnus of the college, dispatched to England to persuade his old enemy to do so. To the college's chancellor, Edmund Gibson, bishop of London, the commissary wrote an introduction for Randolph to present on arrival:

The Gentleman who is to deliver this to your Lordship Mr Randolph is one of the Governours of our College; he was one of the earliest Scholars in it, and has improved himself so well in his Studies, that he is now one of our most eminent Lawyers. By his Acquaintance & interest with General Nicholson he hopes that he can prevail with him to joine in the Transfer of the College. I hope your Lordship will favour him with your best advice and Assistance. He is furnished with Materials, and is very capable of transacting such an affair, tho I believe his chief topick must be that after the Transfer the Govrs of the College will have a greater power and I less.[13]

Blair's apprehensions were in vain, for the embittered Nicholson died in 1728 and only Blair and Fouace remained to approve the transfer. So, at last, meeting in London on February 27, 1729, the two aging friends signed over to the president and masters all funds, buildings, and lands they had so long held for the institution.[14] In effect, James Blair as a trustee conveyed the college to James Blair as president.

The articles of transfer contained "certain ordinances and statutes" that the trustees recommended "for the better ordering and governing the said College and all persons enjoying any office or residing therein." These had been drawn in 1727, apparently when Blair was in England. Perhaps to win Nicholson's support, they were declared to be the result of "mature Deliberation" with Archbishop Wake, who was serving an eight-year term as chancellor of the college. However, they were amenable to change whenever subsequent visitors might see fit.[15]

The statutes first outlined duties of the "college senate," as it termed the governors and visitors. These men were to be: "persons of good Morals, and Sound in the Doctrine of the reformed Church of England; and Friends and Patrons of the College and polite Learning; and Gentlemen in good Circumstances, such as by their Interest, if their be occasion, can patronize and serve the College."[16]

They were to concern themselves chiefly with policy but were also to elect persons to faculty positions, with due regard to "their Learning, Piety, Sobriety, Prudence, good Morals, Orderliness and Observance of Discipline." They were also to support the president and masters.[17]

The document proceeded to outline instruction, government, and discipline. The grammar school would teach Latin and Greek. Books were to be those used in England or approved by the president, for the master was to teach no part of any author "as insinuates any Thing against Religion or good Morals." In studying languages, "nothing contributes so much . . . as dayly Diologues, and familiar Speaking together in the languages they are learning." The grammar school master was to use "the Colloquies of Corderius and Erasmus."

Grammar school students were to learn the Anglican catechism in the "vulgar tongue," while the more advanced would memorize it in Latin. On each Saturday and each day before a holiday, a sacred lesson would be studied. Three terms divided the scholastic year for the grammar and Indian schools: Hilary term began on the first Monday after Epiphany, Easter term on the second Monday after Easter, and Trinity term on the Monday after Trinity Sunday.

Four years of Latin and two of Greek were required preceding admittance to the philosophy school, or college. (As grammar school scholars usually entered at twelve, this would normally qualify them at sixteen for admittance to the philosophy school.) Applicants for grants as "foundation scholars" must at this point be examined by president and masters. It was decreed that "no Blockhead or Lazy Fellow in his Studies" should be chosen.

Two professors would teach on the college level. One would impart "Rhetorick, Logick, and Ethicks" and the other "Physicks, Metaphysicks, and Mathematicks." This division followed Edinburgh's practice after 1708, when that university had abandoned the rotating regencies of Blair's days. Aristotle, the keystone of the medieval curriculum, was to be replaced by whatever system the professors chose. This was a concession to the newer philosophical thought of Bacon, Locke, Hobbes, and the Enlightenment as well as to the scientific writings of William Harvey, Sir Isaac Newton, and Robert Boyle.

Oral disputations or debates survived in the curriculum, and a student had to be able to "propugn" and "conpugn" a thesis as Blair had done at Marischal and Edinburgh.[18] It was further required that "the studious Youth be exercised in Declamations and Themes on various Subjects, but not any taken out of the Bible." Biblical analysis was to be left to the divinity school.

The award of degrees followed Scottish practice: "For these Studies, we allot Two years before they attain to the degree of Batchelor, and Four before they attain to the Degree of Master of Arts." This was changed in a few years to conform to the English practice.

Two divinity professors were called for. One would teach Hebrew and "critically expound the literal sense of the Holy Scripture." The other would "explain the common Places of Divinity, and the Controversies with Hereticks" and engage in disputations on these. Here again William and Mary followed Scottish precedent, probably in the belief that the English practice of assigning independent reading for undergraduates, to be supervised by tutors, was ill-advised for young men as unaccustomed to university life as Virginians were.

After 1718, the college used the £1,000 endowment appropriated by the assembly in an effort to attract divinity students, who were to be chosen for "Ingeniousness, Learning, Piety, and good Behaviour, as to their Morals." Applicants seem to have been few. Not until the two divinity professors were installed in 1729 did theological studies take firm root.

The Indian school master was directed by the charter to teach reading, writing, and "vulgar arithmetick." Emphasis was placed on "the Catechism and the Principle of the Christian Religion." Pursuant to the Boyle bequest, the Indian master had been enjoined by the bishop of London and the Earl of Burlington, Boyle's executor, to Christianize the savages and then send them back to civilize their tribesmen.

The 1727 statutes set up a disciplinary code for the grammar school which was evidently intended to govern the others. Among these young men, "special care must be taken of their Morals, that none of the Scholars presume to tell a Lie, or Curse or Swear, or to take or do any Thing Obscene or Quarrel and Fight, or play at Cards or Dice, or set in to Drinking, or to do any thing else that is contrary to good Manners."

To enforce these provisions, masters were to "chuse some of the most trusty Scholars both for Publick and Clandestine Observators." These resembled student "censors" who had assisted the masters at Edinburgh in Blair's student years there.

Scholars were permitted to live either in the college or to board and room in town, for it was the college's "intention that the Youth, with as little charge as they can, should learn the learned Languages and other Arts and Sciences." Hope was expressed that "all Things relating to the Table or Lodging will be so well supplied within the College, that they can no where better be accommodated." Foundation scholars, like Crombie bursars at Marischal, had to reside in the college to perform daily duties.

Over this semimedieval institution was to preside "a man of Gravity, that is in Holy Orders, of an unblemished Life, and good Reputation and not under Thirty Years of Age." The president must attend meetings of the board of visitors and convey its policies to faculty and students. He must also examine students and give weekly lectures of spiritual import, "or on some Controversy against Hereticks." The statutes called for "a Man of prudence, and skillful in business" who could husband the resources that the trustees were about to transfer.

To Blair's credit, the college statutes that he helped devise set clear limits to the president's authority. He could neither employ nor dismiss masters, who were to be answerable to the "senate." In directing his faculty, he could employ "Word of Mouth" only in minor matters not requiring consultation with the faculty. Except where the vote was split equally, his voice in faculty session had no more weight than any other. Such were the rules governing the college as its long process of founding was completed.

Armed at last with adequate funds, President Blair spent much of his time while in England in 1726 and 1727 in an effort to fill out his faculty and make possible the college transfer. With the help of Archbishop Wake and Bishop Gibson, he engaged the masters and by 1729 had assembled them in Williamsburg. The following were selected:

The position of professor of moral philosophy was filled by the Reverend William Dawson, a graduate of the Queen's College, Oxford, who arrived in Williamsburg in 1729 at the age of twenty-nine. He proved an able, temperate, and loyal teacher and succeeded Blair to the presidency in 1743.

Professor of natural philosophy and mathematics was Alexander Irwin, or Irvine, the first incumbent, who also arrived at the college in 1729. He was called "the Learned Orion" by William Byrd in *The History of the Dividing Line Betwixt Virginia and North Carolina*, published in 1728. He was a Scotsman who had studied at Edinburgh and reached Virginia via Philadelphia. Byrd disliked him and implied that he owed his job to a connection with Blair.

Professors of divinity were two worthy ministers serving in Virginia: the Reverend Bartholomew Yates and the Reverend Francis Fontaine. Yates, a graduate of Brasenose College at Oxford and rector of Christ Church, Middlesex County, had come over in 1700. Fontaine, a Huguenot and an Oxonian, had been rector of Yorkhampton Parish in York County before joining the faculty.

For master of the grammar school, Blair chose Joshua Fry, who had been educated at Wadham College, Oxford, and settled in Essex County, Virginia, about 1720. He later moved to upland Virginia and mapped Virginia, Maryland, and Pennsylvania with Peter Jefferson and others.

Master of the Indian school was John Fox, an English minister who emigrated to Gloucester County in 1721. When he later became usher (assistant master) of the thriving grammar school, the Reverend Robert Barret became master of the Indian school. Fox was rector of Ware Parish in 1737 and died in 1742.

At their first meeting after the transfer of authority was received from England, the president and masters each affirmed the traditional Thirty-Nine Articles of Belief, adopted by the Church of England in 1562 and required for Anglican ordination since 1571. (Article 37 declares, "The Bishop of Rome hath no jurisdiction in this Realm of England.") They also took the Latin oath, *De Fideli Administratione*, which Blair had taken on graduating from Edinburgh, swearing to uphold the monarchy.

To attorney John Randolph they voted 50 guineas, and to Stephen Fouace £20 for their services in transferring control of the college.

Once the College of William and Mary acquired its faculty and was legally founded, it was authorized to send a burgess to the Virginia Assembly, as English universities sent representatives to Parliament.[19] The first burgess to be properly elected by the president, masters, and professors under conditions acceptable to the assembly was George Nicholas, who took his seat in the House of Burgesses on May 25, 1730, and represented the college until his death. He was succeeded by the able and admired Sir John Randolph, one of the college's truest friends, who was elected speaker of the House in August 1734. Other prominent men, usually Williamsburg attorneys, served in succession. Through the selection of the college burgess, President Blair reinforced his power.

The fortunes of the college had so greatly improved by the time William Gooch arrived in Virginia as governor in 1727 that President Blair convinced him a chapel wing should be added. This would give the structure three sides of the quadrangular form that English colleges had inherited from medieval times. "We are going to build the Chappel as fast as we can," Gooch wrote the bishop of London in 1728.[20] This was in contradiction to Hugh Jones's recent observation, "There is as yet no great occasion for the [great] hall, so that it might be made a chapel and divinity-school, for which purpose it would serve nobly with little or no alterations."[21]

President Blair was authorized to take bids, and on March 26 the board of the college received an offer from James Hughes:

I understand by the advertisement of a noat set up at the Capitol by the reverend Mr Commisary Blair that a Chappell is to be erected to the said College in form of the Hall and well fitted for the use of a Chappell workmanlike all which building I will doe for Eight Hundred and ninety-Eight pounds currt Except the Sashes and Glasses in the Body of the Building I am Gent
your most obliged
Humble Servt to Comd
James Hughes[22]

The board eventually chose the experienced Henry Cary, Jr., to do the work, and on June 28, 1729, Blair wrote Bishop Gibson, the new chancellor of the college: "I acquainted your Lop [Lordship] in my last that we had laid the foundation of the chappel. That work has been since carried on with that expedition that the walls are now finished and we are going to set on the roof, so that I make no doubt it will be all inclosed before winter."[23]

Three years after Blair had written Bishop Gibson, the chapel was opened with elaborate ceremonies. The president preached a sermon from Prov. 22:6, "Train up a child in the way he should go: And when he is old, he will not depart from it." William Dawson, professor of moral philosophy, described the occasion to the bishop: "My Lord:—I beg to acquaint your Lordship that on June 28th. 1732 our new chapel was opened with great solemnity. The Governor [Gooch] and his family were pleased to honour us with their Presence, and, it being the assembly time, the members of both Houses came in great numbers. An holy Joy appeared in every countenance."[24] Services were held in the chapel daily at 6 A.M. in summer and 7 A.M. in winter as well as at 5 P.M. each afternoon. All students were required to attend.

The muddy crossroads once known as Middle Plantation had by this time become a considerable village. Wrote Hugh Jones in 1724:

Williamsburgh is now incorporated and made a Market Town, and governed by a Mayor and Aldermen; and is well stock'd with rich Stores, of all Sorts of Goods, and well furnished with the best Provisions and Liquors.

Here dwell several very good Families, and more reside here in their own Houses at Publick Times.

They live in the same neat Manner, dress after the same Modes, and behave themselves exactly as the Gentry in London; most Families of any Note having a Coach, Chariot, Berlin, or Chaise. . . .

Thus they dwell comfortably, genteely, pleasantly, and plentifully in this delightful, healthful, and (I hope) thriving City of *Williamsburgh.*

By 1732 the college had again outgrown its revenues, and President Blair was obliged to write to the Board of Trade for more funds. Receipts from the penny-per-pound export duty were "very much sunk" because of deceptions practiced by exporters, and the board of visitors voted to send Attorney John Randolph to England to ask that enforcement be tightened or alternative funds provided.[25] Two years later the assembly tightened tax collections and allocated all revenues from liquor importation duties to the college. Even so, Blair still urged the bishop of London to press Gooch and the assembly for more funds.[26]

Once the chapel was completed, the college began to build a president's house. The statutes of 1727 had renewed the salary of £150 a year originally paid to the president, and they had specified in addition "an House and Garden suitable to the place, so soon as the College Revenues will bear these expenses." Living a mile and a half from the college, at Richneck, had become inconvenient for the seventy-seven-year-old president.

Furthermore, the increase in the number of students made the president's duties more demanding. Though James Blair had an apartment in the college, it was not practical for him to divide his time between it and his plantation.[27]

A site had been set aside for a president's house in the college yard, facing Brafferton hall and at right angles to the college. Immediately behind the location lay the New Kent road. On July 31, 1732, construction was begun, the *Journal of the Meetings of the President and Masters* recording: "The foundation of the President's house at the College was laid, the President, [and the masters] Mr Dawson, Mr Fry, Mr Stith and Mr Fox, laying the first five bricks in order, one after another. The reason of the foundation being laid that day was, that Mr. Henry Cary, the Undertaker, had appointed his bricklayers to be ready that day, and that they could not proceed till the foundation was laid."[28]

Designed and built by Henry Cary, the president's house appeared as a charming small version of the governor's palace, minus cupola and flanking buildings. William Dawson wrote Bishop Gibson after the foundations were laid that the "common brick House" would cost £650 current money and would be completed by October 1733.

Though the college now prospered, it still had problems. In January 1735 Blair wrote Bishop Gibson:

Our College thrives in reputation, and numbers of Scholars, and handsome buildings, the chappel and the President's House making a great addition to the Conveniency and ornament of it. But we had a fatal blow of late in our revenues, the penny per pound, which K. Wm & Q. Mary gave for the suppt of the Presi and Masters being now so sunk that (through the fraud of the exporters to the W. Indies) it doth not yield above 100 lb per annum, instead of 400 it yielded formerly; our late General Assembly have provided a supply out of a more certain revenue; but it will be 18 months before we have any benefit of it; and in the meantime we shall run at least 100 [pounds] in debt. . . . If your Lop could think it proper to sound Sir R Walpole [the prime minister] or his Brother our Auditor on this subject, perhaps a favourable letter might be obtained [to release certain Crown funds in Virginia] for it is a fund solely apppropriated to this country.

Widowed and alone except for his servants, Blair lived his last ten years in the president's house. From his high-ceilinged bedroom he could look out through the vaulted limbs of oaks onto the college yard and see the coming and going of scholars and masters. With William Dawson as his faithful lieutenant, he shed many duties. William Byrd's secret diaries provide informal glimpses of the aging commissary, relaxing in the company of a few old friends.

Byrd himself, who at first disliked the commissary, was a frequent visitor when he came down the Charles City horsepath from Westover to attend the council and general court. The polished Black Swan of Westover differed from the Scotsman in many ways, but they shared a love for classical languages and literature. The commissary frequently invited his old antagonist by for a glass of sherry. Byrd described one of his visits on December 10, 1639: "About 10 Colonel [Robert] Bolling overtook me and came into the chariot and got to Williamsburg about 3. I put myself in order and walked to the Commissary's, where I ate a mutton chop and talked till 8, and then returned to my lodgings and put my house in order and prayed."[29]

The following April 17, Byrd wrote, "About 9 went to the Commissary's and from thence to court. . . ."[30] Three days later, on Sunday, Byrd went to Bruton church and "After church dined with the Commissary and ate chicken and bacon."[31]

The following June 9, Byrd walked to the commissary's house and "discoursed with him." Frequently Byrd breakfasted on chocolate at the commissary's. Blair occasionally read his verses to Byrd, including his account in Latin, titled "The Suppression of the late Rebellion" of Northern Neck slaves, which he presented to Spotswood in 1717 as ceremonial quitrent for the college land. Once, after spending the night at Blair's, Byrd confided to his diary: "I rose at 6 o'clock but neglected to say my prayers because Mr. Commissary kept me to hear a verse he had made for the College."[32]

Blair several times wrote Archbishop Wake and Bishop Gibson to request books for the meager college library. When John Randolph went to England in 1732 on his last mission for the college, he proposed to Robert Boyle's executors that £500 accumulated from the Brafferton bequest be spent for books.[33] With him he took a list of Blair's books, which were to go to the college on his death, to assure that duplicates were not purchased.[34]

Edmund Gibson, who served as bishop of London from 1723 to 1748, proved Blair's strongest ecclesiastical ally since Henry Compton had died in 1714. A fellow graduate with Governor Gooch of the Queen's College at Oxford, Gibson engaged the Reverend William Dawson after his ordination to help Blair build up the faculty of the college in Virginia.

Once Dawson came to William and Mary, the college drew steadily on Queen's for talent. William Stith, master of the grammar school from 1731 to 1737 and early historian of Virginia, was one of these. After Dawson succeeded Blair as president of William and Mary in 1743, three of its five professors were Queen's College graduates.[35] A later addition, who had probably also attended Queen's, was Thomas Dawson, who came to the college after his brother and became president in 1755.

The college showed a natural affinity with Oxford, which had retained an Anglican character throughout the Puritan Revolution. Harvard, on the other hand, had more contact with the more puritanical Cambridge.

Throughout Blair's life, enrollment at William and Mary remained small. On the college level fewer than 50 young men were enrolled under six masters when Blair died in 1743; in the same year Harvard had 104 undergraduates; while Yale, founded in 1701, had 78. Several dozen boys studied in William and Mary's grammar school, while a handful of Indians wrestled unhappily with English verbs and "vulgar mathematicks" in the Brafferton, which never achieved Boyle's objective of training evangelists to the redmen.[36]

A few scions of wealth like the sons and grandsons of Robert "King" Carter of Corotoman, continued to go to England for schooling. This was especially true of students of the law, who found no equivalent of the Inns of Court in the colonies. However, the chief deterrent to the college's growth was the scarcity of qualified matriculants in so rural a colony.

The training of Anglican clergy at William and Mary suffered from the fact that seminarians had to journey to the mother country after graduation to be ordained, there being no bishop in the colonies to perform the required "laying on of hands." Governor Gooch wrote the bishop of London in 1729, complaining of "the great want we are in of ministers, My Lord, many parishes being vacant."[37] Yet virtually nothing was done to alleviate this until about 1770, according to Bishop Meade, when the college offered a grant of £50 to any candidate going to England to enter holy orders. No English bishop ventured to Virginia in all these years.

It was not surprising that few of William and Mary's scholarships went to theological students during Blair's lifetime, for not many young men were interested in or qualified to pursue theological studies.[38] However, the caliber of those who did was notable, one churchman writing that "the best ministers were those educated at the college."[39]

When the Very Reverend George Berkeley, dean of Derry in Ireland and professor at Dublin University, visited Williamsburg in 1731, Governor Gooch urged him to choose William and Mary as the Anglican college for colonists that Berkeley had proposed to create in Bermuda. However, the dean persisted in his misdirected effort until the Crown declined to provide £20,000 for the project, whereupon Berkeley sailed morosely back to Ireland.[40]

The land fever prevalent in Blair's years in Virginia gave little ground to intellectual or cultural pursuits. As a result, the college's humanizing effects were not generally appreciated until the term of Governor Gooch, some three or four decades after its founding. In the rush to amass wealth in the tobacco colonies, it is understandable that few young men undertook training to read the sages of antiquity in Greek and Latin. The dry scholasticism of classical studies seemed hardly relevant to a society of such tone. Much of the past that Europeans accepted was being rejected by the new breed of Americans.

Nevertheless, Blair's college enriched the colonies by asserting the humanistic values of Christianity and the liberal arts in an acquisitive realm. It stood as a reminder that life offered more worthy reward than the mere storing up of riches. It was to elevate Virginian thought with its Lockean concepts of man's right to life, liberty, and immunity from political and religious dictation. On the foundations that the Scotsman helped to lay, Thomas Jefferson, John Marshall, and the great Revolutionary generation would erect a society of surpassing breadth and exalted purpose.

The chief service of the college in Blair's years was to train many of the colonies' ablest sons to share in the leadership of colonial America. Before William and Mary had opened its doors, these men were obliged to cross the Atlantic to study. Although plantation life produced men of considerable breadth, Virginia's first century had been the poorer for its neglect of scholarship, literature, and the arts. The college from its opening began to stimulate these.

Governor Gooch, an Oxonian, was impressed by what the college had become fifty years after its beginning. "If I tell you," he said to the burgesses shortly after Blair's death, "that there is not in any Part of the World, a College, where good Order, Decency and Discipline are better maintain'd, where God Almighty is more constantly and devoutly worshipp'd, and where greater Care is taken to train up young Students in the Rudiments of Religion, Loyalty, Science, and good Manners, and carrying them on towards Perfection, than in This, I am sure I should speak without Artifice or Flattery, and I dare say, within the Bounds of Truth."[41]

Against this judgment one must balance the darker verdict of an English visitor at about the same time. While he thought the college's "masters were men of great Knowledge and Discretion," the institution did not yet equal New England's. He observed that Virginia's youth were "pampered much more in Softness and Ease than their Neighbours more Northward."[42]

Those who inherited control of the college after Blair had no doubts about the value of the Scotsman's contribution. Wrote the Board of Visitors in 1768, "We know that during the Life of that pious and learned Man Mr. Blair whom we look upon as the Father of the College, the Affairs of it were conducted under this charter, such as it is, with Dignity and Honour to

Himself, and much to the Satisfaction and advantage of the colony in general."[43]

Such was the college that James Blair founded and directed for the last fifty years of his troublous life.

CHAPTER XIII

Blair's Changing Church
1721-1739

❧ In December 1739 James Blair invited evangelist George Whitefield, who had come to Williamsburg on a tour of the colonies, to preach in Bruton Parish Church. A large congregation gathered on Sunday, December 16. *The Virginia Gazette* had announced that Whitefield had arrived from Annapolis on his way to Georgia, where he planned to build an orphanage. Interest was high, for the *Gazette* had carried several accounts of the throngs of people who had heard the evangelist as he passed through New York, Pennsylvania, New Jersey, and Delaware.

As Governor Gooch and the council took their pews, the two ministers entered. Commissary Blair, nearing his eighty-fifth birthday, was bent with age. Whitefield, only twenty-five, was slim and erect. Although the young Oxonian was an Anglican, word had reached Virginia that his "enthusiastical" preaching offended orthodox churchmen. In New England he had been accused of disloyalty to Anglicanism, and South Carolina's commissary had forbidden him to minister to that colony. A *Gazette* dispatch of April 27 had reported that the vice chancellor of Oxford refused to let him preach there.

Morning prayers ended, Whitefield removed his surplice, put on his gown and hood, and mounted the pulpit. In obedience to the canons, he began: "Ye shall pray for Christ's holy Catholike Church" and for the king, queen, royal family, Privy Council, nobility, magistrates, commons, and "all those which have departed out of this life in the Faith of Christ."

Then, in a voice that rose to earnest crescendos and faded to whispers, the fervent enthusiast stated his text: "What think ye of Christ?"

Passionately, Whitefield sought to stir the congregation to a more active Christianity. It was far different from the learned homily that James Blair usually read from the pulpit. Some parishioners nodded in approval, but others felt such fervor was undignified. "His Extraordinary manner of Preaching gains him the Admiration and Applause of most of his hearers," William Parks equivocated later in his *Virginia Gazette*. To the impressionable, however, Whitefield's emotional appeal was potent.

Thus the Great Awakening reached Virginia. In the Age of Reason it was to speak up courageously against the moral complacency that was infecting the educated class. Whitefield's appearance was a portent of the contest in Virginia between Anglicanism and the awakening's evangelists: New Light Presbyterians, New Side Baptists, and a few reform-minded Anglican clergy who would begin to rally under the banner of John and Charles Wesley—the so-called Methodists.

Blair's welcome to Anglican Virginia earned Whitefield's gratitude. The evangelist wrote on December 15, 1739:

Paid my Respects to the Rev. Mr. Blair. His Discourse was Savoury, and such as tended to the Use of edifying. He received me with joy, asked me to preach, and Wished my Stay was to be longer. Under God he has been chiefly instrumental in raising a beautiful College in Williamsburgh, in which is a Foundation for about eight Scholars, a President, two Masters, and Professors in the several Sciences. Here the Gentlemen of Virginia send their Children; and, as far as I could learn by Enquiry, they are near in the same Order, and under the same Regulation and Discipline, as in our Universities at Home. The present Masters came from Oxford. Two of them I find were my contemporaries. I rejoice in seeing such a Place in America.[1]

Despite Whitefield's effectiveness, the Great Awakening was slow to penetrate Virginia. Its force was not felt until after Blair's death. Indeed, the denominational amity that the colony enjoyed during most of the Scotsman's commissariat was in happy contrast to credal conflicts in some of the colonies. This comity resulted in part from Virginia's indulgent treatment of dissenters, following the tolerant lead of King William and Queen Mary. It also owed something to the churchmanship of James Blair. In an age of combative creeds, the old Scotsman governed his church in the tolerant spirit of Laurence Charteris, of Gilbert Burnet, and of Henry Compton. Having felt the whiplash of persecution in Scotland, he was indulgent of religious differences, even while he deplored them.

Blair's permissive views thus enabled Virginia's Anglicans to give ground gracefully to the sects that new emigrants brought into the colony. As the Great Awakening spread, it undermined the monolith of the established church in Virginia. As a result, the Anglican monopoly that the Scotsman had found on its shores in 1685 was eroded during his ministry by the advent of Quakers, Presbyterians, Baptists, Lutherans, Moravians, and other sectarians.

The heterodoxy to the north of Virginia—Puritans in New England, Quakers and Germanic Protestants in Pennsylvania, Catholics in Maryland—all fed the stream of settlers flowing into the Valley of Virginia. From Pennsylvania, emigrants' wagons rumbled southward for the last several years of Blair's ministry, bearing hundreds of New Light Presbyterians to take up land on Virginia's frontier.

In this ethnic ferment, the placid Anglicans were pressed increasingly to accord to all denominations an equal status under law. Blair lived to see only the beginning of this disestablishmentarianism, but the outcome must have been clear. He had been dead five years when Samuel Davies, the strongest dissenter ever to stir Virginia, came from Pennsylvania and fired the souls of the Piedmont frontiersmen.

Actually, religious dissent had been spreading in Virginia since Blair's arrival, though it quickened after the Scotch-Irish began to arrive in 1720. This growth had been encouraged when the Whig Parliament, on the accession of King William and Queen Mary in 1689, passed the Toleration Act and revoked penalties previously imposed against dissenters. It was a liberal concession, and it opened the floodgates of nonconformism in the colony. One itinerant Presbyterian, Francis Makemie, soon extended his ministry from Virginia's Eastern Shore to Anglican parishes at Lynnhaven and on the Elizabeth River, near the future Norfolk. Others followed.

Makemie was an Old Light Presbyterian, whose university education and orthodox preaching made him acceptable to Anglicans. Having also trained in the law,[2] he petitioned Governor Nicholson for a proclamation of "freedom and liberty of conscience" in order that he might freely hold services of his own faith. Nicholson promised such liberty, but not until 1699 did the Tory governor proclaim the Toleration Act in effect in Virginia. While it let all sectarians except Romanists and Unitarians worship in the colony, it still did not permit them to hold office nor exempt them from paying taxes to support the established church. Such a half-measure, of course, would inevitably lead to further demands in the future.

The spread of dissenters after passage of the Toleration Act persuaded the Church of England to make more effort to minister to England's colonies. The Reverend Thomas Bray, who returned to London in 1701 after a troubled year as commissary in Maryland, in that year founded the Society for the Propagation of the Gospel in Foreign Parts with the help of Archbishop Tenison and Bishop Compton.[3] Supported by gifts, the S.P.G. in 1702 began sending missionaries to the American colonies. It also sent theological books and encouraged the baptism of Negroes and Indians. A similar Society for Promoting Christian Knowledge had been organized by Bray in 1697 to distribute religious literature. A third body, known as the Associates of Dr. Bray for Founding Clerical Libraries and Supporting Negro Schools, was created in 1723 and later operated classes for blacks in New York, Williamsburg, and several other towns.[4]

Though he was a latitudinarian churchman, the commissary was in his old age concerned by the infiltration of Quakers and Roman Catholics. He worried especially about the growth of the Society of Friends, whose adherents flocked into Virginia and congregated on the Eastern Shore and below the James in Norfolk, Nansemond, and Isle of Wight counties.

Addressing his clergy in 1705, the commissary warned against quarrels within Anglican ranks. "Pray remember," he told the ministers whom Nicholson had aligned against him, "that our divisions will be nuts to the adversaries of the Church, & of the profession of the ministry, the Atheists, the papists, the Quakers, the loose and ungodly livers & several others who have no great respect for our function. It requires our joint labours to withstand all these, but how glad will they be, to see that Zeal which used to be spent against them, now employed in worrying & devouring one another. . . ."[5]

Nowhere did James Blair reveal his conscientious nature more clearly than in his ministry. For fifty-eight years he rode the forest paths of Henrico, James City, and Bruton parishes, comforting the ill and the bereaved and preaching on Sundays and holy days. Occasionally, he was called from his bed at night to offer the church's last rites. A selection of his published sermons, delivered between 1707 and 1721, reveals his faith and his forthright pulpit style.

The collection of sermons was the result of a suggestion made by Bishop Compton to his clergy in 1707 that they should interpret for their parishioners the "whole mind of God so far as relates to things necessary for salvation." He suggested sermons against drunkenness during Advent, against blasphemy and profanity in Lent, and against Sabbath neglect from Easter to Whitsunday.[6] Blair's 117 sermons, which he wrote out and read—a practice deplored by "enthusiastical" preachers—were delivered over the course of years at Jamestown and Williamsburg. They were then published in 1722 in five volumes by J. Brotherton and J. Oswald of London.

The extensive work, underwritten by the Society for Promoting Christian Knowledge, was titled: *Our Saviour's Divine Sermon on the Mount, Contain'd in the Vth, VIth, and VIIth*

Chapters of St. Matthew's Gospel explained, And the Practice of it recommended in divers Sermons and Discourses.—By James Blair, M.A., Commissary of Virginia, President of William and Mary College, and Rector of Williamsburgh in that Colony.[7] It was to spread Blair's name throughout the English-speaking world. Outside Virginia he was better known for *Our Saviour's Divine Sermon on the Mount* than for any other achievement.

So successful was Blair's *Our Saviour's Divine Sermon on the Mount* that a second edition was printed in four volumes in 1740, this time with a preface by a well-known English theologian, Daniel Waterland.[8] Translated into Danish by Diderick de Thurah, the work was published in Copenhagen in 1761. In the British Isles and America it remained in Anglican libraries for a century. Bishop William Meade, who was born in Virginia when the commissary was still remembered by a few elders, recalled that Blair's work was familiar reading in his youth. He wrote:

As an accurate commentary on that most blessed portion of Scripture, I should think it can never have been surpassed. . . . His congregation was often composed of the authority and intelligence, fashion and wealth of the State, besides the youth of the College; nor does he spare any. I do not wonder that some of the Governors and great ones complained of his being personal. From many sources of information, I fear that swearing was most common among the gentlemen of that day, those high in office setting a bad example. . . .

He is throughout a faithful reprover of sin. He admits that there is little or no infidelity known in the Colony, as in England, but a great deal of wickedness. As to Church principles, as some call them, he was no Sacramentarian [one who believes that the sacraments are the symbolic rather than corporeal manifestation of Christ], and denounces Romanism in no measured terms, but is still conservative. . . .[9]

The Sermon on the Mount was a subject suited to Blair's pen. Taking successive texts from St. Matthew, the commissary described the Godly life and inveighed against drunkenness, fornication, adultery, and other sins. Reminding his hearers that Christ in his sermon to his disciples had laid down a revolutionary code, he urged them to live up to its severe demands. "Be ye doers of the word and not hearers only" was his implicit theme.

The author prefaced his volumes with the explanation that Virginia was free of the doctrinal controversies that beset England, "so that we have little or no Occasion in our Sermons to enter the Lists with *Atheists, Deists, Arians* or *Socinians*; nor are we much troubled with either *Popish* or *Protestant* Recusants. . . . Yet we find Work enough (and more than our few Labourers can accomplish) to encounter the usual Corruptions of Mankind, Ignorance, Inconsideration, practical Unbelief, Impenitance, Impiety, Worldlymindedness, and other common Immoralities. . . . I hope the Doctrine will be found Sound and Orthodox, and the Style plain for the Use of the meanest Hearers. . . ."[10]

Blair wrote that he composed the sermons for a "plain Country Audience without any Thoughts at that time of publishing them to the World." Though a few dealt with doctrine, the majority discussed Christian behavior, morality, and ethics. His censures of pride, anger, covetousness, and false witness were so much at odds with Blair's past behavior that those who knew him may have had difficulty reconciling the two. The preacher was on firmer ground when he attacked sins of the flesh; no one except Nicholson had ever accused him of sexual license, though he lived in a lustful age.[11]

The commissary denounced England's declining piety in an age of secular knowledge. Had not "God's Judgments by means of a Barbarous Enemy" (the Indians) lately fallen upon the settlers of the Carolinas? he asked. In his concern for the state of the church, he shared with John and Charles Wesley and with George Whitefield the hope for a spiritual awakening from the top to the bottom of English society: "There is such a general Neglect, or contempt of Religion; There is such an hardness and Impenetrableness of Heart; there is such a Dulness and absence of mind as to all religious performances; there is such a Treachery of memory; and, in short, such an Incorrigibleness of Life and Manners; that we have nothing almost left but the bare Shell and Outside of Religion, and are for the greatest part utter Strangers to the inward Power and Life of it. Not to speak of the Works of Darkness, which are as freely committed among Christians, as if they believed nothing of Heaven or Hell, or God or Devil."

Like the Wesleyans, Blair believed these faults could be corrected within the Church of England. He agreed with dissenters' criticism that the established church suffered from "all the profane, worldly, and atheistical people who are only nominal Christians, but really of no religion at all." He also admitted that many came to church who "do it no real service, but bring a Scandal and Disgrace upon it." Nevertheless, the church merited support. Though the ship leaked, it was sound enough to "make a good Voyage to Heaven."

The sermons also defended the status quo against demands for reform. No longer did Blair oppose political privilege and the rule of wealth as he had twenty years earlier. He denied that it was "every man's Business to reform Abuses and corruptions, not only in their own Station (which would have been right,) but by invading the Stations of others, magistrates, Legislators, Princes, and Governors; which is the High-way, instead of Peace, to drive all Things to Anarchy and Confusion."

On the contrary, Blair wrote, it was God's intention that every man "keep within his own Sphere, and be not a Busybody in other men's matters." If relief were not gained by petition, "private men must wait patiently, and neither stir up Discontents against the Government, nor flee to Arms, or any other irregular Methods of Redress." How the "old Combustion" had changed!

Opposing democratic reform, Blair argued that "bad men mightily outnumber the good, and consequently in all Societies are able to over-top them in Power and Strength." The righteous would be overpowered "if Matters came to be transacted either by the way of Force or Tumult, or if votes come to be number'd instead of Reasons weigh'd, good Men are in Election to come badly off." He warned that the Golden Rule—"Do unto others as you would have them do unto you"—did not imply equality between "superiors and inferiors." The "levelling principle," he observed, "has no Countenance either from this, or from any other Text in Scripture; and would occasion all manner of Anarchy and confusion in the World."

Yet privilege entailed responsibility, Blair conceded. Masters should treat servants and slaves kindly. Those who "by ill usage, overworking, or over correcting" caused servants to die were guilty of murder in God's sight. No qualities "were more frequently or more strongly pressed in the Christian Religion than Love and Charity."

Our Saviour's Divine Sermon on the Mount did not attack slavery. Though the author advocated that servants be baptized and treated kindly, he accepted the institution and owned slaves at Richneck and at the college. York County records for 1723 listed him as a master of eight "servants," who were probably Negro slaves.[12] Like most English clergymen of his period, he tolerated the prevailing practice, though with the reservation that masters must Christianize their servants as they acquired the biblical knowledge that Anglican practice required. As his bishop had directed, he enjoined masters to instruct Negroes "in the Knowledge of the [Apostles'] Creed, *Lord's Prayer*, and *Ten Commandments*."[13] Like most Europeans of his period, he held slavery to be preferable to the savagery of Africa's tribal wars.

One sermon cautioned that Christians should "Lay not up . . . treasures upon earth," for nothing was "more contrary to the Spirit of Christianity than Covetousness, and the inordinate Cares of the World." Wealth should not be enjoyed in "a narrow, pinching or penurious Temper" but generously with family and friends and "to do good in works in Piety and Charity, and in promoting the public Good of the world."

The commissary examined other faiths and pointed out what he felt to be their errors. The Presbyterian concept of predestination was "a very strange conception of God" and contrary to the scriptures, "which in a most serious Manner, by precepts, promises, threatenings, Exhortation, and Expostulations press to our duty, upon the Hopes of Heaven and Fear of Hell." Deists erred in thinking that man could comprehend God and enter heaven without effort. Catholics had practiced "cruel and barbarous methods of massacres, inquisitions, and persecutions." Enthusiasts, like Quakers, "usurp the Liberty of following the unguarded Dictates of the infallible Spirit of God." Any preacher disparaging biblical authority and substituting his own judgment "strikes at the Root of all Revealed Religion, and opens a door for the utter Destruction of it."

Bishop Meade, writing a century after Blair, characterized the commissary as a "moderate Arminian,"[14] or follower of Jacobus Arminius. This sixteenth-century Dutch theologian preached that human freedom was compatible with divine sovereignty; that eternal life was conditioned on individual behavior rather than predestined by God; that Christ's atonement on the cross was for all of mankind; and that none could achieve Christian regeneration except through the working of the Holy Spirit. With Arminius, Blair rejected the Calvinist beliefs so evident in Presbyterianism. His views largely coincided with the doctrine of the Wesleys.

Although Blair in 1722 rejoiced in the orthodoxy of Virginians, he lived to see the philosophy of deism win influential adherents among faculty and students of his college. To these freethinkers, influenced by the Age of Reason, man's intellect alone seemed sufficient to justify his belief in a supreme being, without need for biblical support. Even while Blair was writing *Our Saviour's Divine Sermon on the Mount,* colonists like Benjamin Franklin and Sir John Randolph, who had studied law in England, were professing deistic views. Writing to the bishop of London in 1737, Blair said Randolph "was a good friend to the College and Country," but he added, "I can't say to the Church; for he has some wild, dissenting, and scarce Christian opinions."[15]

While Blair's sermons appealed to Anglican churchmen, they were neither brilliant nor very readable. They show that Blair's strength lay in his clarity and force. The fact that he had carried through so arduous a literary labor also indicates that the old man had achieved a new serenity. Was it the security of entrenched position? A sense of resignation as death bore away his dear ones? Whatever the reason, James Blair seems to have come to terms with himself after he forced Governor Spotswood's removal in 1722.

Because the Scotsman filled Virginia's most prestigious parish for so long, he influenced many ministers who came after him.

His moderate Arminian beliefs, his forceful preaching, and his Protestant simplicity were all part of Blair's bequests to the church he governed. It proved an enduring legacy.

Of Blair's sermons, the Right Reverend William Stevens Perry, late historiographer of the Protestant Episcopal Church of the United States, wrote: "As specimens of practical divinity couched in scholarly language, and enforced with earnestness and power, they are worthy of commendation."[16]

Literary historian Moses Coit Tyler found Blair's sermons admirable for their sound reasoning. "The thought is fairly wrought out," he wrote, "the divisions are sharp and formal: each discourse is short and to the point: The tone of the author's mind is moderate, judicial, charitable, catholic: he is not brilliant: his style is smooth, simple, honest, earnest: there is no diplomacy: he is trying to make people good."[17]

In publishing Blair's sermons, his friend Thomas Bray, former commissary of Maryland, made financial arrangements that did not satisfy the Scotsman.[18] On December 1, 1722, Secretary Henry Newman of the Society for Promoting Christian Knowledge wrote from London to Governor Drysdale in Virginia: "The 5 vols of Mr Commissary's Excellent Sermons are just now finish'd, but I question whether Dr. Bray will be able to send any bound Copies over by this Ship."[19]

Bray wrote to S.P.C.K. members that sets of Blair's works would be distributed to parishes, together with Archbishop of Canterbury William Wake's *Commentary on the Catechism* and Bishop of Salisbury Gilbert Burnet's *Exposition of the Catechism*.[20] In a letter of January 1, 1723, Newman wrote to Drysdale: "Pray give my most humble service to . . . good Mr. Commissary, whose excellent sermons I am so much pleased with that I think that Sunday ill spent in which I don't read one of them."[21]

Newman reported to Blair in 1724 that sales of his book were slow.

If it be ask'd why Mr. Blair's Sermons don't go off, they say it is because the author is unknown & therefore tho his sense is good, his work must be undervalu'd, but do men of the world talk at this

Rate when they are to buy good wine or anything else they want[?] Will they not go to a Cottage wch is good rather than to a Pallace wch is not so[?] 'Tis true the Name of a thing at its first setting out may help something, yet that alone won't carry it through the world if the intrinsic worth of it don't recomend it. In one word, the Booksellers have made themselves so necessary to an author by an association among them that they are really Masters of the means for countermining any Interest that interferes with theirs. . . .[22]

Blair continued to be dissatisfied with his book's sale and in 1725 wrote to his old friend Stephen Fouace and to Secretary Newman at the S.P.C.K. about it. To this, Newman replied:

> Midle Temple
> 10 Decr 1725
>
> Revd Sir,
> Good Mr Fouace and I received your Letters about treating with Dr Bray for a surrender of his Right to the Copy of your Sermons, but either the Dr being out of Town, or Mr Fouace's Indisposition at Chelsea (or that he can't bear the Motion of a Coach, nor the Chillness of the Water) has prevented our Meeting upon it . . . when he consulted Mesrs Brotherton and other Booksellers what they would give him for the Privilege of an Impression, they scrupled to give him so much as 25 Setts of Copies, whereas he has obliged himself to give you that Number and 50 pounds beside. That the Booksellers Alledge the World is overdone with Sermons, so that the Works of the greatest Men among us will hardly bear a second Impression, and instanced in AB [archbishop of York] Sharp's, Bp Bull, Bp Smalridge, and Dr. Maynard's Sermons as what lie upon Stalls to this Day and never came to a second Impression.
> That notwithstanding these Discouragemts and the Loss he has already suffer'd, the Dr has so great an opinion of your Performance that if the 50 £ Premium for the second edit. be remitted, he will, God sparing his Life, cause a 2d Impression to be made next Summer of 750 or 1000 Setts, and give you the 25 Setts as stipulated in the Contract. . . .[23]

Blair attempted to straighten out the matter with the S.P.C.K. when he went to England in 1726 to meet with Archbishop Wake, Bishop Gibson, and Stephen Fouace and to draw up rules to govern the college. In June 1727 the seventy-two-year-old commissary met with Dr. Bray in London to discuss accounts and to consider how *Our Saviour's Divine Sermon on the Mount* might be more widely sold.[24] Evidently they succeeded, for a new edition was printed eighteen years later. It was the last meeting of the two venerable missionaries.

Although he remained commissary until his death, Blair's ecclesiastical authority was never strengthened. When Edmund Gibson succeeded John Robinson[25] as bishop of London in 1723, Blair wrote abject letters asking to be reappointed. On one occasion he sent Gibson six Virginia hams by the ship *Spotswood*. He warned Gibson that Virginia still had ne'er-do-well clergymen. However, he argued, "I believe the Countrey in general is satisfied that my being in that Office is a considerable restraint upon them, and helps to keep things from growing much worse."[26] Two years later he was still pleading for reappointment so that he might discipline two unworthy ministers.[27]

Gibson did not withhold Blair's appointment for lack of confidence but because he was unsure of his authority. He had first intended as bishop of London to name one or more suffragan bishops overseas.[28] Dr. Bray had endorsed Blair for the first of these appointments, writing to Gibson: "If the President [Blair] should be made the Bishop, He will have this peculiar advantage, that the Candidates for Holy Orders will be Persons educated under his own Eyes and Care and Direction in their Studies. In my humble opinion the President at this Time (and it will be a Great Advantage to Sett out well at First) is in every Respect the Best Qualified of anyone Living that can be found, to take such a Charge upon him, whether we consider his Learning as a Divine, or his Sagacity in Discipline and Government. If I may Venture to Speak my own Thoughts, having known him and his conduct, near Thirty years, I know none so fit."[29]

The fact that nothing came of this proposal was again the result of governmental inaction. When Bishop Gibson asked the Privy Council to define his legal authority in the colonies, he found that he had virtually none. After petitioning King George I, he was at last regranted the minimal control that his predecessors had exercised but nothing more.[30]

Though handicapped by his lapse of authority, Blair assured Gibson repeatedly of his obedience to the bishop's instructions.

"Bishop Compton Directed me to make no further use of my commission than to keep the Clergy in order," he explained to Gibson, "so that I have never pretended to set up any spiritual court for the laity; tho' there are enormities among them that want to be redress'd, & as to the Clergy, unless where they are notoriously Scandalous, I have found it necessary to content myself with admonitions; for if I lay them aside by suspension, we have no unprovided Clergymen to put in their place."[31]

While Blair awaited good news from London, situations arose requiring advice from his bishop: Blair wrote to Gibson on May 13, 1724:

We have at present 2 Ministers (Mr. Thos Bailey & Mr. Jno Worden) so very scandalous for drunkenness & fighting & quarreling publicly, in their drink, that many grievous complaints are brought to me against them & indeed the country rings of the Scandal given by them, & I am censured hard for not calling them to account, as I should certainly have done, if my commission had not ceased, upon the death of your Lordship's predecessor. I had proceeded no further than admonitions & threatenings & they were more bold in their extravagancies than ever, bragging that there is no power in the Country to meddle with them. As soon as my commission comes, I intend to make a visitation of their Churches, & if the Scandals are clearly prov'd, (as I doubt they will), to proceed to Suspension of their licence. . . . I have never made but 2 examples of this kind in all the time that I have been Comr, which is now 34 years, and indeed for want of clergymen we are obliged to bear with those we have, much more than we should do, if we had others to supply the vacancies.[32]

In the same vein, the commissary declared, "I choose rather to lean to the gentle than the severe side, yet certainly the Behaviour of some men is so flagrant that we had better be without ministers than to be served with such as are scandals to the Gospel."[33]

Blair also described to his bishop a scandal that illustrates the loose sex morality he combated throughout his ministry: "There is a gentlewoman lately brought to bed of a bastard child, by her own brother [half-brother] of the father's side. I should be glad of your Lordship's direction what to do in this case; for (by advice from Bishop Compton), I have only made use of my commission to keep the Clergy in order without medling with the laity."[34] How the commissary disposed of this Delphic dilemma is not revealed.

Lieutenant Governor Drysdale at length wrote to the bishop to urge Blair's reappointment, praising ". . . Your Lordship's Commissary on whose truth and integrity I assure your Lordshipp may entirely depend. He has discharged that trust with an unblemished reputation under the Commission of many of your Lordshipp's predecessors, and to their great satisfaction. Yet this behaviour cannott secure him from the assaults of ill tongues, whose Malignity brings innocence itself into Suspicion, and makes the truth difficult to bee known by those who have [been] prepossessed by itt."[35]

The commissary had ten parishes vacant in 1724, and he asked Bishop Gibson to send more ministers:

The livings are Settled by law at 16,000 lbs of Tobacco per annum, besides Glebes & perquisites, & this in the sweet scented Parishes is better than £100 Sterlg; & in all the rest about £80. The ministers, where they are sober & good husbands, live very comfortably. One thing is a great discouragement to them (& no doubt hinders Clergymen from coming into this Country), that very few of them are inducted, but are kept upon agreements with vestries in precarious circumstances. This has run on so long by the connivance of our Governors, that tho' our Present Lieut. Govr Major Drysdall is of himself very willing to redress it, yet he thinks it not prudent to do it without an instruction from his Majesty to that purpose. . . .[36]

Disturbed by the odor of moral decay that wafted from the colonies, Bishop Gibson sent to James Blair seven "Queries to be answered by Persons who were Commissaries to my Predecessor." With these went another questionnaire to be answered by parish ministers. The replies from Virginia reflect the difficult role of the established church in that pioneer land.

Of the forty-eight parishes, all had churches except the new county of Spotsylvania, whose church was under construction. Only thirty-three had ministers. Blair described five of the vacant parishes as "Sweet Scented" for the type of tobacco they produced and characterized the other ten as "Oranocco" parishes for their coarser leaf. Of twenty-eight clergy replying, the average stay in Virginia was twenty-five years and the average service in one parish twenty-one years. Despite the unwillingness of vestries to induct their ministers, few had been turned out. Parishes averaged 20 miles square and 150 families.

So scattered a population in Virginia obviously made impossible the type of leadership exercised by bishops and clergy in England. Blair admitted that he no longer visited each church yearly[37] or even called a clergy convention except on accession of a new monarch or a bishop of London. "This was found inconvenient especially when the Country is in Parties, for, or against a Governor," he explained.[38]

When Bishop Gibson finally reappointed Blair in 1729, he assigned him added control of Bermuda, but Blair persuaded him to rescind it. "That island lyes so out of my way," the commissary pled, "that it will but decieve Your Lop to depend on me for it." He suggested that Gibson instead appoint Dean Berkeley, who had come to the colonies from Ireland the year before in hopes of founding a college in Bermuda.

The commissary suggested three measures to strengthen the church in Virginia: (1) obtain more qualified ministers from England, Ireland, and from the College of William and Mary; (2) improve "the precarious circumstances upon which they hold their livings;" and (3) require a parish to pay its usual salary when vacant and devote the money for other parish purposes. He reported that he knew only four Virginia ministers who had been inducted. The rest were hired from year to year, with these consequences:

1st. It discourages the better sort of Clergymen who hear of it, from adventuring into this Country. 2nd. The Glebes are much neglected & unimproved to what they would be if the Ministers were at a certainty as to their possession of them. 3rd. The Precariousness is a great disservice to the ministers in the business of their marriage, whereas if they were well settled, they might expect creditable matches & good portions with their wives. Now if they marry & settle at all they must be contented with poor bargains, & consequently are able to give but mean education & portions to their children in their life time. . . . This same precariousness is a great restraint upon the Minister's freedom in reproving of vice, either in public or in private, being afraid to disoblige any of the gentlemen of their vestry. . . .[39]

Blair's testimony was confirmed by Governor Drysdale, who in a memorandum with Blair's reply, wrote: "I am of the same opinion with Mr. Comy as to the remedies & . . . will readily comply with what instructions your Lordship shall procure in those affairs. . . ." Yet the correctives would require more revenue, and neither Englishmen nor Virginians were willing to pay higher taxes to support a larger religious establishment.

The church continued to ignore the plight of Negro slaves despite efforts by Bishop Gibson to extend its ministry to them. The commissary frequently referred to the problem. Writing on May 14, 1731, he told the bishop:

> The feared insurrection of the Negroes . . . is now all over, and I can not learn there was any more in it but some loose talk. But it is certain that notwithstanding all the precaution we Ministers took to assure them that Baptism altered nothing as to their servitude or other temporal circumstances; yet they were willing to feed themselves with a secret fancy that it did, and that the King designed that all Christians should be made free. I can't say but that this notion made them flock much faster to Baptism than otherwise they would have done. I took care to baptize none but such as repeated to me first the [Apostles'] Creed, and the Lord's prayer and the ten Comandments, and promised to amend their lives particularly as to several Unchristian practices that are among them. And I believe the same course was followed by other Ministers.

The commissary emphasized that slaves misunderstood baptism to mean freedom: "But all this notwithstanding, there was a general rumour among them that they were to be set free. And when they saw nothing came of it, they grew angry and saucy, and met in the night time in great numbers, and talked of rising; and in some places of choosing their leaders. But by patrouling, and whipping all that were found abroad at unseasonable hours, they quietly broke all this design, and in one County, where they had been discovered to talk of a general cutting off of their Masters, there were four of the Ring-leaders hanged. So now all is very quiet, as indeed there is a general quietness and contentment in the Country. . . ." The tragic dilemma continued as long as slavery survived.

In spite of the rights to worship accorded to non-Anglicans in Virginia after 1699 (Blair reassured Gibson in 1724 that "the

English toleration of Dissenters takes place here"),[40] Quakers, Baptists, and Presbyterians remained dissatisfied with their status. Taxed to support the established church, they could not worship entirely as conscience dictated. Instead, they had to first obtain permission from their county court to hold service in a house or barn.

Evangelists like Whitefield pleased them, but Anglican bishops discouraged this evangelism as a threat to parish ministers. As dissenters grew stronger, so did their objections to supporting the Anglican clergy. One of the Presbyterians' reasons for seeking disestablishment of the church in Virginia was to be "exempted from all taxes for the support of any church watsoever."[41]

Thus, as Virginia grew in Blair's long life, its middle-of-the-road church was assailed by both the zealous and the godless. Yet it had accomplished much good. Its educated clergy had raised the standards of life in the tobaccolands around the Chesapeake. Adhering, although imperfectly, to the ideal that the godly and educated should govern, it had begun to create a conception of leadership that would produce a Richard Bland and a Peyton Randolph—both students of Blair's. Service on vestries trained Virginians for public life and stiffened resistance to excessive royal power. Around the church and the college there developed a dedication to the public good that was to flower in the Revolution.

Whatever Blair's faults, his exaltation of Christian and humanistic values enriched the spirit of America. The Scottish commissary cast a shadow far taller than his size.

A Time to Reap
1739-1743

ᛓ Old age can be a triumph of the spirit or a tragedy of failing faculties. For James Blair, there was no let-up as he reached the biblical three-score years and ten. Despite deafness and debility, he clung jealously to his powers. His obsessive will to rule kept him active until his death.

These closing years were Blair's most serene. Like a ship that has sailed through stormy seas to reach its home port, the old man approached the end of his earthly voyage with composure. Always a detached figure, he had made few close friends in his years in Virginia. By the year 1726, when Drysdale died after four years in the governor's palace, most of Blair's family and friends lay buried at Jamestown or Williamsburg.

Lacking children of his own, the old man had fixed his affections on his nephew John, who had married Mary Monro, the daughter of his old ally John Monro, Jr., and on their children. In John Blair's household, near Williamsburg's center,[1] James Blair frequently supped and talked politics. The younger Blair was an able and agreeable man who held a succession of offices through his uncle's influence, including the bursarship of the college, and succeeded him on the council in 1745.[2] After the death of Archibald Blair, James and Johnny Blair (as William Byrd called him) were business partners in Dr. Blair's Store, which had been organized before 1705 by the Blairs and Philip Ludwell II.[3]

During the last sixteen years of James Blair's life, Virginia enjoyed unprecedented good feeling under the governorship of William Gooch. Blair was in London for the college when King George II named Gooch in 1727 to succeed Drysdale as lieutenant governor. The affable Gooch became well acquainted with the commissary on the long voyage to America,[4] and Blair wrote glowingly to the bishop of London on his arrival in Williamsburg: "He is a sober, serious and well tempered man, obliging and courteous to all, never swears, nor gives way to passions, which examples no doubt will do a great deal of good."[5]

As for the good-natured Gooch, he was privately less rapturous about Blair. "I . . . rule without any particular favourite," he reported to his brother from the governor's palace, "which is not liked by the Commissary who used to Govern. He is an unaccountable spark, hated abominably by all men but his countrymen, and when he can't advise nor direct, he's inclined to perplex, but as yet we are good Friends and I intend to keep it so if I can, which will be difficult."[6]

Even when Blair intrigued against him, the urbane Gooch kept his temper. "The Commissary is a very vile old FFellow," the governor wrote his brother, the bishop of Norwich, "but he does not know that I am sensible of it, being still in appearance good Friends; the best Policy will be to kill him with kindness, but there is no perplexing device within his reach, that he does not throw in my way. Unless he has all and does all, he is not satisfied, and if he did, very few in this country besides himself would be so."[7]

Gooch briefly toyed with the thought of deposing Blair as

president of the college. In the same letter he wrote that "there is no good school in the Colledge, which from its foundation was intended by the Commissary to make a penny of, so that I begin to talk of sending him home, if you approve of it." Evidently Thomas Gooch rejected the idea, for the governor made no further move.

Although Gooch believed Virginia's vestries should induct ministers for life, he was wise enough not to inflame the parishes against him as Spotswood had done. A faithful but discreet Anglican, he advised the bishop of London a month after his arrival in Virginia that he would proceed cautiously in reforming the church: "The time is not yet come in which it will be proper to propose the Inducting of ministers: in the mean season I am preparing bye degrees the Country for it; and am making Friends & forming the best methods to introduce it; and I am not without hopes."[8]

Nevertheless, William Gooch never saw fit to press the issue during his twenty-two years as governor of Virginia. Evidently he came to view the clergy's situation as Robert Beverley had in 1705: "yet are they very rarely turn'd out, without some great Provocation; and then if they have not been abominably scandalous, they immediately get other Parishes: For there is no Benefice whatsoever in that Country that remains without a Minister if they can get one, and no qualified Minister, ever yet return'd from that Country, for want of preferment."[9]

Despite Gooch's private misgivings about the commissary, he humored him and kept his goodwill. In this period of growth, abetted by Gooch's skillful leadership, the old factionalism in the council subsided and Blair was less contentious. Except for his occasional authorship of council papers, he was content to sit and let younger men debate measures before voting his "Yea" or "Nay." Often he dozed at the council table.

"Though much failed in all parts of activity," he wrote the bishop of London in his eightieth year, he continued to lead the clergy "both by admonition & example."[10] Three years later, Charles Bridges, an English portrait painter who had come to Virginia in 1735 and was active in church affairs, wrote of Blair's infirmities to Bishop Gibson:

Hanover, in Virginia, Oct. 19, 1738

My Good Bishop,

... your excellent design of instructing the Negroes here according to the method proposed, and pressing the Commissary to follow you and solicit the Governor and his interest ... will, to my great concern, I fear come to nothing. The Commissary and I grow in years, and the world hangs heavy upon us. I am rous'd sometimes and then call upon him, and then he is asleep perhaps & answers nothing, & I am ready to sleep too. Would to God your powerful voice would sound in our ears to get up and be doing a little more good, while there is time and opportunity. . . .[11]

The ancient commissary had become an embarrassment to his bishop, for new clergy needed stronger leadership than he could now give. One of them, the Reverend Anthony Gavin, a former Roman Catholic who served a frontier parish in Goochland, wrote Dr. Gibson that he regularly preached at three churches, while four clerks read the services at his seven other sites. His views typified the sentiment of frontiersmen that the Established Church was not concerned for their welfare. Although Gavin had recently baptized 229 whites, 172 Negroes, 15 Quakers, and two "Annabaptists,"[12] he was discouraged

to see Episcopacy so little regarded in this colony, and the cognizance of spiritual affairs left to the Governor & council by the laws of this colony. And next to this, it gives me a great deal of uneasiness to see the greatest part of our Brethren taken up in farming and buying slaves which in my humble opinion is unlawful for any Christian and in particular for a clergyman. . . .

The Revd Mr. Blair, I really believe, is a good man, and has been a good minister, but he can not act in his commission as is required, & I have always wish'd that your Lordship would send us a Deputy Commissary a Clergyman of known zeal, courage, & resolution, & such as could redress some great neglects of duty in our brethren, & bring Episcopacy to be better regarded, for even some of the clergymen born and educated in this colony are guilty in this great point. . . .[13]

Blair devoted less effort each year to his role as commissary.[14] He spent his energies instead on the college and on his inescapable functions at Bruton Parish, assisted, after his hearing and his voice began to fail, by William Dawson and his brother, Thomas. No longer was he able to go on horseback to visit other parishes. He indulged his taste for Greek and Latin authors and dozed before the hearth in the president's house. Occasionally he bought or sold a piece of land.[15] He had become a venerated elder, living above mundane daily concerns. His portrait, painted in these years, presumably by his friend Charles Bridges, shows him with solemn mien, his left arm resting on an open Greek testament, alongside the mythological phoenix rising from the ashes of the 1705 fire. The college stands behind him.[16]

"I am glad to hear the Venerable Mr. Commissary Blair is still living to do the good his heart is always inclin'd to," wrote Secretary Henry Newman of the Society for Promoting Christian Knowledge to a Virginia cleric in 1741.[17] To Blair, Newman wrote:

London, 3 March, 1742/43

Revd & Dear Sr:

I heartily rejoyce that it has pleas'd God to prolong your life to do so much good as you have in America, a large field where a Gent of yr. experience & learning was necessary to lay a wise & good foundation for Posterity; I am witness of many things that you have done with Success for the benefit of the Colony & College where you preside. May it please God still to continue you to be that great Blessing you have many years past been. . . .

I heard abt. 3 weeks ago that our Old friend Mrs. Drysdale [widow of the previous governor] was well at Cheswick, but not without the infirmities of Age as must be expected at our time of life. May God fit us for that State which is exempt from all infirmities & give us the hapiness of meeting in the Mansions of the Blessed is the sincere wish of

Revd. & Dr. Sr.[18]
[Henry Newman]

Newman was pleased that Blair had lived to see a second edition of his sermons, "notwithstanding the embarrassments which attended it." He referred to difficulties in selling the first printing and the consequent delay in Blair's receipt of royalties.

To the bishop of London, Blair frequently referred to his approaching death. In a letter introducing William Stith, a William and Mary graduate who went to England in 1735 to be ordained, he concluded: ". . . I beg your Lop's Benediction and prayers, particularly that I may make an happy exit, being now full of years and infirmities." The next year he observed: "It is a great comfort to me that I shall leave the college under the protection of so good friends."

Aspirants for Blair's offices became active as his strength waned. An attorney named Wagener let it be known that his father, a minister in England, would like to become commissary, but Gooch pooh-poohed the idea to the bishop of London. He had inquired and found the elder Wagener "much better remembered as a bad painter, than a Divine. But if we here might be allowed to name, our Philosophy Professor Mr. [William] Dawson, is the man."

He listed the Oxonian's qualifications, adding, "And I make no question, on the first occasion after the Commissary's Death, he will be unanimously Elected President of the College, and have his Parish." Dawson's appointment would "do the Church and Religion good service [in Virginia], which doth not yet know what a visitation means," Gooch wrote.[19]

Blair's last years saw him elevated at the age of eighty-five to the role of temporary governor of Virginia. When Colonel Robert Carter of Corotoman died in 1732, Blair became the senior member of the twelve-man council, entitling him to preside in the absence of the governor. In the case of prolonged gubernatorial lapse, custom would also entitle Blair as president of the council and commander-in-chief of Virginia to a salary and perquisites to some £1,200 a year.[20]

To the chagrin of Gooch and of Blair's younger colleagues, such a vacancy did occur in 1740, when Colonel Gooch was obliged to lead Virginia's troops in the British expedition to dislodge the Spanish at Cartagena, as Alexander Spotswood died just as the troops were to sail from Chesapeake Bay. This was the War of Jenkins' Ear, which England entered in October 1739 in the effort to expel Spain from Florida, liberate the Spanish West Indies, and capture the key cities in South America, such as Cartagena.

Byrd, who was next in seniority to Blair, attempted to supersede the deaf old commissary on the grounds that a clergyman was ineligible to govern, but the Scotsman reacted with savage vigor. He invoked an "old standing instruction," never revoked by governor or council, that conferred the office on whoever was senior in the absence of the king's appointee. Blair insisted he had "not the least desire or hope that the Presidentship will fall in my time," but he thought the standing instruction "well contrived to keep all things easy and to give a general content."[21] The commissary prevailed.

But Blair found Governor Gooch reluctant to part with his salary during a campaign that he expected to be brief. Gooch's wife and family would continue to reside in the governor's palace,[22] and their establishment must be maintained. After negotiating with Blair, His Excellency grudgingly agreed to pay his stand-in at the rate of £600 a year. "Being very unwilling to enter into a Controversy with the Governour," Blair wrote his Bishop, "I chose rather to make it up with loss to myself."[23] Gooch confided to his brother in England that the Scotsman was a hard bargainer.[24]

Fortunately for President Blair, no Indians or pirates threatened his eight-month governorship. He found no occasion to convene the assembly and could report to the Board of Trade that all was "peace and quietness."[25] William Byrd, who was nineteen years younger, painted a pathetic picture of the old man, now too deaf to preside over the general court as was the governor's duty. "This I am forct to perform in his stead," Byrd wrote, "being next Oars, while he now and then nods in his chair." He thought Virginians a "little dissatisfied with being Governd by an Ecclesiastick, and the rather because of his Great age & Infirmity," but he observed that Blair's mind remained clear.[26]

Among the licenses which Blair signed as president of the council was one to nineteen-year-old Edmund Pendleton to practice law in county courts, which was issued April 25, 1741.

When acting governor Blair was host at the annual king's birthday ball in the Capitol in October 1740, Byrd attended and conceded that "the President entertained well."[27] The old man kept a sharp eye on the government and made twice yearly reports to the Board of Trade. To able young William Dawson he entrusted most of his college and parish duties.

When William Gooch returned from South America in July 1741, Blair declared himself glad to retire from "Company and business."[28] Virginians warmly welcomed the wounded warrior, even though Cartagenians had stood off England's three-month siege and forced her troops to retire without attaining their object. "The Virginians were mightely rejoyced at my Return, Day and Night firing Guns, Bonfires and Illuminations," Gooch wrote his brother, though "the good Commissary kept believing he should never see me again."[29]

Blair and Gooch were briefly at odds over the appointment of a naval officer for the York River, the governor having proposed to name his son, and Blair favoring another man. However, this impasse was resolved by the untimely death of young William Gooch in 1742.

Despite his advanced age, Blair still discharged ceremonial duties of commissary. He wrote Bishop Gibson to recommend a young applicant who was about to set sail for England to apply for holy orders:

Williamsburg, February 19, 1741–2

MY LORD:—This comes by an ingenious young man, Mr. James Maury, who though born of French parents, has lived with them in this county of Va., since he was a very young child. He has been educated at our college and gave a bright example of diligence in his studies and of good behavior in his morals. He has made good proficiency in the study of Latin and Greek authors, and has read some systems of philosophy and divinity. I confess as to this last I could wish he had spent more time in it before he had presented himself for Holy Orders, that his judgment might be better settled in the serious study of the Holy Scriptures and other books both of practical and polemical Divinity. But his friends have pushed him on too fast. He looks, too, much younger than he is, being of a brood that are of low stature.

He will be, by the time this comes to your Lordship's hands, about 24 years, having been born about the 1st April, 1718. I doubt not your Lordship encouraging our Virginia students. It is a great advantage that one have them from their infancy. They generally prove very solid good men.

My time here must be very short, being in my 87th year.

JAS. BLAIR[30]

As Blair predicted, James Maury proved a worthy minister. In his Latin school he was to teach Thomas Jefferson, Dabney Carr, and James Madison—later the president of William and Mary and first bishop of Virginia. From his parish in Louisa County, Maury in 1762 brought the "Parson's Cause" litigation in which Patrick Henry won fame.

The commissary did not long survive. Death stilled his tired heart on April 18, 1743, after a rupture had become gangrenous. Presumably he died in his bedroom in the president's house, probably attended by Dr. George Gilmer, a graduate of Edinburgh who had married his niece Harrison Blair and was at that time practicing medicine and maintaining an apothecary shop and store in Williamsburg.[31] So strong was his constitution that he lived ten days after doctors thought his death was imminent.[32] The wary Gooch, soon to be knighted for long service to his king, sent the news to England: "Old Blair died last moneth in his 88 Year, and to the great comfort of his Nephew, his Heir, has left £10,000 behind him. A Rupture he has had above 40 Years concealed from every Body but one Friend, mortified and killed him. If his Belly had been as sound as his head and Breast, he might have lived many years longer."[33]

Blair's wealth, which had aroused envy in his lifetime, probably exceeded Gooch's estimate. It included 1,250 acres in New Kent,[34] 100 acres of the Richneck tract,[35] a half interest in the Blair-Prentis store with a value of £6,000, Negro servants, and other property. Among his bequests was £100 for teaching poor children. He left the college his library and £500 for a scholarship for "breeding a young divine." Though his will was lost in the destruction of James City County records in 1865, it is referred to in the Blair-Prentis store papers as having been dated April 5, 1743.[36] The purchasing power of his estate would be almost $1,000,000 today.

Although a crypt had been built beneath the college chapel,[37] Blair chose to be buried beside his wife Sarah in the Jamestown churchyard. Befitting his scholarly calling, his tomb was inscribed in Latin, as John Locke's had been thirty-nine years earlier. Some said Blair composed his own epitaph, which was translated thus:

Here lies buried
The Reverend and Honorable
James Blair A.M.
Born in Scotland,
Educated in the University of Edinburgh,
He came
First to England, then to Virginia;
In which part of the world
He filled the offices
For 58 years of Preacher of the Gospel,
For 54 of Commissary,
Of President of William and Mary,
Of a Councillor
to the British Governors,
Of President of the Council,
Of Governor of the Colony.
The comeliness of a handsome face
adorned him.

He entertained elegantly, in a cheerful, hospitable manner,

without luxury;
most munificently
he bestowed charity upon all needy persons;
in affability
he excelled.
For the College a well varied Library
he had founded.
Dying, his own Library
by will he bequeathed
for the purpose of informing students in Theology
and instructing the poorer youth.
He departed this life the XIV day before the Calends of May
MDCCXLIII
At the age of LXXXVIII.
Works more lasting than marble
will commend to his nephews
The surpassing praise of a well beloved old man.[38]

Standing between the tombs of James and Sarah Blair, the
trunk of an ancient sycamore today casts its shadows over their

crumbling marble. Snakes nest in the dead tree, slithering to the ground on summer days to cool themselves on the brick floor inside Jamestown's church. Cardinals, which Blair called "Virginian nightingales," serenade the ivied churchyard. It is a scene of peace and of desolation. And here James Blair sleeps, an ocean away from the dark Scottish coast where most of his kinsmen lie.

What manner of man was this solitary Scot, whose passionate voice was raised so often in Virginia's early debates? Unknown and unknowable, unloved and almost unlovable, he must nevertheless be reckoned as a force for good in the colony's growth. Though he wore the cassock of humility, his life was one long protest against the exploitations of a selfish age. Reared in a Scotland of civil and religious strife, he yearned for a land where men might live in Christian concord. It was that idealism that lured James Blair to Virginia.

Yet, like many an idealist, Blair gave way to bitterness when other imperfect men threatened his visions. Despite his virtues, his anger and avarice alienated many people and several times almost destroyed him. His record is spotted with contradiction and intrigue. But we must remember that Blair lived at a time of violent name-calling and dispute, when outrageous insults went unpunished by law or public opinion. When he is fairly judged in the context of his times, his assaults against Andros, Nicholson, and Spotswood become understandable and even admirable. Had Blair lacked his steely disposition, he could never have founded his college or curbed the chronic usurpations of royal governors.

In his thirst for power he was much like the Reverend Cotton Mather, his Congregationalist contemporary in New England who led the Boston revolt against Sir Edmund Andros in 1689. Both men were at times reminiscent of the ambitious and politically ruthless churchmen of the Renaissance. Yet each contributed to his times.

James Blair was first of all important as one of the most enlightened early critics of British rule in Virginia. "Perhaps the Commissary . . . had a little of the spirit of American independence in him," Bishop Meade wrote of his conflict with Spots-wood.[39] His attacks on Andros, Nicholson, and Spotswood were a logical sequel to Nathaniel Bacon's challenge of Governor Berke-ley in 1676. The gradual stiffening of Virginia's resistance to English policy was in part the result of the Blair faction's courage in opposing the Board of Trade's policies after 1695. And the suc-cess of council objections in time encouraged similar action by the House of Burgesses, which became more independent as the eighteenth century unfolded.

Blair's memorials against Andros were among the first pro-tests from the American colonies in the eighty years before the Revolution. In the same vein followed "The Case of the Planters in Virginia," authorized by the House of Burgesses in 1732; "A Vindication of the Said Representation," probably written by John Randolph in 1733 when he presented the burgesses' peti-tion to London;[40] and Richard Bland's farsighted "An Enquiry into the Rights of the British Colonies," which in 1766 proposed a British commonwealth of nations, linked to the mother country through loyalty to the crown.[41]

At his best, Blair spoke for indignant Virginians in his lifetime much as Thomas Jefferson did two generations later. Both men had an acquaintance with history and philosophy that enabled them to see the great opportunity facing Americans. Of all his contemporaries in Virginia, only William Byrd II besides Blair had the mind and erudition for such a role, but the easy-going Black Swan of Westover lacked the granite hardness for the job.

In giving form to spiritual and intellectual life in Virginia, Blair was opposed by the apathy of a materialistic age. His hoped-for reformation was slow, for scientific rationalism was beginning to undermine the prevailing religiosity by the time he arrived in 1685 in Virginia. Yet, through his acquaintance with secular as well as theological thought—of the Hellenistic as well as the Christian tradition—he could reconcile the two and lead Virginia away from the narrow colonialism of Sir Wil-liam Berkeley toward the wider humanism of George Mason. To the literary historian Moses Coit Tyler, Blair was "the creator of the healthiest and the most extensive intellectual influence that was felt in the Southern group of colonies before the Revolution."

Of all his endeavors, the college was the most successful. After a slow start, it became by the end of his life an uplifting influence in colonial America. By the time of the Revolution, most of Virginia's clergy and many of her statesmen had trained at the college. In the outpouring of settlers from the Tidewater to the west and south, William and Mary's graduates planted schools and churches over a wide span for a hundred years after Blair's death. The Carolinas, Kentucky, Tennessee, and the Ohio Valley especially felt his influence for, as Vernon Louis Parrington was to observe, "Virginia was the mother of the agrarian west."

Jefferson, with the perspective of years, suggested in 1781 why Blair's college had grown slowly: "The admission of the learners of Latin and Greek filled the college with children. This rendering it disagreeable and degrading to young gentlemen already prepared for entering on the sciences, they were discouraged from resorting to it, and thus the schools for mathematics and moral philosophy, which might have been of some service, became of very little."[42] Not until the great Revolutionary generation of George Washington, thirty years after Blair's death, did the full bloom of Blair's life work become fully evident.

It is worthy of note that four of the seven Virginia signers of the Declaration of Independence had attended Blair's college: George Wythe, Carter Braxton, Benjamin Harrison V, and Thomas Jefferson. Again, of Virginia's seven delegates to the Constitutional Convention in 1787, four had studied at William and Mary: Wythe, Edmund Randolph, the commissary's great-nephew John Blair II,[43] and Dr. James McClurg, an alumnus who became the first professor of medicine at William and Mary.

In his preoccupation with politics and the college, Blair after 1693 shamefully neglected his role as commissary. His influence over Virginia's clergy declined sharply after he became involved in Virginia's politics and threw himself into factional disputes with the governor. Thereafter the commissary was for twenty-five years so embroiled that he paid only token attention to his commission from the bishop of London. Only after 1722, when Governor Drysdale replaced Spotswood, did Blair at last return to nonpolitical concerns. Then it was too late for him to recoup the loyalty of his clergy.

William Meade, facing many of Blair's problems as bishop of Virginia's Episcopal diocese a century later, recognized the commissary as a sound leader and doctrinarian, whatever his shortcomings: "Our impression of him is, that, though he could not be otherwise than busy, considering all the offices he held and the relation he bore to others, yet that the charge brought against him by some, that he was *too busy*, had truth in it. . . . Still, we must esteem him a sincere Christian and a most laborious man in the performance of duty in all his official relations. The College owed its existence to him, and was probably as well managed by him as times and circumstances allowed; and it is probable that his faithful preaching and correct moral deportment did much to stem that torrent of wickedness which, in his day, flowed over England and America."[44]

Blair's effectiveness suffered, through no fault of his, from the cloudy circumstances of his acceptance into the Church of England's ministry, which did not satisfy Virginia's requirement of Anglican ordination. The fault here, however good the intention, lay with Bishop Compton, who had sent him to Virginia in ignorance or disregard of Virginia law. The commissary's hold on his clergy also suffered from his Scottish nationality. Many mild and kindly clerics were put off by his disputatiousness, for Blair had mannerisms for which Scotsmen were criticized as well as praised:

. . . an economy and even parsimony of words, which does not always betoken a poverty of ideas; an unsuperable dislike to wear his heart upon his sleeve, or make a display of the deeper and more tender feelings of his nature; a quiet and undemonstrative deportment which may have great firmness and determination behind it; a dour exterior which may cover a really genial disposition and kindly heart; much caution, wariness, and reserve, but a decision, energy of character, and tenacity of purpose . . . a very decided practical faculty which has an eye on the main chance, but which may co-exist with a deeplying fund of sentiment; a capacity for hard work and close application to business, which, with thrift and patient persistence, is apt to bear fruit in considerable success; in short, a reserve of strength, self-reliance, courage, and endurance which, when an emergency demands . . . may surprise the world.[45]

The human side of James Blair will never be fully known for lack of family papers. Even knowledge of his appearance is slight, based on his three portraits and on the description gathered by a nineteenth-century chronicler: "He was a hale, hearty, red-faced old gentleman, dressed entirely in black velvet, with ruffles at his wrists, and broad, shining silver buckles at his knees and shoes, and much addicted to taking snuff, a box for which he carried often in his hand. He was a lively old gentleman, though grave at times."[46]

Leaving no children, the commissary bequeathed no legends as kindly husband or father. Only his epitaph testifies to his "affability," his generosity to the poor, and his liberality to the college. Byrd's reference to Sarah Blair's resort to her cup for "consolation" has even raised a question about their marriage. However, Sarah's ill-health and childlessness seem the source of her discontent, for large families were usual in her age, and the dynastic urge ran strong in the Harrisons.[47] Relations between Blair and her kinsmen remained good, and it is significant that when the commissary died he was buried beside Sarah and the Harrisons at Jamestown.

Few men are privileged to live as long as Blair did. Born during Cromwell's rule, he survived seven royal reigns. King George II ascended the throne sixteen years before Blair died. Three archbishops of Canterbury were his friends: John Tillotson, Thomas Tenison, and William Wake. He was chosen by Henry Compton to be the first commissary of the Church of England in America, and he knew as friends Compton's successors John Robinson and Edmund Gibson. He talked philosophy with John Locke and sent him Virginia peach stones to satisfy his curiosity. In the realm of politics he served with every governor of Virginia from 1685 to 1743. More than fifty "Great men" sat with him in the council, and several hundred lesser ones were elected burgesses during that period of gathering strength.

In the Church of England, he knew illustrious preachers like Gilbert Burnet, Edward Stillingfleet, and George Whitefield, who brought the Great Awakening to much of America. Kindly Thomas Bray, founder of the Society for the Propagation of the Gospel, was his friend for forty years. Among the young clergy whom he influenced were three who succeeded him as president of the college: William Dawson (1743–52), William Stith (1752–55), and Thomas Dawson (1755–60).

Despite his long stewardship in Virginia, James Blair never became the typical "Great man" that Byrd or Carter was. He never acquired the love of luxury, of outdoor life, of good-natured camaraderie in alehouse or tavern which enlivened burgesses' meetings in Jamestown or Williamsburg. He found his pleasure instead in the play of power and the implementation of ideas. He remained an abstemious Scottish pedant even when he grew rich and powerful. As with many a preacher's son, his spartan memory of rectory life goaded him to work, save, and create a better life for his posterity. The hardships of youth left him tough and ambitious.

This, then, was James Blair, who forsook the old world of Alvah, Aberdeen, Edinburgh, Cranston Parish, and London for a new one of Henrico, Jamestown, and Williamsburg. Born in the Age of Faith, he lived to know and welcome the dawning Age of Reason. A child of seventeenth-century Scotland, he helped make Virginia something more than an obedient colony. "Between the older colonial America and later industrial America," wrote Parrington, "stand the ideals of the Old Dominion, more humane and generous than either, disseminating the principles of French romantic philosophy, and instilling into the provincial American mind, static and stagnant in the grip of English colonialism, the ideal of democratic equalitarianism and the hope of humane progress. The nineteenth century first entered America by way of the James River."[48]

No man contributed more to Virginia's intellectual maturation than did James Blair.

Sixteen days before Blair died, the embodiment of that new age was born, on April 2, 1743, a hundred miles west of Williamsburg on Virginia's frontier. He was Thomas Jefferson, and he would help to build a new society on the firm foundations that Blair, dying of gangrene, left behind him in that bright Virginia springtime.

Appendixes

Notes

Bibliography

and

Index

A Note *on the* Blair Families

of Virginia,

Pennsylvania, *and* Kentucky

ᴕ Several families bearing the proud Scottish surname Blair were conspicuous in colonial America. The most prominent of these was planted by the subject of this book, the Reverend James Blair, who came to Virginia in 1685, and by his brother Archibald, who followed him by 1690. They were sons of the Reverend Robert Blair, a Church of Scotland minister of Banffshire in northern Scotland.

James Blair died childless, but Archibald Blair married three times and had at least two sons, John and James, and three daughters who left a number of progeny in Tidewater Virginia. One daughter, Elizabeth, married first John Bolling, Jr. (great-grandson of Pocahontas and John Rolfe) and after his death, the pre-Revolutionary statesman and pamphleteer, Richard Bland. A second daughter, Harrison, married Dr. George Gilmer, a Scottish physician of Williamsburg. The third, Anne, married a Mr. Whiting of Gloucester.

John Blair I, who died in Williamsburg in 1771 at age eighty-four, was the father of three sons—one of whom died unmarried—and five daughters. One son, John Blair II, had three daughters, none of whom left surviving issue. The other, James Blair II, was survived by a son, Archibald, an "infant orphan" when James II died in 1773. This Archibald Blair married Molley Whiting of Gloucester and became clerk of the Virginia Council and of the Virginia Committee of Safety during the Revolution. He died in 1825, the father of three sons and a daughter.

A second family of Blairs, apparently unrelated to the first, settled in Richmond and in western Virginia in the eighteenth century.

These descended from the Reverend John Blair, a Scotch-Irish emigrant of Ayrshire ancestry who settled in Pennsylvania in the early 1700's. This worthy became the schoolmaster of a wilderness "Log College" at Fagg's Manor in Bucks County. One of his sons, James, became an attorney in western Virginia before moving into pioneer Kentucky. This James was the father of Francis Preston Blair, who was born at Abingdon, Virginia, in 1791 and founded and edited the influential Washington *Globe* in the nineteenth century. Francis Preston Blair was a friend of Andrew Jackson and of Martin Van Buren, the father of Civil War General Francis Preston Blair and Postmaster General Montgomery Blair, and the builder of the handsome Blair House in Washington, which survives today as the nation's guest house for visiting foreign heads of state.

Another son of the Pennsylvanian John Blair was the Reverend John Durburrow Blair, who was born at Fagg's Manor and was educated at the College of New Jersey, which became Princeton. John D. Blair came to Virginia about 1785 and conducted the Washington Henry Academy in Hanover County. After a period there, he moved to Richmond to open another school and to minister to the first Presbyterian congregation in Virginia's post-Revolutionary capital city.

John D. Blair and the Reverend John Buchanan of the Episcopal church were known to John Marshall's generation in Richmond as "the two parsons." From 1792 until 1814 they held their services on alternate Sundays in the newly built Virginia Capitol. Descendants of John Durburrow Blair are numerous through intermarriage with the Winston, Mayo, Scott, Beirne, and Carter families.

No relationship apparently existed between either of these clans and the nineteenth-century Virginia historian, Hugh Blair Grigsby. Grigsby was named instead for a Scottish clergyman, Hugh Blair, who was admired in the United States for his sermons and writings.

Other Blairs, chiefly of Scottish origin, emigrated to America in the colonial period or later, but their relationship to the subject of this book was remote, if it existed at all. Variant spellings of the name (Blayre, Blaire, etc.), once common, have largely disappeared.

_____

Blair Family
of Banffshire, Scotland
and James City County, Virginia

A Partial Genealogy

_____

(*see following page*)

Blair Family
of Banffshire, Scotland,
and James City County, Virginia
A Partial Genealogy

ROBERT (?-?)
m. ———
Minister, Alvah,
1636–79

WILLIAM (?-?)
m. ———
Parish Minister,
1667–88
Rector, Marischal
College, 1688–91

JOHN (?-?)
m. (1) Mary M'Lurge
(2) Elizabeth
Pearson
Apothecary
Burgess, Edinburgh

MARJORY (?-?)

JAMES (c. 1655–1743)
m. Sarah Harrison
(1670–1713)
Commissary, Virginia
President,
William and Mary
President, Council

ARCHIBALD
(c. 1665–1733)
m. (1) ———
(2) Sarah Archer
Fowler
(3) Mary Wilson
Roscow Cary
Physician
Burgess

JOHN (1687–1771)
m. Mary Monro
President, Council

JAMES (?-?)

ELIZABETH
(c. 1710–75)
m. (1) John
Bolling, Jr.
. (2) Richard Bland

ANNE (?-?)
m. ———Whiting

HARRISON (1715–55)
m. George Gilmer
Physician

CHRISTIAN (1727–84)
m. Armistead
Burwell

JOHN (1731–1800)
m. Jean Balfour
Councillor
Delegate, Constitu-
tional Convention,
1787
Justice, U.S. Supreme
Court

MARY (1734–?)
m. (1) George
Braxton
(2) Robert
Burwell
(3) R. Prescott

SARAH (1738–1804)
m. Wilson Cary

JAMES (1741–73)
m. Katharine
Eustice
Physician

ARCHIBALD (1745–?)

ANNE (1746–?)
m. John Banister

ELIZABETH (?-?)
m. Samuel
Thompson
Captain, R.N.

Harrison Family
of Yorkshire, England,
and Surry County, Virginia
A Partial Genealogy

SARAH (1670–1713)
  m. James Blair
  (1655–1743)

BENJAMIN III
  (1673–1710)
  m. Elizabeth Burwell
  (1677–1734)
Attorney General

NATHANIEL
  (1677–1727)
  m. Mary Cary Young
Councillor

BENJAMIN I
  (in Va. c. 1632)
  m. Mary——
Burgess, 1646–?

BENJAMIN II
  (1645–1713)
  m. Hannah Churchill
  (1651–98)
Burgess
Councillor

HANNAH (1678–1731)
  m. Philip Ludwell II
  (1672–1727)
  Councillor

HENRY (1682–1732)
  m. Elizabeth Smith
Burgess

ELIZABETH (?-?)
  m. William Edwards
    Secretary. Council

Officialdom
of England *and* Virginia
in the Lifetime *of* James Blair

Rulers of England

OLIVER CROMWELL, *1649–58*
RICHARD CROMWELL, *1658–59*
CHARLES II, *1660–85*
JAMES II, *1685–89*
WILLIAM III, & MARY II, *1689–94*

WILLIAM III, *1694–1702*
ANNE, *1702–14*
GEORGE I, *1714–27*
GEORGE II, *1727–60*

Archbishops of Canterbury

No appointment, *1644–60*
WILLIAM JUXON, *1660–63*
GILBERT SHELDON, *1663–77*
WILLIAM SANCROFT, *1677–91*

JOHN TILLOTSON, *1691–95*
THOMAS TENISON, *1695–1716*
WILLIAM WAKE, *1716–37*
JOHN POTTER, *1737–47*

Bishops of London

No appointment, *1644–60*
GILBERT SHELDON, *1660–63*
HUMFREY HENCHMAN, *1663–75*

HENRY COMPTON, *1675–1714*
JOHN ROBINSON, *1714–23*
EDMUND GIBSON, *1723–48*

Governors, Lieutenant Governors, and Acting Governors of Virginia

EDWARD DIGGES, *Governor, 1655–56*
SAMUEL MATHEWS, JR., *Governor, 1656–60*

SIR WILLIAM BERKELEY, *Governor, 1660–77*
FRANCIS MORYSON, *Lieutenant Governor, 1661–62*
COLONEL HERBERT JEFFREYS, *Lieutenant Governor, 1677–78*
THOMAS CULPEPER, *Baron Culpeper of Thoresway, Governor, 1677–83*
SIR HENRY CHICHELEY, *Deputy Governor, 1678–82*
NICHOLAS SPENCER, *President of the Council, 1683–84*
FRANCIS HOWARD, *Baron Howard of Effingham, Governor, 1683–92*
NATHANIEL BACON, SR., *President of the Council, 1684–90*
CAPTAIN FRANCIS NICHOLSON, *Lieutenant Governor, 1690–92*
SIR EDMUND ANDROS, *Governor, 1692–98*
RALPH WORMELEY, *President of the Council, 1698*
COLONEL FRANCIS NICHOLSON, *Governor, 1698–1705*
WILLIAM BYRD I, *President of the Council, 1700–1704*
COLONEL EDWARD NOTT, *Governor, 1705–6*
EDMUND JENINGS, *President of the Council, 1706–9*
COLONEL ROBERT HUNTER, *Governor, 1707–9*
EDMUND JENINGS, *Lieutenant Governor, 1708–10*
GEORGE HAMILTON, *Earl of Orkney, Governor, 1710–37*
COLONEL ALEXANDER SPOTSWOOD, *Lieutenant Governor, 1710–22*
COLONEL HUGH DRYSDALE, *Lieutenant Governor, 1722–26*
COLONEL ROBERT "KING" CARTER, *President of the Council, 1726–27*
WILLIAM GOOCH, *Lieutenant Governor, 1727–49*
WILLIAM ANNE KEPPEL, *Earl of Albemarle, Governor, 1737–54*
THE REVEREND JAMES BLAIR, *President of the Council, 1740–41*

Notes

1. *Bartlett's Familiar Quotations*, 14th ed. (Boston: Little, Brown & Co., 1968), p. 205. Citing Richard Horne Shepherd.

2. Blair's tombstone at Jamestown, Virginia, inscribed in Latin, notes, "He departed this life the XIV Day before the Calends of May, 1743. At the age of 88 years." In March 1735, he referred to himself as "being now entered into my eightieth year." William Stevens Perry, ed., *Historical Collections Relating to the American Colonial Church*, 5 vols. (Hartford: Printed for the Subscribers, 1870–78), 1:358.

3. Peter John Anderson, ed., *Fasti Academiae Mariscallanae: Selections from the Records of the Marischal College and University, 1593–1860*, 3 vols. (Aberdeen: New Spalding Club, 1898), 2:196–98. In 1860 the college was combined with neighboring King's College to become the University of Aberdeen.

4. John Spalding, *Memorialls of the Trubles in Scotland and in England, A.D. 1624–A.D. 1645*, 2 vols. (Aberdeen: Spalding Club, 1850–51), 1:420–23.

5. Hew Scott, ed., *Fasti Ecclesiae Scoticanae*, 7 vols. (Edinburgh: Oliver and Boyd, 1926), b:247.

6. Ibid.

7. John Malcolm Bulloch, *The Lord Rectors of the Universities of Aberdeen* (Aberdeen: D. Wyllie & Son, 1890), p. 51; Anderson, *Fasti Academiae*, 2:13. William Blair is buried in the churchyard of St. Nicholas' (Section D, Grave 523), the Mother Church of Aberdeen.

8. From a document in the Scottish Record Office, Edinburgh, signed by James Blair and dated November 10, 1682, designating "my brother german, John Blair, apothecarie in Edinburgh" his factor and procurator during James's absence from Scotland.

9. Charles B. Boog Watson, ed., *Roll of Edinburgh Burgesses and Guild Brethren, 1406–1707* (Edinburgh: Printed for the Scottish Record Society by J. Skinner & Co., Ltd., 1929), p. 49.

10. Henry Paton, ed., *The Register of Marriages for the Parish of Edinburgh, 1595–1700* (Edinburgh: Printed for the Scottish Record Society by James Skinner & Company, 1905), p. 27.

11. From letter from W. H. Makey, city archivist of Edinburgh, to the author, dated February 3, 1969.

12. University records list him as a member of class ninety-seven, which graduated in 1865, "freed from the discipline of D. Robert Lidderdale." Apparently Archibald's medical training followed his graduation from Edinburgh, as the first medical professors of the university were not appointed until that year. *A*

Catalogue of the Graduates in the Faculties of Arts, Divinity, and Law of the University of Edinburgh since its Foundation (Edinburgh: Neill and Company, 1858).

13. J. Grant, *History of the Burgh and Parish Schools of Scotland* (London: William Collins & Sons, Ltd. 1876), p. 98; William Cramond, *The Annals of Banff*, 2 vols. (Aberdeen: Printed for the New Spalding Club, 1893), 2:165–74.

14. Gordon Donaldson, *Scotland: James V to James VII* (Edinburgh and London: Oliver & Boyd, 1965), pp. 388–89.

15. From "bec jaune" (yellow beak), as a fledgling scholar was called at the Sorbonne.

16. John Malcolm Bulloch, *A History of the University of Aberdeen, 1495–1895* (London: Hodder and Stoughton, 1895), p. 93.

17. Robert Sangster Rait, *The Universities of Aberdeen: A History* (Aberdeen: James Gordon Bissett, 1895).

18. Ibid., p. 288.

19. Ibid., p. 257.

20. Ibid., p. 288.

21. Bulloch, *A History of the University of Aberdeen*, p. 95.

22. Ibid., p. 93.

23. Ibid.

24. Ibid., p. 124.

25. Ibid., p. 128.

26. In 1717, Blair as president of the College of William and Mary wrote an account in Latin of a threatened slave insurrection, presenting it to Governor Spotswood as a ceremonial rental for the college land.

27. David Bayne Horn, *A Short History of the University of Edinburgh, 1556–1889* (Edinburgh: University Press, 1967), p. 41.

28. *A Catalogue of the Graduates*, p. 103.

29. Horn, *A Short History*, p. 25.

30. Ibid., p. 30.

31. William A. Caruthers, *The Knights of the Horseshoe* (New York: A. L. Burt Company, 1904), p. 6.

32. George David Henderson, *Religious Life in Seventeenth-Century Scotland* (Cambridge: University Press, 1937), p. 143.

33. Thomas Middleton, *An Appendix to the History of The Church of Scotland: Containing the Succession of the Archbishops and Bishops in Their Several Sees, from the Reformation of Religion, until the Year 1676* (London: E. Flesher, 1677), pp. 30–31.

34. Gilbert Burnet, *Bishop Burnet's History of His Own Time: With the Suppressed Passages of the First Volume, and Notes by the Earls of Dartmouth and Hardwicke, and Speaker Onslow, Hitherto Unpublished*, 6 vols. (Oxford: Clarendon Press, 1823), 1:302.

35. Donaldson, *Scotland*, p. 363.

36. Burnet, *History*, 2:19.

37. Perry, *Historical Collections*, 1:247. From undated, unsigned letter.

38. Burnet, *History*, 2:166.

39. *The Register of the Privy Council of Scotland*, 8 vols., 3d ser., edited by P. Hume Brown (Edinburgh: H. M. Register House, 1915), 3:296–97.

40. Ibid., p. 308.

41. Burnet, *History*, 2:168, 318–19.

42. It was rumored that Grimston had paid the Earl of Clarendon £8,000 for the office, which he held until his death. *Dictionary of National Biography*, 63 vols. ed., Leslie Stephen and Sidney Lee (London: Smith, Elder & Co., 1892–1912), 23:258.

43. The term "german," from the Middle English "germayn," was commonly

used to indicate full blood relationship, through common parentage. The word "factor," commonly used in England to designate an agent, had special meaning in Scotland as "a person who manages an estate for another; steward; bailiff." *Webster's New World Dictionary of the American Language* (Cleveland and New York: World Publishing Company, 1966), pp. 520, 607.

44. *Register of Deeds* (Edinburgh: Scottish Record Office), 59:439, no. 1192.

45. Burnet, *History*, 2:167–68.

46. Services continued to be held in the Rolls Chapel until 1895. It was torn down in 1896 and in 1902 the present Museum of the Public Record Office was built on the site.

47. Samuel Pepys, *The Diary and Correspondence of Samuel Pepys*, 4 vols. (London: George Allen & Unwin, Ltd., 1929), 2:162, for entry of April 16, 1665.

48. Compton won the name "the Protestant bishop." According to S. L. Lee in the *Dictionary of National Biography*, 11:446, "He spent all his fortune in helping Irish protestants, Scottish episcopalians, and refugees who fled to England from the persecution of foreign countries . . . he died a poor man." It was Compton who in 1677 performed the marriage of fifteen-year-old Princess Mary to William of Orange, who was twelve years her senior.

49. Perry, *Historical Collections*, 1:247. Blair was to produce this certificate at a convention of Anglican clergy in Virginia in 1719 as evidence that he had been properly ordained by a bishop. An opponent, the Reverend Hugh Jones, insisted that "presbyter" meant he was in Presbyterian orders. However, in the Church of Scotland during the reign of Charles II, "presbyter" was equivalent to "priest" in England. Evidently Compton so accepted it in 1684.

50. *Calendar of State Papers Domestic, James II, February-December, 1685*, 2 vols., edited by E. K. Timings (London: H. M. Stationery Office, 1960), 1:440, lists names of the fifty-seven "to embark on the shipp William, John Bennet commander, bound for Jamaica." It is probable that the *William* docked at Port Royal, which was the chief English port in the Caribbean until largely destroyed by an earthquake in 1692.

CHAPTER II

1. Arthur Pierce Middleton, *Tobacco Coast* (Newport News, Virginia: Mariners Museum, 1953), p. 187.

2. Annie Lash Jester, *Newport News, Virginia: 1607–1960* (Newport News, Virginia: City of Newport News, 1961), p. 15.

3. Charles E. Hatch, Jr., *America's Oldest Legislative Assembly & Its Jamestown Statehouses* (Washington: Government Printing Office, 1956), p. 29.

4. *Appleton's Cyclopaedia of American Biography*, 6 vols., edited by James Grant Wilson and John Fiske (New York: D. Appleton and Company, 1891), 12:28.

5. *Encyclopedia of Virginia Biography*, 5 vols. (New York: Lewis Historical Publishing Company, 1915), 1:53.

6. These were Gloucester, formed in 1651; Lancaster, 1651; Middlesex, about 1669; Nansemond, originally Upper Norfolk, 1637; New Kent, 1654; Norfolk, originally Lower Norfolk, 1637; Northampton, 1643; Northumberland, 1645; Stafford, 1664; Surry, 1652; and Westmoreland, 1653. *A Hornbook of Virginia History* (Richmond: Virginia State Library, 1965), pp. 14–30.

7. Ibid., p. 68.

8. William W. Hening, *Statutes at Large: Being a Collection of All the Laws of Virginia from the First Session of the Legislature in 1619*, 13 vols. facs. ed. (Charlottesville: University Press of Virginia, 1969), 2:518–43. Lord Culpeper bought out Lord Arlington's share in 1681 and in 1684 sold his proprietorship of Virginia south of the Rappahannock back to the king for an annual pension of £600, to run for the remaining twenty-one years of the original 1674 grant.

See Fairfax Harrison, *Virginia Land Grants: A Study of Conveyancing in Relation to Colonial Politics* (Richmond: Privately printed, 1925), pp. 54–55. By the marriage of Culpeper's daughter to Lord Fairfax, the holding became known as the Fairfax Grant.

9. George MacLaren Bryden, *Virginia's Mother Church and the Political Conditions under Which It Grew*, 2 vols. (Richmond: Virginia Historical Society, 1947), 1:279. No relics of the settlement remain visible and the exact location is unknown. The county seat was moved about 1742 and the parish church, sometimes known as Varina Church, was replaced by another on the present site of Richmond, at the fall line of the James. A Virginia state highway marker near Varina reads: "At Varina, a short distance south, John Rolfe and Pocahontas lived after their marriage in 1614. The place became the first county seat of Henrico County and here also was the glebe house of Reverend James Blair, founder of William and Mary College. Under the name of Aiken's Landing, Varina was a point of exchange for prisoners in 1862. Fort Harrison nearby was one of the principal works in the Richmond defenses, 1862–64. It was captured on September 29, 1864."

10. Philip Alexander Bruce, *Social Life in the Seventeenth Century*, 2d ed. (Lynchburg, Virginia: J. P. Bell Co., Inc., 1927), p. 138.

11. Henrico County Records, [Deeds and Wills], 1677–92, pt. 2, Virginia State Library, Archives Division, original, p. 418.

12. From a "List of Parishes in Virginia and the Ministers in Them," dated June 3, 1680, and sent by Secretary Jenings to London. Brydon, *Virginia's Mother Church*, 1:190, 203–4.

13. William Stevens Perry, ed., *Historical Collections Relating to the American Colonial Church*, 5 vols. (Hartford: Printed for the Subscribers, 1870–78), 1:360.

14. Middleton, *Tobacco Coast*, p. 458.

15. Wakefield, Surry County, is not to be confused with the later Washington family plantation of the same name on Pope's Creek, Westmoreland County, where George Washington was born in 1732. Harrison family tradition claimed relationship to Major General Thomas Harrison, a Cromwellian, who was one of the regicides of King Charles I in 1660. Samuel Pepys noted in his diary for October 16 of that year: "I went to Charing Cross to see Major-General Harrison hanged, drawn, and quartered, which was done there, and he looked as cheerful as any man could in that condition."

16. The author is indebted to Thomas E. Thorne, professor of fine arts of the College of William and Mary, for his study of the Blair portraits. These include the single surviving life portrait of Sarah Harrison Blair, painted by J. Hargreaves in 1705 in London. It was given to the college in 1829 by Mrs. Mary Monro Peachy, great granddaughter of Archibald Blair, and hangs in the Board of Visitors' Room.

17. "Hon. John Blair, Jr.," an address by Henry T. Wickham, Esq., of Virginia, at a special session of the U.S. Circuit Court of Appeals, Philadelphia, Pennsylvania, May 6, 1913, p. 11.

18. From Blair tombstones in the Jamestown churchyard, now obliterated. Lyon G. Tyler, "Diary of John Blair," *William and Mary Quarterly*, 1st ser., 7 (July 1898–April 1899): 133.

19. *Papers Relating to an Affidavit made by His Reverence James Blair, Clerk, pretended President of William and Mary College, and Supposed Commissary to the Bishop of London in Virginia, against Francis Nicholson, Esq., London,* (n.p., 1727; photostat, Massachusetts Historical Society), p. 104.

20. The will of Benjamin Harrison II, written in 1711 and probated February 18, 1713, left £400 each to his daughters Sarah and Hannah and land to each son. It also bequeathed £20 to buy "ornaments" for a new chapel and granted for perpetual church use five acres of land on which "The old chapel now

stands." A new chapel was built beginning in 1711, but Harrison and his wife remain interred in the burial ground of the old. His epitaph read: "Here lyeth the Body of the Hon. Benjamin Harrison, Esqr. Who did Justice, Loved Mercy and walked Humbly with His God, Was Always Loyal to His Prince & a great Benefactor to his Country." A. W. Bohannan, *Old Surry* (Petersburg: Plummer Printing Company, Inc., 1927), p. 44.

21. *Papers Relating to an Affidavit*, p. 104.

22. Years later, when Sarah and James Blair had been buried beneath raised tombs in the Jamestown churchyard, a sycamore tree grew beneath them, lifting them high above their original places. The late sexton, Sam Robinson, delighted in telling the story of the "mother-in-law tree" to thousands of visitors, including Queen Elizabeth, the Queen Mother, in 1954, and Queen Elizabeth II and Prince Philip in 1957.

23. The tombstone of Elizabeth Harrison Edwards, now illegible, was partly readable until a century ago. Lyon G. Tyler in *The Cradle of the Republic: Jamestown and the James River* (Richmond: Hermitage Press, 1906), p. 130, deciphered its text as: "Here lies interred the body of [Elizabeth Edwards], wife of William Edwards of [James] Citty, Gent and daughter of [Benjamin Harrison] of ye [county of Surry, who was born the] sixth day of January -----, [and died] the 14th. day of -----, [aged] seventeen years and ----- dayes."

24. Ethel Armes, *Stratford Hall: The Great House of the Lees* (Richmond: Garrett and Massie, Inc., 1936), quoting an unidentified source, p. 22.

25. Henrico County Record Book, No. 2 [Orders and Wills], 1678–93, Virginia State Library, Archives Division, p. 286.

26. Ibid., 319.

27. He was also first cousin to Francis Bacon, Lord Verulam.

28. Land Office Patent Book 8, 1689–95, Virginia State Library, Archives Division, p. 37.

29. Ibid., pp. 340–41.

30. William Byrd, *The Secret Diary of William Byrd of Westover, 1709–1712*, edited by Louis B. Wright and Marion Tinling (Richmond: Dietz Press, 1941), p. 11.

31. Effingham served as governor from September 28, 1683, until March 1, 1692. He was in Virginia from February 21, 1684, until February 1689. During most of his absence he was represented by Nathaniel Bacon, Sr., president of the council.

32. From "Instructions to Francis Nicholson, Esq., His Majesty's Lieut. and Governor-Gen'l of Virginia," *Virginia Magazine of History and Biography* 4 (July 1896): 51.

33. Public Record Office, Colonial Office 5, London, copy in Library of Congress (hereinafter cited as P.R.O./C.O., in L.C.) 5, 1305, dated December 15, 1689. Cited by George MacLaren Bryden in *Virginia's Mother Church*, 1:280.

34. *Executive Journals of the Council of Colonial Virginia*, 4 vols., edited by H. R. McIlwaine (Richmond: Virginia State Library, 1925–30), 1:116.

35. P.R.O./C.O. 5, in L.C. 1305.

36. Ibid.

37. *Executive Journals*, 1:120 for entry of July 24, 1690.

38. Ibid., pp. 154–55.

39. The Reverend James Sclater was rector of Charles Parish in York County.

40. *Journal of the House of Burgesses of Virginia, 1619–1776*, 13 vols., edited by J. P. Kennedy and R. H. McIlwaine (Richmond: Colonial Press, E. Waddey, Co., 1915), 2:366–67, for entry of May 20, 1691.

41. Perry, *Historical Collections*, 1:250, 252.

42. *Journal of the House of Burgesses*, 2:344.

43. Robert Beverley, in *The History and Present State of Virginia*, wrote that

the first new plan for the college was presented to the council in 1689, but Beverley said no further action could be taken immediately because the House of Burgesses was not in session.

44. "Vital Facts: A William and Mary Chronology, 1693–1963" (Williamsburg: College of William and Mary, 1963), p. 2.

45. The originals of the addresses are in the papers of the Society for the Propagation of the Gospel in London. They are published in the *William and Mary Quarterly*, 2d ser., vol. 10 (1930): 323–37, and quoted in Richard L. Morton, *Colonial Virginia* (Chapel Hill: University of North Carolina Press, 1960), 1:357–59.

CHAPTER III

1. During the centuries of the Holy Roman Empire, church took precedence over state in Europe. The domination of state over church, which accompanied the rise of nationalism after the Middle Ages, came to be known as Erastianism, after the German-Swiss theologian Thomas Erastus, who lived from 1524 to 1583.

2. A prayer to be said "upon the court of guard" at Jamestown was included in Sir Thomas Dale's "Lawes Divine, Morall, and Martiall," brought to Jamestown about 1611. It read in part: "We know O Lord, we have the divel and all the gates of hel against us, but if thou O Lord be on our side, we care not who be against us. . . . And seeing by thy motion and work in our harts, we are left our warme nests at home, and put our lives into our hands principally to honour thy name, and advance the kingdome of thy son, Lord, give us leave to commit our lives into thy hands. . . ."

3. Susan Myra Kingsbury, ed., *Records of the Virginia Company of London*, 4 vols. (Washington: Government Printing Office, 1906–35), 2:19, 26.

4. *Dictionary of National Biography*, edited by Leslie Stephen and Sidney Lee, 63 vols. (6 supp.) (London: Smith, Elder & Co., 1892), 32:187.

5. Arthur L. Cross, "Schemes for Episcopal Control in the Colonies," *Annual Report of the American Historical Association for the Year 1896* (Washington: Government Printing Office, 1897), p. 234.

6. *Calendar of State Papers, Domestic Series of the Reign of Charles I, 1633–34*, edited by John Bruce (London: Longmans, Green, Longmans, Roberts and Green, 1863), p. 225.

7. *Proceedings of the General Assembly of Virginia, July 30–August 4, 1619*, edited by William J. Van Schreeven and George H. Reese (Jamestown, Virginia: Jamestown Foundation, 1969), p. 63.

8. William W. Hening, *The Statutes at Large: Being a Collection of All the Laws of Virginia from the First Session of the Legislature in 1619*, 13 vols. facs. ed. (Charlottesville: The University Press of Virginia, 1969), 1:122–24.

9. John Smith, *The Works of Captain John Smith*, 2 vols., edited by Edward Arber (Birmingham, England: Privately printed, 1884), 2:958.

10. John Hammond, *Leah and Rachel, or, The Two Fruitfull Sisters Virginia and Maryland: Their Present Condition Impartially Stated and Related* (London, 1656), in W. Q. Force, ed., *Tracts and Other Papers* (Washington: W. Q. Force, 1844), vol. 3, no. 14, p. 9.

11. George MacLaren Brydon, *Religious Life of Virginia in the Seventeenth Century* (Williamsburg: Virginia 350th Anniversary Celebration Corporation, 1957), pp. 10–11.

12. Ibid., p. 11.

13. Ibid.

14. Ibid., pp. 10–11. Whitaker's remark has been misunderstood as meaning that the surplice was not then in use in Virginia. From other documentary sources, it is clear that it was. Apparently Whitaker meant that it was not the subject of controversy in Virginia as it was in England at that time.

15. Hening, *Statutes at Large*, 1:277.

16. Brydon, *Religious Life*, p. 34.

17. Ibid., p. 35.

18. Ibid., p. 37.

19. James Stuart Murray Anderson, *The History of the Church of England in the Colonies and Foreign Dependencies of the British Empire*, 3 vols. (London: F. & J. Rivington, 1845–56), 2:341.

20. Governor Berkeley reported in 1671 that there were forty-eight parishes. However, authorized parishes were sometimes tardily organized. For lack of clergy, some had no ministers.

21. Hening, *Statutes at Large*, 1:44.

22. "The setting up of a vestry of laymen as temporal head of the Church in a parish or congregation was first developed in Virginia. It was extended later to other colonies as the Anglican Church spread through them all, and it came over into the life of the Protestant Episcopal Church in the United States." Brydon, *Religious Life*, p. 13.

23. Hening, *Statutes at Large*, 2:51–52.

24. Ibid., p. 45.

25. Ibid., p. 47.

26. Ibid., p. 54.

27. Charles E. Hatch, Jr., *The First Seventeen Years, Virginia, 1607–1624* (Williamsburg: Virginia 350th Anniversary Celebration Corporation, 1957), p. 16.

28. The 1662 revision of the Book of Common Prayer continues to be used with minor alterations in the Church of England. The version in use by the Episcopal church in the United States was revised in 1789, in 1892, and in 1928.

29. The first organ in a Virginia church was ordered for Petsworth Parish, Gloucester County, in 1735. In 1737 the organ arrived, a gallery for it was ordered built "at the west End of the Church," and an organist was employed. *The Vestry Book of Petsworth Parish, Gloucester County, Virginia, 1677–1793*, transcribed, annotated and indexed by C. G. Chamberlayne (Richmond: Virginia State Library Board, 1933), pp. 234, 236, 242, 243, 244–46.

30. From *The Whole Book of Psalmes, Collected into English Meeter by Thomas Sternhold, John Hopkins, and Others . . .* (London: Printed by I. H. for the Company of Stationers, 1638). An adaptation of this standard English psalter was published at Cambridge, Massachusetts, in 1640, as *The Whole Book of Psalms Faithfully Translated into English Metre*. This Bay Psalm Book, written by Richard Mather, John Eliot, and Thomas Weld, was to Massachusetts' Puritans what *The Whole Book of Psalmes* was to Virginia Anglicans.

31. Burke Davis, *A Williamsburg Galaxy* (New York: Holt, Rinehart and Winston, 1968), p. 50.

32. Saint George was the patron saint of England. According to tradition, he was a soldier who was beheaded after his conversion to Christianity. Saint Andrew, the patron saint of Scotland, was brother to Simon Peter and one of the twelve apostles.

33. Brydon, *Religious Life*, p. 30.

34. Ibid., pp. 38–39.

35. Nicholas Trott, ed., *The Laws of the British Plantations in America, Relating to the Church and the Clergy, Religion and Learning* (London: Printed for B. Cowse, 1721), pp. 119–20.

36. "A Memorial of What Abuses are crept into the churches of the plantations," P.R.O./C.O. in L.C., vol. 4, p. 47.

37. "Declaration of Colonel Jeffreys," *The Virginia Magazine of History and Biography* 22 (January 1914): 44–47.

38. William Stevens Perry, *Historical Collections Relating to the American Colonial Church*, 5 vols. (Hartford: Printed for the Subscribers, 1870–78), 1:2–3.

39. P.R.O./C.O. in L.C., 1356, pp. 217–18. This arbitrary division was to create friction between Commissary Blair and several royal governors.

40. Henry Compton was suspended from his diocese by James II in 1686 but was restored to duty after the Revolution of 1688.

CHAPTER IV

1. Blair wrote Nicholson and asked his intercession for Sarah Blair "if it should please God that I dye in this service & my poor wife be called to account by the Assembly." Blair to Nicholson, June 19, 1691, "Papers Relating to Nicholson and the College," *Virginia Magazine of History and Biography* 7 (July 1899–April 1900): 159–60.

2. Presumably from the Scottish "whigg," meaning soured whey. The word came to imply a liberal, populist attitude. *The Gentleman's Magazine, or Monthly Intelligencer*, published in London in 1731, wrote: "The Principles of an old Whig were, that all Men are by Nature equal, that no Man hath a right to Power but by consent; that Men were born to be free; that every Government ought to be a free Government, consisting in security of Person and Property by strong and equal Laws, which ought to be the standing measure of the Prince's Action, and the People's Obedience; and in a liberty of speaking and writing upon all Subjects, and of worshipping God that way every Man thinks best."

3. The account of Blair's appearance before the king and queen is quoted and paraphrased from his letter of December 3, 1691, to Nicholson. From manuscript in the possession of the Society for the Propagation of the Gospel in Foreign Parts, printed in William Stevens Perry, ed., *Historical Collections Relating to the American Colonial Church*, 5 vols. (Hartford: Printed for the Subscribers, 1870–78), 1:3–8. "William and Mary College: Recently Discovered Documents," *William and Mary Quarterly*, 2d ser., 10 (1930): 239–42.

4. Jeffrey Jeffreys, colonial agent for Virginia, had previously presented several petitions from the colony. *Journal of the House of Burgesses of Virginia, 1619–1776*, 13 vols., edited by J. P. Kennedy and H. R. McIlwaine (Richmond: Colonial Press, E. Waddey, Co., 1915), 2:374.

5. Gilbert Burnet had become bishop of Salisbury in 1689. He gave Blair a letter of introduction to the archbishop of Canterbury, who received Blair kindly, recalled his services to the master of the rolls, and suggested that Blair write him a memorandum that would predispose the king to the proposal. This Blair did. Blair to Nicholson, December 3, 1691, "William and Mary College: Recently Discovered Documents," *William and Mary Quarterly*, 2d ser., 10 (1930): 239.

6. William Lloyd, who later became bishop of Lichfield and bishop of Worcester.

7. Gilbert Burnet, *Bishop Burnet's History of His Own Time: With the Suppressed Passages of the First Volume, and Notes by the Earls of Dartmouth and Hardwicke, and Speaker Onslow, Hitherto Unpublished*, 6 vols. (Oxford: Clarendon Press, 1823), 4:205.

8. The governor designated for Virginia by the Crown frequently remained in England and left the administration of the colony to a lieutenant in Virginia. During his several absences from the colony, Lord Howard of Effingham was represented first by Councillor Nathaniel Bacon, Sr., and later by Lieutenant Governor Francis Nicholson.

9. Blair to Nicholson, December 3, 1691, "William and Mary College: Recently Discovered Documents," *William and Mary Quarterly*, 2d ser., 10 (1930): 242.

10. From London on November 21, 1691, Blair wrote Kirkwood that the bishop of London "intends to ask a stipend for whosoever shall be Commissary in Virginia . . . and he seems to have very kind intentions towards me in the thing, for tho I dissuaded him from making it a place of profit, he tells me he will

ask no less than 200 pounds a year for it. . . ." The commissary also recited progress in behalf of the college. Advocates' MS 29.3.4, fol. 5, National Library of Scotland.

11. Blair to Nicholson, February 27, 1692, "William and Mary College: Recently Discovered Documents," *William and Mary Quarterly*, 2d. ser., 10 (1930): 242. The Royal household and troops were transported to Holland during part of the conflict so that the king could direct his forces in person.

12. Henry Hartwell, James Blair, and Edward Chilton, *The Present State of Virginia, and the College*, edited by Hunter Dickinson Farish (Williamsburg: Colonial Williamsburg, Inc., 1940), p. xv.

13. Arthur Pierce Middleton, *Tobacco Coast* (Newport News, Virginia: Mariners Museum, 1953), p. 293.

14. Blathwayt had served since 1681 as "Surveyor and Auditor General of all his Majesty's Revenues arising in America." P.R.O./C.O. in L.C., 1318, pp. 225–27.

15. "A Memoriall Concerning £2000 raised out of the Quitt Rents now begg'd for ye Colledge of Virginia," P.R.O./C.O.5 in L.C., 1306, no. 118.

16. Perry, *Historical Collections*, 1:8. Though Blair wrote Nicholson that he had obtained money from the Boyle estate, several legalities remained to be cleared up. The Manor of Brafferton from which it was to come was not purchased until 1695, and regulations concerning the part to go to William and Mary were not drawn up until December 1697, during Blair's next visit to London.

17. Richard L. Morton, *Colonial Virginia*, 2 vols. (Chapel Hill: University of North Carolina Press, 1960), 1:348.

18. Blair to Nicholson, February 27, 1692, "William and Mary College: Recently Discovered Documents," *William and Mary Quarterly*, 2d ser., 10 (1930): 243.

19. *Calendar of Treasury Books, 1689–1692*, edited by William A. Shaw (London: H. M. Stationery Office, 1931), vol. 9, pt. 5.

20. "A Memoriall Concerning £2000 raised out of the Quitt Rents now begg'd for ye Colledge of Virginia." P.R.O./C.O.5 in L.C., 1306, no. 118.

21. Ibid., no. 118.

22. Ibid., no. 119.

23. These objections were written in the margin of a copy of Blair's memorial, ibid., no. 118.

24. Ibid., no. 116.

25. Burnet, *History*, 3:165.

26. Benjamin Franklin to Mason Weems and Edward Gant, July 17, 1784. Albert H. A. Smyth, ed., *The Writings of Benjamin Franklin*, 10 vols. (New York: Macmillan Co., 1905–7), 9:240. No reference to such an incident occurs in any of Blair's surviving correspondence. One author, Samuel R. Mohler, surmises that Franklin may have heard or read the story when he visited William and Mary in 1756 to receive the honorary M.A. degree. Samuel R. Mohler, "Commissary James Blair, Churchman, Educator, and Politician of Colonial Virginia" (Ph.D. diss., University of Chicago, 1940), p. 172.

27. Thomas Babington Macauley describes Sir Edward Seymour as "licentious, profane, corrupt, too proud to behave with common politeness, yet not too proud to pocket ellicit gain." Macauley further describes him as "a Tory and a Churchman" who "had been persecuted by the Whigs in the day of their prosperity." Thomas Babington Macauley, *The History of England from the Accession of James the Second*, 10 vols. (Boston and New York: Houghton Mifflin & Co., 1899) 2:229–30.

28. *Acts of the Privy Council, Colonial Series*, 6 vols., edited by W. L. Grant and James Munro (Hereford: H. M. Stationery Office), 2:212.

29. "Papers Relating to Nicholson and the College," *Virginia Magazine of History and Biography*, 7 (October 1899): 159.

30. Hartwell, Blair, and Chilton, *The Present State of Virginia*, pp. 72–73.

31. *Journal of the House of Burgesses of Virginia*, 2:368.

32. Mohler, "Commissary James Blair," p. 177.

33. Wormeley had attended Oriel College, Oxford.

34. "An Abstract of the Design and Institution of the College of William and Mary in Virginia," Fulham Palace MSS, papers relating to Virginia, 1st box, no. 48, London.

35. Burnet, *History*, 2:209.

36. Blair to Nicholson, December 3, 1691, "Papers Relating to Nicholson and the College," *Virginia Magazine of History and Biography* 7 (July 1899–April 1900): 160–63.

37. Ibid., p. 161.

38. Ibid., p. 162.

39. Ibid., p. 160.

40. Blair to the Earl of Nottingham, dated "Portsmouth, March 29, 1693," indicates that he departed that port.

41. *Calendar of Treasury Books* (1689–1692), vol. 9, pt. 1, p. 275.

42. *Journal of the House of Burgesses of Virginia*, 2:491.

43. *Executive Journals of the Council of Colonial Virginia*, 4 vols., edited by H. R. McIlwaine (Richmond: Virginia State Library, 1925–30), 1:301.

44. "Papers Relating to Nicholson and the College," p. 163.

45. Morton, *Colonial Virginia*, 1:348. This church, completed in 1683, was the predecessor of the present Bruton Parish Church, completed in 1715.

46. P.R.O./C.O.5 in L.C., 1309, no. 16, p. 88.

47. Middleton, *Tobacco Coast*, p. 459.

48. "Papers Relating to Nicholson and the College," p. 391.

49. *Dictionary of American Biography*, 20 vols., edited by Allen Johnson and Dumas Malone (New York: Charles Scribner's Sons, 1928–36), 13:300–301.

CHAPTER V

1. *Executive Journals of the Council of Colonial Virginia*, 4 vols., edited by H. R. McIlwaine (Richmond: Virginia State Library, 1925–30), 1:116 for June 4, 1690.

2. P.R.O./C.O.5 in L.C., 1305, no. 73. See also ibid., no. 116.

3. "A Memorial Concerning Sir Edmund Andros, Governor of Virginia, by John Blair," in William Stevens Perry, ed., *Historical Collections Relating to the American Colonial Church*, 5 vols. (Hartford: Printed for the Subscribers, 1870–78), 1:19.

4. *Calendar of Treasury Books* (1660–March 1704/5), 19 vols., edited by William A. Shaw (London: H. M. Stationery Office, 1904–35), vol. 9, pt. 3, p. 1258. P.R.O./C.O.5 in L.C., 1309, no 49, p. 285. *Calendar of State Papers, Colonial Series, America and West Indies* (1697–98), edited by J. W. Fortescue and Cecil Headlam (London: H. M. Stationery Office, 1901–16), p. 289. *Executive Journals of the Council*, 1:400, 402.

5. Thomas Jefferson Wertenbaker, "The Attempt to Reform the Church of Colonial Virginia," *Sewanee Review* 25 (July 1917): 257.

6. "Conference at Lambeth, December 27, 1697," in Perry, *Historical Collections*, 1:49.

7. Blair to Nicholson, January 2, 1694, *Papers Relating to an Affidavit made by His Reverence James Blair, Clerk, pretended President of William and Mary College, and Supposed Commissary to the Bishop of London in Virginia, against Francis Nicholson, Esq.*, (n.p., 1727), p. 75.

8. Samuel R. Mohler, "Commissary James Blair, Churchman, Educator, and Politician of Colonial Virginia" (Ph.D. diss., University of Chicago, 1940), p. 240.

9. P.R.O./C.O.5 in L.C., 1308, no. 45. *Calendar of State Papers, Colonial Series, America and West Indies* (1693–96), p. 256.

10. Precedent in Virginia discouraged clergy participation in politics, and no minister had sat in the assembly. William W. Hening, *The Statutes at Large: Being a Collection of All the Laws of Virginia from the First Session of the Legislature in 1619*, 13 vols., facs. ed. (Charlottesville: University Press of Virginia, 1969) 1:378.

11. William E. Dodd, *The Old South: Struggles for Democracy* (New York: Macmillan Company, 1937), p. 108.

12. William and Mary College Papers, Lambeth MSS, vol. 942, no. 50, p. 6 (typed copy), Bodleian Library, Oxford University.

13. Evidently Hannah and Philip Ludwell II lived briefly at Richneck, for their daughter Hannah was born there in 1701. Ethel Armes, *Stratford Hall: The Great House of the Lees* (Richmond: Garrett & Massie, Inc., 1936), p. 20.

14. From deed no. 21 of the Lee-Ludwell Papers in possession of the Virginia Historical Society. No acreage is mentioned, but a plat drawn in 1770 showed 3,865 acres. The Blairs agreed that the property should revert to Philip Ludwell II or his descendants in event there were no "lawfull heirs of either of their bodies." The property had first been owned by Richard Kemp. It passed to Thomas Ludwell, a bachelor, who left it to his brother Philip on his death, October 1, 1678. When Bruton Parish was created in 1674, it was named for Ludwell's native town of Bruton in Somerset, England.

15. Another deed in the Lee-Ludwell Papers of the Virginia Historical Society, dated August 5, 1707, conveys an additional one hundred acres adjoining the Richneck tract from Ludwell to James and Sarah Blair. It refers to "the Plantation on which the said James Blair now lives" and describes the land as being bounded on one side by Archer's Hope Mill Swamp and on another by the lands "now or late belonging to Mr. John Page on the road leading to the County of New Kent." The principal Richneck house stood not far off the road to Jamestown, near the present Walsingham Academy. The author is indebted to Arthur Hill for pointing out the site, which is unmarked.

16. Henrico County Records [Deeds and Wills], 1697–1704, no. 68–3590, Archives Division, Virginia State Library. Bartholomew Fowler's widow, born Sarah Archer, became the second wife of Blair's brother Archibald after 1700.

17. Blair held Andros responsible for the decline. Perry, *Historical Collections,* 1:45.

18. *Executive Journals of the Council,* 1:327.

19. *Journal of the House of Burgesses of Virginia, 1619–1776,* 13 vols., edited by J. P. Kennedy and H. R. McIlwaine (Richmond: Colonial Press, W. Waddey Co., 1915), 3:74.

20. Blair to Nicholson, May 8, 1695, *Virginia Magazine of History* 7 (July 1899–April 1900): 275–76.

21. The "Instrument Appointing Commissioners for Taking Subscriptions Toward a College" lists "Mr. James Blair, Commissary, Capt. William Randolph, Col. Edward Hill, Mr. Francis Eppes, and Captain Joseph Foster, Mr. Patrick Smith, minister of Southwark, Mr. Benj. Harrison, Mr. Henry Baker, Col. Thos Milner, Col. Joshua Lawson, and Col. Lemuel Mason, Mr. Samuel Eburne, minister of Bruton, Edmund Jennings, Esq., Capt. Francis Page, Mr. Henry Hartwell, & Mr. William Sherwood & Captain Henry Duke.

"Mr. Dewel Pead, minister of Middlesex, Mr. Christopher Robinson, Mr. John Buckner, Major Lewis Burwell, Capt. Phillip Lightfoot, Major Henry Whiting, Captain John Smith, Mr. Thomas Foster, Col. Richard Johnson, Mr. William Leigh.

"Mr. John Farnifold, minister of Bowtracey, Capt. George Cooper, Mr. Christopher Neale, Capt. William Hardwick, Capt. Lawrence Washington, Col. William Fitzhugh, Captain William Ball, Captain John Pinkard, Mr. Robert Carter, Capt. William Lee.

"Mr. Teagle, Minister of Accomack, Col. Daniel Jenefer, Col. Charles Scarborough, Col. John West, & Capt. John Custis . . . ," P.R.O./C.O.5, in L.C., 1306, no. 23.

22. Conference at Lambeth, December 27, 1697, Perry, *Historical Collections*, 1:44.

23. Ibid., pp. 42–43.

24. "Papers Relating to Nicholson and the College," *Virginia Magazine of History* 7 (July 1899–April 1900): 391.

25. Wormeley to Blathwayt, August 16, 1695. Blathwayt Papers, Colonial Williamsburg Archives.

26. Blair to Nicholson, May 8, 1695, MS, Virginia Historical Society, printed in *Virginia Magazine of History and Biography* 7 (July 1899–April 1900): 275–76.

27. William and Mary College Papers, Lambeth MSS, folder 8, vol. 942, no. 50, Bodleian Library.

28. William H. Browne, ed., *Proceedings of the Council of Maryland, 1687/ 8–93: Archives of Maryland*, 70 vols. (Baltimore: Maryland Historical Society, 1890), 20:237.

29. Ibid., p. 235.

30. *Papers Relating to an Affidavit*, p. 37.

31. Hugh Jones, *The Present State of Virginia, Giving a Particular and Short Account of the Indian, English and Negroe Inhabitants of that Colony*, edited by Richard L. Morton (Chapel Hill: University of North Carolina Press, 1956), p. 67.

32. The original college differed markedly from that rebuilt on the same foundation after the 1705 fire. For an excellent account of its design and construction, see Marcus Whiffen, *The Public Buildings of Williamsburg: Colonial Capital of Virginia* (Williamsburg: Colonial Williamsburg, 1958), pp. 18–33.

33. The issue was aired at a hearing before the archbishop of Canterbury at Lambeth in 1697 at which William Byrd II represented Andros. Perry, *Historical Collections*, 1:54–57.

34. *Executive Journals of the Council*, 1:324. *Journal of the House of Burgesses*, 3:4–5.

35. *Executive Journals of the Council*, 1:324.

36. Ibid., p. 325. Blair evidently referred to James II's replacement of offending ministers during his ill-fated reign.

37. Ibid.

38. Ibid. "His restless Comport I ever passed by till the whole Councill for his Demeanor before them cauling him as unfitt to be in Council I thought it my duty . . . to suspend him . . . till further Order," Andros to the Duke of Shrewsbury, June 4, 1695, P.R.O./C.O.5/1307, f.f. 175–76.

39. Andros to the Lords Commissioners of Trade and Plantations, June 4, 1695, P.R.O./C.O.5, in L.C., 1307, no. 72.

40. Andros to the Duke of Shrewsbury, Principal Secretary of State, June 4, 1695. P.R.O./C.O.5 in L.C., 1307, no. 24.

41. Blair to Nicholson, May 8, 1695, *Virginia Magazine of History and Biography* 7 (July 1899–April 1900): 277.

42. Ibid.

43. The Commissary convened the clergy in June 1696 at Jamestown, where they drew up an address to the governor. They asked that their benefices be restored to the value they had before tobacco had declined in price. They also asked the governor to obtain from King William and Queen Mary improvement

in the glebes, which had been "so Ornamentally described by the said House of Burgesses" but which were often "destitute of houses, orchards and other conveniences." Andros to the Duke of Shrewsbury, June 27, 1696, P.R.O./C.O.5 in L.C., 1307, no. 34.

44. Blair to Nicholson, February 12, 1697. Edmund B. O'Callaghan, ed., *Calendar of Historical Manuscripts in the Office of the Secretary of State, Albany, N.Y.* (Albany: Weed, Parsons and Company, 1866), pt. 2, p. 342.

45. P.R.O./C.O.5, in L.C., 1309, no. 52. *Executive Journals of the Council*, 1:364 for April 20, 1697.

46. Ibid. Eight members of the council to the Lords Commissioners, April 24, 1697.

47. Conference at Lambeth, December 27, 1697. Perry, *Historical Collections*, 1:58–59.

48. Eight councillors to the Lords Commissioners, April 24, 1689, P.R.O./C.O.5, in L.C., 1309, no. 17. *Executive Journals of the Council*, 1:364.

49. Conference at Lambeth, December 27, 1697. Perry, *Historical Collections*, 1:59.

50. Ibid., pp. 58–62.

51. With the removal of Philip Ludwell I to England after 1700, his son took over Greenspring, Chippokes, and the property at Jamestown. Ludwell senior died in England after 1711.

52. Alexander Wilbourne Weddell, ed., *Virginia Historical Portraiture* (Richmond: William Byrd Press, 1930), pp. 148–49.

CHAPTER VI

1. A memorandum by Blair at the end of the trip reads: "To all my Expences living in *London* and solliciting Business [£] 200.0.0. To my Passage at Sea and Travelling by Land [£]50.00.0." *Papers Relating to an Affidavit made by His Reverence James Blair, Clerk, pretended President of William and Mary College, and Supposed Commissary to the Bishop of London in Virginia, against Francis Nicholson, Esq.*, n.p., 1727, p. 86.

2. Blair to Nicholson, June 2, 1698, Ibid., p. 85.

3. "Mr. Commissary Blair's Memorial against Governor Nicholson," in William Stevens Perry, ed., *Historical Collections Relating to the American Church*, 5 vols. (Hartford: Printed for the Subscribers, 1870–78), 1:75.

4. William H. Browne, ed., *Proceedings of the Council of Maryland, 1687/8–93: Archives of Maryland*, 70 vols. (Baltimore: Maryland Historical Society, 1890), 20:365–66.

5. Nicholson to the Lords Commissioners, August 20, 1696, Ibid., (1697–98), 23:492.

6. Henry Hartwell, James Blair, and Edward Chilton, *The Present State of Virginia and the College*, edited by Hunter Dickinson Farish (Williamsburg: Colonial Williamsburg, Inc., 1940), pp. xv–xvi.

7. Peter Laslett, "John Locke, the Great Recoinage, and The Origins of the Board of Trade, 1695–1698," *William and Mary Quarterly*, 3d ser., 14 (1957): 370.

8. The manuscript for "Some of the Cheif Greivances of the present Constitution of Virginia with an Essay towards the remedies thereof" is in the Lovelace Collection of Locke manuscripts in the Bodleian Library, Oxford University. In one passage, Blair observed, "Governors are sent over thither not such as are to stay and Live with the people: but such as are to make a little money for four or five years, and then to return again. Now it is not likely that men goeing in this design will promote towns or any other improvements, but such as will quit cost, and pay them for their pains, in their own time." Michael G. Kammen, ed., "Virginia at the Close of the Seventeenth Century: An Ap-

praisal by James Blair and John Locke," *Virginia Magazine of History and Biography* 74 (1966): 156.

9. Chilton was married to Hannah, daughter of Colonel Edward Hill of Shirley, in Charles City County. Hill was later named a trustee of the College of William and Mary.

10. Hartwell died in England in 1699.

11. Laslett, "John Locke, the Great Recoinage," p. 400.

12. From a photostatic copy of the covering note, endorsed "October 9 & 10th 1697./to William Popple, Esq. Secretary to the Lords Commissioners of the Council of Trade at Whitehall," in the manuscript collection, University of Edinburgh.

13. The report was not published until 1727. After slight revision, it was issued by John Wyat, in London, apparently for the benefit of the College of William and Mary, with the charter appended and its title changed to *The Present State of Virginia, and the College.* A new edition, edited by Hunter Dickinson Farish, was published by Colonial Williamsburg in 1940. See ibid., p. xviii.

14. Ibid., p. 70.

15. Ibid., p. 59.

16. Ibid., p. 68.

17. Ibid.

18. This independent governmental body had been appointed in May 1696 to replace the committee of the Privy Council that had supervised colonial affairs since 1675.

19. "Memorial Concerning Sir Edmund Andros, Governor of Virginia, by Dr. Blair" [1697], Perry, *Historical Collections,* 1:10–17.

20. Ibid., p. 11.

21. Ibid., pp. 12–13.

22. Ibid., p. 16.

23. Ibid., p. 15.

24. Ibid., p. 14.

25. Ibid.

26. Ibid., p. 18.

27. Ibid., pp. 18–19.

28. Ibid., p. 22.

29. Ibid., pp. 23–24.

30. Ibid., p. 25.

31. Ibid., pp. 27–28.

32. Frances Culpeper, whose former husband was Sir William Berkeley, continued to be known as Lady Berkeley despite her marriage to Philip Ludwell I.

33. "Memorial Concerning Sir Edmund Andros," Perry, *Historical Collections,* 1:26–27.

34. Ibid., p. 29.

35. Tenison had succeeded John Tillotson as archbishop of Canterbury in 1695.

36. Marshall later wrote the Board of Trade, requesting that a "letter of Revocation" be sent Andros in Virginia, "there having been no Complaint against Sir Edmund Andros of Mismanagement in his Government in Virginia." P.R.O./C.O.5, in L.C., 1309, no. 48.

37. Richmond Croom Beatty, *William Byrd of Westover* (Boston: Houghton Mifflin Company, 1932), pp. 14, 22.

38. Perry, *Historical Collections,* 1:37. This charge was evidently based on a letter from the Reverend Nicholas Moreau in Virginia to the Bishop of Lichfield and Coventry, dated April 12, 1697. He wrote: "This clergy is composed for the most part of Scotchmen, people indeed so basely educated and so little

acquainted with the excellency of their charge and duty, that their lives and conversation are fitter to make Heathens than Christians." Ibid., p. 30.

39. "Conference at Lambeth," December 27, 1697. Ibid., pp. 39–40.

40. Ibid., p. 37.

41. Ibid., pp. 40–43.

42. Ibid., p. 42.

43. Ibid., pp. 43–65.

44. William Stevens Perry, *The History of the American Episcopal Church*, 1587–1883, 2 vols. (Boston: James R. Osgood and Co., 1885), 1:121.

45. The manuscript, in Byrd's hand, was found by Louis B. Wright in the Byrd papers at the Henry E. Huntington Library. Originally titled "A Vindication of Sir Edmond Andros before the Arch Bishop of Canterbury and the Bishop of London at Lambeth by Mr. Byrd anno 1697," it had been shortened by a line drawn through "by Mr. Byrd anno 1697." In it Byrd correctly surmised that Blair was conniving to replace Andros with Nicholson. He wrote that Blair "has been a Constant Stickler for ecclesiastical courts in Virginia: which woud be worth to him as commissary about 200 pound a year. This project Colonel Nicholson drove on him very furiousle dureing his time, but Sir Edmund succeeding him, and percieving the impracticableness of that scheme, by rason of the corruption of the Clergy and the irreconcilable aversion of the Laity[,] he [Andros] forbore to prosecute this affair so zealously as the other had done. This offended Mr Blair, because he found himself disappointed in that hopefull Project and therefore makes this unjust War upon Sir Edmond Andros . . . that . . . he might possibly get his righteous Patron Mr. Nicholson to succeed Him. And coud that be brough about my lords he expects to be his first minister . . . But if he [Nicholson] should prove restiff I expect he will blacken him as much as he has done Sir Edmond Andros." Louis B. Wright, "William Byrd's Defense of Sir Edmund Andros," *William and Mary Quarterly*, 3d ser., 2 (1944): 62.

46. Beatty, *William Byrd*, p. 27.

47. Locke MSS in the Bodleian Library, Oxford University, by permission. Photostat in possession of Colonial Williamsburg. No reply from Locke has been found.

48. P.R.O./C.O.5, in L.C., 1309, no. 52. *Calendar of State Papers, Colonial Series, America and West Indies* (1697–98), pp. 294, 322.

49. *Calendar of State Papers, Colonial Series, America and West Indies* (1697–98), pp. 296, 329, 399.

50. The Bishop of London to Sir Philip Meadows, August 9, 1698. P.R.O./C.O.5, 1309, no. 59.

51. Stephen Webb, "Officers and Governors: The Role of the British Army in Imperial Politics and the Administration of the American Colonies, 1689–1722" (Ph.D. diss., University of Wisconsin, 1965), p. 231.

The Reverend Nicholas Moreau in Virginia wrote to the Bishop of Lichfield and Coventry on April 12, 1697, to observe that Andros' "time is over." In his fascinating study of British governors, Stephen Saunders Webb deems this to be "a recognition that governors' terms were usually limited to five years or less. . . . This was the time usually required for political tides to cycle out an officer's political patrons and substitute men with clients of their own." At the time Moreau wrote, Andros had already served five and half years in Virginia.

52. Nicholson to Locke, May 26, 1698, and February 4, 1699. Locke MSS C. 16, Lovelace Collection, Bodleian Library, Oxford University.

53. Secretary James Vernon to the Lords Commissioners, May 31, 1698, P.R.O./C.O.5, in L.C., 1309, no. 45.

54. *Papers Relating to an Affidavit*, pp. 84–85.

55. P.R.O./C.O.5, in L.C., 1359, p. 210.

56. A burning candle was used to measure the time permitted for bidding.

57. William Blathwayt, colonial auditor-general, sat as a member of the Board of Trade. Blathwayt opposed Locke's reforms and championed Andros when Locke favored his removal. He was clerk to the Privy Council under Charles II, James II, William and Mary, and Queen Anne. From 1692 to 1702 he was also secretary of state.

58. Locke MSS in the Bodleian Library, Oxford University, by permission. A photostat is in the possession of Colonial Williamsburg. Blair goes on to report that as his last vindictive act, Andros named Dudley Digges of York to the council, though Digges had not yet been seated. "For our College's sake," he asked, "I would beg that such a man as this may be left out of the Council, as he is at present out of it, not having been nominated in the Governours Instructions. . . ."

59. A baroscope shows the approximate weight of the atmosphere. A thermoscope indicates changes in temperature without accurately measuring them.

60. Perry, *Historical Collections*, 1:66–67.

CHAPTER VII

1. Three of its houses had been inherited by Philip Ludwell I on the death of his brother Thomas in 1678. Foundations of the State House group were unearthed by Samuel H. Yonge in 1903 and are described in his *The Site of Old "James Towne," 1607–1698* (Richmond: Hermitage Press, 1907), pp. 85–97.

2. From an address by Miss Jane Carson to the Jamestowne Society, Williamsburg Conference Center, May 13, 1967.

3. *Journal of the House of Burgesses of Virginia, 1619–1776*, 13 vols., edited by J. P. Kennedy and H. R. McIlwaine (Richmond: 1915), 3:xxx, 135, 161, 162, 165.

4. Louis B. Wright, *The First Gentlemen of Virginia: Intellectual Qualities of the Early Colonial Ruling Class* (San Marino: Huntington Library, 1940), p. 110.

5. For an account of the five addresses, see "Speeches of the Students, 1699" *William and Mary Quarterly*, 2d ser., 10 (1930): 323–24.

6. Jones was the third scholar to sign an address on May 17, 1699, from "the President, Masters and Scholars of the Royal College of William and Mary in Virginia," expressing their pleasure in the assembly's visit and their expectation of continued "Blessings and Prayers of all good men." He was the son of Rowland Jones, first rector of Bruton Parish, whose gravestone describes him as "Pastor, primus & delectissimus."

7. Blair to the archbishop of Canterbury. William Stevens Perry, ed., *Historical Collections Relating to the American Colonial Church*, 5 vols. (Hartford: Printed for the Subscribers, 1970–78), 1:112–13.

8. P.R.O./C.O.5, in L.C., 1359, p. 399. Ibid., 1312, no. 5.

9. Nicholson to the Archbishop of Canterbury, Perry, *Historical Collections*, 1:120.

10. "Report of the Journey of Francis Louis Michel from Berne, Switzerland, to Virginia, October 2, 1701–December 1, 1702," *Virginia Magazine of History and Biography* 24 (1916): 26.

11. Spotswood to Blathwayt, July 28, 1711. Robert A. Brock, ed., *Official Letters of Alexander Spotswood: Lieutenant Governor of Virginia, 1710–1722*, n.s., 2 vols. (Richmond: The Virginia Historical Society, 1882–85), 1:103.

12. Ibid., pp. 156–57.

13. John Oldmixon, *The British Empire in America*, 2 vols. (London, 1741), 1:437.

14. Marcus Whiffen, *The Public Buildings of Williamsburg: Colonial Capital of Virginia* (Williamsburg: Colonial Williamsburg, 1958), p. 9.

15. Robert Beverley, *The History and Present State of Virginia*, edited by

Louis B. Wright (Chapel Hill: University of North Carolina Press, 1947), p. 105.

16. Blair to [Earl of Nottingham], March 29, 1693, *Calendar of State Papers, Colonial Series, America and West Indies* (1693–96), edited by J. W. Fortescue and Cecil Headlam (London: H. M. Stationery Office, 1930), no. 227, p. 69.

17. Burke Davis, *A Williamsburg Galaxy* (New York: Holt, Rinehart and Winston, 1968), p. 11.

18. Richard L. Morton, *Colonial Virginia*, 2 vols. (Chapel Hill: University of North Carolina Press, 1960), 1:377–78. Nicholson explained, in his affidavit of March 3, 1705, that he objected to Blair's funeral oration because "he reflected, to give it no worse an epithete[,] upon their Matys King Charles the Second, & especially on King James." P.R.O./C.O.5, in L.C., 1314.

19. Davis, *A Williamsburg Galaxy*, p. 12.

20. Beverley, *The History and Present State of Virginia*, pp. 103–5.

21. "A President and Six Masters," an address delivered by W. Melville Jones on the 268th anniversary of the granting of the Royal Charter, February 8, 1693 (Williamsburg: The College of William and Mary, 1961), p. 15.

22. Ibid.

23. Inglis to Nicholson in Perry, *Historical Collections*, 1:140. Inglis left, but when Blair offered him the mastership of the grammar school again in 1716, he returned and remained until his death. Blair wrote the bishop of London in 1717 that Inglis "had a good talent for teaching and was a sober and good man. Under him the school thrives. . . ." Inglis remained in York County from 1705 on, and records of Bruton Parish list the deaths of his daughters Mary and Anne in 1710, of his wife Anne in 1711, and of his son David in 1714. William A. R. Goodwin, *The Record of Bruton Parish Church*, edited by Mary Frances Goodwin (Richmond: Dietz Press, 1941), pp. 164–65.

24. Beverley, *History and Present State of Virginia*, pp. 266–67. The historian erred. Blair's salary was £150.

25. "Conference at Lambeth, December 27, 1697," Perry, *Historical Collections*, 1:42.

26. Samuel R. Mohler, "Commissary James Blair, Churchman, Educator, and Politician of Colonial Virginia" (Ph.D. diss., University of Chicago, 1940), p. 203.

27. "Mr. Commissary Blair's Memorial against Governor Nicholson," 1701. Perry, *Historical Collections*, 1:76.

28. Ibid.

29. Nicholson to the Lords Commissioners, March 1705. *Calendar of State Papers, Colonial Series, America and West Indies* (1704–5), pp. 422–23.

30. "Mr. Commissary Blair's Memorial," ibid., pp. 79–80.

31. Nicholson to the Bishop of London. S.P.G. MSS, ser. B.1, no. 752, p. 930, Library of Congress transcripts.

32. *Executive Journals of the Council of Colonial Virginia*, 4 vols., edited by H. R. McIlwaine (Richmond: Virginia State Library, 1925–30), 2:146.

33. The manuscript remained in the files of the Lords Commissioners of Trade and Plantations until 1727, when it was published. Henry Hartwell, James Blair, and Edward Chilton, *The Present State of Virginia, and the College*, edited by Hunter Dickinson Farish (Williamsburg: Colonial Williamsburg, Inc., 1940).

34. Beverley, *History and Present State of Virginia*, p. 104.

35. Nicholson to the Lords Commissioners. *Calendar of State Papers, Colonial Series, America and West Indies* (1699), p. 311.

36. Nicholson to the Lords Commissioners, October 22, 1703. P.R.O./C.O.5, in L.C., 1313, no. 33.

37. *Calendar of State Papers, Colonial Series, America and West Indies* (1699), p. 312.

38. Quary to the Lords Commissioners, October 15, 1703. *Calendar of State Papers, Colonial Series, America and West Indies* (1702–3), p. 732.

39. Manuscript in the possession of Colonial Williamsburg, originally in the collection of the Society for the Propagation of the Gospel.

40. Stephen Fouace to Archbishop of Canterbury, September 28, 1702. Fulham Palace MSS, papers relating to Virginia, 1st box, no. 95, Library of Congress.

41. Lucy Burwell eventually married Edmund Berkeley, who became a member of the council.

42. Stephen Fouace to Archbishop of Canterbury. Fulham MSS, 1st box, no. 95. Nicholson mistakenly wrote that Monro married James Blair's sister, but this was not the case.

43. Bishop of London to Blair, December 10, 1702. *Papers Relating to an Affidavit made by His Reverence James Blair, Clerk, pretended President of William and Mary College, and Supposed Commissary to the Bishop of London in Virginia, against Francis Nicholson, Esq.* (n.p., 1727), p. 8. Photostat, Massachusetts Historical Society.

44. Council of Virginia to the Queen, May 20, 1703. Perry, *Historical Collections*, 1:80–81.

45. Evidently a reference to the Reverend Stephen Fouace, one of Blair's few supporters among the Virginia clergy, and to Philip Ludwell I, both in England.

CHAPTER VIII

1. Subsequently impounded by a dam, the creek is known today as Lake Matoaka. It adjoins the campus of the College of William and Mary.

2. James Blair, *Our Saviour's Divine Sermon on the Mount, Contained in the Vth, VIth, and VIIth Chapters of St. Matthews' Gospel explained: and the Practice of it Recommended in Divers Sermons and Discourses*, 4 vols. 2d ed., (London: J. Brotherton, 1740).

3. That was the case of Grace Sherwood, of Princess Anne County, who was ducked in 1706 on suspicion of having evil powers.

4. William Meade, *Old Churches, Ministers, and Families of Virginia*, 2 vols. (Philadelphia: J. B. Lippincott & Co., 1906), 1:112.

5. The building, given to the Association for the Preservation of Virginia Antiquities by the Colonial Dames in the United States of America, in 1907, follows in some respects the form of St. Luke's Church, Isle of Wight County, built after 1632. The first brick Jamestown Church continued in use until the governorship of Robert Dinwiddie (1751–58), when it was supplanted by a more accessible church on the mainland, near Greenspring, called the Upper Church of James City Parish. The abandoned Jamestown church was in ruins by 1800.

6. From *The Whole Book of Psalmes, Collected into English Meeter by Thomas Sternhold, John Hopkins, and others* . . . (London: Printed by I.H. for the Company of Stationers, 1638).

7. Samuel H. Yonge, *The Site of Old "James Towne," 1607–1698* (Richmond: Hermitage Press, Inc., 1907), p. 72.

8. Ibid., p. 65.

9. Cobblestone foundations, evidently of the 1617 church, were uncovered in an archeological examination in 1902. Ibid., pp. 67–68.

10. Ibid., pp. 65–66.

11. Lyon Gardiner Tyler, *The Cradle of the Republic: Jamestown and James River* (Richmond: Hermitage Press, Inc., 1906), p. 133.

12. Ibid., p. 129.

13. The earliest death recorded on any of the gravestones is 1682. According to the *Report of the Proceedings of the Late Jubilee at Jamestown, Va.*, published after the bicentennial of 1807, "the discovery of the oldest stone became an object of general emulation . . . beyond 1682, nothing legible could be traced. . . ." Yonge, *Site of Old "James Towne,"* p. 68.

14. Tyler, *Cradle of the Republic*, p. 145. Keith, born in Aberdeen of the family that had created Marischal College, was a Quaker before joining the Church of England and emigrating to the colonies in 1689. His great-grandson was George Wythe.

15. Nicholson to the High Sheriff of New Kent County, Virginia, March 3, 1700. William Stevens Perry, *Historical Collections Relating to the American Colonial Church*, 5 vols. (Hartford: Printer for the Subscribers, 1870–78), 1:66.

16. Nicholson to the Clergy of Virginia, April 10, 1700. Ibid., p. 115.

17. The Clergy of Virginia to the Governor, April 11, 1700. Ibid., pp. 116–17.

18. This lengthy document is erroneously identified in Perry, *Historical Collections*, as an appendix to a letter from the Reverend Alexander Forbes of Upper Isle of Wight Parish on July 21, 1724, to the bishop of London. However, internal evidence and Blair's signature on the original indicate his authorship. The author is indebted to Samuel R. Mohler for this identification.

19. Perry, *Historical Collections*, 1:344.

20. Eight Councillors to the Lords Commissioners of Plantations, April 24, 1697. *Calendar of State Papers, Colonial Series, America and West Indies* (May 1696–October 1697), edited by J. W. Fortescue and Cecil Headlam (London: H. M. Stationery Office, 1901–16), pp. 461–62.

21. Robert Beverley, *The History and Present State of Virginia*, edited by Louis B. Wright (Chapel Hill: University of North Carolina Press, 1947), p. 263.

22. Samuel R. Mohler, "Commissary James Blair, Churchman, Educator, and Politician of Colonial Virginia" (Ph.D. diss., University of Chicago, 1940), p. 105.

23. Philip Ludwell II to Philip Ludwell, Esq., March 11, 1703. P.R.O./C.O.5, in L.C., 1314, no. 15(a).

24. Nicholas Moreau to the Right Honorable the Lord Bishop of Lichfield and Coventry, His Majesty's High Almoner, April 12, 1697. Perry, *Historical Collections*, 1:29–32.

25. Nicholson to Bishop of London, July 29, 1702, draft letter. Francis Nicholson Papers, MSS Colonial Williamsburg Archives, Colonial Williamsburg microfilm M-59. Nicholson wrote a briefer letter on July 28, 1702, to the archbishop of Canterbury in criticism of Blair. Both were penned "On board her Majtys Ship ye Southampton by ye Capes of Virginia." Fulham Palace Papers, Colonial Williamsburg microfilm M-287 #103.

26. Carl Bridenbaugh, *Mitre and Sceptre: Transatlantic Faiths, Ideas, Personalities, and Politics, 1689–1775* (New York: Oxford University Press, 1962), p. 119.

27. Twenty of the Clergy to the Bishop of London, September 22, 1703. Rawlinson MSS, c933 fo. 40, Library of Congress.

28. Memorandum by Six of the Clergy, 1703–4, Fulham Palace MSS, papers relating to Virginia, 3d box, no. 27, Library of Congress.

29. Twenty of the Clergy to the Bishop of London, September 22, 1703, ibid., 3d box, no. 48.

30. The opinion was in response to Nicholson's request for clarification of his instructions as governor, which had left it unclear as to whether governor or vestry held the initiative in inducting a parish minister. Northey made no objection to the Virginia vestries' traditional role as patrons in selecting their ministers and presenting them to the governor for induction, but he held that they could not delay action unduly. "If the Parishioners do not present a Minister to the Governor within six months after any Church shall become void, the Governor as Ordinary shall and may collate a Clerk to such Church by Lapse and his Collate shall hold the Church for his Life. If the Parishioners have never presented, they may have a reasonable Time to present a Minister, but if they will not present, being required so to do, the Governor may also in their Default collate a Minister." R. T. Barton, ed., *Virginia Colonial Decisions: The Reports*

by *Sir John Randolph and by Edward Barradall of Decisions of the General Court of Virginia*, 2 vols. (Boston: Boston Book Co., 1909), 2:13. B3.

31. *Executive Journals of the Council of Colonial Virginia*, 4 vols., edited by H. R. McIlwaine (Richmond: Virginia State Library, 1925–30), 2:353.

32. Mohler, "Commissary James Blair," pp. 111–12.

CHAPTER IX

1. Though sometimes erroneously referred to as Sir Francis Nicholson, he was never knighted.

2. Burke Davis, *A Williamsburg Galaxy* (New York: Holt, Rinehart and Winston, 1968), p. 9.

3. Robert Beverley, *The History and Present State of Virginia*, edited by Louis B. Wright (Chapel Hill: University of North Carolina Press, 1947), pp. 103–4.

4. *Journal of the Commissioners of Trade and Plantations* (1704–8) 14 vols. (London: H. M. Stationery Office, 1920–38), pp. 5–8. See *Calendar of State Papers, Colonial Series, America and West Indies* (1704–5), edited by J. W. Fortescue and Cecil Headlam (London, H. M. Stationery Office, 1901–16), pp. 105–10.

5. Nicholson to the Lords Commissioners, March 6, 1705. *Calendar of State Papers, Colonial Series, America and West Indies* (1704–5), p. 433.

6. Lords Commissioners to the Queen, June 13, 1704, Ibid., p. 166.

7. Blair to Philip Ludwell II, January 6, 1705. "Colonial Letters," *Virginia Magazine of History and Biography* 5 (July 1897–April 1898): 52–53.

8. *Executive Journals of the Council of Colonial Virginia*, 4 vols., edited by H. R. McIlwaine (Richmond: Virginia State Library, 1925–30) 2:414–16.

9. Ibid., p. 415.

10. *Calendar of State Papers, Colonial Series, America and West Indies* (1704–5), p. 370. The shipmaster, Richard Smith, said that when taken by a French privateer off the Scilly Isles, "I threw pacquetts I had on board from the Governor of Virginia and Maryland overboard."

11. The ensuing digest and quotations of Blair's affidavits are based on their texts as printed in William Stevens Perry, *Historical Collections Relating to the American Colonial Church* (Printed for the Subscribers, 1870–78), 1:93–112; 131–38.

12. "Jurat. 25 *to* die Aprilis anno regni Dominae Nostrae Annae Dei gratia Angliae Scotiae Franciae et Hiberniae Reginae Fidei Defensoris, &c., tertio annoque Domini 1704 . . ." ("Sworn—25th day of April in the reign of our Queen Anne by the Grace of God—Queen of England, Scotland, France, and Ireland. Defender of the Faith, etc., In the third year of the Reign.")

13. Blair used the word "mistress" in its innocent sense, meaning sweetheart or intended bride. Lucy Burwell eventually married Edmund Berkeley.

14. That is, inmates of Newgate Prison, or "jailbirds."

15. Perry, *Historical Collections*, 137–38. Blair's nephew John was a grammar school student at the college and apparently took part in the "barring out," judging from the affidavit in the 1705 of Jane Newman, a former servant of the Blairs.

16. "Affidavit of STEPHEN FOUACE relating to the maladministration of Col. Nicholson, Governor of Virginia, April 25, 1704." Ibid., pp. 87–93. In a letter to the archbishop of Canterbury on September 28, 1702, Fouace wrote of Nicholson: "Whatever cometh in his head about any thing Strikes him as strongly & carrieth him as infallibly as if it were inspiration, so that he becometh incapable of examining the solidity & the truth of it himself by second Thoughts & of consulting with others."

17. Thomas Jefferson Wertenbaker, *Give Me Liberty: The Struggle for Self-Government in Virginia* (Philadelphia: American Philosophical Society, 1958), p. 22.

18. P.R.O./C.O.5, in L.C., 1304, no. 36. *Journals of the Commissioners* (1704–8), p. 85. The abstracts were presented January 25, 1705.

19. Hugh Peters was an English minister, deeply involved in the political controversies of Stuart times, who was put to death in 1660 for abetting the execution of Charles I.

20. Perry, *Historical Collections*, 1:179–81.

21. *Calendar of State Papers, Colonial Series, America and West Indies* (1704–5), pp. 477–78, 397–402.

22. Ibid., p. 485.

23. Ibid., pp. 413–15.

24. Ibid., pp. 413–23.

25. Ibid., p. 419.

26. Ibid., pp. 413–15.

27. Ibid., pp. 426–27.

28. Ibid., p. 432.

29. *Journal of the House of Burgesses of Virginia*, 1619–1776, 13 vols., edited by J. P. Kennedy and H. R. McIlwaine (Richmond: Colonial Press, E. Waddey Co., 1915), 4:xxiv, 107–8.

30. *Calendar of State Papers, Colonial Series, America and West Indies* (1704–5), pp. 430–31.

31. *Papers Relating to an Affidavit made by His Reverence James Blair, Clerk, pretended President of William and Mary College, and Supposed Commissary to the Bishop of London in Virginia, against Francis Nicholson, Esq.* (n.p., 1727), pp. 25–26.

32. Ibid., pp. 29, 44–45.

33. Ibid., p. 73.

34. Perry, *Historical Collections*, 1:146.

35. Ibid., p. 147.

36. Ibid., pp. 141–54. The twenty-three clerics who signed were Solomon Whateley, Guy Smith, Daniel Taylor, James Sclater, Edward Portlock, Ralph Bowker, John Carnegie, William Williams, Emanuel Jones, Jacob Ware, Arthur Tillyard, Bartholomew Yates, Lewis Latané, William Rudd, Peter Wagener, James Burtell, James Boisseau, Orlando Jones, Andrew Monro, Thomas Sharp, James Clack, Peter Kippax, and Richard Squire.

37. Ibid., pp. 149–50.

38. Monro experienced difficulties similar to Blair's. Some of the vestry of St. John's Parish once addressed Governor Nicholson thus: "We do solemnly Declare that we have no personal prejudice against the Rev. Jno Monro, our present minister, upon account of his being of the Scotish Nation (though we must confess an Englishman would be more acceptable), but we are extremely dissatisfied with his behavior in Gen'l towards Government, insomuch that if all the Clergy of the Colony should follow his steps, the country would soon be in an uproar, if not endeavor for a revolt to the Dishonor of her Majty's Crown and Dignity. . . ."

39. Robertson, Anderson, and Brechin were identified by Blair's opponents as "Blair's countrymen," or Scotsmen.

40. Perry, *Historical Collections*, 1:151.

41. Ibid., p. 165.

42. Ibid., pp. 168–69.

CHAPTER X

1. The original, in the British Public Record Office, was redrawn in 1940 and published as an illustration for Rutherfoord Goodwin's *A Brief and True Report Concerning Williamsburg in Virginia* (Williamsburg: Colonial Williamsburg, Inc., 1941), p. xi.

2. P.R.O./C.O.5, 1318, p. 200 (Colonial Williamsburg microfilm M-240, reel 41). Mary R. M. Goodwin, "The Colonial Store," Colonial Williamsburg House Report, 1966, p. 245. James Blair and Philip Ludwell II supported each other in politics and business. Blair wrote Ludwell from London in 1705 as "Dear Brother," sending "my service to my Sister[-in-law] and blessing to the girlies," Ludwell's three daughters.

3. Nicholson to Bishop of London, July 29, 1702, MS letter, in possession of Colonial Williamsburg.

4. Philip Alexander Bruce, *Economic History of Virginia in the Seventeenth Century*, 2 vols. (New York: Macmillan and Company, 1896), 2:382–83. Archibald's third wife had first married William Roscow of Warwick, who originally contracted to marry Sarah Harrison. Roscow died in 1700.

5. In addition to his son John, who became president of the council, Archibald Blair had three daughters: Anne, who married a Mr. Whiting of Gloucester; Elizabeth, who married, first John Bolling, Jr., of Henrico, and second the pre-Revolutionary pamphleteer Richard Bland of Prince George County; and Harrison, who married Dr. George Gilmer, an Edinburgh University graduate who practiced medicine and kept a store in Williamsburg. A younger son, James Blair, who became a physician, was mentioned in the elder James Blair's will.

6. Mary R. M. Goodwin, "Colonial Store," p. 246.

7. Ibid., pp. 246–49. Prentis operated the store after 1733 as William Prentis and Company. Edward M. Riley, "William Prentis & Co.," *Financial Executive*, April 1968, pp. 35–41.

8. The Archibald Blair house has been acquired by Colonial Williamsburg and partially restored to its original state.

9. "Report of the Journey of Francis Louis Michel from Berne, Switzerland, to Virginia, October 2, 1701–December 1, 1702," translated by W. J. Hinke, in *Virginia Magazine of History and Biography* 24 (1916): 126–27.

10. Manuscript in Fulham Palace library, dated 1697. William Stevens Perry, *Historical Collections Relating to the American Colonial Church*, 5 vols. (Hartford: Printed for the Subscribers, 1870–78), 1:36.

11. "Testimony to the Burning of the College of William and Mary, 1705," *Virginia Magazine of History and Biography* 6 (July 1898–April 1899): 275.

12. Mungo Inglis to Francis Nicholson, Fulham MSS, printed in *William and Mary Quarterly*, 2d ser., 10 (1930): 73.

13. Nicholson Papers, quoted in Marcus Whiffen, *The Public Buildings of Williamsburg: Colonial Capital of Virginia* (Williamsburg: Colonial Williamsburg, 1958), pp. 32–33.

14. Blair to Archbishop Tenison, September 2, 1706. Perry, *Historical Collections*, 1:83–84.

15. Governours and Visitors to the Archbishop, William and Mary College Papers, 1721–1818, Ac 1808, Library of Congress.

16. Lord Chancellor Macclesfield, *Ex Parte* William and Mary College, April 1722. *Papers Relating to an Affidavit made by His Reverence, James Blair, Clerk, pretended President of William and Mary College, and Supposed Commissary to the Bishop of London in Virginia, against Francis Nicholson, Esq.* (n.p., 1727), p. 32.

17. Louis B. Wright and Marion Tinling, eds., *The Secret Diary of William Byrd of Westover, 1709–1712* (Richmond: Dietz Press, 1941), p. 67.

18. Ibid., p. 82.

19. Ibid., p. 99.

20. Ibid., p. 116.

21. "Proceedings of the Visitors of William and Mary College, 1716," *Virginia Magazine of History and Biography* 4 (July 1896–April 1897): 170–71, 173.

22. Stephen Hawtrey to Edward Hawtrey, March 26, 1765. "Description of

William and Mary College, 1765," *Virginia Magazine of History and Biography* 16 (July–October 1908): 210.

23. Henry Compton, "Present Rules and Methods . . . for the disposition of the Rents and proffits of the Mannor of Brafferton . . . ," *William and Mary Quarterly*, 2d ser., 10 (1930): 68.

24. Perry, *Historical Collections*, 1:123–24.

25. Masters of the Indian school were: Christopher Jackson, before 1716; Christopher Smith, 1716; the Reverend Charles Griffin, about 1720; Richard Cocke, before 1729; the Reverend John Fox, 1729; the Reverend Robert Barret, 1737; the Reverend Thomas Dawson, 1738. Lyon G. Tyler, "The College of William and Mary: Its Work, Discipline, and History, from Its Foundation to the Present Time," *Bulletin of the College of William and Mary*, May 1917, p. 32.

26. Hugh Jones, *The Present State of Virginia, Giving a Particular and Short Account of the Indian, English and Negroe Inhabitants of that Colony*, edited by Richard L. Morton (Chapel Hill: University of North Carolina Press, 1957), p. 67.

27. Ibid., p. 114.

28. "Proceedings of the Visitors of William and Mary College, 1716," p. 169.

29. Thomas Story, *A Journal of the Life of Thomas Story: Containing an account of his remarkable convincement of, and embracing the principals of truth, as held by the people called Quakers, and also, of his Travels and labors in the Service of the Gospel: With many other occurrences and observations* (Newcastle-upon-Tyne: Isaac Thompson and Company, 1747), pp. 387–88.

30. "Proceedings of the Visitors of William and Mary College, 1716," p. 165.

31. Nott was buried in Bruton churchyard after a state funeral conducted by James Blair. A handsome tomb marks the site.

32. *Executive Journals of the Council of Colonial Virginia*, 4 vols., edited by H. R. McIlwaine (Richmond: Virginia State Library, 1925–30), 3:117–18.

33. Ibid., p. 118.

34. *Calendar of State Papers, Colonial Series, America and West Indies* (1716–18), edited by J. W. Fortescue and Cecil Headlam (London: H. M. Stationery Office, 1901–16), p. 1901–16.

35. The earliest masters and their dates of appointment were: The Reverend Mungo Inglis, 1694; the Reverend Arthur Blackamore, 1706; the Reverend Mungo Inglis (reappointed 1716, died 1719); the Reverend Hugh Jones, 1719; Joshua Fry, 1729; the Reverend William Stith, 1731; the Reverend Edward Ford, 1737; the Reverend Thomas Robinson, 1742. Tyler, "The College of William and Mary," p. 32. Inglis was a master of arts of Edinburgh University.

36. Jordan D. Fiore, "Jonathan Swift and the American Episcopate," *William and Mary Quarterly*, 3d ser., 11 (1954): 429.

37. Jones, *The Present State of Virginia*, p. 96.

38. William Keith, *The History of the British Plantations in America*, (London: Printed at the Expence of the Society for the Encouragement of Learning by S. Richardson, 1738), p. 172.

39. Blair conducted Whateley's funeral at Bruton Parish Church on November 19, 1710. William Byrd wrote in his diary for that date: "In the afternoon we walked to church again to hear Mr. Blair preach Mr. Whately's funeral sermon, which he performed very well. . . ." Wright and Tinling, *The Secret Diary of William Byrd of Westover*, p. 260.

40. William A. R. Goodwin, *Historical Sketch of Bruton Church, Williamsburg, Virginia* (Petersburg, Virginia: Franklin Press Company, 1903), p. 28.

41. Whiffen, *Public Buildings of Williamsburg*, p. 77.

42. Ibid. (No source given.)

43. Jones, *The Present State of Virginia*, p. 70.

44. Whiffen, *Public Buildings of Williamsburg* p. 83. (No source given.)

45. William A. R. Goodwin, *The Record of Bruton Parish Church*, edited by Mary Frances Goodwin (Richmond: Dietz Press, 1941), pp. 31–33.

46. Sarah Blair was buried in the Jamestown churchyard, near the remains of other Harrisons. Her tombstone, no longer legible, read: "Memoriae Sacrum/ Here lyes in the hope of a Blessed Resurrection/ ye body of Mrs. Sarah Blair, wife of/ Mr. James Blair, Commissary of Virginia,/ Sometime Minister of this Parish,/ She was daughter of/ Col. Benjamin and Mrs. Hannah Harrison of/ Surry. Born Aug. ye 14th 1670. Married June ye 2d 1687./ Died May ye 5, 1713 exceeding beloved and lamented." Lyon G. Tyler, *The Cradle of the Republic: Jamestown and the James River* (Richmond: Hermitage Press, 1906), p. 133.

CHAPTER XI

1. Robert A. Brock, ed., *The Official Letters of Alexander Spotswood, Lieutenant Governor of Virginia, 1710–1722*, 2 vols. (Richmond: The Virginia Historical Society, 1882–85), 2:291–92.

2. Burke Davis, *A Williamsburg Galaxy* (New York: Holt, Rinehart and Winston, 1968), p. 28.

3. "Miscellaneous Colonial Documents," *Virginia Magazine of History and Biography* 17 (1909): 41–43.

4. Alexander Spotswood to Lord Orkney, December 22, 1718. P.R.O./C.O.5, in L.C., 1318, p. 585.

5. William Byrd II in 1717 listed these: "James Blair and Philip Ludwell II, married sisters of Nathaniel Harrison; William Byrd II married Ludwell's half-niece; William Bassett and Edmund Berkeley married Ludwell's nieces, the Burwell sisters." He did not include Carter as a member.

6. After the death of Benjamin Harrison II in 1712, his son Nathaniel was named to the council.

7. "The Councils Representations to the Govr touching commissions of Oyer and Terminer." Brock, *Official Letters of Alexander Spotswood*, 2:24–28.

8. The Council of Virginia to the Lords Commissioners, May 4, 1717.

9. P.R.O./C.O.5, in L.C., 1418, pp. 241–42.

10. Richmond Croom Beatty, *William Byrd of Westover* (Boston: Houghton Mifflin Company, 1932), pp. 92–96.

11. Northey to the Lords Commissioners, December 24, 1717. P.R.O./C.O.5, in L.C., 1318, pp. 297–301.

12. *Executive Journals of the Council of Colonial Virginia*, 4 vols., edited by H. R. McIlwaine (Richmond: Virginia State Library, 1925–30), 3:470.

13. Ibid., pp. 493–94.

14. Ibid., pp. 464–65, 479–80.

15. Spotswood to the Lords Commissioners, March 20, 1718, P.R.O./C.O.5, in L.C., 1318, pp. 371–88.

16. Spotswood to the Lords Commissioners, June 24, 1718. *Calendar of State Papers, Colonial Series, America and West Indies* (1717–18), edited by J. W. Fortescue and Cecil Headlam (London: H. M. Stationery Office, 1901–16), p. 277.

17. Ibid.

18. Spotswood to Orkney, July 1, 1718. P.R.O./C.O.5, in L.C., 1318, pp. 533–37.

19. Ludwell-Paradise House was the first building acquired by John D. Rockefeller, Jr., in 1926, in the restoration of Williamsburg.

20. *Journal of the House of Burgesses of Virginia, 1619–1776*, 13 vols., edited by J. P. Kennedy and H. R. McIlwaine (Richmond: Colonial Press, E. Waddey Co., 1915), 5: xxxvii, 200–201. Spotswood to the Lords Commissioners, June 11 and August 14, 1718. Brock, *Official Letters of Alexander Spotswood*, 2:278–79, 288.

21. "A Narrative of the Steps & Proposals made during the Session of the

Assembly for Accommodating Our Differences." P.R.O./C.O.5, in L.C., 1318, pp. 541–55.

22. Spotswood to the Lords Commissioners, June 24, 1718. Brock, *Official Letters, of Alexander Spotswood*, p. 284.

23. Achitophel, also spelled Ahithophel in the biblical account, was King David's counselor, who treacherously joined with Absalom against David.

24. Spotswood to Orkney, July 1, 1718. P.R.O./C.O.5, in L.C., 1318, pp. 533–34.

25. Ibid.

26. Ibid.

27. *Journal of the House of Burgesses* (1712–26), 5:xxxix, 194, 210, 216, 228–29, 230–31.

28. Ibid., p. 230.

29. Spotswood to Orkney, December 22, 1718. P.R.O./C.O.5, in L.C., 1318, pp. 567–71.

30. *Journal of the House of Burgesses* (1712–26), 5:240.

31. P.R.O./C.O.5, in L.C., 1318, pp. 647–66, 808–9.

32. Spotswood to Orkney, December 22, 1718, ibid., p. 569. The Grymes referred to was John Grymes of Middlesex, elected a burgess in 1715 in opposition to Spotswood. He was Ludwell's son-in-law. Corbin was Gawin Corbin of Middlesex, also elected in 1715 as an anti-Spotswood leader.

33. *Journal of the Commissioners for Trade and Plantations, 1704–82*, 14 vols., edited by Cecil Headlam (London: H. M. Stationery Office, 1920–38), 3:425–26.

34. Spotswood to the Lords Commissioners, May 5, 1720. P.R.O./C.O.5, in L.C., 1318, p. 847.

35. Spotswood to the Lords Commissioners, January 16, 1720. Ibid., pp. 9–20.

36. William Stevens Perry, ed., *Historical Collections Relating to the American Colonial Church*, 5 vols. (Hartford: Printed for the Subscribers, 1870–78), 1:246.

37. William Waller Hening, *The Statutes at Large: Being a Collection of All the Laws of Virginia from the First Session of the Legislature in 1619*, 13 vols., facs. ed. (Charlottesville: The University Press of Virginia, 1969) 2:46 for Act IV in the Code of 1662.

38. Perry, *Historical Collections*, 1:202.

39. Ibid.

40. Ibid., p. 203.

41. Ibid., p. 207.

42. "HISTORICAL REMARKS for the better understanding the PROCEEDINGS of the Convention of the Clergy at Williamsburg, in April, 1719." *Ibid.*, p. 219.

43. The anti-Blair clergy were Ralph Bowker, George Robertson, Emanuel Jones, Bartholomew Yates, William Finney, Lewis Latané, Thomas Sharpe, John Skaife, Alexander Scott, John Worden, Benjamin Pownal, William Brodie, John Bagge, Hugh Jones, Andrew Thomson, George Seagood, James Robertson, and James Falconar. Virginia clergy absent from the meeting were Alexander Forbes, James Tennant (out of country), Daniel Taylor (excused by letter), Samuel Bernard (ill), James Clack (ill), Owen Jones, John Prince, John Bell, Giles Rainsford, James Brechin, John Span, and William Black. "The Journal of the Proceedings of the Convention Held at the College of William and Mary, in the City of Williamsburg, in April, 1719," ibid., pp. 199–200.

44. Ibid., pp. 212–13.

45. Ibid., p. 213.

46. Ibid., pp. 213–14.

47. Ibid., p. 218.

48. Ibid., p. 223.

49. Blair and Monro's "Historical Remarks." *Ibid.*, p. 225.

50. "To the Honble Alexander Spotswood His Majties Lt Govr & Commander in Chief of the Colony." *Ibid.*, pp. 223–24.

51. Besides Blair, signers were John Monro, Jr., John Cargill, Peter Fontaine, John Brunskill, Guy Smith, Francis Milne, and James Sclater. *Ibid.*

52. "An Answer to the Accusations contained in the Governour's Letter to the Convention; which Letter is to be seen in the Journal of the Proceedings of the Said Convention," and "Mr. COMMISSARY's Remarks on the Governour's Letter to the Parish of St. Anne's, relating to Collations. . . ." *Ibid.*, pp. 266–42.

53. *Ibid.*, pp. 218–20.

54. "To the Honble Alexander Spotswood. . . ." *Ibid.*, p. 220.

55. Blair from Spotswood, April 9, 1719. *Ibid.*, p. 222.

56. Brock, *Official Letters of Alexander Spotswood*, 2:293.

57. Perry, *Historical Collections*, 1:243–45.

58. *Executive Journals of the Council*, 3:517.

59. *Ibid.*, p. 524; Brock, *Official Letters of Alexander Spotswood*, p. 335; Perry, *Historical Collections*, 2 314–15.

60. William A. R. Goodwin, *The Record of Bruton Parish Church*, edited by Mary Frances Goodwin (Richmond: Dietz Press, 1941), p. 134.

61. *Ibid.*, pp. 17–29.

62. Leonidas Dodson, *Alexander Spotswood, Governor of Colonial Virginia, 1710–1722* (Philadelphia: University of Pennsylvania Press, 1932), p. 272. Spotswood to Bishop of London, May 26, 1721, Rawlinson MSS, H 376 fo 260B, Library of Congress.

63. Dodson, *Alexander Spotswood*, 273. In a letter to his London agent, Micajah Perry, John Custis wrote in 1721 to ask that he provide cash, if needed, to James Blair, who had gone there "to seek his just right." John Custis Letter Book, 1717–41, Manuscript Division, Library of Congress.

64. The commission was dated April 3, 1722. P.R.O./C.O.5, in L.C., 1319, p. 85.

65. *Ibid.*, p. 533.

66. Walter Havighurst, *Alexander Spotswood: Portrait of a Governor* (New York: Holt, Rinehart & Winston, 1967), pp. 103–4.

CHAPTER XII

1. Hugh Jones, *The Present State of Virginia, Giving a Particular and Short Account of the Indian, English and Negroe Inhabitants of that Colony*, edited by Richard L. Morton (Chapel Hill: University of North Carolina Press, 1956), pp. 80–81.

2. Blair to Nicholson, December 3, 1691. "Papers Relating to the Administration of Governor Nicholson and to the Founding of William and Mary College," *Virginia Magazine of History and Biography* 7 (July 1899–April 1900): 160–63.

3. Elizabeth Dabney Coleman and W. Edwin Hemphill, "Founding Virginia's First College," *Virginia Cavalcade Magazine*, Summer 1957, p. 191.

4. *Ibid.*

5. John M. Jennings, *The Library of the College of William and Mary in Virginia, 1693–1793* (Charlottesville: The University Press of Virginia, 1968), pp. 15–35.

6. P.R.O./C.O.5, in L.C., 1319, p. 664.

7. Jones, *The Present State of Virginia*, p. 108.

8. *Ibid.*, p. 67.

9. "Memorandum for His Excellency," *William and Mary Quarterly*, 2d ser., X, p. 248. The account is unsigned and undated.

10. Spotswood to the Bishop of London, May 26, 1721. Rawlinson MSS, H 376 fo 260B, Library of Congress.

11. *The Charter, Transfer, and Statutes of the College of William and Mary* (Williamsburg: William Hunter, 1758), p. 113.

12. Blair to Nicholson, December 3, 1691. William Stevens Perry, ed., *Historical Collections Relating to the American Colonial Church* (Hartford: Printed for the Subscribers, 1870–78), 1:3–8.

13. Blair to Bishop of London, June 8, 1728. Fulham Palace MSS, papers relating to Virginia, 1st box, no. 124, Library of Congress.

14. The transfer of authority was completed August 15, 1729. *Vital Facts of the College of William and Mary in Virginia* (Compiled by the College, 1963), p. 5.

15. The statutes were dated at London on June 24, 1727, but were not printed until 1736. *William and Mary Quarterly*, 1st ser., 12 (April 1914): 285.

16. Ibid.

17. Ibid., p. 286.

18. The practice of requiring advancing or graduating students to deliver an oral argument and to defend it against assault by professors continued at William and Mary at least until 1792, when Littleton Waller Tazewell described such an ordeal precedent to his graduation. Lynda Rees Heaton, "Littleton Waller Tazewell's Sketch of His Own Family . . . 1823," pp. 173–76, MSS collection, College of William and Mary.

19. The first faculty choice for burgess was Peter Beverley, but the House of Burgesses in 1715 refused to seat him on grounds that the college had no right to elect until it was legally founded. *Journal of the House of Burgesses of Virginia* (1619–1776), 13 vols., edited by J. P. Kennedy and H. R. McIlwaine (Richmond: Colonial Press, E. Waddey Co., 1915), 5:138.

20. William Gooch to Bishop of London, February 14, 1727–28. Herbert L. Ganter, "Documents Relating to the Early History of the College of William and Mary and to the History of the Church in Virginia," *William and Mary Quarterly*, 2d ser., 19 (October 1939): 456.

21. Jones, *The Present State of Virginia*, p. 111.

22. William and Mary College Papers, folder 241, printed in "The Walls of the College," *William and Mary Quarterly*, 1st ser., 11 (January 1903): 175n.

23. Ganter, "Documents Relating to the Early History," p. 467.

24. "Unpublished Letters at Fulham, in the Library of the Bishop of London," *William and Mary Quarterly*, 1st ser., 9 (April 1901): 220.

25. Blair to Bishop of London, August 14, 1732. Fulham Palace MSS, 1st box, no. 164. Randolph was the fifth son of Blair's former Henrico neighbors, William and Mary Isham Randolph, of Turkey Island plantation. His sister Mary married William Stith, who was president of the college from 1752–1755.

26. Blair to Bishop of London, September 18, 1733. Ibid., 2d box, no. 112.

27. Blair had the use of the three-hundred acre glebe lands of Bruton Parish, located in York County, and also apparently retained ownership of one hundred Richneck acres adjoining the college land. The remainder of Richneck reverted to the Ludwells, from whom he had leased it. Inherited by Philip Ludwell III on his father's death in 1727, Richneck was bequeathed on his death in 1767 to his daughter, Frances, and subsequently divided.

28. "Journal of the Meetings of the President and Masters of William and Mary College" [1729–84], *William and Mary Quarterly*, 1st ser., 1 (July 1892–April 1893): 137. William Stith became master of the grammar school about 1732.

29. *Another Secret Diary of William Byrd of Westover, 1739–1741*, Maude H. Woodfin, ed., translated and collated by Marion Tinling, (Richmond: Dietz Press, 1942), pp. 16–17.

30. Ibid., p. 58. During the last stages of the American Revolution, the presi-

dent's house was used briefly as headquarters by the British General Lord Cornwallis.

31. Ibid., p. 59.

32. Louis B. Wright and Marion Tinling, eds., *The Secret Diary of William Byrd of Westover, 1709–1712*, (Richmond: Dietz Press, 1941), p. 102.

33. "Journal of the Meetings of the President and Masters," pp. 215–18.

34. According to William Dawson, one of the masters of philosophy, Blair had "not many good editions of the fathers." Dawson to the Bishop of London, August 11, 1732, Fulham Palace MSS, 1st box, no. 16.

35. Courtlandt Canby, "A Note on the Influence of Oxford University upon William and Mary College," *William and Mary Quarterly*, 2d ser., 21 (1941): 244.

36. Spotswood wrote the Bishop of London in 1712: "There are now 14 Indian Children at the College and I speedily expect six more from our Neighboring Nations. . . ." Robert A. Brock, ed., *The Official Letters of Alexander Spotswood, Lieutenant Governor of Virginia, 1710–1722*, 2 vols. (Richmond: The Virginia Historical Society, 1882–85), 1:156.

37. Gooch to the Bishop of London, June 29, 1729, Gooch Transcripts, 1721–51, from P.R.O. and Fulham Papers, Colonial Williamsburg Research Department, Microfilm records, I, 134.

38. Such grants were made from the Nottoway Foundation, which had been created with the gift of £1,000 from the General Assembly in 1718, and the King Carter Fund, which was endowed by a bequest on that worthy's death in 1732, leaving to his family 300,000 acres, nearly 1,000 blacks, and substantial cash.

39. Paul Micou, "Services of Commissary James Blair to the Colony of Virginia," *South Atlantic Quarterly* 8 (April 1909): 164–73.

40. Gooch to Bishop of London, June 29, 1729, *William and Mary Quarterly*, 2d ser., 19 (1939): 463. After his return to Ireland from North America, Berkeley was made bishop of Cloyne in 1734. On his death Bishop Berkeley made a bequest to Yale College, which named its divinity school in his honor.

41. *Journal of the House of Burgesses* (1742–49), p. 154.

42. "Observations in Several Voyages and Travels in America," *London Magazine*, July 1746, reprinted in *William and Mary Quarterly* 1st ser., 15 (July 1906–January 1907): 143–59.

43. Visitors of the College to the Bishop of London, July 1, 1768, Fulham MSS, 2d box, no. 26.

CHAPTER XIII

1. Lyon G. Tyler, *The College of William and Mary in Virginia: Its History and Work, 1693–1907* (Richmond: Whittet & Shepperson, 1907), p. 32. Blair was apparently unaware that the bishop of London had forbidden Whitefield's preaching in his diocese. Blair wrote the Bishop in 1740 that he had heard, subsequent to Whitefield's sermon, that Whitefield was not in good standing. If this was correct, Blair wrote, he apologized. Blair to the Bishop of London, May 29, 1740. William Stevens Perry, ed., *Historical Collections Relating to the American Colonial Church*, 5 vols. (Hartford: Printed for the Subscribers, 1870–78), 1:362–64.

2. A governor of New York denounced Makemie for his evangelical services and described him as a "preacher, a doctor of physics, a merchant, an attorney, and what is worst of all, a disturber of government."

3. Bray was sent to the colonies in 1695 to ascertain the state of the church. On his return he wrote "A Memorial Representing the State of Religion in the Continent of North America." As a consequence, the Society for the Propagation of the Gospel in Foreign Parts was incorporated, under royal charter, in 1701.

4. Upon his death in 1728, Nicholson left most of his estate to the Society for the

Propagation of the Gospel in Foreign Parts. "Francis Nicholson," *Dictionary of American Biography*, 20 vols., edited by Allen Johnson and Dumas Malone (New York: Charles Scribner's Sons, 1928–36), 13:501.

5. "Account of the Proceedings of the Clergy of Virginia at the Church in Williamsburg, 1705." Perry, *Historical Collections*, 1:147.

6. From the Bishop of London's Eleventh Conference. Edward F. Carpenter, *The Protestant Bishop* (New York: Longmans, Green and Company, 1956), p. 212.

7. James Blair, *Our Saviour's Divine Sermon on the Mount, Contained in the Vth, VIth, and VIIth Chapters of St. Matthew's Gospel explained: and the Practice of it Recommended in Divers Sermons and Discourses*, 4 vols., 2d ed., (London: J. Brotherton, 1740), Rare Book Collection, the College of William and Mary. The author gave his books to friends. A copy of the third volume of the 1722 edition, inscribed "Robert Carter Ex dono Jacobi Blair Esq 1723," is at Shirley plantation in Charles City County.

8. Dr. Waterland, who was well known for his sermons and writings opposing deism, dated his preface to Blair's *Sermons* at Windsor, England, on December 24, 1739. "The worthy author living (if yet he lives) at too great a Distance to attend this edition . . ." he wrote, "I was desired to take the small trouble upon me." He noted that the sermons were first printed "by the particular Encouragement of then Metropolitan Archbishop Wake, and of Dr. Robinson, then Bishop of London, to whom the Sermons were dedicated." Blair revised the work slightly in 1732. Ibid., 1:v.

9. William Meade, *Old Churches, Ministers, and Families of Virginia*, 2 vols. (Philadelphia: J. B. Lippincott Co., 1906), pp. 155–56. Sermons in Virginia Episcopal churches in his youth were modeled after Blair's, Meade wrote: "The books most in use were Blair's *Sermons*, Sterne's *Works*, the *Spectator*, *The Whole Duty of Man*, sometimes Tillotson's *Sermons*. . . . But Blair's *Sermons*, on account of their elegant style and great moderation in all things, were most popular. . . ." P. 24.

10. Blair, *Our Saviour's Divine Sermon*, 1:xx.

11. Nicholson to the Bishop of London. Society for the Propagation of the Gospel in Foreign Parts MSS, B–1, no. 113, p. 422, Library of Congress.

12. William Hunter's *Virginia Gazette* for December 12, 1755, p. 4, included an advertisement by Daniel Parke Custis for two runaway slaves which mentioned that one "formerly belonged to the late Commissary Blair."

13. Bishop Gibson sent circular letters in 1727 to ministers and slave-holders in the colonies urging greater effort to educate and Christianize slaves. Blair reported in 1729 that the letters had had effect and that many slaves were "very desirous of becoming Christians." He thought most of these "are in hopes that they will meet with so much the more respect and that . . . Christianity will help them to their freedom." Blair to the Bishop of London, June 28, 1729, Fulham Palace MSS, papers relating to Virginia, 2d box, no. 109, Library of Congress. He expressed stronger support a year later. Blair to the Bishop of London, July 30, 1730, ibid., 1st box, no. 131. A threatened slave insurrection in 1731 cooled his ardor for slave baptism. Blair to Bishop of London, May 14, 1731, ibid., 2d box, no. 110.

14. Meade, *Old Churches*, 1:155.

15. Blair to Bishop of London, March 11, 1737. Fulham MSS, box 15, no. 51, M 287. Randolph's statement of religious views in his last testament was printed in William Parks's Virginia Gazette for May 6, 1737.

16. William Stevens Perry, *The History of the American Episcopal Church, 1587–1883*, 2 vols. (Boston: James R. Osgood and Co., 1885), 1:120.

17. Moses Coit Tyler, *A History of American Literature during the Colonial Period, 1607–1765* (New York: G. P. Putnam's Sons, 1904), p. 262.

18. Blair had been appointed as Virginia correspondent for the society on

August 19, 1701. Society for Promoting Christian Knowledge, GM i, p. 167, Archives, London.

19. Henry Newman to Lieutenant Governor Hugh Drysdale, December 1, 1722, ibid., CN 3/1, p. 50.

20. Thomas Bray to the Society for Promoting Christian Knowledge, April 26, 1723, ibid., ALB 12/7394.

21. Henry Newman to Drysdale, January 1, 1722/23. Ibid., CN 3/1, pp. 50–51.

22. Henry Newman to Thomas Bray, September 24, 1724. Ibid., CS2/15, p. 4.

23. Henry Newman to James Blair, December 10, 1725. Ibid., CN 3/2, pp. 5–7.

24. Memorandum of notification from Blair in London, to the society, dated June 8, 1727. Ibid., ALB 14/9272. The books had been sold by 1740, when a second edition was published.

25. Robinson was a younger brother of Christopher Robinson, who had emigrated to Virginia about 1666 and settled on the Rappahannock River, becoming secretary of the colony and a trustee of the college. His son John, appointed to the council in 1720, became its president, and was father to John Robinson II, who became speaker of the House of Burgesses in 1738.

26. Blair to the Bishop of London, July 9, 1723. Fulham MSS, 2d box, no. 105.

27. Blair to the Bishop of London, May 25, 1725. Ibid., 2d box, no. 108.

28. Ibid.

29. Thomas Bray to the Bishop of London, October 28, 1723. Ibid., 3d box, nos. 44–45.

30. *Acts of the Privy Council of England, Colonial Series*, 6 vols., edited by W. L. Grant and James Munro (Hereford: H. M. Stationery Office, 1906–12), 3:88–90. E. B. O'Callaghan and B. Fernow, eds., *Documents Relative to the Colonial History of the State of New-York* (Albany: Weed, Parsons and Company, 1856), p. 363.

31. James Blair to the Bishop of London, February 10, 1724. Perry, *Historical Collections, Papers*, 1:250/51.

32. Blair to the Bishop of London, May 13, 1724. Ibid., pp. 252–53.

33. Blair to the Reverend Mr. Forbes, June 20, 1723. Ibid., pp. 251–52.

34. Blair to the Bishop of London, May 13, 1724. Ibid., p. 253.

35. Hugh Drysdale to the Bishop of London, May 7, 1724. Dawson Papers on microfilm in the Research Department, Colonial Williamsburg, M–22–4.

36. Blair to the Bishop of London, February 10, 1724, Perry, *Historical Collections*, 1:250.

37. The Reverend Hugh Jones wrote that parishes resented visits from the commissary. "Visitations have been attempted by Mr. Commissary; but he met with so many Difficulties from the Church Wardens refusing to take the oath of a Church Warden, or to make presentments, and from the General aversion of the people to everything that looks like a Spiritual Court, that little has been done that way." Convention of the Clergy to the Bishop of London, April 10, 1719. Ibid., p. 214.

38. In 1718 Commissary Christopher Wilkinson of Maryland wrote the Bishop of London that "the Commissary in Virginia does nothing at all in the exercising of his Commission." Wilkinson to the Bishop of London, May 26, 1718. William Stevens Perry, ed., *Historical Collections Relating to the American Colonial Church*, 5 vols., (Hartford: Printed for the Subscribers, 1870–78), 4:108–9. In 1738 the Reverend Anthony Gavin wrote the Bishop that no convocation had been held in ten years. Ibid., 1:360–61.

39. "Queries to be answered by Persons who were Commissaries to my Predecessor," with responses by James Blair, July 17, 1724. Ibid., 1:257–60.

40. Ibid., p. 257.

41. From a memorial by the Presbytery of Hanover to the General Assembly of Virginia in 1776. *Journal of the House of Burgesses of Virginia, 1619–1776*, 13

vols., edited by J. P. Kennedy and H. R. McIlwaine (Richmond: Colonial Press, E. Waddey Co., 1915), p. 189.

Earlier, the Presbyterian Synod of Philadelphia, in May 1738, had written Governor Gooch of the concern for "civil and religious liberties" of Scotch-Irish emigrants coming to Virginia. Gooch replied that he had "always been inclined to favour the people who have lately removed from other provinces, to settle on the western side of our great mountains" and that "no interruption shall be given to any minister of your profession [denomination] who shall come among them, so as they conform themselves to the rules prescribed by the act of toleration in England, by taking the oaths enjoined thereby, and registering the places of their meeting, and behave themselves peaceably towards the government. . . ."

CHAPTER XIV

1. The exact location is uncertain, but an early deed indicates that it stood in the vicinity of Chowning's Tavern.

2. In 1745 Governor Gooch explained to London that he had not previously recommended John Blair's appointment because "during his Uncle's the late Commissary's lifetime, he was in narrow Circumstances." He later became president of the council and was acting governor in 1758 and 1768.

3. During 1716 and 1717 a frame structure was built for the Blair store on Duke of Gloucester Street. About 1740 a brick storehouse was built next door to it. Later known as William Prentis & Company, the business flourished until the Revolution. The brick Prentis store is exhibited by Colonial Williamsburg.

4. Blair had also sailed from England on the vessel that brought Drysdale to Virginia in 1722.

5. Blair to the Bishop of London, October 28, 1727. William Stevens Perry, ed., *Historical Collections Relating to the American Colonial Church*, 5 vols. (Hartford: Printed for the Subscribers, 1870–78), 1:352–53. The governor had unusual faith in the power of fasting. He wrote the bishop of London on June 29, 1729: "We are again this Year under Apprehensions from the caterpillars, for which reason I appointed a Fast, and can now inform your Lordship that by the peculiar Favour of Heaven that danger is over. . . ."

6. Gooch to Thomas Gooch, Bishop of Norwich, March 27, 1728. Sir William Gooch Papers, 1727–51, Colonial Williamsburg Archives.

7. Gooch to the Bishop of Norwich, June 9, 1728. Ibid.

8. Gooch to the Bishop of London, October 18, 1727, Fulham Palace MSS, papers relating to Virginia, 2d box, no. 164, Library of Congress.

9. Robert Beverley, *The History of Virginia in Four Parts*, 2d ed. (London: F. Fayram and J. Clarke, 1722), p. 229. On May 11, 1742, the council heard the complaint of the Reverend James Pedin against the vestry of Nottoway Parish for ousting him. It found Pedin guilty of "many Immoralities as Drunkenness, Profane Swearing & Lude, Debauched Actions" and recommended to the commissary that he deny him the pulpit.

10. Blair to the Bishop of London, March 24, 1735. Perry, *Historical Collections*, 1:358.

11. Bridges to the Bishop of London, October 19, 1738. Ibid., pp. 361–62. Another evaluation of Blair was contained in a letter from the Reverend Emanuel Jones of Petsworth Parish, Gloucester, to Gibson on June 1, 1724: "I believe no man can [provide a more knowledgeable account of Virginia's church than Blair] (provided he will do it as *impartially* as he is able to do it fully and clearly). . . . Ever since I came to this Colony . . . I have had more Kindness, Civility, and Respect shewn to me than I could possibly expect, being chose these many years past (altogether unknown to myself) one of the Governors of

Wm & Mary Colledge, tho Mr Commissary with all his Interest set up his brother-in-law (another Clergyman) in Opposition to me. . . ."

12. Anabaptists (from the Greek, meaning "to baptize again") originated in Switzerland about 1522 and spread to Europe and America, becoming known as Baptists. They practiced adult baptism and opposed baptism of infants.

13. Anthony Gavin to the Bishop of London, August 5, 1738. Perry, *Historical Collections*, 1:360–61.

14. On October 13, 1736, Blair used the columns of the *Virginia Gazette*, founded the same year by William Parks, to announce, "In obedience to an Instruction lately received, the ministers of this Colony of Virginia, are desired and required, in their Prayers for the Royal Family, (next after His Royal Highness, Frederick Prince of Wales,) to pray for the Princess of Wales, thus: [Our Gracious Queen Caroline, Their Royal Highnesses, Frederick Prince of Wales, The Princess of Wales, the Duke, the Princesses and all the Royal Family.] James Blair, Commissary." It was published in the issue of October 8–15, 1736.

15. A fragmented manuscript of a deed among the Tyler papers at the College of William and Mary records Blair's purchase of a tract in Bruton Parish, York County, on October 17, 1732, from John Mundell. A 1782 map of Williamsburg identifies this as "Blair's Quarter" and locates it east of the town. Mundell had come to Virginia in 1719 as a "rebel prisoner," presumably a follower of the Jacobite pretender taken in the battle of Preston in 1715. In 1727 Mundell was appointed doorkeeper of the Virginia House of Burgesses.

16. The unsigned portrait of Blair has also been attributed to William Dering, who painted in Williamsburg at this period. However, research by Miss Susanne Neale of Colonial Williamsburg suggests that Bridges, who was associated closely with the commissary from 1735 to 1738, was the painter.

17. Henry Newman to the Reverend John Thompson, Orange County, Va., September 18, 1741. Society for Promoting Christian Knowledge, CN 2/8, p. 20, Archives, London.

18. Newman to Blair, March 3, 1743. Original draft, unsigned. Ibid., CN 2/9, p. 58.

19. Gooch to the Bishop of London, May 21, 1739. Gooch Papers. In a letter four years later, Gooch announced Blair's death, and told his bishop of William Dawson's "being by the unanimous vote of the Visitors elected President of William and Mary College." The Bruton Parish vestry chose William Dawson as rector, and Bishop Gibson appointed him commissary. Blair's seat on the Governor's Council was filled by William Fairfax.

20. Blair to the Bishop of London, August 14, 1732. Fulham MSS, 1st box, no. 164.

21. Ibid.

22. William Gooch II, son of the Governor and Lady [Rebecca Stanton] Gooch, attended the College of William and Mary. He died in the governor's palace in 1742.

23. Blair to the Bishop of London, October 11, 1740. Fulham MSS, 1st box, no. 96.

24. William Gooch to the Bishop of Norwich, June 12, and August 22, 1740. Gooch Papers.

25. Blair to the Lords Commissioners, October 15 and November 6, 1740. P.R.O./C.O.5, in L.C., 1325.

26. Byrd to Major Francis Otway, February 1740. "Letters of the Byrd Family," *Virginia Magazine of History and Biography* 37 (1929): 29–30.

27. Maude H. Woodfin, ed. *Another Secret Diary of William Byrd of Westover, 1739–1741*, translated and collated by Marion Tinling, (Richmond: Dietz Press, 1942), p. 107.

28. Blair to the Bishop of London, September 17, 1741. Fulham MSS, 2d box, no. 212.

29. William Gooch to the Bishop of Norwich, October 13, 1741. Gooch Papers.

30. Philip Slaughter, *Memoir of Joshua Fry* (Richmond: Randolph & English, 1880), pp. 68–69. Maury was plaintiff in the "Parsons' Cause" suit in 1763 wherein Patrick Henry represented the defendants.

31. A Williamsburg dispatch in the May 12 issue of the *Pennsylvania Gazette* read: "April 22. On Monday last, about the hour of 7 in the Morning, departed this Life in the 88th year of his Age, the Hon. and Reverend Mr. James Blair, Commissary of this Colony; President of the College of William and Mary; Rector of Bruton Parish, and one of His Majesty's Honourable Council in Virginia; and some Time President of this Colony." No copy of the *Virginia Gazette* for this period has been found. The *South Carolina Gazette* carried under date of July 25, 1743: "From Virginia we hear, that on the 18th of April had died there, in the 88th year of his age, the Hon. and Reverend Mr. James Blair, Commissary of that Colony; President of the College of William and Mary; Rector of Bruton Parish, and one of His Majesty's Honorable Council in Virginia; and some time President of that Colony."

32. John Blair described James Blair's death in a letter to the Bishop of London dated May 28, 1743: "It having pleased the Sovereign Disposer of all Things to Call to his Mercy the Sould of my late Revd. & Honble Uncle, your Lops Commissary here (who after three weeks struggle with a most painful Attack of the stone and gravel left us the 18th of last month to mourn our great loss of so worthy a Friend and Benefactor to this poor Country, & to the Church and College here) I thought it my duty in his behalf to acknowledge the receipt of your Lop's last to him . . . The Governor having before mentioned that he intended the Rev Mr Wm Dawson (who is now chosen President of the College) should act as Commissary in some things as there should be occasion, till your Lop's pleasure should be known, I thought it most proper to deliver them to him. . . .

. . . Mr. Dawson attended [Commissary Blair] frequently and gave him the Sacrament, and Mr. Commissary, not doubting he would be chosen President, more than once earnestly recommended to him to be careful of the Youth of the College that they might be well instructed in the Doctrine of the Church of England, and added in my hearing that he hoped he would be appointed Commissary too; though he said at the same time your Lop had not signified anything to him in the matter. But the Commissary had been witness of his behavior for many years; for he had got him to assist him in his Church soon after coming to this Country, and had been his constant hearer for some years, which, to the gen'l satisfaction of all the parish he assisted him as his Curate, when his [Blair's] voice began to fail. . . ."

33. Gooch to the Bishop of Norwich, May 14, 1743. Gooch Papers. In his will, Blair left his one-half of the stock in the Blair-Prentis store to five children of his brother Archibald Blair: John, James, Elizabeth, Ann, and Harrison. John was to manage the estate and receive "the Profits thereof" until the children came of age or married.

34. A copy of a deed signed by John Blair and dated 1778 refers to 1,250 acres as "being the land lately the property of Doctor James Blair deceased" and lying in Blisland Parish, New Kent County. The deed is in possession of the College of William and Mary.

35. The remainder of Richneck's acreage, leased by Blair from Philip Ludwell II, was willed by the latter to his son Philip III. On the latter's death in 1767 he left it to his daughter Frances, who died unmarried in 1768, leaving Richneck to her two sisters.

36. Mary R. M. Goodwin, "The Colonial Store," Colonial Williamsburg House Report, 1966, p. 297.

37. Sir John Randolph, an alumnus, a member of the board of visitors, and the representative of The College of William and Mary in the House of Burgesses from 1734 until his death in 1737, had been interred in the crypt.

38. Lyon G. Tyler, *The Cradle of the Republic: Jamestown and the James River* (Richmond: Hermitage Press, Inc., 1906), pp. 131–32. Tyler arrived at the Latin text and the English translation by collating fragments of the tomb which remained legible in 1906 with the version of the inscription printed in Bishop Meade's *Old Churches, Ministers, and Families of Virginia*. Tyler was assisted by Dr. Lyman B. Wharton, professor of ancient and modern languages at the College of William and Mary from 1870 to 1881 and from 1886 to 1906, who reconstructed the Latin text as follows: "H.S.E. [Hic sepultus est]/ Vir Reverendus et Honorabilis/ JACOBUS BLAIR, A.M./ In Scotia natus,/ In Academia Edinburgensi nutritus/ Primo Angliam deinde Virginiam/ venit:/ In qua parte terrarum/ Annos LVIII Evangelii Preconis,/ LIV Commissarii/ Gulielmi et Mariae Praesidis,/ e Britanni[a] Principum/ Conciliarii/ Concilii Presidis,/ Coloniae Prefecti,/ munera sustinuit;/ ornavit/ eum oris venusti Decus;/ [Accepit orn]ate, hilari, sine Luxu, hospitali [modo;]/ munificent-/ issimo egenis [dedit] largo/ omnibus; comi [animo]/ superavit./ Collegio bene diversam/ fundaverat,/ moriens Bibliothecam suam/ ad alendum Theologiae studiosum/ [et] juventutem pauperiorem instituendam/ Testamento legavit./ [ante] Cal. Maii in die [XIV decessit],/ MDCCXLIII/ aetat: LXXXVIII./ [exim]iam desideratissimi/ senis Laudem/ suis nepotibus commendabunt/ [o]pera marmore perenniora."

39. Bishop William Meade, *Old Churches, Ministers, and Families of Virginia*, 2 vols. (Philadelphia: J. B. Lippincott Company, 1906), 1:160.

40. Randolph was knighted in 1733 for his presentation of the Virginia Burgesses' plan for regulating the tobacco trade, which Prime Minister Sir Robert Walpole expected to increase England's revenues. In 1734 Randolph was elected by the president and masters to represent the College of William and Mary in the House of Burgesses and served as Speaker until his death in 1737. He was the father of Peyton Randolph, president of the first Continental Congress, and of John Randolph the Tory.

41. Bland, who attended William and Mary about 1725–27, married Elizabeth Blair Bolling, widowed daughter of John and Mary Monro Blair.

42. Thomas Jefferson, *Notes on Virginia* (Philadelphia: H. C. Cary and I. Lee, 1825), p. 206.

43. John Blair II was appointed by President Washington in 1790 to be associate justice of the Supreme Court of the United States. He resigned on account of ill health in 1796. He was described as "blameless of disposition, pious, and possessed of great benevolence and goodness of heart."

44. Meade, *Old Churches*, 1:164.

45. James G. Leyburn, *The Scotch-Irish: A Social History* (Chapel Hill: University of North Carolina Press, 1962), pp. 78–79.

46. William A. Caruthers: *The Knights of the Horseshoe* (New York: A. L. Burt Company, 1904), p. 6.

47. On April 29, 1709, William Byrd dined at "Mr. Bland's" and recorded: "Mrs. Blair was sick and talked very [simply]." Louis B. Wright and Marion Tinling, eds., *The Secret Diary of William Byrd of Westover, 1709–1712* (Richmond: Dietz Press, 1941), p. 27.

48. Vernon Louis Parrington, *The Romantic Revolution in America*, (New York: Harcourt Brace and Company, 1927), p. 6.

Bibliography

"An Abstract of the Design and Institution of the College of William and Mary in Virginia." Fulham Palace MSS, papers relating to Virginia, 1st box, no. 48, London. Transcripts in Library of Congress.

Acts of the Parliaments of Scotland, A.D. MCDXXIV–A.D. MDCCVII. 13 vols. Edited by Thomas Thompson. Edinburgh: n.p., 1820.

Acts of the Privy Council of England, Colonial Series. 6 vols. Edited by W. L. Grant and James Munro. Hereford: H. M. Stationery Office, 1906–12.

Anderson, James Stuart Murray. *The History of the Church of England in the Colonies and Foreign Dependencies of the British Empire.* 3 vols. London: F. & J. Rivington, 1845–56.

Anderson, Peter John, ed. *Fasti Academiae Mariscallanae: Selections from the Records of the Marischal College and University, 1593–1860.* 3 vols. Aberdeen: New Spalding Club, 1898.

Appleton's Cyclopaedia of American Biography. 6 vols. Edited by James Grant Wilson and John Fiske. New York: D. Appleton and Company, 1891.

Armes, Ethel. *Stratford Hall: The Great House of the Lees.* Richmond: Garrett and Massie, Inc., 1936.

Bartlett's Familiar Quotations. 14th ed. Edited by John Bartlett. Boston: Little, Brown & Co., 1968.

Barton, Robert Thomas, ed. *Virginia Colonial Decisions: The Reports by Sir John Randolph and by Edward Barradall of Decisions of the General Court of Virginia.* 2 vols. Boston: Boston Book Company, 1909.

Batsford, Harry, and Charles Fry. *The Face of Scotland.* 4th ed., rev. London: B. T. Batsford, Ltd., 1942.

Beatty, Richmond Croom. *William Byrd of Westover.* Boston: Houghton Mifflin Company, 1932.

Beverley, Robert. *The History and Present State of Virginia.* Edited by Louis B. Wright. Chapel Hill: University of North Carolina Press, 1947.

————. *The History of Virginia, in Four Parts: By a Native and Inhabitant of the Place.* 2d ed. London: F. Fayram and J. Clarke, 1722.

Biographia Britannica: or, the Lives of the Most Eminent Persons who have Flourished in Great Britain and Ireland, From the Earliest Ages, Down to the Present Times. 6 vols. London: n.p., 1747–63.

Blair, James. *Our Saviour's Divine Sermon on the Mount, Contained in the Vth, VIth, and VIIth Chapters of St. Matthew's Gospel explained: and the Practice of it Recommended in Divers Sermons and Discourses.* 4 vols. 2d ed. London: J. Brotherton, 1740.

————. *A Paraphrase on Our Saviour's Sermon on the Mount, contained in V, VI, VII Chap. of St. Matthew's Gospel.* London: John Booth Bookseller, 1729.

Blathwayt Papers, Colonial Williamsburg Archives, Williamsburg, Virginia.

Bohannan, A. W. *Old Surry.* Petersburg: Plummer Printing Company, Inc., 1927.

Book of Common Prayer and Administration of the sacraments, and other rites and ceremonies of the church, according to the use of the Church of England: etc. Cambridge: J. Baskerville, 1761.

Brewer, Clifton Hartwell. *A History of Religious Education in the Episcopal Church to 1835.* New Haven: Yale University Press, 1924.

Bridenbaugh, Carl. *Mitre and Sceptre: Transatlantic Faiths, Ideas, Personalities, and Politics, 1689–1775.* New York: Oxford University Press, 1962.

Brock, Robert A., ed. *The Official Letters of Alexander Spotswood, Lieutenant Governor of Virginia, 1710–1722.* 2 vols. Richmond: Virginia Historical Society, 1882–85.

Browne, William H., ed. *Proceedings of the Council of Maryland, 1687/8–93: Archives of Maryland.* 70 vols. Baltimore: Maryland Historical Society, 1890.

Bruce, Philip Alexander. *Economic History of Virginia in the Seventeenth Century.* 2 vols. New York: Macmillan and Company, 1896.

————. *Social Life in the Seventeenth Century.* 2d ed. Lynchburg, Virginia: J. P. Bell Co., Inc., 1927.

Brydon, George MacLaren. *Religious Life of Virginia in the Seventeenth Century.* Williamsburg: Virginia 350th Anniversary Celebration Corporation, 1957.

————. *Virginia's Mother Church and the Political Conditions under Which It Grew.* 2 vols. Richmond, Virginia Historical Society, 1947–52.

Bulloch, John Malcolm. *A History of the University of Aberdeen, 1495–1895.* London: Hodder and Stoughton, 1895.

————. *The Lord Rectors of the Universities of Aberdeen.* Aberdeen: D. Wyllie & Son, 1890.

Burnet, Gilbert. *Bishop Burnet's History of His Own Time: With the Suppressed Passages of the First Volume, and Notes by the Earls of Dartmouth and Hardwicke, and Speaker Onslow, Hitherto Unpublished.* 6 vols. Oxford: Clarendon Press, 1823.

————. "Thoughts on Education." Edited by John Clarke, in his *Bishop Burnet as Educationist.* Aberdeen University Studies, no. 67. Aberdeen, 1917.

Burton, Lewis W. *Annals of Henrico Parish, Diocese of Virginia, and especially of St. John's Church, the present mother church of the parish, from 1611 to 1884.* Richmond: Williams Printing Company, 1904.

Byrd, William. *The Secret Diary of William Byrd of Westover, 1709–1712.* Edited by Louis B. Wright and Marion Tinling. Richmond: Dietz Press, 1941.

Calendar of State Papers, Colonial Series, America and West Indies, 1689–92, 1693–96, 1696–97, 1697–98, 1699, 1700, 1701, 1702–3, 1704–5. Edited by J. W. Fortescue and Cecil Headlam. London: H. M. Stationery Office, 1901–16.

Calendar of State Papers Domestic, James II, February–December, 1685. 2 vols. Edited by E. K. Timings. London: H. M. Stationery Office, 1960.

Calendar of State Papers, Domestic Series of the Reign of Charles I, 1633–34. Edited by John Bruce. London: Longmans, Green, Longmans, Roberts and Green, 1863.

Calendar of Treasury Books, 1660–March 1704/5. 19 vols. Edited by William A. Shaw. London: H. M. Stationery Office, 1904–35.

Carpenter, Edward F. *The Protestant Bishop.* New York: Longmans, Green and Company, 1956.

Caruthers, William A. *The Knights of the Horseshoe.* New York: A. L. Burt Company, 1904.

A Catalogue of the Graduates in the Faculties of Arts, Divinity, and Law of the University of Edinburgh since Its Foundation. Edinburgh: Neill and Company, 1858.

"The Charter of the College of William and Mary in Virginia," *Bulletin of the College of William and Mary* 6 (January 1913): 3–19.

Clark, G. N. *The Later Stuarts, 1660–1714.* Vol. 10. The Oxford

History of England. 14 vols. Edited by G. N. Clark. Oxford: Clarendon Press, 1934.

Clarke, John, ed. *Bishop Burnet as Educationist.* Aberdeen University Studies, no. 67. Aberdeen, 1917.

Clarke, T. E. S., and H. C. Foxcroft. *A Life of Gilbert Burnet: Bishop of Salisbury.* Cambridge: University Press, 1907.

Cleaveland, George J. *Reformation and Reunion.* New York: Carlton Press, 1963.

Coleman, Elizabeth Dabney, and W. Edwin Hemphill. "Founding Virginia's First College." *Virginia Cavalcade Magazine* 7 (Summer 1957) : 14–22.

Cramond, William. *The Annals of Banff.* 2 vols. Aberdeen: Printed for the New Spalding Club, 1893.

Cross, Arthur Lyon. *The Anglican Episcopate and the American Colonies.* New York: Longmans, Green and Company, 1902.

————. "Schemes for Episcopal Control in the Colonies," in *Annual Report of the American Historical Association for the Year 1896.* Washington: Government Printing Office, 1897.

Daiches, David. *The Paradox of Scottish Culture: The Eighteenth-Century Experience.* London: Oxford University Press, 1964.

Davis, Burke. *A Williamsburg Galaxy.* New York: Holt, Rinehart and Winston, 1968.

Dawson Papers. Microfilm, Research Department, Colonial Williamsburg, Inc., Williamsburg, Virginia.

"Declaration of Colonel Jeffreys," *The Virginia Magazine of History and Biography* 22 (January 1914) : 44–47.

Dictionary of American Biography. 20 vols. Edited by Allen Johnson and Duman Malone. New York: Charles Scribner's Sons, 1928–36.

Dictionary of National Biography. 63 vols. (6 supp.) Edited by Leslie Stephen and Sidney Lee. London: Smith, Elder & Co., 1892–1912.

Dodd, William E. *The Old South: Struggles for Democracy.* New York: Macmillan Company, 1937.

Dodson, Leonidas. *Alexander Spotswood, Governor of Colonial Virginia, 1710–1922.* Philadelphia: University of Pennsylvania Press, 1932.

Donaldson, Gordon. *Scotland: Church and Nation through Sixteen Centuries.* London: SCM Press, Ltd., 1960.

————. *Scotland: James V to James VII.* Edinburgh and London: Oliver & Boyd, 1965.

Encyclopedia of Virginia Biography. 5 vols. New York: Lewis Historical Company, 1915.

Executive Journals of the Council of Colonial Virginia. 4 vols. Edited by H. R. McIlwaine. Richmond: Virginia State Library, 1925–30.

Fiore, Jordan D. "Jonathan Swift and the American Episcopate." *William and Mary Quarterly*, 3d ser. 11 (1954) : 425–33.

Fiske, John. *Old Virginia and Her Neighbours*. 2 vols. Boston and New York: Houghton, Mifflin and Company, 1900.

Fontane, Theodor. *Across the Tweed*. London: Phoenix House, 1965.

Fulham Palace MSS, papers relating to Virginia. Transcripts in the Library of Congress.

Fulham Papers, Vol. 11, Lambeth Palace Library.

The Gentlemen's Magazine, or Monthly Intelligencer. London: n.p., 1731.

Gooch Papers, Sir William, Colonial Williamsburg Archives. Williamsburg, Virginia.

Goodwin, Mary R. M. "The College of William and Mary." Research Department, Colonial Williamsburg, June 1967.

——. "The Colonial Store." Colonial Williamsburg House Report, 1966.

——. "Historical Notes: The College of William and Mary." Research Department, Colonial Williamsburg, March 1954.

Goodwin, Rutherfoord. *A Brief and True Report Concerning Williamsburg in Virginia*. Williamsburg: Colonial Williamsburg, Inc., 1941.

Goodwin, William A. R. *Historical Sketch of Bruton Church, Williamsburg, Virginia*. Petersburg, Virginia: Franklin Press Company, 1903.

——. *The Record of Bruton Parish Church*. Edited by Mary Frances Goodwin. Richmond: Dietz Press, 1941.

Grant, James. *History of the Burgh and Parish Schools of Scotland*. London: William Collins & Sons, Ltd., 1876.

Hamilton. Henry. *An Economic History of Scotland in the Eighteenth Century*. Oxford: Clarendon Press, 1963.

Hammond, John. *Leah and Rachel, or, The Two Fruitfull Sisters Virginia and Maryland: Their Present Condition Impartially Stated and Related*. London: n.p., 1656. Reprinted in W. Q. Force, *Tracts and Other Papers*, vol. 3, no. 14. Washington: W. Q. Force, 1844.

Harrison, Margaret Scott. "Commissary James Blair of Virginia: A Study in Personality and Power." M.A. thesis, College of William and Mary, 1958.

Harrison, Fairfax. *Virginia Land Grants: A Study of Conveyancing in Relation to Colonial Politics*. Richmond: Privately printed, 1925.

Hartwell, Henry, James Blair, and Edward Chilton. *The Present State of Virginia, and the College.* Edited by Hunter Dickinson Farish. Williamsburg: Colonial Williamsburg, Inc., 1940.

Hatch, Charles E., Jr. *America's Oldest Legislative Assembly & Its Jamestown Statehouses.* Washington: Government Printing Office, 1956.

————. *The First Seventeen Years, Virginia, 1607–1624.* Williamsburg: Virginia 350th Anniversary Celebration Corporation, 1957.

Havighurst, Walter. *Alexander Spotswood: Portrait of a Governor.* New York: Holt, Rinehart & Winston, 1967.

Heaton, Lynda Rees. "Littleton Waller Tazewell's Sketch of His Own Family . . . 1823." MSS Collection, College of William and Mary.

Henderson, George David. *Religious Life in Seventeenth-Century Scotland.* Cambridge: University Press, 1937.

Hening, William W. *The Statutes at Large: Being a Collection of All the Laws of Virginia from the First Session of the Legislature in 1619.* 13 vols. Facs. ed. Charlottesville: University Press of Virginia, 1969.

Henrico County Record Book, no. 2 [Orders and Wills], 1678–93. Archives Division, Virginia State Library.

Henrico County Records [Deeds and Wills], 1677–92, pt. 2. Archives Division, Virginia State Library.

Henrico County Records [Deeds and Wills], 1697–1704. Archives Division, Virginia State Library.

"Hon. John Blair, Jr." An address by Henry T. Wickham, Esq., of Virginia at a special session of the U.S. Circuit Court of Appeals, Philadelphia, Pennsylvania, May 6, 1913.

Horn, David Bayne. *A Short History of the University of Edinburgh, 1556–1889.* Edinburgh: University Press, 1967.

A Hornbook of Virginia History. Richmond: Virginia State Library, 1965.

Horner, Frederick. *The History of the Blair, Banister, and Braxton Families before and after the Revolution, with a brief Sketch of their Descendants.* Philadelphia: J. B. Lippincott Company, 1898.

"Instructions to Francis Nicholson, Esq., His Majesty's Lieut. and Governor-Gen'l of Virginia." *Virginia Magazine of History and Biography* 4 (1896): 49–54.

Jefferson, Thomas. *Notes on Virginia.* Philadelphia: H. C. Cary and I. Lea, 1825.

Jennings, John M. *The Library of the College of William and Mary in Virginia, 1693–1793.* Charlottesville: University Press of Virginia, 1968.

Jester, Annie Lash. *Newport News, Virginia: 1607–1960.* Newport News, Virginia: City of Newport News, 1961.

Jones, Hugh. *The Present State of Virginia, Giving a Particular and Short Account of the Indian, English and Negroe Inhabitants of that Colony.* Edited by Richard L. Morton. Chapel Hill: University of North Carolina Press, 1956.

Journal of the Commissioners for Trade and Plantations, 1704–82. 14 vols. Edited by Cecil Headlam. London: H. M. Stationery Office, 1920–38.

Journal of the House of Burgesses of Virginia, 1619–1776. 13 vols. Edited by J. P. Kennedy and H. R. McIlwaine. Richmond: Colonial Press, E. Waddey, Co., 1905–15.

"Journal of the Meetings of the President and Masters of William and Mary College." *William and Mary College Quarterly Historical Magazine,* 1st ser. 1 (July 1892–April 1893): 130–37, 214–20.

Kammen, Michael G., ed. "Virginia at the Close of the Seventeenth Century: An Appraisal of James Blair and John Locke." *Virginia Magazine of History and Biography* 74 (1966): 144–69.

Keith, William. *The History of the British Plantations in America.* London: Printed at the Expence of the Society for the Encouragement of Learning by S. Richardson, 1738.

Kingsbury, Susan Myra, ed. *The Records of the Virginia Company of London.* 4 vols. Washington: Government Printing Office, 1906–35.

Land Office Patent Book 8, 1689–1695. Archives Division, Virginia State Library.

Laslett, Peter. "John Locke, the Great Recoinage, and the Origins of the Board of Trade, 1695–1698." *William and Mary Quarterly,* 3d ser. 14 (1957): 370–402.

————. *John Locke—Two Treatises of Government: A Critical Edition with an Introduction and Apparatus Criticus.* Cambridge: University Press, 1960.

Lee-Ludwell Papers, Virginia Historical Society, Richmond, Virginia.

Leyburn, James G. *The Scotch-Irish: A Social History.* Chapel Hill: University of North Carolina Press, 1962.

Locke MSS, Bodleian Library, Oxford University.

Macauley, Thomas Babington. *The History of England from the Accession of James the Second.* 10 vols. Boston and New York: Houghton, Mifflin & Co., 1899.

Mackinnon, James. *The Social and Industrial History of Scotland.* London: Longmans, Green and Company, 1921.

Manross, William Wilson. *A History of the American Episcopal Church.* 2d ed. New York: Morehouse-Gorham Co., 1950.

Maxwell-Lyte, Henry Churchill. *Historical Notes on the Use of the Great Seal of England.* London: H. M. Stationery Office, 1926.

Meade, Bishop William. *Old Churches, Ministers, and Families of Virginia.* 2 vols. Philadelphia: J. B. Lippincott Company, 1906.

"A Memorial by the Presbytery of Hanover to the General Assembly of Virginia" (1776). *Journal of the House of Burgesses (1773–76),* edited by J. P. Kennedy. Richmond: The Colonial Press, 1905.

"A Memorial of What Abuses are crept into the churches of the plantations." Public Record Office, Colonial Office 1/41, folios 48–49, London. Copy in Library of Congress.

"A Memoriall Concerning £2000 raised out of the Quitt Rents now begg'd for ye Colledge of Virginia." Public Record Office, Colonial Office 5/1358, pp. 195–99. Copy in Library of Congress 1306, no. 118.

Micou, Paul. "Services of Commissary James Blair to the Colony of Virginia." *South Atlantic Quarterly* 8 (April 1909) : 164–73.

Middleton, Arthur Pierce. *Tobacco Coast.* Newport News, Virginia: Mariners Museum, 1953.

Middleton, Thomas. *An Appendix to the History of the Church of Scotland: Containing the Succession of the Archbishops and Bishops in Their Several Sees, from the Reformation of Religion, until the Year 1676.* London: E. Flesher, 1677.

Mohler, Samuel R. "Commissary James Blair, Churchman, Educator, and Politician of Colonial Virginia." Ph.D. diss., University of Chicago, 1940.

Morton, H. V. *In Search of Scotland.* New York: Dodd, Mead and Company, 1932.

Morton, Richard L. *Colonial Virginia.* 2 vols. Chapel Hill: University of North Carolina Press, 1960.

Motley, Daniel Esten. *Life of Commissary James Blair.* Johns Hopkins University Studies in Historical and Political Science, no. 10, ser. 19. Baltimore: Johns Hopkins University Press, 1901.

Notestein, Wallace. *The Scot in History.* New Haven: Yale University Press, 1946. "Observations in Several Voyages and Travels in America," *London Magazine,* July 1746. Reprinted in *William and Mary Quarterly,* 1st ser. 15 (July 1906–April 1907) : 143–59.

O'Callaghan, Edmund B., ed. *Calendar of Historical Manuscripts in the Office of the Secretary of State, Albany, N.Y.,* Pt. 2. Albany: Weed, Parsons and Company, 1866.

———. and Berthold Fernow, eds. *Documents Relative to the Colonial History of the State of New York.* 15 vols. Albany: Weed, Parsons and Company, 1856–87.

Oldmixon, John. *The British Empire in America*. 2 vols. London: n.p., 1741.

Papers Relating to an Affidavit made by His Reverence James Blair, Clerk, pretended President of William and Mary College, and Supposed Commissary to the Bishop of London in Virginia, against Francis Nicholson, Esq. n.p., 1727. Photostat, Massachusetts Historical Society.

"Papers Relating to Nicholson and the College." *Virginia Magazine of History and Biography* 7 (October 1899–April 1900) : 153–72, 275–86, 386–401.

Parrington, Vernon Louis. *The Romantic Revolution in America*. New York: Harcourt Brace and Company, 1927.

Paton, Henry, ed. *The Register of Marriages of the Parish of Edinburgh, 1595–1700*. Edinburgh: Printed for the Scottish Record Society by James Skinner & Company, 1905.

The Pennsylvania Gazette, Philadelphia, 1743.

Pepys, Samuel. *The Diary and Correspondence of Samuel Pepys*. 4 vols. London: George Allen & Unwin, Ltd., 1929.

Perry, William Stevens. *The History of the American Episcopal Church, 1587–1883*. 2 vols. Boston: James R. Osgood and Co., 1885.

————, ed. *Historical Collections Relating to the American Colonial Church*. 5 vols. Hartford: Printed for the Subscribers, 1870–78.

"Peyton Randolph House: Block 28, Colonial Lots 207 and 237." Report prepared by Mary Stephenson, May 1952; revised by Jane Carson. Colonial Williamsburg, December 1967.

"A President and Six Masters." Address delivered by W. Melville Jones, on the 268th anniversary of the granting of the Royal Charter. Williamsburg: College of William and Mary, 1961.

Proceedings of the General Assembly of Virginia, July 30–August 4, 1619. Edited by William J. Van Schreeven and George H. Reese. Jamestown, Virginia: Jamestown Foundation, 1969.

Rae, T. I. "Scotland in the Time of Shakespeare." Folger Booklets on Tudor and Stuart Civilization. Ithaca, New York: Cornell University Press, 1965.

Rait, Robert Sangster. *Life in the Medieval University*. Cambridge: University Press; and New York: G. P. Putnam's Sons, 1912.

————. *The Universities of Aberdeen: A History*. Aberdeen: James Gordon Bissett, 1895.

———— and George S. Pryde. *Scotland*. 2d ed. New York: Frederick A. Praeger, 1954.

Rawlinson MSS, papers relating to Virginia. Library of Congress c933 fo. 40.

Register of Deeds. Vol. 59. Scottish Record Office, Edinburgh.

The Register of the Privy Council of Scotland. 8 vols., 3d ser. Edited and abridged by P. Hume Brown. Edinburgh: H. M. Register House, 1915.

"Report of the Journey of Francis Louis Michel from Berne, Switzerland, to Virginia, October 2, 1701–December 1, 1702." Translated and edited by William J. Hinke. *Virginia Magazine of History and Biography* 24 (1916) : 1–43, 113–41, 275–303.

Riley, Edward M. "William Prentis & Co." *Financial Executive* (April 1968) , pp. 35–41.

Smith, John. *The Works of Captain John Smith.* 2 vols. Edited by Edward Arber. Birmingham, England: Privately printed, 1884.

Schmitz, Robert Morell. *Hugh Blair.* New York: King's Cross Press, 1948.

Scott, Hew, ed. *Fasti Ecclesiae Scoticanae: The Succession of Ministers in the Church of Scotland from the Reformation.* 7 vols. new ed. Edinburgh: Oliver and Boyd, 1926.

Shepperson, Archibald Bolling. *John Paradise and Lucy Ludwell of London and Williamsburg.* Richmond: Dietz Press, Inc., 1942.

Slaughter, Philip. *Memoir of Joshua Fry.* . . . Richmond: Randolph & English, 1880.

Smyth, Albert H. A., ed. *The Writings of Benjamin Franklin.* 10 vols. New York: Macmillan Co., 1905–7.

Society for the Propagation of the Gospel in Foreign Parts MSS, Series B.1, Library of Congress.

Society for Promoting Christian Knowledge, Archives, London.

Spalding, John. *Memorialls of the Trubles in Scotland and in England, A.D. 1624–A.D. 1645.* 2 vols. Aberdeen: Spalding Club, 1850–51.

Story, Thomas. *A Journal of the Life of Thomas Story: Containing an account of his remarkable convincement of, and embracing the principals of truth, as held by the people called Quakers, and also, of his Travels and labors in the Service of the Gospel: With many other occurrences and observations.* Newcastle-upon-Tyne: Isaac Thompson and Company, 1747.

Trott, Nicholas, ed. *The Laws of the British Plantations in America, Relating to the Church and the Clergy, Religion and Learning.* London: Printed for B. Cowse, 1721.

"Twenty of the Clergy to the Bishop of London, September 22, 1703." Rawlinson MSS, Library of Congress.

"Two Hundredth Anniversary of the Charter of the College of William and Mary—1693–1893." College of William and Mary, Williamsburg, Virginia.

Tyler, Lyon G. "The College of William and Mary: Its Work, Discipline, and History, from its Foundation to the Present Time." *Bulletin of the College of William and Mary* (May 1917) , 38 pp.

————. *The College of William and Mary in Virginia: Its History and Work, 1693–1907*. Richmond: Whittet & Shepperson, 1907.

————. *The Cradle of the Republic: Jamestown and the James River*. Richmond: Hermitage Press, Inc., 1906.

————. "Diary of John Blair." *William and Mary Quarterly*, 1st ser., 7 (July 1898–April 1899) : 133.

————. *Narratives of Early Virginia, 1606–1625*. New York: Charles Scribner's Sons, 1907.

Tyler, Moses Coit. *A History of American Literature during the Colonial Period, 1607–1765*. New York: G. P. Putnam's Sons, 1904.

Tyler Papers, Archives, College of William and Mary.

University of Edinburgh Manuscript Collection.

The Vestry Book of Petsworth Parish, Gloucester County, Virginia, 1677–1793. Transcribed, annotated, and indexed by C. G. Chamberlayne. Richmond: Virginia State Library Board, 1933.

The Virginia Gazette. Published at Williamsburg by William Hunter, 1755.

"Vital Facts: A William and Mary Chronology, 1693–1963." Williamsburg: College of William and Mary, 1963.

Vital Facts of the College of William and Mary in Virginia. Complied by the College, 1955.

Virginia Magazine of History and Biography. Richmond: Published Quarterly by the Virginia Historical Society, 1893——.

Watson, Charles B. Boog, ed. *Roll of Edinburgh Burgesses and Guild Brethren, 1406–1707*. Edinburgh: Printed for the Scottish Record Society by J. Skinner & Co., Lts., 1929.

Webb, Stephen Saunders. "Officers and Governors: The Role of the British Army in Imperial Politics and Administration of the American Colonies, 1689–1722." Ph.D. dissertation, University of Wisconsin, 1965.

————. "Strange Case of Francis Nicholson." *William and Mary Quarterly*, 3d ser., 23 (1966) : 513–48.

————. "William Blathwayt, Imperial Fixer." *William and Mary Quarterly*, 3d ser., 25 (1968) : 3–21.

————. "William Blathwayt, Imperial Fixer: 1689–1717." *William and Mary Quarterly*, 3d. ser. 26 (1969) : 373–415.

Webster's New World Dictionary of the American Language. Cleveland and New York: World Publishing Company, 1966.

Weddell, Alexander Wilbourne, ed. *Virginia Historical Portraiture*. Richmond: William Byrd Press, 1930.

Wertenbaker, Thomas Jefferson. "The Attempt to Reform the Church of Colonial Virginia." *Sewanee Review* 25 (July 1917): 257–82.

————. *Give Me Liberty: The Struggle for Self-Government in Vir-

ginia. Philadelphia: American Philosophical Society, 1958.

Whiffen, Marcus. *The Public Buildings of Williamsburg: Colonial Capital of Virginia.* Williamsburg: Colonial Williamsburg, 1958.

The Whole Booke of Psalmes, Collected into English meeter by Thomas Sternhold, John Hopkins, and Others. . . . London: Printed by I. H. for the Company of Stationers, 1638.

William and Mary College Papers, 1721–1818, Library of Congress.

William and Mary College Quarterly Historical Magazine, 1st ser., 26 vols., Williamsburg, 1892–1919. 2d ser., Williamsburg, 1921–44.

"William and Mary College: Recently Discovered Documents." *William and Mary Quarterly,* 2d ser., 10 (1930) : 239–43.

William and Mary Quarterly, 3d ser., Williamsburg, 1944——.

Williams, David Alan. "Political Alignments in Colonial Virginia Politics, 1698–1750." Ph.D. diss., Northwestern University, 1959.

Woodfin, Maude H., ed. *Another Secret Diary of William Byrd of Westover, 1739–1741.* Translated and collated by Marion Tinling. Richmond: Dietz Press, 1942.

Wright, Louis B. *The First Gentlemen of Virginia: Intellectual Qualities of the Early Colonial Ruling Class.* San Marino: Huntington Library, 1940.

————. "William Byrd's Defense of Sir Edmund Andros." *William and Mary Quarterly,* 3d ser. 2 (1944) : 47–62.

———— and Marion Tinling, eds. *The Secret Diary of William Byrd of Westover, 1709–1712.* Richmond: Dietz Press, 1941.

Yonge, Samuel H. *The Site of Old "James Towne," 1607–1698.* Richmond: Hermitage Press, 1907.

Index